Psychological Interventions and Research with Latino Populations

Related Titles of Interest

Psychological Interventions and Cultural Diversity
Joseph F. Aponte, Robin Young Rivers, and Julian Wohl
ISBN: 0-205-14668-6

**Cognitive and Behavioral Interventions: An Empirical Approach to Mental
   Health Problems**
Linda W. Craighead, W. Edward Craighead, Alan E. Kazdin,
   and Michael J. Mahoney (Editors)
ISBN: 0-205-14586-8

Multicultural Assessment Perspectives for Professional Psychology
Richard H. Dana
ISBN: 0-205-14092-0

Psychology and African Americans: A Humanistic Approach, Second Edition
Adelbert H. Jenkins
ISBN: 0-205-16488-9 Case 0-205-16489-7 Paper

Research Design in Clinical Psychology, Second Edition
Alan E. Kazdin
ISBN: 0-205-14587-6

**Psychotherapy and Counseling with Minorities: A Cognitive Approach to
   Individual and Cultural Differences**
Manuel Ramirez III
ISBN: 0-205-14461-6

Psychological Interventions and Research with Latino Populations

Edited by

Jorge G. García   **María Cecilia Zea**
The George Washington University

Allyn and Bacon
Boston • London • Toronto • Sydney • Tokyo • Singapore

Library of Congress Cataloging-in-Publication Data

Psychological interventions and research with Latino populations /
    Jorge G. García, María Cecilia Zea, editors.
        p.   cm.
    Includes bibliographical references and index.
    ISBN 0-205-16095-6
    1. Hispanic Americans—Mental health services.   2. Hispanic
Americans—Psychology.   3. Hispanic Americans—Health risk
assessment.   I. García, Jorge G.   II. Zea, María Cecilia.
    RC451.5.H57P77 1997
    362.2'08968073-dc2O

                                                        96-19256
                                                          CIP

Printed in the United States of America

10 9 8 7 6 5 4 3 2 1   00 99 98 97 96

To my parents, Eduardo and Silvia,
who gave me the opportunities at the right times,
and to my daughters, Fernanda and Amaya,
who gave me the affection needed to undertake this work.
Jorge

A mis padres, Aureliano y Delma,
por su fé en mí y su afecto incondicional.
María Cecilia

Contents

PART II   *Mental Health Treatment, Research, and Interventions*

PART III   *Health and Rehabilitation Research and Intervention*

Preface

The purpose of this book is to describe state-of-the-art psychological conceptualizations, interventions, and research with Latino groups living in the United States. A central underlying assumption is the presence of commonalities and differences among Latino groups. Therefore, Latinos are not treated as a single group but instead as specific groups—Mexican Americans, Cubans, Puerto Ricans, Central Americans and so on—as pertinent throughout the book. The influence of the African diaspora in Latino cultures is deliberately included, as Latino researchers oftentimes refrain from taking race as a topic of inquiry. Some chapters cover several Latino groups, but only in cases where the authors focus on commonalities across groups.

Although it can be argued that the first writing on this subject goes back to the work of George I. Sánchez in the 1930s, it was not until the 1970s that this topic became salient in the psychological literature. It was then that conceptualizations such as acculturation began to emerge, and that issues such as language and cultural bias in assessment and intervention practices were originally explored. A major compendium of theory, research, and practice with Latinos was the book entitled *Chicano Psychology,* edited by Mendoza and Martinez in the early 1980s. That book described psychological developments and applications with Mexican Americans (or Chicanos) living in the southwestern states annexed to the U.S. territory after the U.S.–Mexican war. At about the same time, historical forces such as the first wave of Cuban immigration inspired Latino psychologists in the Southeast to begin exploring issues of acculturation and intergenerational conflict. The 1980s witnessed the emergence of publications describing research and interventions with Puerto Rican populations, particularly women, as represented by authors such as Comas-Díaz.

Since these earlier experiences, psychological theory, research, and applications with Latino groups have grown steadily. This growth has paralleled the changes experienced by the Latino population in this country in terms of cultural diversification and the resulting emergence of new challenges. Psychological study involving Latinos covers many other Latino groups that have immigrated to this country during the 1980s and 1990s, such as new waves of people from Cuba, Central America (mostly from El Salvador and Nicaragua), and South America.

The scope of psychological research and applications has also widened dramatically in the 1990s, extending into the areas of education, mental health, organizations, health, and rehabilitation. Psychologists today have to deal with problems in the Latino community that either did not exist or were not as prevalent twenty years ago, such as youth violence, posttraumatic stress disorder (particularly related to terror campaigns and war in Central and South America), the AIDS epidemic, and disability. In addition, current research has led to a deeper understanding of phenomena such as the effects of immigration stress, intergenerational cultural gap, enculturation, acculturation, biculturalism, ethnic identity development, interactive cultural strain, bilingualism, and adjustment to disability, among others.

As the editors of this book, we have made an explicit attempt to capture the evolution of basic conceptualizations of Latino psychology that have been developed in the last twenty years by inviting contributors to address these issues throughout the book. A vast range of psychological interventions that represent current challenges in the areas of mental health, health psychology, and rehabilitation psychology with Latinos today are addressed. Assessment issues were added as appropriate in chapters describing specific interventions aimed at a particular problem. We also sought contributions covering the entire spectrum of Latino groups living in the United States. Consequently, the reader can find specific interventions and studies with Mexican Americans (Chapters 2, 4, 5, 7, and 11), Central Americans (Chapters 3 and 12), Cubans (Chapters 10 and 14), and Puerto Ricans (Chapters 8 and 14). Four chapters refer to all the different Latino groups, which probably reflects the fact that professionals now provide services in communities formed by a conglomeration of a variety of Latino groups. Finally, we included chapters containing original empirical and theoretical research and chapters summarizing research in a particular area.

This book is organized into three sections, and with a few exceptions (Chapters 1 and 14, which are mostly descriptive), each one comprises chapters that combine original conceptual developments, research, and interventions. Part I contains conceptual issues and prevention research and interventions. Part II deals with mental health treatment research and interventions. The focus of Part III is on the description of health and rehabilitation research and interventions.

Chapter 1, by Jorge G. García and Sylvia Marotta, presents a characterization of the Latino population in the United States. The authors utilize data from the latest U.S. census to construct original frequency and percentage tables depicting demographic information across the different Latino groups, namely Mexican Americans, Puerto Ricans, Cubans, and Central and South Americans. This chapter contains information on projections of population growth and distribution of the Latino population by geographic region, gender, age, marital status, family size, and household type. When appropriate, these figures are compared against the data for the U.S. population as a whole. Finally, the reader of this chapter will find current data on socioeconomic variables such as income, poverty level, education, occupation, health insurance, and languages spoken at home, both for Latinos as a whole and for each specific Latino group. According to the data presented in this chapter, the Latino population is growing at a rapid pace and will represent 15% of the total U.S. population by 2015. Latinos as a group are younger than the total population; they have larger families, have significantly less income and education, and for the most part hold unskilled occupations that generally do not provide adequate health insurance. The authors of this chapter discuss the mental health implications of these characteristics and indicate how they may affect access to services and the nature of mental and physical health problems experienced by this population.

In Chapter 2, by Martha E. Bernal and George P. Knight, readers will find a description of the authors' long-term research on ethnic identity, particularly that of Mexican-American children. The data presented in this chapter support the development of an ethnic identity socialization model in preschool to school-age children which is consistent with cognitive development theory. The authors also analyze the role of intragroup cultural variability on the transmission of ethnic identity from parents to children. It appears that recent immigration correlates with stronger transmission of the native cultural heritage. More importantly, the researchers introduce data indicating a relationship between ethnic identity and social behavior, such as cooperative versus competitive behavioral preferences. The authors of this chapter offer a substantial discussion of the theoretical and methodological implications of their findings for future research, and delineate ways in which their research can be utilized to facilitate cognitive and social development in Latino children. Although the sample in their study includes primarily Mexican-American children, the authors suggest that their findings may be applicable to children from other Latino groups as well.

Chapter 3, by María Cecilia Zea, Virginia A. Diehl, and Katherine S. Porterfield, contributes to the sparse literature on Central American immigrants, perhaps the newest arrivals to the United States. The personal histories of these immigrants are replete with war-related experiences, traumatic stress associated with the event of crossing the border, and the struggle of adjusting to a new culture. The authors offer a model for research, based on their earlier research with this population, as well as on related research by other authors, that includes risk and protective factors mediating the trauma of war.

Latino youth violence is a theme that has received much public and professional coverage in recent years. Chapter 4, written by Jerald Belitz and Diana M. Valdez, condenses research about this topic and presents a conceptualization and intervention model addressing this problem. These authors examine psychosocial and cultural variables associated with gang affiliation in young Mexican-American males. Included in these variables are factors of cultural identity, acculturation level, transcultural family conflict, and immigration. In addition, these authors discuss assessment issues, such as cultural bias in using personality measures, language of test administration, the need for collateral and ethnocultural information, and the potential for overdiagnosing. Of particular interest is their section on intervention strategies for male youth violence. They recommend a program that balances cultural sensitivity, awareness of sociocultural and spiritual issues, and grounding in family therapy principles. Its main components are the treatment of transcultural family conflict, successive-generation family systems, identity development within a group orientation, and a well-defined role for the therapist.

Chapter 5, by Barbara VanOss Marín and Cynthia A. Gómez, includes an analysis of the influence of a myriad of factors that may affect sexual behaviors, specifically those such as condom use that relate to prevention of transmission of the HIV virus and other STDs. The authors report comparative data from their own studies and other sources about the frequency of multiple sexual partners, condom use with primary and secondary partners, anal intercourse, age at onset of sexual activity, and adolescent sexual activity. The data appear to indicate that Latinos do not differ from Caucasians in terms of sharing a relatively high frequency of condom use with secondary partners and a high rate of early adolescent sexual activity; but, on average, they have more sexual partners and have anal intercourse more frequently than Caucasians. The authors warn, however, that this information is inconsistent and may contain reporting bias. This chapter also addresses five behaviors and skills necessary for successful HIV-preventive sexual behavior, and how each of these behaviors is determined by specific cultural values and norms held by men and women of Latino descent. Finally, the authors summarize strategies that practitioners can use to increase HIV-preventive sexual behaviors, including sexual socialization, fostering comfort in talking about sexuality, a focus on empowerment of women, an understanding of gay and lesbian issues, self-efficacy goals, and the use of persons infected with HIV as agents of behavior change.

Problems of accessibility and use of mental health services have long been acknowledged within the Latino community. John J. Echeverry addresses these treatment barriers in Chapter 6. He analyzes several factors that may contribute to this endemic problem, particularly client and organizational or systemic variables. Client variables are classified into demographic, cultural, and individual factors, and the author establishes how each of these may play a role in the creation and maintenance of barriers to service availability and accessibility. Demographic characteristics listed by the author are age, gender, education level, and legal immigration status. Cultural factors include religious beliefs, degree of acculturation, national origin, level of English proficiency, resource preference, and beliefs about mental illness and treatment. Presenting mental health problems and personality variables contribute to individual factors that may affect help-seeking behaviors. In the final section of this chapter, the author provides some recommendations for the remediation of barriers to mental health services.

The authors of Chapter 7, Augustine (Gus) Barón and Madonna G. Constantine, introduce the reader to the concept of interactive culture strain as it applies to college students of Chicano descent. Their thesis is that this strain is the result of the stress associated with the cognitive, emotional, and behavioral demands stemming from interactive processes of acculturation, ethnic identity development, and gender-role socialization. Counseling Chicano college students implies in most cases the need to address the processes that may explain their feelings of distress. These authors state that much of their therapeutic effort concerns the management of interactive culture stress. This chapter is organized into three sections. First, the authors define and describe the process of acculturation, ethnic identity development, and gender-role socialization. The second section is dedicated to the issue of assessment of each of these three core processes and makes the case for the use of clinical interviews as the primary assessment tool. The authors actually developed an assessment protocol, which they present in this section as a model. The third part illustrates assessment and intervention practices based on a hypothetical case study, which helps the reader to understand the elements involved in their innovative approach.

Chapter 8 is focused on the treatment of *ataques de nervios* (nervous attacks) in Puerto Rican women. As defined by Migdalia Rivera-Arzola and Julia Ramos-Grenier, this is a frequent phenomenon involving trembling, heart palpitations, numbness, loss of consciousness, breathing difficulty, and temporary hyperkinesis. To understand this phenomenon, they provide a conceptual framework that explains the role of emotions in personality development through a constructivist view. This theory may consider anger as a conflictive emotion that at the psychological level may be aimed at the correction of a perceived wrong, and at the sociocultural level may function to maintain accepted standards of conduct. According to the authors, *ataques de nervios* represent uncontrolled anger that cannot be manifested in an assertive manner within a dominant patriarchal system that views women's anger as incongruent with a preconceived feminine ideal. The cultural concepts of *machismo, marianismo,* and *hembrismo* in Puerto Rican society help to explain sexual roles that direct the expressions of anger in Puerto Rican women, as well as other cultural practices discussed in this chapter. The authors provide a psychosocial and cultural model of intervention that combines elements of critical consciousness, feminist psychology, assertiveness training, posttraumatic stress treatment, developmental consciousness therapy, and social support.

In Chapter 9, Lillian Comas-Díaz analyzes the mental health needs of Latino professionals through the interface of environmental, ethnocultural and individual factors. Environmental factors discussed here include sociopolitical context, organizational dynamics, and affiliation with a minority group. Ethnocultural factors comprise values such as collectivism, familism, *personalismo,* and *simpatía.* The extent to which Latinos hold such values depends on their level of acculturation, socioeconomic status, and family and gender roles. At the individual level, the author analyzes occupational shock, occupational socialization failure, stress, and distress. In addition, she addresses gender differences in the workplace. At several points throughout the chapter, Comas-Díaz illustrates her conceptualizations with case studies. The final section in this chapter emphasizes mental health treatment strategies for Latino professionals experiencing depression, stress reactions, anxiety, psychosomatic disorders, and addiction, all related to the interaction of organizational and ethnocultural conflicts at the workplace. The author argues for the use of psychodynamic, cognitive-behavioral, and interpersonal psychotherapy approaches to help professionals restore a sense of competence, self-reliance, and balanced functioning, as well as to address the person–occupational environment transaction. For assessment purposes, Comas-Díaz advocates the use of the ethnocultural occupational inventory, which is summarized graphically at the end of the chapter.

Chapter 10 constitutes a summary of research and interventions conducted over a period of twenty years with Latino families (predominantly Cuban) in Florida. The authors, a team of nine professionals led by José Szapocznik, have high visibility in the field, and their work can be characterized as seminal and pioneer. What they have contributed is the development of an ecosystemic model to approach mental health needs of Latino families, which they have modified through the years to make it more responsive to changes in the cultural environment. In this chapter, the authors trace the history of their research focus and interventions, providing evaluation data and descriptions of some of their key programs of intervention. Their original goal was to address problems of behavior and drug abuse among Latino youth in the Miami area. They soon discovered, however, that to have successful outcomes they had to intervene at the family and contextual level. Their original approach was labeled structural family therapy, which they found more effective than other traditional intervention modalities such as individual psychodynamic therapy and group counseling. Given societal changes such as declining conditions in the inner city and a diversification of the

Latino community in the region, they articulated a structural ecosystemic approach that works at different contextual levels (macrosystems, microsystems, mesosystems, and exosystems) and which is based primarily in the social ecological theory of Bronfenbrenner. In this chapter, readers will find a thorough description of their approaches, along with evaluation results, and a discussion of the implications of their work with families.

Chapter 11 concerns both mental health and rehabilitation. In this chapter, Felipe G. Castro and Helen M. Tafoya-Barraza describe their research and treatment/rehabilitation programs with Mexican Americans addicted to cocaine and heroin. The authors first provide a description of the sociocultural context of drug abuse by summarizing epidemiological data and analyzing the role of acculturation, income, education, and health insurance. Later in the chapter they deal with treatment needs and the process of drug addiction in Mexican Americans from an integrative theory–oriented perspective. Following this discussion they describe general and culturally relevant approaches, which include elements of family systems and gender-role expectations. The final section in this chapter presents the results of an HIV prevention program with users of heroin and cocaine who engaged in injection and needle sharing. The goals of this 14-week program were to modify high-risk behaviors for HIV infection. The first phase involved mostly psychoeducational sessions. The middle phase consisted of detoxification from methadone, training in job-seeking skills, and exploration of feelings. The final phase emphasized self-sufficiency and focused on money management, job placement, and finding living arrangements. Results showed significant increases in self-efficacy behaviors and a reduction in drug use via injection. The authors discuss the implications of these findings as well as directions for future research and interventions.

Chapter 12 concerns socioeconomic, cultural, and rehabilitation issues involving Latinos with disabilities. The authors, María Cecilia Zea, Jorge G. García, Faye Z. Belgrave, and Tirsis Quezada, begin the chapter with comprehensive data about disability in the Latino population. Most of the data were extracted from original government sources that have rarely been condensed together into one document before. Variables include incidence and projected growth of disability, work age incidence, employment rates, occupation and earnings, rates of income and insurance, and educational level of Latinos with disabilities. The authors also provide information on frequent types of disability. Ensuing sections address the relationship between ethnocultural values and disability, as well as the relationship between socioeconomic factors and employment barriers. Some core values and beliefs discussed in this chapter that affect adjustment to disability include familism and allocentrism, interdependence, gender roles, respect, aspects of time orientation, informality, spirituality, and beliefs about causation of disability. Employment barriers analyzed here include work disincentives, lack of transferable skills, discrimination, testing issues, and labor market trends.

The subject matter of Chapter 13 is essentially the interaction of health services and language. Juan Preciado and Manuel Henry focus on the barriers faced by Latinos with limited English proficiency when dealing with a health system that uses predominantly English. They study the impact of language barriers in public health education, health services utilization, research, health professionals, and patient–therapist communications. Insufficient English skills may lead to an inability to benefit from prevention information, low use of primary health services, unreliable and invalid data in research, lack of trust in health professionals, and communication misunderstandings with the therapist resulting in misdiagnosis and inadequate treatment. In addition, the authors offer specific innovative recommendations and techniques to help close the linguistic gap in written and oral communications. Finally, they explore the language variations within the Latino community and provide strategies to communicate effectively with both linguistically heterogeneous and homogeneous Latino groups. This chapter is primarily aimed at service providers, who need to become aware of this serious linguistic problem and to develop effective ways of dealing with it.

María Cecilia Zea, Tirsis Quezada, and Faye Z. Belgrave wrote the final chapter of this book. Its substance is the interconnection between culture and health, and its implications in the practice of health psychology with Latino groups. To illustrate their point, the authors researched African cultural roots in certain Latino cultures. Specifically, they describe the practice of the Yoruba religion as a means to conceptualize and deal with health and illness from a perspective that departs radically from the dominant Western medical model under which health psychologists in the United States normally operate. The message of this chapter is that health psychology applications need to incorporate a cultural perspective without which much of its effectiveness and utilization will be very limited, particularly with Latino populations.

In summary, this book is primarily directed to educators who can use it as a textbook or reference source in courses dealing with multicultural psychology, counseling, social work, and related disciplines. Researchers and practitioners also can benefit from this book because it contains significant research methodology issues and theoretically grounded interventions at the individual, group, family, and systemic levels. Readers can find relevant and original information about key issues in mental health prevention and treatment across several specific Latino groups, information that has seldom been compiled into one comprehensive volume. Although we are aware of the impossibility of presenting a complete history and description of every Latino group in the United States, we expect that this undertaking will stimulate other researchers to expand the knowledge in this subject and to make it a priority. Finally, to the extent that Latinos living in this country share many cultural similarities with Latino Americans, we hope that this book will help promote collaborative research with professionals living in Latin America.

Acknowledgments

Our deepest thanks to all the excellent contributors who dedicated their valuable time and energy to this project and had the kindness to endure a long review process. We are indebted to Melba J. T. Vásquez from Vásquez & Associates Mental Health Services of Austin, Texas; Ernest L. Chávez of Colorado State University; and Steven López from the University of California at Los Angeles for their thoughtful review of this book and helpful feedback. We would like to recognize Lillian Comas-Díaz and Martha E. Bernal for their encouragement and expert advice; Melinda Hernández, who played a key role in formatting the chapters; Laura Jones for her indispensable and highly competent role in formatting, editing, and indexing the chapters; Kim Asner for her input about some of the chapters; and Mylan Jaixen and Sue Hutchinson of Allyn and Bacon, who were such a positive force in completing this book.

The Editors

Jorge G. García is an associate professor in the Department of Counseling, Human, and Organizational Studies at The George Washington University. He received a degree in Psychology at The Universidad Católica de Chile in Santiago, Chile in 1977 and a doctorate in rehabilitation (Rh.D.) from Southern Illinois University at Carbondale in 1988. Dr. García has over 15 years of experience as a psychologist in Chile and as licensed professional counselor and rehabilitation counselor in Washington, D.C. His publications and presentations in mental health and rehabilitation with Latinos deal primarily with behavioral adjustment after traumatic head injuries and coping with HIV/AIDS.

María Cecilia Zea is an associate professor of Psychology at The George Washington University. She received a degree in psychology at Javeriana University in Bogotá, Colombia in 1981 and her M.A. (1987) and Ph.D. (1990) degrees in Clinical/Community Psychology at the University of Maryland at College Park. Prior to coming to the United States, Dr. Zea taught at the Department of Psychology at Javeriana University and held a private practice in Bogotá. Her research interests include cross-cultural issues and adaptation of ethnically diverse and immigrant populations.

The Contributors

Sergio Aisenberg
University of Miami

Augustine (Gus) Barón
University of Texas at Austin

Jerald Belitz
University of New Mexico

Martha E. Bernal
Arizona State University

Faye Z. Belgrave
The George Washington University

Felipe G. Castro
Arizona State University

J. Douglas Coatsworth
University of Miami

Lillian Comas-Díaz
Transcultural Mental Health Institute

Madonna G. Constantine
Temple University

Virginia A. Diehl
Western Illinois University

John J. Echeverry
The George Washington University

Jorge G. García
The George Washington University

Cynthia A. Gómez
University of California,
San Francisco

Manuel Henry
Universidad de la Laguna
Islas Canarias

George P. Knight
Arizona State University

William Kurtines
Florida International University

Yolanda Mancilla
University of Miami

Barbara VanOss Marín
University of California,
San Francisco

Silvia Marotta
The George Washington University

Scott McIntosh
University of Miami

Hilda Pantín
University of Miami

Angel Pérez-Vidal
University of Miami

Katherine S. Porterfield
The George Washington University

Juan Preciado
Hostos Community College

Tirsis Quezada
The George Washington University

Julia Ramos-Grenier
Grenier Associates
Hartford, Connecticut

Migdalia Rivera-Arzola
Saint Joseph College

Daniel Santisteban
University of Miami

Mercedes Scopetta
University of Miami

José Szapocznik
University of Miami

Helen M. Tafoya-Barraza
Arizona State University

Diana M. Valdez
University of New Mexico

María Cecilia Zea
The George Washington University

Chapter 1

Characterization of the Latino Population

JORGE G. GARCÍA
SYLVIA MAROTTA
The George Washington University

It is a fairly presumptuous undertaking to try to define the characteristics of the Latino population in one chapter. There is no single Latino population; rather, there are distinct groups that identify with a specific language, culture, or place. Definitions themselves are a function of the variables that describe personhood and of the environments that press upon people who identify themselves as Latinos, Hispanics, or any of the other myriad labels that are used. That being said, this is nevertheless an attempt to shed some light on Latino demographics and on the issues that may affect their psychological health.

When the authors of this chapter first began our collaboration, we realized that our personal experiences of culture led to different definitions for the same concept. In defining the meaning of the words *Latino* and *American*, we were filtering our conceptual frameworks through the life experience of someone of Latino heritage who is third-generation American, versus someone of Latino heritage who is a Chilean citizen but resides permanently in the United States. Both identify themselves as "American," but the word carries a different meaning for each of them. To a person born in Chile and emigrating here 12 years ago, nationality is the basic identification ("I am Chilean"). Being an American to him is a given, because Chile is in South America, which is part of the American continent, as it is taught in Chile. To a person born in Texas from a family with long Texan roots, the basic identification is American ("I am American"), meaning the United States. The label *American* then becomes an ideological construct defined according to their respective experiences of ethnic identification and of identification with the dominant U.S. culture.

The question "What is your ethnic background?" yields a different answer, one based on nationality (Chilean) and the other on ethnicity (Mexican-American). Questions about nationality may or may not evoke an ethnic response. The context of the question—*where* the question is asked—may produce a different answer as well. A Chilean in Chile may choose *Criollo* (the Spanish–Native mix) or *Mapuche* (the main remaining native tribe in Chile) to answer this question. The same person, in a different context, may answer *Chilean*. The variations in this dialogue are endless because the definitions and conceptual frameworks individuals create for themselves are as diverse as the different contexts in which they navigate. Latinos, as a group, are more distinguished by their within-group diversity than they are by monolithic descriptions. Who is asking the question and where it is asked may influence the answer significantly.

The goal of this chapter is to give readers an overview of demographic characteristics of Latinos in the United States. Much of the descriptive data in this chapter come from the U.S. government. The way in which the U.S. Census Bureau asks questions delimits the descriptors and the described and does not reflect the ethnic identification of many Latinos. As a consequence, this chapter is limited in capturing the rich diversity of Latinos and the cultural spectrum that exists among them.

One of the first limiting choices that the editors of this book had to make was the decision to use the term *Latino* as opposed to *Hispanic,* the term traditionally used by the Census Bureau. As noted by Padilla and Salgado de Snyder (1985), there are many ways of labeling those groups and individuals whose culture, language, and/or geography have Latin roots. One can choose a definition based on the way that others have defined a group (e.g., the government) or on how an individual or group defines itself. Some groups identify themselves as Hispanic American, but others are incensed by this same term because it was chosen by the U.S. government to collect census information. Indeed, this term has become the dominant label in the last decade and has been defined as a descriptor for people of Spanish origin and descent (Baptiste, 1987). According to this author, however, the term *Hispanic* may be offensive to individuals or groups who would rather be identified in terms of their nationality or who want to dissociate from Spanish heritage because of its colonialist implications.

Within the Latino population, a historical point in time sometimes determines the label, as in the use of *Chicano* during the militant 1970s period in the United States. Geography is another determining factor in choosing a label. Anecdotal experience indicates that the word *Latino* appears to be the term accepted most often in the northeastern and mid-Atlantic regions of this country. The word *Hispanic* is the term most often heard in the Southern and Western regions of the United States, where it is often used interchangeably to mean Mexican-American—the group that forms the majority of Latinos in the United States (U.S. Bureau of the Census, 1992). The editors of this book have nevertheless chosen the word *Latino,* while realizing its limitations and strengths. The goal in this selection is to be as inclusive as possible while respecting geographical differences and the characteristics of the most recent arrivals to this country. The label *Latino* may be more inclusive than *Hispanic* because the latter is restricted to the use of the Spanish language, whereas the former includes immigrants from Latin America who do not necessarily speak Spanish (some second- or third-generation Latinos and Brazilians) and who may not feel represented by the label *Hispanic*.

Latinos in the United States: A Snapshot

This chapter describes the various Latino groups in terms of the proportion of the general population they represent, as well as their proportion within the Latino population. Other data will be presented to describe this population with respect to geography, immigration, education, occupation, income, poverty level, and other relevant demographic information.

In reading comparison data in this chapter, it should be noted that Latinos constitute a subset of the total U.S. population. Numerical differences are therefore not independent. In cases where Latinos are compared to non-Latino whites, these comparisons are indicated. The "other" category warrants specific attention because on most demographic variables there are differences in this collective category that deviate from the larger Latino groups. All data included in the tables described in this chapter are calculations and groupings made by the authors on the basis of raw data provided by the 1990 U.S. Census of the Population (García, 1992).

Geographic Distribution

According to the 1990 U.S. Census, Latinos can be found in all areas of the country; however, the highest concentrations occur in the southwestern states and in New York. The Latino population in the United States is more geographically concentrated than the total population, with 87% residing in ten states: California, Texas, New York, Florida, New Jersey, Arizona, New Mexico, Colorado, Massachusetts, and Illinois. Approximately two-thirds of all Latinos can be found in California, Texas, and New York. Within each of these areas, however, Latinos represent a variable proportion of the total population. For example, in California and Texas, the Latino population represents 25% of the whole population; in New York, Latinos represent only 11% of the population. California alone has 7.7 million Latinos. In New Mexico, more than one-third of the population is Latino (U.S. Bureau of the Census, 1992). In the decade since 1980, there has been a 69% increase in the Latino population. Since 1960, the representation of Mexican Americans has increased from 2.1 million to 13.3 million (National Council of La Raza, 1990). High concentrations of Latinos are found in other regions of the country. For example, Latinos represent more than half of the total population of Miami, and the United States has the fifth largest Latino population in the world.

There are regional distribution differences among the various groups of Latinos as well. For example, Salvadorans are clustered in Los Angeles; Washington,

D.C.; and Houston (Bean & Tienda, 1987). In Florida, the largest group is Cuban in origin, followed by other Central and South American immigrants (Bean & Tienda, 1987). California and Texas are the residence areas preferred by Mexicans (Council on Scientific Affairs, 1991; Zambrana, Silva-Palacios, & Powell, 1992). These differences in the proportion of Latinos found in various parts of the country affect the way in which mental health services are conceptualized, as well as how they are delivered. In parts of the country where the concentration of Latinos is high, it is likely that some members of the Latino groups may be deeply involved in policy decisions, educational practices, and other systemic frameworks for service delivery. Those parts of the country with recent immigrant populations, on the other hand, may not yet have begun to address the systemic level of mental health delivery or may be in the early stages of recognizing the need to alter service delivery in response to the needs of large numbers of newly arrived Latinos.

Latinos and Immigration

Immigration accounts for the majority of the increase in the Latino population in recent years (Zambrana et al., 1992). Almost one-third of all immigrants to the United States come from Latin American countries, and approximately one-half of all Latinos in the United States have lived in this country for less than 12 years (Schick & Schick, 1991). The average length of residence for Latinos in the United States is 15 years. The immigrant experience is vastly affected by the legal status of the newly arrived person. Most recent immigrants are undocumented (Schick & Schick, 1991). Persons with work credentials have a much different acculturating experience than those who must remain invisible to the systems that have power to deport them.

The newest arrivals to the United States are primarily from Central America, especially Salvadorans. These immigrant groups have been exposed to the traumatic effects of civil war (see Chapter 3 by Zea, Diehl, and Porterfield). They do not, for the most part, enjoy the refugee status of previous immigrant groups such as Vietnamese and Cubans. Because of these factors, newer immigrants are acculturating at differential rates. In addition, their socioeconomic conditions, educational levels, and physical and mental health status can be expected to be different from those of groups who immigrated under protected status.

The remaining Latino population—Mexican, Puerto Rican, and Cuban—comprises the groups from which most demographic data have been collected. In reading the descriptors provided in this chapter, one must continually question the context in which these data were collected, and decisions based on them must be applied flexibly, to reflect the larger demographic context.

Population Size and Distribution

Tables 1.1 and 1.2 describe information about the Latino population as a whole and by groups. Latinos now constitute about 10% of the total U.S. population and 36% of the ethnic minority population (U.S. Bureau of the Census, 1993). Mexicans, the

TABLE 1.1   Latino Groups as Percentage of Total U.S. Population

Groups	Number	Percentage
Total U.S. population	248,709,873	100
All Latino	22,354,059	10
Mexican	13,495,938	5
Puerto Rican	2,727,754	1
Cuban	1,043,932	0.5
Other	5,086,435	2

TABLE 1.2   Latino Groups as Percentage of Total Latino Population

Description	Number	Percentage
Total Latino	22,354,059	100
Mexican	13,495,938	60
Puerto Rican	2,727,754	12
Cuban	1,043,932	5
Other	5,086,435	23

largest Latino group in the United States, represent 5% of the total population. Puerto Ricans and Cubans represent 1% and 0.5% of the U.S. population, respectively. When compared to the overall Latino population, Mexicans represent about 60% of all Latinos, with Puerto Ricans forming the next largest group at 12%. The category of "other" represents a very diverse group comprising mainly Central and South American cultural groups, among others.

Projected Growth

Projections for comparative population growth rates indicate that the Latino population will increase at a rate three to five times faster than the general population (U.S. Bureau of the Census, 1992). This means that the Latino population is the fastest growing group in the United States and will be the largest minority group in the United States (Hayes-Bautista, Shink, & Chapa, 1988; Schick & Schick, 1991). By 2020 it is expected that Latinos will be about 15% of the total U.S. population. This represents a growth rate of approximately 20% (Schick & Schick, 1991) compared to the 10% growth experienced by Latinos from 1980 to 1990. Much of this growth rate can be attributed to a currently larger proportion of young people of childbearing age and to the flow of immigrants across the U.S. borders (Amaro & Russo, 1987). The Mexican-American group is expected to grow the most, followed by Central and South Americans, and then Cubans.

Table 1.3 presents projective data on growth of the Latino population over the next 20 years by age categories. This information indicates that the greatest change

TABLE 1.3   Projected Growth Rates by Age Groups

Age Groups	1990	2010	Percentage Change
0–17	7,107	9,700	27
18–44	8,804	12,108	27
45–64	2,851	6,510	56
65+	1,126	2,477	5

will occur in the 45 and older group (approximately 55% growth). This means that the age structure of the Latino population, currently much younger than the total U.S. population (see Table 1.4), will change dramatically in the years to come, becoming more similar to the age structure for the total population. However, this will largely depend on immigration patterns in the future.

Gender and Age Distribution

When compared to the U.S. population, the gender distribution of Latinos is very similar (see Table 1.5). Table 1.4 shows that age distribution, on the other hand, is strikingly different. For example, 38% of the Latino population is under the age of 19, while only 29% of the U.S. population is less than 19. Almost 75% of the Latino population is under 39 years of age, versus 60% for the total population. Given the birth rates, this age difference is likely to become more pronounced in the coming years. Among those people 65 years of age and above, only 7% of Latinos are 65 and above, compared to 17% of the total U.S. population.

TABLE 1.4   Percentage Distribution of
Latinos by Age

Age	U.S.	Latino
Under 19	29	38
20–39	32	36
40–64	27	20
65+	17	7

TABLE 1.5   Percentage Distribution of Population
by Gender

Gender	U.S.	Latino
Males	49	50
Females	51	50
Total population	248,709,873	22,354,059

Marital Status and Family Size

Marital status for both Latinos and the total U.S. population appears to be very similar (see Table 1.6). Most people are married, and approximately one-third of both populations have never married. Table 1.7 shows that family size for Latinos differs from that for the total population. Latino family size is predominantly larger than 3 members (65%). For the total U.S. population, 57% of families have fewer than 2 members. Among the larger families, three times as many Latino families have more than 6 members.

Household Type and Size

Table 1.8 compares the percentage of family households and nonfamily households of the total U.S. population against the Latino population. These data indicate that family households are much more frequent than nonfamily households in both groups, and that Latinos tend to have more family households than the total population (81% versus 70%).

Regarding household size comparisons within the Latino population, the subgroup with the largest household size is the Mexican. The Cuban population, on the other hand, mirrors the household size of the total U.S. population more closely (see Table 1.9).

TABLE 1.6   Percentage Distribution of U.S. and Latino Population by Marital Status

Marital Status	U.S.	Latino
Never married	27	33
Married	58	56
Widowed	7	4
Divorced	8	7

Note: Population 15 years of age and older.

TABLE 1.7   Percentage Distribution by Size by Family

Number of Persons	U.S.	Latino
<2	57	35
3–5	39	53
>6	4	12

Note: Mean number of family persons, U.S.: 2.6; Latino: 3.5.

TABLE 1.8   Percentage Distribution by
Household Type

Household Type	U.S.	Latino
Family (married, male and female householders, no spouse present)	70	81
Nonfamily (male or female householders)	30	19

TABLE 1.9   Percentage Distribution of Latino Groups by Size of Household

Number of Persons	Mexican	Puerto Rican	Cuban	Central and South American
>2	30	44	52	34
3–5	54	50	45	57
6+	16	7	3	9

Urban and Rural Distribution

By far the largest proportion of Latinos live in cities (91%). Table 1.10 describes the distribution. Some studies indicate that Central American immigrants come mostly from rural areas (Leslie & Leitch, 1989), contributing to the need to adjust to a new culture that is also nonrural.

Socioeconomic Status

As illustrated in Table 1.11, almost twice as many total U.S. households are in the highest income category ($50,000 or more) as Latino households (26% versus 15%). At the low end of the income spectrum, 21% of Latinos make less than $10,000, compared to 15% for the total U.S. population.

Intragroup comparisons illustrated in Table 1.12 reveal that the Cuban population has the highest median income when compared to the other three groups. Puerto Ricans have the lowest median income. Mexican and Central/South Americans have similar household income profiles.

Table 1.13 shows that Latinos are twice as likely to be below the poverty level than the total U.S. population. Within the Latino group, 39% of Puerto Ricans are below the poverty level, exceeding the proportion (29%) of the entire Latino population below poverty level by 10 percentage points. Again, the Cuban population more closely resembles the U.S. population as a whole.

TABLE 1.10   Percentage Distribution by Urban/Rural Residence

Description	U.S.	Latino
Urban	64	91
Rural	26	9

TABLE 1.11   Percentage Distribution by Household Income

Income	U.S.	Latino
Less than $10,000	15	21
$10,000–$24,999	27	34
$25,000–$49,999	33	31
$50,000+	26	15

Note: Median household income for United States: $30,126; Latino: $ 22,688

TABLE 1.12   Percentage Distribution of Household Income by Latino Group

Income	Mexican	Puerto Rican	Cuban	Central and South American
<$10,000	19	33	20	18
$10,000–$24,999	36	29	27	34
$25,000–$49,999	32	22	30	33
$50,000+	13	17	24	16
Median incomes	$22,477	$ 7,967	$ 26,593	$ 24,157

TABLE 1.13   Percentage of Latinos Below Poverty Level

Poverty	U.S.	Latino	Mexican	Puerto Rican	Cuban	Central/ South American
<$14K	14	29	30	39	18	24

TABLE 1.14 Percentage Distribution by Education Level

Education	U.S.	Latino
High school	80	53
College	21	9

Note: Population 25 years of age and older.

TABLE 1.15 Percentage Distribution by Occupation

Description	U.S.	Latino
Professional/technical	16	6
Administration	7	3
Sales	4	4
Service and support	32	31
Farm and forestry	6	4
Labor/crafts	35	52

Education and Language

Table 1.14 illustrates dramatic differences in the percentage of the Latino population and total U.S. population completing high school and college. Only half of Latinos 25 years of age and older have completed high school, compared to 80% for the total population. Only 9% of Latinos have college degrees, compared to 21% for the total population.

Approximately 80% of the U.S. population speak only English at home, whereas 8% of the U.S. population speak only Spanish at home. For the Latino population, 77% speak Spanish at home. The remaining 23% speak English or other languages. When discussing language spoken in the home, it is important to note the length of time that people have been in the United States. Approximately 75% of Latinos speak English after having resided in the United States for 15 years or more.

Occupation and Employment

As can be seen in Table 1.15, the majority of the Latino population fall under the labor and craft occupations (52%) while only 6% are employed in professional or technical occupations. These data correlate with the educational attainment levels

TABLE 1.16   Percentage Distribution of Occupations by Latino Groups

Description	Mexico	Cuba	Central/South	Total
Professional	3	6	11	6
Service	25	34	42	31
Labor/craft	62	53	36	52

Note: These data, reported by Schick and Schick (1991), exclude Puerto Ricans.

TABLE 1.17   Percentage Distribution of Unemployment by Gender

Description	U.S.	Latino
Males	7.5	12.2
Females	5.4	9.8

cited in Table 1.14, which indicated that about 50% of Latinos over 25 years of age have not completed high school. The fact that some Latinos may have immigrated from rural areas in their home country may also correlate with a high rate of Latinos whose occupations are in the labor category.

Table 1.16 provides data about occupations across Latino groups. It is apparent that Central and South American groups deviate from the norm for the total Latino group. A higher percentage of workers in this subgroup are employed in professional and technical occupations, and a lower percentage in labor occupations. This is difficult to explain but may reflect the heterogeneous characteristics of the population immigrating from South America.

In terms of employment by gender, the Latino population as a whole closely resembles the U.S. population. The labor force in both groups is almost equally divided in terms of gender, but there are important differences in unemployment rates for male and female Latinos (see Table 1.17). Latino males' unemployment rate was 12.2%, compared to 7.5% for non-Latino white males. For females, there is an unemployment rate of 9.8% for Latinos, compared to 5.4% for non-Latinos (García, 1992).

Latinos and Health Care

Two major factors that contribute to understanding Latinos and mental health are Latino usage of physical and mental health services, and insurance coverage among Latinos. When compared to whites, Latinos have very different patterns of usage of health delivery systems. (Council on Scientific Affairs, 1991). Latinos tend to use emergency services for routine health care. Often, treatment administered to them in emergency rooms is influenced by their ethnic background as was noted in a study indicating that analgesics are inadequately provided to Latinos (Todd, Samaroo, & Hoffman, 1993). They also have less access to preventive health care. Latinos do not have regular sources of health care when compared to whites. For prenatal care, Latinos are less likely than whites to have medical attention. Latino dependence on emergency or nontraditional sources of health care puts them at risk for more serious illnesses and consequently for longer and more expensive hospital stays. Although Latinos represent only 10% of the population, they are disproportionately represented among the population diagnosed with human immunodeficiency virus (HIV), and their knowledge about HIV is lower (Marín, 1989). Mental health service-seeking by Latinos is affected by language, accultura- tion levels, and the assessment and treatment practices of mental health practitio- ners (Malgady, Rogler, & Costantino, 1987).

In the United States most health care is mediated by insurance. When com- pared to the general U.S. population, Latinos tend not to be covered by insurance. On a national level, twice as many Hispanics do not have health insurance com- pared to the general population (Schick & Schick, 1991; U.S. Bureau of the Census, 1993). Latinos with limited English skills were noted to have the lowest insurance coverage, further limiting access to health care. In addition, Latino employment situations are more tenuous and underpaid and often preclude their obtaining insurance coverage through their employers (Council on Scientific Affairs, 1991). Within the Latino population there are differences as well. Cuban Americans rep- resent the group most likely to be covered by insurance. The subgroup found most often on Medicaid rosters are Puerto Ricans. Although they are the majority of the Latino population in this country and are the oldest group in the United States, Mexican Americans are the group least likely to be covered by insurance. Latinos whose language is predominantly Spanish make less use of health care services than those who are English speakers (Council on Scientific Affairs, 1991).

Summary and Conclusions

This chapter has provided demographic information about the Latino population that is relevant to the mental health status of this group. Most demographic data were taken from the 1990 U.S. Census. Variables included the size of the Latino population by the various Latino groups; geographic distribution in the United States; projections of growth; and distribution by gender, age, and marital status. Other variables described included family size and household type. This chapter provided data on economic variables such as household income, poverty level, occupation, and employment rates, as well as data on education and language spo- ken at home. Finally, this chapter included data on health care coverage and acces- sibility drawn from the literature as well as from the 1990 U.S. census data.

By 2020, 15% of the total population will be Latino, representing a 50% increase from the current proportion. Mexican Americans constitute the largest group of Latinos in the United States. Latinos are also a relatively young population when compared to the total, with 38% being under the age of 19. Thus, issues associated with youth, such as drug use, early pregnancy, and gang violence, will continue to exert systemic pressure. The size of the Latino family when compared to the total population is striking as well, with 65% having more than three persons, compared to only 43% for the total population. When comparing groups of Latinos, a finding of significance is the number of times that the Cuban population parallels the total population, whereas Puerto Ricans seem to depart the most. Latinos seem to reside in urban areas much more than is true for the total U.S. population. This fact may prove problematic because many of the newer immigrant Latinos come originally from rural areas, so that the potential for serious complications resulting from adjustment issues is greater.

The median income for Latinos is considerably less than that for the total population ($22,000 versus $30,000, respectively). Twice as many Latinos as Whites live below the poverty level. This affects access to health care and correlates with the fact that Latinos are less likely to have health insurance. A higher unemployment rate for Latinos than for non-Latino Whites also limits access to health care, as does the fact that Latinos most frequently hold jobs in labor or crafts occupations which are usually unstable and carry little or no health insurance. Insufficient education may compound the access problem in that it prevents Latinos from gaining access to jobs that would provide more stability and better health insurance. This fact is particularly costly for Latinos who suffer a disability and who may not have adequate insurance and may lack transferable skills to reenter the work force.

Throughout the different chapters in this book implications of the demographic factors described here for the physical and mental health of Latinos in the United States are addressed. Latinos are a rapidly growing and diverse group, and this trend will likely force a significant change in the way mental and physical health services are delivered to members of this group. These demographic changes will also affect the practices of mental health professionals, especially in the areas of assessment, communication, intervention strategies, and research. Some of these aspects are the primary focus of discussion in the ensuing chapters.

References

Amaro, H., & Russo, N. F. (1987). Hispanic women and mental health: An overview of contemporary issues in research and practice. *Psychology of Women Quarterly, 11*, 393–407.

Baptiste, D. A. (1987). Family therapy with Spanish-heritage immigrant families in cultural transition. *Contemporary Family Therapy, 9*, 229–251.

Bean F., & Tienda, M. (1987). *The Hispanic population of the United States.* New York: Russell Sage Foundation.

Council on Scientific Affairs. (1991). Hispanic health in the United States. *Journal of the American Medical Association, 265*(2), 248–252.

García, J. M. (1992). *The Hispanic population in the U.S.: March 1992.* Washington, DC: U.S. Department of Commerce, Bureau of the Census.

Hayes-Bautista, D. E., Shink, W. O., & Chapa, J. (1988). *The burden of support: Young Latinos in an aging society.* Stanford, CA: Stanford University Press.

Leslie, L. A., & Leitch, M. L. (1989). A demographic profile of recent Central American immigrants: Clinical and service implications. *Hispanic Journal of the Behavioral Sciences, 11,* 313–329.

Malgady, R. G., Rogler, L. H., & Costantino, G. (1987). Ethnocultural and linguistic bias in mental health evaluation of Hispanics. *American Psychologist, 42,* 228–233.

Marín, G. (1989). AIDS prevention among Hispanics: Needs, risk behaviors and cultural values. *Public Health Reports, 104,* 411–415.

National Council of La Raza. (1991). *Hispanic education: Statistical portrait 1990.* Washington, DC.: Author.

Padilla, A. M., & Salgado de Snyder, N. (1985). Counseling Hispanics: Strategies for effective intervention. In P. Pedersen (Ed.) (1987), *Handbook of cross-cultural counseling and therapy* (pp. 157–164). New York: Praeger.

Schick, F. L., & Schick, R. (1991). *Statistical handbook on U.S. Hispanics.* Phoenix, AZ: Oryx Press.

Todd, W. H., Samaroo, N., & Hoffman, J. R. (1993). Ethnicity as a risk factor for inadequate emergency department analgesia. *Journal of the American Medical Association, 269,* 1537–1539.

U.S. Bureau of the Census (1992). *1990 Census of population and housing summary: Tape file 3A.* Washington DC: Department of Commerce, Data User Services Division.

U.S. Bureau of the Census (1993). *Latino Americans today.* Washington DC: U.S. Government Printing Office.

Zambrana, R. E., Silva-Palacios, V., & Powell, D. (1992). Parenting concerns, family support systems and life problems in Mexican-origin women: A comparison by nativity. *Journal of Community Psychology, 20,* 276–288.

Chapter *2*

Ethnic Identity of Latino Children

MARTHA E. BERNAL
GEORGE P. KNIGHT
Arizona State University

This chapter deals with the ethnic identity of children of Latino background who live in the United States—that is, children whose families share a heritage that blends their Hispanic with their indigenous Native American roots and, in Cuba and Puerto Rico especially, with their African roots as well. These families are of Mexican, Cuban, Puerto Rican, Central American, or Latin American descent. Although the term *Latino* is not an ethnic identity, it has been used to refer collectively to people of such Indo-Hispanic background who live in the Americas. Furthermore, in the United States, the term encompasses people of this heritage who either are newly arrived or have been in this country for one or more generations, and are anchored in an Anglo-American cultural environment. Commonly, people of Mexican, Cuban, or other background are said to belong to the ethnic group defined by the nation in which they originated.

Several considerations motivate the study of the ethnic identity of Latino children. One that is most important to the social and political scientist concerns self-identification as an ethnic minority. In 1970, the Bureau of the Census began to rely on self-identification as the primary means of counting members of racial and ethnic groups. Thus, the psychological view of oneself as a group member became the focus of this count. As a result of the use of self-identification, scientific understanding of the following kinds of questions has gained importance: How is ethnic identity transmitted from one generation to the next? What are the determinants of the persistence of ethnic identity? What makes people, children and adults, willing to self-identify or not? How do factors such as acculturation affect their ethnic identity?

Stimulated by pressures on educators and health and mental health professionals to understand and serve the rapidly growing population of Latino children in this country, behavioral scientists also have demonstrated increasing interest in the ethnic identity of Latino children. This interest stems in part from the realization that Latino families have distinctive histories, nationalities, and cultures, and their accompanying customs, values, behaviors, and beliefs. On the basis of this background, Latinos vary in the extent to which they both express their culture in their lives and view themselves as members of their respective groups. It has been recognized that efforts to relate important psychological variables to Latino children differentiated simply by the label *Latino*, or even by more specific ethnic labels, are fruitless unless this distinctiveness is assessed. Several kinds of cultural characteristics distinguish Latino children in addition to their specific ethnic label; among the most important of these characteristics is ethnic identity. These characteristics include the value of respect for their elders, a strong sense of familism expressed as family loyalty, good manners, cooperation for the common goal, and—most important of all for the purpose of this chapter—ethnic identity.

Two processes determine the ethnic identity of Latino children: enculturation and acculturation. *Enculturation* refers to the socialization of ethnic group children in their respective cultures, and *acculturation* refers to a process of culture change which occurs as they adapt to the host society. Latino children learn from their families and communities the values, customs, behaviors, and language of their ethnic group. And, because they live in a dominant cultural surrounding, they learn from their peers, schools, and the media the values, customs, behaviors, and language of the host culture. In addition, they become knowledgeable about the various attitudes held by Anglo-Americans toward them. One way of conceptualizing the difference between Latino children and their Anglo peers is in terms of this process of culture change. Such change occurs in both directions, with children of both groups learning about one another's cultural differences. However, the flow of culture change is primarily from the Anglo to the Latino cultures, since the former is dominant. Because Latino children must adapt to pressure to change, they are bound to experience, at different times in their lives, greater conflict and psychological distress. This distress is heightened by prejudice and discrimination toward Latinos. For example, the non-English-speaking Latino child who enters a U.S. school environment must learn the rules of conduct of the Anglo-American culture, including use of the English language. But the child also may learn that Latinos are regarded as inferior to Anglos in various ways. Via these two processes of enculturation and acculturation, Latino children learn about their group membership, Latino culture and language, the views and feelings of their group toward itself and others, and their ethnic identity.

Conceptualizations of Ethnic Identity: Historical Perspectives

Ethnic identity may be defined as a psychological construct, an abstract set of ideas that we have about our own ethnic group membership and about who we are (Bernal, Knight, Garza, Ocampo, & Cota, 1990). Ethnic identity is also one of the social identities that form one's conception of self, or self-concept (Tajfel, 1978). As a part of the self-concept, the ethnic identity of Latino children contributes to their adaptation within their families as well as within their Anglo-American surroundings. In our research, we have emphasized the complexity and multidimensionality of ethnic identity. According to our conceptualization, children's ethnic identity is composed of a number of components: (1) self-identification or categorization of oneself into the ethnic group, which is based on one's knowledge of the cues distinguishing the group, and on the ethnic label one chooses to use; (2) ethnic knowledge or information regarding the cultural values, styles, customs, traits, and so on that are characteristic of one's group; (3) ethnic preferences and feelings about being a member of one's group, about own-group members, speaking the language, and values; (4) ethnic constancy—knowing that one's ethnic characteristics are permanent; and (5) use of ethnic role behaviors. Children may not know that the ethnic behavior and customs in which they engage with their families are based on their culture, but they can tell you whether they use those behaviors. As they get older, engaging in these ethnic behaviors may help them understand that they are members of their ethnic group. Both (1) and (3) reflect the evaluation one places on ethnic identity, or one's ethnic self-concept. Individuals may or may not choose to self-identify in ways that affirm their ethnic heritage and group membership, and may have either positive or negative feelings about their ethnic group membership and about using the language and following the customs of their group (what some investigators call ethnic group loyalty).

The Earlier Literature on Minority Children's Identity.   The vast majority of the early literature relating to children's racial/ethnic identity focused on the identities of Black children. This early research provided a literature that has drawn scientific attention to different aspects of ethnic socialization, among them racial awareness (e.g., Goodman, 1964; Moreland, 1966; Stevenson & Stewart, 1958), racial attitudes (e.g., Porter, 1971; Williams & Moreland, 1976), and racial or ethnic identification and preference (e.g., Brand, Ruiz, & Padilla, 1974; Clark & Clark, 1947). However, the terms *race* and *ethnicity* often have been used interchangeably in the literature, as if their meanings were identical, and there has been poor realization of the possibility that the processes of racial identification and ethnic identification may not occur at the same developmental rate and at the same age. Indeed there is a growing literature suggesting that racial awareness among Black children may occur at a younger age than does ethnic awareness among Latino children (Bernal et al., 1990; Fox & Jordan, 1973; George & Hoppe, 1979; Ocampo, Bernal, & Knight, 1993; Rice, Ruiz, & Padilla, 1974; Rosenthal, 1974). Bernal et al.

(1990) have suggested that racial awareness may develop earlier than ethnic awareness because ethnic awareness may require an understanding of relatively complex cues such as customs, beliefs, and values in addition to the perception of physical cues, which are most often relatively obvious in the development of racial awareness. Another criticism of this body of literature concerns the reliability and validity of several identity measures (Ballard, 1976). Aboud (1987) has reviewed this earlier literature on minority children's racial/ethnic attitudes and preferences.

It was also fairly common in this early research to rely exclusively on measures of children's attitudes and preferences toward their own and other racial or ethnic groups as indicators of self-identification and self-concept. That is, a positive attitude toward a group was often interpreted as an identification with that group (Tajfel, 1978), and ethnic children's preferences for a White doll over a Black or ethnic doll were often interpreted as an indication of a poor self-concept. The more recent research, in addition to differentiating between racial and ethnic identity, has differentiated the evaluative and self-defining dimensions of ethnic identity (e.g., Aboud, 1987; Bernal, Knight, Ocampo, Garza, & Cota, 1993; Phinney & Rotheram, 1987).

The Sequencing of Social Identities. Ocampo et al. (1993) examined the sequencing of social identities by reviewing the literature bearing upon the emergence of key aspects of gender, racial, and ethnic identity. Figure 2.1 displays a graphic illustration of the sequencing of social identities using data taken from 13 different studies cited in the figure caption. The methods used to assess the components of awareness, self-identification, and constancy within each realm of gender, race, and ethnicity varied widely, and the reader is referred to the original papers for descriptions of the measures. This figure presents the age range in which 70% or more of the children were reported to demonstrate an understanding of each of three identity components. These findings suggest that children develop ethnic awareness and ethnic self-identification well after the respective gender and racial components, and that neither racial nor ethnic constancy is attained until a few years after gender constancy.

Ethnic Children's Self-Concept. A review of the psychological literature on the self-concept of ethnic minority children examines the theory that they experience low self-concept and self-esteem because of social and ethnic derogation by society (Rosenberg, 1979). The large body of literature that examines the self-worth or self-esteem of ethnic minority children in comparison to White children has yielded inconsistent findings. There are several criticisms of this research—for example, that most of the research has been conducted on preschool children, who are too young to have developed an ethnic identity. Furthermore, Rosenberg (1979) has pointed out that in order for it to be the case that minority children have lower esteem, they have to be aware of how their group is evaluated, they have to agree with that evaluation, they have to believe that the evaluation applies to them

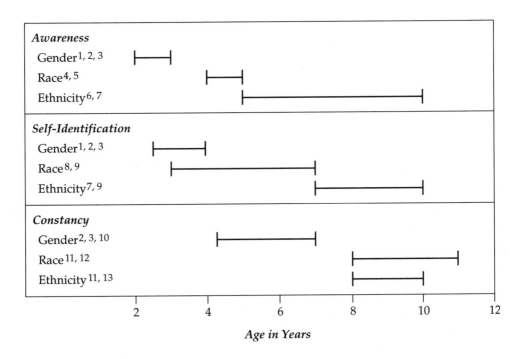

FIGURE 2.1   The Development of Social Awareness, Self-identification, and Constancy for the Concepts of Gender, Race, and Ethnicity: (1) Thompson (1975); (2) Slaby & Frey (1975); (3) Martin & Little (1990); (4) Clark & Clark (1947); (5) Rice, Ruiz, & Padilla (1974); (6) Aboud & Mitchell (1977); (7) Vaughn (1987); (8) Marsh (1970); (9) Fox & Jordan (1973); (10) Emmerich, Goldman, Kirsh, & Sharabany (1977); (11) Aboud (1984); (12) Semaj (1980); (13) Bernal, Knight, Garza, Ocampo, & Cota (1990)

personally, they have to have high regard for the person(s) making the evaluation, and they have to use Whites as their comparison reference group. Nevertheless, most of the research comparing the self-esteem of Mexican-American with that of Anglo-American children has yielded no differences (e.g., Burke, Balow, & Hunt, 1988; Franco, 1983; Larned & Muller, 1979; Maldonado & Cross, 1977). A major problem with all of the minority children's self-concept literature is that ethnic identity, or ethnic self-concept, has not been measured separately, nor has it been compared with global self-concept. Consequently, the relationships between ethnic identity and self-worth have not been examined.

The mixed findings generated by the literature comparing the self-worth scores of Latino and majority children may be the result of researchers examining this issue in rather simplistic ways. That is, the self-worth of minority children may well be a function of the degree to which the ethnic identity–related behaviors of these children match the demands placed upon them by the groups of individuals with whom they interact and that they see as most important to them. For example, if Rosenberg (1979) is correct regarding the requisites for children to have lower self-esteem, highly identified children will have high self-worth if the individuals who are important to them and who evaluate them are highly ethnically identified, if the children connect their ethnic identity to the same group as these important individuals, and if the children interpret the evaluations of these significant others as positive. Thus, the relationship between ethnic identity and self-worth may be moderated by the nature of the environment the child encounters.

Latino Children's Ethnic Identity

This section describes the current state of the literature on the ethnic identity of Latino children. Specifically, we shall describe the evidence bearing upon the structure of ethnic identity components, and on age differences in ethnic identity components.

Measurement of Latino Children's Ethnic Identity

The Children's Ethnic Identity Questionnaire
We shall first briefly describe the Children's Ethnic Identity Questionnaire, which we developed for measuring each of the five components of ethnic identity (Bernal et al., 1990). It is important to note that the measure was tailored specifically to children of Mexican descent rather than to Latino children generally. Details of the procedure varied because the methodology was being improved as it was used, and it required developmentally appropriate adaptations. Therefore, some of the items for preschool children were different from those used with school-age children. The components and their measures were as follows:

Ethnic self-identification.   Several tasks and measures were included in this component. The *Ethnic Label* task required children to identify, from among a set of 10 ethnic terms (Japanese, Hispanic, Italian, Spanish, Chicano, Anglo, Chinese, Black, Mexican, and German), the terms that characterized them. Each term was read separately and children were asked, "Are you a _____?" Then they were asked which term was more like them than the others. The Ethnic Grouping of Others task used individual photographs of 12 unknown children, six of whom were Mexican-American and six Anglo-American. Children were asked to sort the children into a "Mexican" or a "Not Mexican" box. In the Ethnic Self-Grouping task, children were shown a self-photograph and asked to put it in the box where it belonged. Then they gave their Reason for Self-Grouping when they were asked in what way they were like the children in the box holding their photograph. Five different variables were derived: Correct Ethnic Label, Number of Correct Ethnic Labels, Correct Ethnic Group of Others (the number of correct choices made in grouping Mexican and non-Mexican children), Correct Self-Grouping, Reason for Self-Grouping (reasons were scored for their level of complexity and use of concrete or psychological trait terms).

Ethnic Constancy.   A set of six questions was used to assess children's awareness that their ethnicity would remain constant over time, settings, and transformations (e.g., "When you become a grown-up person will you be Mexican?"). The questions were modeled after Slaby and Frey's (1975) gender constancy scale, and yielded a score consisting of the number of constancy responses to the six questions.

Use of Ethnic Role Behaviors.   Fourteen questions relating equally to Mexican and Anglo behaviors were used to ask children whether they did them (e.g., "Do you ever have piñatas at your birthday party?"). The score was the sum of "yes" responses to the Mexican questions.

Ethnic Knowledge.   Two hypothetical towns labeled as Mexican or Anglo were described to the children, and they were asked about things people did in each town. Specifically, they were asked about the frequency of certain events happening in each town, for example, "How many of the people in the Mexican town eat *menudo*?" The children indicated their response by pointing to one of three circles: a small "none" with no faces in it, a medium-sized "some" circle that was half-filled with faces, and a large "all" circle that was completely filled with faces. The difference scores between the rated frequency of each item (none = 1, some = 2, all = 3) were computed and then averaged across the 20 items. A high score indicated a greater expected frequency of the items in the Mexican town.

Ethnic Preferences and Feelings.   Structured after Harter and Pike's (1980) Pictorial Scale of Perceived Competence and Acceptance for Young Children, a set of ten items was presented, each of which contained a pair of line drawings of a same-sex child and two verbal descriptions expressing different preferences of a particular type. Each description had a Mexican and a non-Mexican preference. Children were shown the figures; then their attention was directed toward the drawing on the left, and they were told, for example, "This Mexican boy/girl invites mostly Mexican friends to his/her birthday party." Then children were directed to the drawing on the right and told, "This Mexican boy/girl invites mostly Anglo friends to his/her birthday party." Then children were asked, "Which boy/girl is most like you?" They responded by pointing to one of two circles beneath the drawing indicating "a lot like you" (large circle) or "a little like you" (small circle). Each item was scored on a four-point scale ranging from a low Mexican preference (a lot like the Anglo figure) to a high Mexican preference (a lot like the Mexican figure). Then these responses were averaged. A high score indicated a preference for the Mexican alternatives.

Description of the Samples

We have generated evidence bearing upon the structure of ethnic identity and its development, using our Ethnic Identity Questionnaire, in several samples of Mexican-American children ages 3½ to 10 years old—that is, in preschool and early school-age children of Mexican descent. Given the heterogeneity of the subgroups constituting the Latino population, it is necessary that the research on the ethnic identity of Latino children clearly specify the nature of the sample investigated. Table 2.1 presents some basic descriptive information regarding the nature of the Mexican-American samples in our investigations.

The first sample consisted of preschool children ages 3½ to 6 years who were enrolled in Headstart programs in Denver, Colorado. Most of these children were English monolingual, but about one-third were bilingual or Spanish monolingual, and the latter were tested in Spanish. The second sample comprised 46 children ages 6 to 10 years who were recruited from a community youth center, a Catholic church, and a local park. The third sample consisted of a larger and broader sample of 151 children aged 4 years 8 months to 10 years 4 months who were from a Headstart program and from three different elementary schools. All children in samples 2 and 3 were fluent in English, a small number were bilingual, and all were located in Phoenix, Arizona. Families of the children were primarily of low socioeconomic status (SES). In the case of samples 2 and 3, the mothers of the children were administered questionnaires to assess their own ethnic identity as well as several other variables such as their Mexicanism and Americanism, and their ethnic socialization, or enculturation, of their children.

TABLE 2.1   Characteristics of the Three Samples—Development of Ethnic Identity

| | | | Parents' Generation | | | | | |
| | | | Mothers | | | Fathers | | |
Sample	N	Ages	1	2	3+	1	2	3+
1. Denver—Headstart	46	3–7 to 6–4	10	4	31	10	4	31
2. Phoenix—Community	45	6 to 10	2	14	29	18	6	21
3. Phoenix—Schools	151	4–8 to 10–4	16	53	34	na	na	na

Note: The ages are expressed in years-months.

The Structure of Ethnic Identity among Mexican-American Children

Conceptualizations of Children's Ethnic Identity

Historically, ethnic identity has often been defined simply as ethnic labeling (e.g., Brand, Ruiz, & Padilla, 1974). More recently, more complex multidimensional conceptualizations of ethnic identity have been developed (e.g., Elias & Blanton, 1987; García, 1982; Hutnik, 1986) suggesting that ethnic identity is composed of dimensions including self-categorization, knowledge, attitudes and feelings, and behaviors related to one's culture (Bernal et al., 1990; Driedger, 1975; García, 1982; Rosenthal & Hrynevich, 1985). However, few investigators have assessed the multidimensional nature of ethnic identity in Latino children (Phinney, 1990). Furthermore, the dimensions and structure of ethnic identity among Latino adults may not generalize directly to Latino children because of the normal developmental changes in self-concept. That is, the evidence that the structure of self-concept in childhood is different from that in adulthood (Harter, 1983; Rosenberg, 1979) suggests that the structure of ethnic identity, which is a part of self-concept, also may differ in childhood and adulthood. The evidence that features of self-concept become more differentiated with development suggests that the dimensions of ethnic identity among children may become similarly differentiated with age.

The Multidimensional Nature of Children's Ethnic Identity

Our conceptualization of the structure of ethnic identity among Mexican-American children (Bernal et al., 1990; Knight, Bernal, Garza, Cota, & Ocampo, 1993) emphasized the multiple interrelated dimensions or components of ethnic identity. To test these interrelationships, we examined the structure of the ethnic identity components in the data obtained from the third sample described earlier (Knight, Garza, & Bernal, 1994). A confirmatory factor analysis of the data from sample 3 and the intercorrelations among the ethnic identity components in the first two samples (Bernal et al., 1990; Knight, Bernal, Garza, Cota, & Ocampo, 1993) indicated that the ethnic identity of Mexican-American children appears to be a multidimensional construct composed of distinct but related components.

The Development of Ethnic Identity

Theoretical Developmental Framework

The information that ethnic minority children gain about their ethnicity and ethnic group memberships is acquired through social learning experiences provided by families and communities, as well as by the dominant society. As they grow older, they learn increasingly more complex information and integrate past learning with present learning. Cognitive developmental constraints may limit children's ability to grasp and incorporate the content of their ethnic identity. The developmental framework for changes in the components of minority children's ethnic identity shown in Table 2.2 has been extended from Harter's self-system theory (1983).

This table predicts developmental shifts in the ethnic identity components from preschool to early school levels. At the preschool level, the content of children's ethnic identity components is characterized by simple, concrete descriptions of physical attributes, appearance, and behaviors. Their ethnic labels have little meaning, and they may not have ethnic constancy, feelings, and preferences. They engage in the customs and behaviors of their culture because their families do, and they do as their parents say. They probably do not associate these customs and behaviors with their ethnicity.

At the early school level, the content of children's ethnic identity components is more complex and traitlike. Ethnic labels have meaning, and they understand the constancy of their ethnicity. They engage in more ethnic role behaviors, know more about the ethnic relevance of these behaviors, and demonstrate feelings and preferences about their ethnic group.

Age Differences in Ethnic Identity

We found that the Headstart children of the first sample had very limited knowledge of their ethnic identity (Bernal et al., 1990). As can be seen in Table 2.3, the older of these children more frequently used correct ethnic labels such as Spanish or Mexican. However, few of the children had a correct ethnic label, and even these children could not give a reason that the label applied to them; they had *empty*

TABLE 2.2   Descriptive Shifts in the Components of Ethnic Identity with Age

Ethnic Identity Components	Preschool Level	Early School Level
Ethnic self-identification	Empty labels: "I'm Mexican because my mother said so."	Meaningful labels: "I'm Mexican because my parents come from Mexico."
Ethnic constancy	Don't understand.	Understand permanence of their ethnicity.
Ethnic role behaviors	Engage in and describe behaviors, may not know why behaviors are ethnic.	Engage in more role behaviors, know more about their ethnic relevance.
Ethnic knowledge	Simple, global knowledge.	More complex and specific knowledge, including cultural traits.
Ethnic feelings and preferences	Undeveloped; do as their families do.	Have feelings and preferences.

TABLE 2.3　The Percentage of Preschool Children of Sample 1 with Some Knowledge on Each Ethnic Identity Variable and the Correlation of Each Variable with Age and Language Use

		Coefficients	
Variable	Percentage Knowledgeable	Age	Spanish Speaking
Correct ethnic label	37.0	.26[*]	−.22
Correct ethnic grouping of others	23.9	.06	.28[*]
Correct self-grouping	45.7	−.10	.20
Reason for self-grouping	6.5	−.02	.06
Ethnic constancy	37.0	−.03	−.01
Knowledge of ethnic behaviors	10.9	−.09	−.20
Use of ethnic behaviors	NA	−.06	.51[**]

Source: M. E. Bernal, G. P. Knight, C. A. Garza, K. A. Ocampo, & M. K. Cota, "The Development of Ethnic Identity in Mexican-American Children," *Hispanic Journal of Behavioral Sciences*, Vol. 12, 1990, pp. 3–24.

Note: Pearson correlations when both variables are continuous, point biserial correlations when there is one continuous and one dichotomous variable, and Kendall tau-B coefficients when both are dichotomous.

[*]p < .05; [**]p < .01.

labels. Most of the children did not have ethnic constancy, and their knowledge of ethnic role behaviors was quite limited. The Spanish-speaking children also had a slight advantage; they were more likely to group their ethnic peers correctly into the Mexican box, and they more often used ethnic role behaviors. These findings were consistent with the theoretical predictions from Table 2.1 regarding preschool children's ethnic identity.

The analyses of the data provided by the second sample of children, who were older, provided some complementary findings (Bernal et al., 1990). In comparison to the preschoolers, the 6- to 8-year-olds had a considerably greater understanding of their ethnic identity: 86% could give a correct ethnic label, 71% could group themselves correctly as Mexican (though few could give a reason for the grouping), they answered 4 of 6 ethnic constancy questions correctly on average, and they showed some ethnic knowledge and preferences (see Table 2.4). The increase in the children's understanding of ethnic identity with age was evident in the 8- to 10-year-old column. In the case of all variables, the older children showed a greater awareness of their ethnic identity. All except two of the measures used were significantly related to age, indicating that the older children knew more about their ethnic identity. We also found that Spanish-speaking children had a greater awareness of their ethnic identity than non-Spanish-speaking children. It may be theorized that the parents of Spanish-speaking children are themselves Spanish-speaking and are likely to teach their children more about their culture than non-Spanish-speaking parents.

Finally, the age-related findings obtained in the second sample were repeated in the third sample (see Table 2.5). In this larger sample, age was positively associ-

TABLE 2.4   Performance of the Children of Sample 2 on Ethnic Identity Variables by Age Groups and Correlations Relating Each Variable to Age and Spanish Language Use

Child's Ethnic Identity	Percentage Correct or Mean (Standard Deviation)[a]		Correlations[b]	
	6–8 (n = 21)	8–10 (n = 24)	Age	Spanish-Speaking
Self-identification:				
Correct ethnic label	86.7%	95.8%	.10	−.10
Number of correct ethnic labels	1.30(.80)	2.17(.76)	.43**	.26*
Correct ethnic grouping of others	9.00(4.40)	11.46(.88)	.41**	.37***
Ethnic self-grouping	71.4%	91.7%	.26*	−.02
Reason for self-grouping at early school level	9.5%	37.5%	.46***	.28*
Ethnic constancy	4.43(1.69)	5.38(1.10)	.31*	.06
Use of ethnic role behaviors	4.76(2.64)	5.50(1.44)	.06*	.35*
Ethnic knowledge	0.45(.58)	0.92(.53)	.50***	.51***
Ethnic preferences	2.74(.32)	3.02(.47)	.34*	.25*

Source: M. E. Bernal, G. P. Knight, C. A. Garza, K. A. Ocampo, & M. K. Cota, "The Development of Ethnic Identity in Mexican-American Children," *Hispanic Journal of Behavioral Sciences*, Vol. 12, 1990, pp. 3–24.

[a]The sample was split at the age of 96 months to provide these descriptive data; in the analyses, "months of age" was used as a continuous variable.

[b]Pearson correlations as when both variables are continuous, point biserial correlations when there is one continuous and one dichotomous variable, and Kendall tau-B coefficients when both are dichotomous.

*$p < .05$; **$p < .01$; ***$p < .001$.

ated with ethnic self-identification (a composite of number of correct ethnic labels, correct ethnic grouping of others, and ethnic self-grouping), ethnic constancy, ethnic knowledge, and use of ethnic role behaviors (Knight, Garza, & Bernal, 1994).

Thus, predictions from Table 2.1 were supported by these results: Ethnic identity follows a progression from early childhood to age 10 as predicted. Furthermore, children who speak their native language at home are likely to have higher scores and thus to have a clearer sense of their identity.

However, there are a number of limitations to our knowledge regarding the development of ethnic identity among Latino children. A majority of children in this research were of low SES, and the parents were not well educated. Although low SES and education do not necessarily reflect the quality of child-rearing, it is important to collect data from a broader SES and educational range to ascertain the generalizability of the results across SES and parent education. Perhaps an even more glaring limitation is that the sample comprised only Latino children of Mexican descent. While there is little reason to believe that the development of ethnic identity follows a different course in other Latino populations, this is an empirical question that needs to be addressed.

TABLE 2.5 The Means, Standard Deviations, and Correlations with Age for Each Ethnic Identity Dimension for Sample 3 Children

Ethnic Identity	Mean	Standard Deviation	Correlation with Age
Ethnic self-identification	−0.50[a]	0.63	.62[***]
Ethnic constancy	3.45	1.98	.50[***]
Ethnic knowledge	0.61	0.56	.37[***]
Ethnic preferences	2.94	0.57	.11
Ethnic role behaviors	3.54	1.35	.29[**]

Source: G. P. Knight, C. A. Garza, & M. E. Bernal, "The Structure of Ethnic Identity among Mexican-American Children," unpublished manuscript, Arizona State University.

[a]The index of ethnic self-identification was a composite of three standardized scores. Further, the negative mean standard score occurred because there was a clear ceiling effect for each of the three scores that were used to form this composite (i.e., the distributions of these scores were negatively skewed).

[**]$p < .01$, [***]$p < .001$.

The Socialization of Ethnic Identity in Latino Children

A Model of the Socialization of Children's Ethnic Identity

Several interesting questions followed from our results on the development of Latino children's ethnic identity: What do parents teach their children about their ethnic identity? Does this teaching lead to more robust ethnic identities in their children? Is the parents' ethnic background related to the ethnic teaching of their children, and to their children's ethnic identity? There is a broader question of which these several questions are subsamples: What are the socialization mechanisms that lead to the development of ethnic identity? Our theorizing about this question has led to a model or organizational structure for thinking about the answers. The model includes several sets of variables that describe the socialization of ethnic identity: the characteristics of the family's social ecology, the joint socialization effects of familial and nonfamilial agents, the child's ethnic identity, the child's cognitive abilities, and the child's social behaviors, some of which are based on his or her ethnic socialization. In this model, both the enculturation and acculturation of children are taken into account.

In our model (see Knight, Bernal, Garza, Cota, & Ocampo, 1993; or, for an expanded version, see Knight, Bernal, Garza, & Cota, 1993) of the socialization of ethnic identity, there are several causal links among the variables. Children's family background (generation, acculturation, ethnic identity, language, cultural knowledge, education), family structure (status relationships, familial interdependence, family size), and the broader social ecology (urbanization level of community, SES of family and community, minority status, dominant group characteristics) are causally linked to the content that is socialized by the familial and nonfamilial agents. These socialization agents include the children's family, peers, teachers, and the media who transmit information and views about ethnicity and ethnic group membership to the children. Familial and nonfamilial agents may transmit views, values, and other information that creates conflict between the children's homes and schools, such as views about children's adoption of ethnic versus Anglo customs, language, and identity (see Figure 2.2).

This socialization content then is causally linked to the nature of the children's ethnic identity. Thus, socialization processes lead to the characteristics and qualities of ethnic identity, and in addition cognitive developmental processes affect the rate of acquisition and the complexity of ethnic identity. As cognitive maturation proceeds, children begin to understand more abstract concepts, and these reasons for their self-identification as ethnic group members become more complex with age.

Children's ethnic identity, in turn, mediates the effects of familial and nonfamilial socialization on their social behaviors, including the use of Spanish or English, cooperation-competition, cognitive style, and any behaviors that are linked to ethnicity. Finally, children's cognitive development determines the complexity of the influence of socialization agents on ethnic identity, the influence of ethnic identity on social behavior, and the influence of socialization agents generally on children's social behaviors.

The Role of Parents

To answer the questions regarding the role of parents in the socialization of children's ethnic identity, we focused on the role played by the socialization content that Mexican-American parents provide for their children. This content transmit-

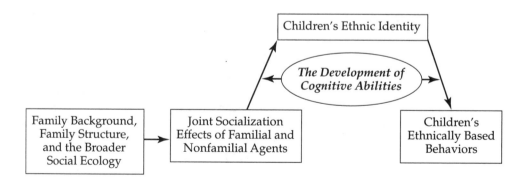

FIGURE 2.2   A Social Cognitive Model of the Development of Ethnic Identity and Behaviors among Mexican-American Children

ted by parents to their children is influenced by their family background and other social ecology variables. Parents in turn influence the nature of children's ethnic identity, which also influences subsequent behavior. Thus, parents' socialization content is said to "mediate" the link between family background variables and children's ethnic identity. The model predicts a pattern of relationships among these variables:

1. Families who have greater contact with their ethnic roots are more likely to teach their children about their ethnic background.
2. Parents' teaching their children about their ethnic background is related to their children's ethnic identity.
3. Children's ethnic identity is related to children's ethnically based behaviors (e.g., cooperation, respect, use of Spanish).
4. Children's cognitive development determines (moderates) the complexity of the influence of socialization agents on ethnic identity, the influence of children's ethnic identity on ethnically based social behavior, and the influence of socialization agents generally on children's social behaviors.

The mothers of sample 2, the school-age Mexican-American children, provided information about the generation of migration of both parents, responded to a scale of acculturation that revealed the degree of *Mexicanism* and *Americanism* of the mothers (their comfort with each of the two cultures), and answered a questionnaire about what they taught their children about being Mexican, which included aspects of Mexican culture, and ethnic pride and discrimination (Knight et al., 1993).

Table 2.6 presents the correlations among family background and teaching variables. As can be seen in this table, the interrelations among the family background variables and among the teaching variables are consistent with general expectations. Perhaps most important for the present purposes, the family background variables are related to the teaching variables in a manner consistent with the socialization model. That is, the mothers who teach about the ethnic culture and who have cultural objects in the home are less acculturated mothers (as indexed by their comfort with the Mexican and American cultures) and have husbands who are more recent immigrants.

Table 2.7 presents the correlations of the family background and teaching variables with the children's ethnic identity variables. The family background and teaching variables are also related to the children's ethnic identity variables in a manner consistent with the socialization model. Mothers who are less acculturated (as indexed by their comfort with the Mexican and American cultures) and fathers who are more recent immigrants have children who more correctly self-identify as members of their ethnic group, more often use ethnic role behaviors, and have more ethnic knowledge and preferences.

Additional support for the socialization model described here has been provided in a study of the mothers and children of sample 3 (Knight, Cota, & Bernal,

TABLE 2.6 Correlations among the Family Background and the Teaching Variables from Sample 2

	Teaching Variables			Family Background Variables		
	Teaching about Mexican Culture	Teaching about Ethnic Pride and Discrimination	Mexican Objects in the Home	Americanism	Mother's Generation	Father's Generation
Family background variables:						
Mexicanism	.51***	.49***	.53***	-.47***	-.06	-.57***
Americanism	-.36**	-.33**	-.42**		.29*	.39**
Mother's generation	.04	.07	.09			.20
Father's generation	-.55***	-.38**	-.50***			
Teaching variables:						
Teaching about Mexican culture		.49***	.65***			
Teaching about ethnic pride and discrimination			.48***			

Source: G. P. Knight, M. E. Bernal, C. A. Garza, M. K. Cota, & K. A. Ocampo, "Family Socialization and the Ethnic Identity of Mexican-American Children," *Journal of Cross-Cultural Psychology*, Vol. 24, 1993, pp. 99–114.

*p < .05, **p < .01, and ***p < .001.

TABLE 2.7 Correlations of the Family Background and Teaching Variables with the Children's Ethnic Identity Variables from Sample 2

	Children's Ethnic Identity Variables				
	Number of Correct Ethnic Labels	Correct Ethnic Grouping of Others	Use of Ethnic Role Behaviors	Ethnic Knowledge	Ethnic Preferences
Family background variables:					
Mexicanism	.32*	.36**	.40**	.31*	.35**
Americanism	-.19	-.47***	-.11	-.02	-.16
Mother's generation	-.14	-.13	.09	-.08	-.06
Father's generation	-.22+	-.24+	-.38**	-.34**	-.29*
Teaching variables:					
Teaching about Mexican culture	.24+	.18	.44***	.09	.23+
Teaching about ethnic pride and discrimination	.07	.32*	.22+	.15	-.16
Mexican objects in the home	.23+	.16	.34*	-.02	.24+

Source: G. P. Knight, M. E. Bernal, C. A. Garza, M. K. Cota, & K. A. Ocampo, "Family Socialization and the Ethnic Identity of Mexican-American Children," *Journal of Cross-Cultural Psychology,* Vol. 24, 1993, pp. 99–114.
$^+p < .10$, $^*p < .05$, $^{**}p < .01$, and $^{***}p < .001$.

1993). This investigation examined the socialization of cooperative, competitive, and individualistic preferences among Mexican-American children using structural modeling. In this study, 59 of the Mexican-American children from the third sample completed an individually administered resource allocation task designed to assess their preferences for cooperative, competitive, or individualistic allocations of resources between themselves and a same-sex peer. Figure 2.3 presents the results of the Structural Equations Modeling analysis designed to test the fit of these data to a model derived from the socialization perspective described above. Because it was necessary for all endogenous variables to be continuous in nature, including the index of resource allocation preferences, standardized regression coefficients obtained in the scoring of the resource allocation behavior were used in these analyses. Cooperative resource allocation preferences produced large positive coefficients for the *concern for other* or the *concern for equal* indices. Competitive resource allocation preferences produced large positive coefficients for the *concern for own* index and large negative coefficients for the *concern for other* index. Individualistic resource allocation preferences produced large positive coefficients for the *concern for own* index. (More thorough details regarding the scoring procedure and the data analysis are available in Knight, Cota, & Bernal, 1993).

The results of this causal modeling analysis supported the viability of a model indicating that: the mother's ethnic knowledge and preferences influence her teaching about the ethnic culture; the mother's teaching about ethnic culture influ-

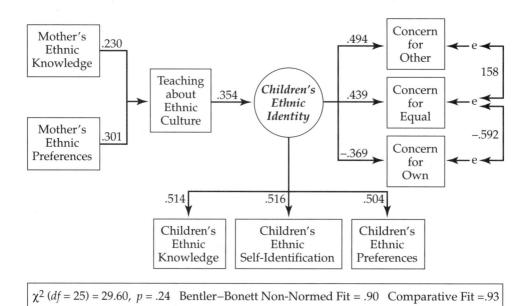

χ^2 (*df* = 25) = 29.60, *p* = .24   Bentler–Bonett Non-Normed Fit = .90   Comparative Fit = .93

FIGURE 2.3   **The Socialization of Cooperative, Competitive, and Individualistic Preferences among Mexican-American Children**

ences the child's ethnic identity; and the child's ethnic identity in turn influences the child's cooperative, competitive, and individualistic resource allocation preferences in a manner consistent with the theory.

Summary and Discussion

In summary, we have developed and refined theory and methodology for studying the formation and transmission of Mexican-American identity in preschool to school-age children, and have presented a socialization model that invites empirical exploration. The formation data are consistent with cognitive developmental theory and, in combination with data from other representative samples of Mexican-American children, are useful in setting developmental expectations regarding children's ethnic identity. The data on the transmission of ethnic identity from parents to their children remind us of the intragroup variability that exists in the cultural characteristics of parents, as well as in the extent to which they teach their children about their cultural background and thus contribute to the formation of their ethnic identity. The finding that recently immigrated parents teach their children more about their cultural heritage and more strongly influence their children's ethnic identity may not be surprising, but this is its first documentation in the ethnic identity literature. Clearly, the stream of immigration from Mexico must play a strong hand in the maintenance of Mexican-American identity. More novel is the relationship between children's ethnic identity and children's cooperative/ competitive behavioral preferences. This particular finding emphasizes the role of ethnic identity in human behavior, and directs attention to the exploration of its role in other ethnically related social behaviors.

Implications of These Findings

Cognitive understanding.   These results have numerous implications. First, the results regarding the development of ethnic identity suggest that it is important to recognize restrictions on children's cognitive capacity when they are asked about their ethnicity. Young children may not have the ability to describe their ethnicity in an abstract way, but such incapacity is not due to a low sense of pride, weakening or rejection of their ethnic identity, "cultural deprivation," or low IQ. The preschool child who gives you a "Chicano handshake" and then cannot answer a query about what the word *Chicano* means is neither lacking in cultural heritage nor ignorant. When he is older, he will be able to answer that it means being from Mexico, and by the age of 10 he also will be able to explain the handshake as a way of greeting other Mexican people, which is a psychological trait. Another implication concerns multicultural educational materials for children, which must be pitched at the level of understanding of the child as suggested by developmental shifts demonstrated by our data.

Mental health and psychological adaptation.   To begin to formulate concerns about how other groups view them, to understand negative stereotypes, or to maintain a strong sense of their ethnic identity as a buffer against the prejudice that they are likely to experience, Mexican-American children must develop some basic abilities. These abilities include self-identification with their ethnic group, awareness of their ethnicity, and a clear sense of the permanency of their ethnic characteristics. Assuming that our data are generalizable across socioeconomic status and parental education, they suggest that Mexican-American children may not develop all these abilities until about 8 to 10 years of age. Practitioners working with children who are 8 years or older should be cognizant that Mexican-American children are likely to have sufficient information and cognitive development to have an ethnic identity, and that this ethnic identity may be of relevance to any psychological or social problems a Latino child may be experiencing. Thus, for example, if family conflict is the issue, it is possible that an incompatibility in ethnic identity between one or both parents and the child leads to serious culturally based differences in values, and thus to differences in behavioral expectations. In working with families and in other clinical contexts, such as in institutional settings where ethnic children are in the minority, the practitioner may wish to provide multicultural experiences for Mexican-American children regardless of their age so as to promote ethnic identity development and thus strengthen their sense of who they are as ethnic persons and enable them to withstand negative stereotypes. Eventually, when children reach adolescence, such experiences may result in the achievement of a more secure ethnic identity, as suggested by Phinney (Phinney, 1993; Phinney, Lochner, & Murphy, 1990).

Future Research and Theory

Our methodology can be used to assess the effects of a variety of factors that may differentially affect ethnic identity components—in particular, contextual variables, child-rearing styles, gender values, and variables related to mental health. In addition, extension of the methodology for measurement of ethnic identity to Mexican-American adolescents is a logical next step because of the importance of the process of identity achievement during adolescence (Erickson, 1968; Phinney, 1992). A number of investigators have developed models of ethnic identity development and methodologies for assessing ethnic identity across ethnic groups (e.g., Cross, 1978; Helms, 1985; Kim, 1981; Phinney, 1990). A needed development, however, is the theoretical and methodological *link* from childhood through adolescence in a manner that permits continuity in the understanding and assessment of the development of ethnic identity across the lives of young people. The theoretical part of the *link* would need to identify those relevant variables experienced by younger children in their more restricted social ecologies, and the effects of these on ethnic self-concept, and to integrate them with those variables and effects that operate in the increasingly broader social ecologies of preadolescence and adolescence.

This theoretical *link* also would need to be extended so that it encompasses four processes that affect the ethnic identity of the young person: enculturation, acculturation, development or maturation, and life changes or transitions, which are common as youths move across schools and communities. Addition of theoretical consideration of these processes, however, complicates the research methodology immeasurably because the effects of these kinds of processes are extremely difficult to sort out, particularly given that other variables, such as socioeconomic background, recency of immigration, and education, also prevail.

As an example of the complications involved, suppose that one wanted to compare the following groups in order to identify the varying effects of the four processes on ethnic identity. Although adolescents already have experienced considerable enculturation into the Mexican-American culture by their families and communities, and thus one would expect minimal enculturative effects, they still may be undergoing rapid acculturative, maturational, and transitional changes. If one were interested in assessing the effects of acculturation on ethnic identity in these youths, a possible research design would be to compare groups of youths: (1) making the transition from a junior high school with high representation of the youths' own ethnic group to a high school with high majority culture representation (acculturation group), with (2) youths where no own-ethnic-group representation change is encountered during the same transition (transition group), with (3) youths attending a four-year high school where there is a high own-ethnic-group representation across grades (maturation group). The difficulty of locating such groups would be heightened by the need to match the schools for socioeconomic background and recency of immigration. Thus, attempts to study these processes encounter substantial obstacles.

In Mexican-American culture, gender differences in enculturation may lead to differential emphases on children's ethnic identity components. For example, females may be expected to maintain cultural traditions and values, in part because they have less freedom to interact with members of the dominant culture, but also because they must behave according to culturally preconceived notions of appropriate feminine behavior, and they are expected to provide cultural continuity across generations in their role as homemakers and mothers. If ethnicity is linked to their enculturation as females, and their ethnic identity becomes fused with their gender identity, then the additive strength of both identities would be greater, and lesser strength in one would affect the other identity as well. Males, by contrast, may be capable of a strong ethnic identity that mediates culturally based behaviors independently of gender identity. Data on such possible differences do not exist, although greater involvement in ethnicity by women than by men has been reported by one reviewer (Phinney, 1990). Exploration of such gender differences in the socialization of ethnic identity may elucidate the large differences in social behaviors often observed among men and women of Latino background.

References

Aboud, F. E. (1984, January). *The development of ethnic identity and attitudes.* Paper presented at the Society for Research on Child Development Study Group on Children's Ethnic Socialization. Los Angeles, California.

Aboud, F. E. (1987). The development of ethnic self-identification and attitudes. In J. S. Phinney & M. J. Rotheram (Eds.), *Children's ethnic socialization: Pluralism and development* (pp. 32–55). Newbury Park, CA: Sage Publications.

Aboud, F. E., & Mitchell, F. G. (1977). Ethnic role taking: The effects of preference and self-identification. *International Journal of Psychology, 12,* 1–17.

Ballard, B. (1976). Development of racial awareness: Task consistency, reliability, and validity. *Journal of Genetic Psychology, 129*(1), 3–11.

Bernal, M. E., Knight, G. P., Garza, C. A., Ocampo, K. A., & Cota, M. K. (1990). The development of ethnic identity in Mexican-American children. *Hispanic Journal of Behavioral Sciences, 12,* 3–24.

Bernal, M. E., Knight, G. P., Ocampo, K. A., Garza, C. A., & Cota, M. K. (1993). Development of Mexican American identity. In M. E. Bernal & G. P. Knight (Eds.), *Ethnic identity: Formation and transmission among Hispanics and other minorities* (pp. 31–46). Albany, NY: SUNY Press.

Brand, E. S., Ruiz, R. A., & Padilla, A. M. (1974). Ethnic identification and preference: A review. *Psychological Bulletin, 81,* 860–890.

Burke, J. P., Balow, C. E., & Hunt, J. P. (1988). *Self-concept comparisons among Black, Mexican American, and White children in low-SES integrated schools.* Unpublished manuscript, Arizona State University, Tempe.

Clark, K. B., & Clark, M. P. (1947). Racial identification and preference in Negro children. In T. M. Newcomb & E. L. Hartley (Eds.), *Readings in social psychology* (pp.169–178). New York: Holt.

Cross, W. (1978). The Thomas and Cross models of psychological nigrescence: A literature review. *Journal of Black Psychology, 4,* 13–31.

Driedger, L. (1975). In search of cultural identity factors: A comparison of ethnic students. *Canadian Review for Sociology and Anthropology, 12,* 150–161.

Elias, N., & Blanton, J. (1987). Dimensions of ethnic identity in Israeli Jewish families living in the United States. *Psychological Reports, 60,* 367–375.

Emmerich, W., Goldman, K. S., Kirsh, B., & Sharabany, R. (1977). Evidence for a transitional phase in the development of gender constancy. *Child Development, 48,* 930–936.

Erickson, E. H. (1968). *Identity: Youth and crisis.* New York: Norton.

Fox, D. J., & Jordan, V. D. (1973). Racial preference and identification of Black, American Chinese, and White children. *Genetic Psychology Monographs, 88,* 229–286.

Franco, J. N. (1983). A developmental analysis of self-concept in Mexican-American and Anglo school children. *Hispanic Journal of Behavioral Sciences, 5,* 207–218.

García, J. (1982). Ethnicity and Chicanos: Measurement of ethnic identification, identity, and consciousness. *Hispanic Journal of Behavioral Sciences, 4,* 295–314.

George, D. M., & Hoppe, R. A. (1979). Racial identification, preference, and self-concept: Canadian Indian, and White school children. *Journal of Cross Cultural Psychology, 10,* 85–100.

Goodman, M. K. (1964). *Race awareness in young children.* New York: Collier.

Harter, S. (1983). Developmental perspectives on the self-system. In E. M. Hetherington (Ed.), *Handbook of child psychology: Socialization, personality, and social development* (Vol. 4, pp. 275–385). New York: Wiley.

Harter, S., & Pike, R. (1980). *The pictorial scale of perceived competence and acceptance for younger children.* Unpublished manuscript, University of Denver.

Helms, J. (1985). Toward a theoretical explanation of the effects of race on counseling: A Black and White model. *Counseling Psychologist, 12,* 153–165.

Hutnik, H., (1986). Patterns of ethnic minority identification and modes of adaptation. *Ethnic and Racial Studies, 9,* 150–167.

Kim, J. (1981). *The process of Asian-American identity development: A study of Japanese American women's perceptions of their struggle to achieve positive identities.* Unpublished Ph.D. dissertation, University of Massachusetts.

Knight, G. P., Bernal, M. E., Garza, C. A., & Cota, M. K. (1993). A social cognitive model of the development of ethnic identity and ethnically-based behaviors. In M. E. Bernal & G. P. Knight (Eds.), *Ethnic identity: Formation and transmission among Hispanics and other minorities* (pp. 213–234). Albany, NY: SUNY Press.

Knight, G. P., Bernal, M. E., Garza, C. A., Cota, M. K., & Ocampo, K. A. (1993). Family socialization and the ethnic identity of Mexican-American children. *Journal of Cross-cultural Psychology, 24,* 99–114.

Knight, G. P., Cota, M. K., & Bernal, M. E. (1993). The socialization of cooperative, competitive, and individualistic preferences among Mexican American children: The mediating role of ethnic identity. *Hispanic Journal of Behavioral Sciences, 15,* 291–309.

Knight, G. P., Garza, C. A., & Bernal, M. E. (1994). *The structure of ethnic identity among Mexican American children.* Unpublished manuscript, Arizona State University.

Larned, D. T., & Muller, D. (1979). Development of self-concept in Mexican American and Anglo students. *Hispanic Journal of Behavioral Sciences, 11,* 279–285.

Maldonado, B. M., & Cross, W. (1977). Today's Chicano refutes the stereotype. *College Student Journal, 11,* 146–152.

Marsh, A. (1970). Awareness of racial differences in West African and British children. *Race, 11,* 289–302.

Martin, C. L., & Little, J. K. (1990). The relation of gender understanding to children's sex-typed preferences and gender stereotypes. *Child Development, 61,* 1427–1439.

Moreland, K. (1966). Comparison of racial awareness in Northern and Southern children. *American Journal of Orthopsychiatry, 36,* 22–32.

Ocampo, K. A., Bernal, M. E., & Knight, G. P. (1993). Gender, race, and ethnicity: The sequencing of social constancies. In M. E.

Bernal & G. P. Knight (Eds.), *Ethnic identity: Formation and transmission among Hispanics and other minorities* (pp. 11–30). Albany, NY: SUNY Press.

Phinney, J. S. (1990). Ethnic identity in adolescents and adults: Review of research. *Psychological Bulletin, 108,* 499–514.

Phinney, J. S. (1992). The multigroup ethnic identity measure: A new scale for use with adolescents and young adults from diverse groups. *Journal of Adolescent Research, 7,* 156–176.

Phinney, J. S. (1993). A three-stage model of ethnic identity development in adolescence. In M. E. Bernal & G. P. Knight (Eds.), *Ethnic identity: Formation and transmission in Hispanics and other minorities* (pp. 61–79). Albany, NY: SUNY Press.

Phinney, J. S., Lochner, B. T., & Murphy, R. (1990). Ethnic identity development and psychological adjustment in adolescence. In A. R. Stiffman & L. E. Davis (Eds.), *Ethnic issues in adolescent mental health* (pp. 53–72). Newbury Park: Sage.

Phinney, J. S., & Rotheram, M. J. (1987). *Children's ethnic socialization: Pluralism and development.* Newbury Park, CA: Sage Publications.

Porter, J. D. R. (1971). *Black child, White child.* Cambridge: Harvard University Press.

Rice, A. S., Ruiz, R. A., & Padilla, A. M. (1974). Person perception, self-identity, and ethnic group preference in Anglo, Black, and Chicano preschool and third-grade children. *Journal of Cross-Cultural Psychology, 5,* 100–108.

Rosenberg, M. (1979). *Conceiving the self.* New York: Basic Books.

Rosenthal, B. G. (1974). Development and self-identification in relation to attitudes toward the self in the Chippewa Indians. *Genetic Psychology Monographs, 90,* 43–141.

Rosenthal, D. A., & Hrynevich, C. (1985). Ethnicity and ethnic identity: A comparative study of Greek-, Italian-, and Anglo-Australian adolescents. *International Journal of Psychology, 20,* 723–742.

Semaj, L. (1980). The development of racial evaluation and preference: A cognitive approach. *Journal of Black Psychology, 6,* 59–79.

Slaby, R. G., & Frey, K. S. (1975). Development of gender constancy and selective attention to same sex models. *Child Development, 46,* 849–856.

Stevenson, H. W., & Stewart, E. C. (1958). A developmental study of racial awareness in young children. *Child Development, 29,* 399–409.

Tajfel, H. (1978). *Differentiation between social groups: Studies in the social psychology of intergroup relations.* London: Academic Press.

Thompson, S. K. (1975). Gender labels and early sex role development. *Child Development, 46,* 339–347.

Vaughn, G. M. (1987). A social psychological model of ethnic identity. In J. S. Phinney & M. J. Rotheram (Eds.), *Children's ethnic socialization* (pp. 73–91). Newbury Park, CA: Sage Publications.

Williams, J. A., & Moreland, J. K. (1976). *Race, color, and the young child.* Chapel Hill: University of North Carolina Press.

$Chapter\ 3$

Central American Youth Exposed to War Violence

MARÍA CECILIA ZEA
The George Washington University

VIRGINIA A. DIEHL
Western Illinois University

KATHERINE S. PORTERFIELD
The George Washington University

In the 1980s the civil war and human rights abuses in Central American countries caused a tremendous influx of immigrants into the United States. The vast majority of these immigrants were children and youth (Benjamin & Morgan, 1989). Children living in El Salvador and Guatemala in the 1980s were repeatedly exposed to a kind of war violence different from that of traditional wars. As described by Melville and Lykes (1992), this so-called low-intensity warfare (LIW) is "characterized by random government-sponsored terrorism, often coming unexpectedly from the sky by means of helicopters, the use of medium to small military units that sneak up on isolated rural villages, and the attempted destruction of all social relationships, networks, and solidarity among the targeted civilian population" (p. 535). Almost 70,000 Salvadorans died as a consequence of political repression in the form of low-intensity warfare between 1977 and 1987 (García & Rodríguez, 1989; Martín-Baró, 1989, 1990a; Montes & García, 1988). In Guatemala it is estimated that between 50,000 and 100,000 people were killed and over 400 villages were destroyed between 1981 and 1983 (Melville & Lykes, 1992).

Hundreds of thousands of Central Americans (one out of four in the case of Salvadorans) have been uprooted by force, military pressure, or war destruction, becoming refugees either in their own countries or abroad. There are more than a million Salvadoran and about 200,000 Guatemalan refugees in the United States alone (Melville & Lykes, 1992), and, as mentioned earlier, most of them are children or young adults (Benjamin & Morgan, 1989). The first of these young people came to the United States in 1980, and for the most part they are here to stay. They constitute the most recent influx of Latinos to the United States, and as a consequence of their war-related experiences (e.g., exposure to brutality, threats to their lives, deprivation) and recent immigration they present special problems such as posttraumatic stress disorder, academic difficulties, and adjustment problems. Consequently, this is a group whose urgent needs require special attention from Latino psychology in the 1990s.

The fact that most Central American youth migrated to the United States in order to escape civil war makes them a unique population among Latinos. Although at first glance it might seem that these youth are here by choice, in fact they migrated in order to survive. Massive exposure to violence characterizes this population. Many Central American children witnessed or experienced mutilations, torture, disappearances of family members, killings, massacres of entire communities, bombings, and relocation. Families were dislocated as a consequence of the war, with children being separated from their parents. Fathers were frequently forced to leave their families and country to avoid being drafted. Mothers often joined them later in the United States, but the costs and dangers of the trip forced parents to leave their younger children behind. Once the parents had a secure financial situation in the host country, they would send for their children. In the meantime, these children were exposed to war violence without the protective buffering typically provided by the presence of a parent (Aron, 1990; Diehl, Zea, & Espino, 1994; Ronstrom, 1989).

Cristina's[1] story exemplifies the experiences of Central American youth. Cristina is a young Salvadoran woman who as a girl witnessed war-related violence in her neighborhood on the outskirts of San Salvador. Cristina described becoming so accustomed to hearing about and observing killings that "a part of your feelings freeze, and you stop suffering about it." When somebody from the town disappeared for a few days, the mothers and relatives would start searching for the missing person in the nearby garbage dump. People in the neighborhood would spread the news each time new corpses were found there. Cristina described how "sometimes you could only find pieces, like a hand, and you would try to identify your relative with just that information." One of the worst incidents she witnessed took place when the army came to take away her neighbor, a woman in her early twenties. It was particularly painful for Cristina to listen to the young woman's mother yelling for help, to hear the noise the soldiers made while they took her away, and not to be able to do anything. "I was very afraid if I helped her they would take me.... Later on, when they found her body, I had to go see her, I had to see with my own eyes. They had mutilated her breasts. I can never forget that image." Even many years after this episode, Cristina still has nightmares in which somebody is after her to rape, mutilate, and then kill her, as happened to her neighbor. She wakes up startled from these dreams but does not talk about this recurrent nightmare with anyone because she fears descriptions of her experiences in El Salvador will hurt those who care about her.

---

[1] Cristina's name is a pseudonym.

Even before Cristina fled her country she was presenting some symptoms characteristic of posttraumatic stress disorder, for example the *freezing* or numbness of her feelings. She describes becoming so numb that she could no longer feel anything except the desire to survive. It appears that her feelings were so overwhelming that she suppressed them in order to survive, and the casual observer might believe that she had become so completely accustomed to the violence and the pain of others that the horror no longer mattered.

Cristina migrated alone to the United States when her mother began to fear that she would be picked up and hurt by the army. At that time, she spoke no English, and although she had started college in El Salvador, she could find only menial jobs in the United States. She did not know anyone in the city where she originally settled, and the process of adjusting to the new culture was slow. Even now, stressful events such as moving to a different city will trigger flashbacks of corpses completely covered by blood, like the ones she saw in El Salvador.

Cristina's story exemplifies the trauma experienced by many war survivors. According to Eth and Pynoos (1985), trauma is "an overwhelming event resulting in helplessness in the face of intolerable danger, anxiety, and instinctual arousal" (p. 173). This event is perceived as a direct threat to the victim's life and/or to the lives of one's significant others, generating fear that is often paralyzing.

We can further paint a picture of the lives of Central American young people with these experiences reported by 30 Salvadoran youth between the ages of 14 and 18 (Mancilla, 1987). They had migrated to the Washington, D.C., area between 1983 and 1984 in order to avoid the war (47%), to avoid being recruited (10%), or to reunite with parents who had migrated earlier (50%). Among the aspects they liked least about El Salvador they cited war (66.7%), poverty (10%), danger of being drafted (10%), and unemployment (6.7%). Fifty-seven percent of these youth had lost friends to the war, 33% had lost a family member, 30% had witnessed massacres, 17% had witnessed torture, 53% had witnessed shootings, 50% had witnessed explosions, 43% witnessed killings, 30% witnessed beatings, 23% witnessed abductions. Many had friends and relatives who disappeared.

The drawings in Figure 3.1, made by Salvadoran children in refugee camps in Honduras and obtained by William Vonberger (1986), illustrate beyond words the horror of the experiences these refugee children endured.

Although war's impact on children from various countries has been discussed previously (e.g., Freud & Burlingham, 1943), each wartime situation is different. For instance, though introduced earlier in history, low-intensity warfare was perfected in Central America. There have been no studies comparing the effects on children of exposure to traditional war (e.g., World War II) and exposure to low-intensity warfare. It is unclear whether there are cultural differences in coping styles that affect children's ability to deal with the stress generated by war. It is also unclear whether the types of support provided to the children by the adults in their lives vary across cultures or societally.

At present we do not have an adequate body of research addressing the needs of Central American youth exposed to war violence. Only recently have some measures of war-related trauma been developed. Espino, Sanguinetti, Moreno, Diehl,

FIGURE 3.1   Drawings Made by Salvadoran Refugee Children While They Were in Honduran Camps

Source: From *Fire in the Sky: Salvadoran Children Drawings* by William Vonberger (Ed.). Copyright 1986 by Writers and Readers, New York. Used by permission.

and Zea (1987) developed a scale to measure levels of exposure to war-related violence in Central American children. Hjern, Angel, and Höjer (1991) designed a scale to measure exposure to violence and the impact of separation and loss in Chilean immigrant children. Mollica and colleagues (1992) developed the Harvard Trauma Questionnaire for Indochinese adults. Pynoos and Eth (1986) developed an interview technique to assess trauma in children that is useful for various clinical settings but not specifically directed at war situations.

The psychological impact of trauma on Central American children exposed to war violence has only recently begun to be examined. Arroyo and Eth (1984) conducted one of the most widely cited studies of Central American youth. They interviewed 28 Salvadoran and two Nicaraguan youth and their parents and found that the impact of exposure to violence included "suicidal behavior, multiple somatic complaints without organic etiology, various serious antisocial acts, insomnia, separation anxiety, defiance, and multiple school related problems" (p. 107). Clearly, the effects of exposure to war violence can be far-reaching and severe (Freud & Burlingham, 1943; Kinzie, Sack, Angell, Manson, & Rath, 1986). But why are some children profoundly and chronically affected by war violence, while others are only moderately or temporarily affected? Are these differences attributable to risk and protective factors that moderate or mediate the impact of war violence?

A Model of the Impact of Exposure to War Violence

On the basis of investigations of children who have experienced war situations, we propose a framework that can provide a foundation for future research and could lead to the development of a broader theory of the traumatic effects of exposure to war on children. This model includes both risk and protective factors as mediators of the consequences of war-related trauma (see Figure 3.2). Although in many

Risk Factors

Nontraditional warfare
Uprooting and migration
Fear of deportation
Economic hardships

Outcomes

Negative socialization of children
Posttraumatic stress disorder
Other psychological symptoms
Academic difficulties

Trauma →   →

Protective Factors

Social support
Psychosocial competence
Cognitive factors

FIGURE 3.2   Model of Risk and Protective Factors on the Impact of Trauma Induced by War-Related Violence

cases the absence of a protective factor becomes a risk factor, the inverse is not true of the risk factors. For example, lack of social support makes the children more susceptible to developing PTSD symptoms. Staying in the home community, however, does not necessarily serve a protective function. Therefore, we have chosen to consider risk and protective factors separately. Nevertheless, it is implied that children who lack social support, psychosocial competence, and cognitive abilities will be more likely to develop negative outcomes.

Risk Factors

The risk factors denoted in Figure 3.2 contribute to or exacerbate the negative impact of exposure to war violence on Central American children and youth. One of the difficult experiences shared by many of these children is the *type of warfare* that they have endured. Many Central Americans were exposed to low-intensity warfare, which is different from traditional war (e.g., World War II) in that it relies on random acts of terrorism and the blurring of the distinctions between enemy and friend and between civilian and combatant (Melville & Lykes, 1992). For children living under these conditions, the unpredictability of their experiences and the confusion generated by them constitutes a major source of added stress.

Mancilla (1987) interviewed 30 Salvadoran youth between the ages of 14 and 18 who had been in the United States for an average of 4.5 years. It appeared that the type of warfare they had experienced (involving sudden disappearances and atrocities committed before their eyes) had a clear impact on their emotional well-being. These youth ranked as particularly stressful the disappearance of friends and relatives and their own direct witnessing of violent acts toward others. Youth exposed to the stress of violence exhibited anxiety, fear, and depression. These findings support the conclusion of the American Psychological Association Task Force on War-Related Stress (Hobfoll et al., 1991): "The greater the threat of loss or the actual loss to which individuals were exposed, the greater their level of risk" (p. 848).

Psychological warfare was another tactic utilized during the Central American conflict. Ignacio Martín-Baró (1990b) characterized psychological warfare as any type of operation that includes "demoralizing the rival (military or civilian, individual or group), [and] convincing the enemy that it would be useless to continue fighting" (p. 95). These tactics include propaganda campaigns, news reports, rumors, or the use of religion to instill insecurity in individuals about their own beliefs and feelings, which makes them accept and "submit to the 'established order' " (p. 96). People surrender to the situation and give up hope when psychological warfare is used. If the victims are forced to relocate, having given up hope might make the transition to a new culture more difficult.

Uprooting and migration are a consequence of the destruction of communities and involves the loss of both roots and of place of origin. Many of the youth in our sample and in Mancilla's study reported missing their hometown and their country as one of the burdens they had to bear. Migration per se is a risk factor that generates considerable stress. This stress is exacerbated when the immigration is illegal, particularly when the child travels alone or with only part of the family, when the situation at the destination is unknown, or when the child is victimized during the border crossing. Add to these problems the difficulty of adapting to a new culture, including the stress of adopting the behavior, attitudes, and beliefs of the host culture (Berry, 1990), and the problems and fears associated with having undocumented status.

Cervantes, Salgado de Snyder, and Padilla (1989) found that in addition to exposure to war violence, the experience of migration contributed to the development of PTSD symptoms in young adults. Their sample compared immigrants to nonimmigrants. Among the immigrants there were 120 Central American (44 who reported migrating because of the war and 76 who reported migrating for other reasons) and 138 Mexican adults who had migrated to the United States. Among the nonimmigrants there were 188 Mexican Americans born in the United States and 141 Anglo-Americans. They found significant differences in generalized psychological distress between immigrants and nonimmigrants as measured by the Center for Epidemiology Depression Scale (CES-D) developed by Radloff (1977). Immigrants reported "loneliness and isolation, concentration difficulties, lower interest levels, and feelings of hopelessness about the future" (Cervantes et al., 1989, p. 617). However a cautionary note should be made, and it is that in this study the impact of migration may be confounded with the impact of war on Central Americans. However, the fact that PTSD scores of Mexican immigrants ($M = 5.34$) significantly differed from those of Mexican Americans ($M = 3.73$) and Anglo Americans ($M = 3.27$) indicates that the migration did contribute to stress.

The perpetual fear of deportation is another considerable stressor which Central American children and their parents must endure. The U.S. policy of strict restrictions against immigration of Central Americans (i.e., not granting them refugee status) forces most Central Americans to live in the United States as undocumented individuals.

Once in this country, undocumented individuals find few social services available to them or capable of meeting their needs. Language and monetary barriers abound. Medical, mental health, family counseling, school, and job assistance are a few of the unmet needs of this undocumented population. When services are offered to them, many times they hesitate to accept them because they fear being reported to the Immigration and Naturalization Service (INS).

Economic hardships add to the pressures on Central American children. For the Guatemalan children interviewed by Melville and Lykes (1992), one of the hardest parts of their ordeal while fleeing their towns was the hunger they had to endure until they arrived at the refugee camps. Poverty and economic difficulties both in transit and on arrival in the United States are reported as sources of stress once these children have survived the war. Their parents may have difficulty finding a job, whether day labor or steady employment, because they do not speak English well or because of their undocumented status. Many times families have to move, often because co-workers, employers, or neighbors hint at or threaten a call to the INS.

Protective factors.   Although a host of protective factors play a role when a child is exposed to war violence and subsequently attempts to adapt to a new environment, we have identified a few in the literature and in our own research that seem to be most salient. These are social support, psychosocial competence, and cognitive factors.

Social support.   Since the initial literature on social support appeared (Caplan, 1974, 1976; Cobb, 1976) research has demonstrated the benefits of perceiving the availability of social support, whether it gets accessed or not (Cohen & McKay, 1984; Cohen & Wills, 1985; Holahan & Moos, 1981; Lakey & Heller, 1988; Zea, Jarama, & Bianchi, 1995). This support can consist of either tangible or intangible forms of assistance that lead individuals to believe that someone cares for them (Barrera, Sandler, & Ramsay, 1981). This belief seems to increase resilience and acts as a protective factor during stressful periods such as wartime. It may be provided by parents, other family members, or the community.

Social support provided by parents or other family members has been discussed as one of the most important determinants of positive or negative outcomes after exposure to war violence. Freud and Burlingham (1943) found that children who lived through World War II had a more positive psychological outcome if a supportive parent was available. Similarly, Kinzie, Sack, Angell, Manson, and Rath (1986) found that among Cambodian children exposed to severe war violence, those who had remained with a nuclear family member were less likely to receive a psychiatric diagnosis such as posttraumatic stress disorder or severe depression than those who had lived with a foster family or alone. In the Melville and Lykes (1992) study, Guatemalan children attributed their recovery from trauma to the supportive role of their parents.

Diehl et al. (1994) investigated 63 Latino youth between the ages of 7 and 16 who were members of a community center in Washington, D.C. Eighty-three percent of these youth were from Central America, predominantly from El Salvador. The trauma variable examined in this study was exposure to war violence as measured by the scale developed by Espino et al. (1987). One of the protective factors that this study investigated was the maintenance of the nuclear family. With respect to psychological effects, children exhibited more PTSD symptoms when they had endured more extreme exposure to war violence and when they had been separated from their fathers. However, separation from mother accounted for less of the variance in PTSD symptoms than did separation from father. This surprising finding is partially explained by the fact that generally, children who were separated from their mothers were also separated from their fathers. Another factor might be that in strongly patriarchal cultures such as those in Central America, the mother nurtures the children, but the presence of the father is a symbol of protection. Therefore, the absence of the father may have been perceived by the children as more threatening than was the absence of the mother. With the father absent, the mothers might have been frequently victimized during the war, and therefore their presence did not buffer the children's fears.

Additionally, there was a weak developmental trend between age of separation from father and PTSD; the older the child was when the father was separated from the family, the greater the number of PTSD symptoms the child presented. This finding is consistent with reports of younger children appearing to be more resilient than older children in response to major disasters (Masten, Best, & Garmezy, 1990). Our data also showed that when the separation was caused by the death of a family member, the effects were more severe. Those children who heard of or saw a family member killed (or dead) as a result of war had more PTSD symptoms. Obviously, when children witness their family members being killed, this is more traumatic than having a family member leave to avoid persecution. War has become very personal, and the trauma of this experience is extreme.

In our study, both separation from the mother and separation from the father were negatively related to reading achievement (as measured by the WRAT-R). However, neither of the separation measures was significantly related to verbal or performance IQ scores on the WISC-R. From these findings it appears that separation of a child from his or her parents is a better predictor of academic achievement than of IQ. This is consistent with Green's (1985) findings of trauma affecting the ability to focus attention on the task at hand.

Mancilla (1987) examined social support and psychosocial competence as protective factors, and psychological symptoms as outcomes in a sample of Salvadoran youth living in the Washington, D.C., area. Her findings underscore the importance of receiving social support, particularly while being exposed to war violence. She found that the social support the children had received while in El Salvador was a more important predictor of how well they coped in the United States than was the social support they were now receiving in the United States. The support received in El Salvador probably helped buffer the impact of war violence and might have enhanced the children's coping ability. A few studies suggest that some children become more active copers under extremely challenging circumstances, and that this helps them deal with the chronic exposure to violence typical of war-related situations or urban neighborhoods (Fitzpatrick, 1993; Tyler, Tyler, Echeverry, & Zea, 1992). Moreover, children exposed to war situations adapt better when their parents' coping ability is adequate, when they can function under stress, and when they provide social support to their children (Masten et al., 1990).

Social support provided by other family members in the permanent or temporary absence of parents has also been considered an important protective factor. Alternative caregivers can serve as role models in times of stress and can provide emotional support that may compensate for the absence of the parents (Garbarino, Dubrow, Kostelny, & Pardo, 1992).

Social support provided by the community has also been shown to buffer war-related stress. Ziv and Israeli (1973) found that in kibbutzim that had been bombarded, children who received support from their teachers experienced the event as less traumatic. In some instances it even became a source of pride to be part of a bombarded kibbutz. Melville and Lykes (1992) investigated the relationship between social support in refugee camps and emotional coping. There were several differences among four camps for Guatemalan refugees. Two of these were in Guatemala and two were in Mexico. In one of the Guatemalan camps there was a commitment by the camp staff to encourage and maintain Mayan culture and language, while this effort was not put forth in the other three camps. However, Melville and Lykes found no conclusive evidence that social support in the form of retaining one's own culture was positively related to emotional coping. One factor that may have obscured this relationship is that the children in the Mexican camps felt and literally were safer than those in Guatemalan camps. In the camps in Mexico children were encouraged to talk about their experiences, whereas in the camps in Guatemala they were not encouraged because in their situation talking could have been dangerous. Therefore, the positive effects of safety and self-expression may have balanced out the influence of support for the children's cultural heritage.

In a study of Latin American children who migrated to Canada, Allodi (1989) found no differences in emotional health and social adjustment between children exposed to war violence and those not exposed. He attributes these findings in part to the host country; Canada has been a country supportive of refugees. These findings contrast with those of Mancilla (1987), who found that social support in the host country (the United States) was not as important as that in the country of origin. The discrepancy could be accounted for by the fact that the United States historically has not provided as much social support as Canada. The role of a supportive community seems to be of particular importance to Central Americans given that Latino culture is relational. That is, instead of focusing on individual needs, people focus on relationships with others. Supportive community interventions may be more culturally congruent with this population than individual interventions.

Psychosocial competence. Tyler (1978) and Tyler, Brome, and Williams (1991) defined psychosocially competent individuals as those who have moderate self-efficacy, believe they can control the outcomes of their lives, have moderate trust in the world around them, and have an active coping and planful behavioral style. Psychosocially competent individuals display resilience, which is defined as "the process of, capacity for, or outcome of successful adaptation despite challenging or threatening circumstances" (Masten et al., 1990, p. 426). Colombian street children living under the most adverse circumstances demonstrated resilience; they sustained competence under threat and seemed to endure life on the streets successfully. These children survived trauma comparable to that of war: In a sample of 94 boys, 25% had been shot or stabbed and 25% had been raped before they were 12 years old (Tyler et al., 1992). It is common for these children to be persecuted by paramilitary groups who aim to "cleanse" the streets of the "disposable," a term frequently used to refer to the street children. Tyler et al. found that those children who had experienced some kind of personal support while still at home and fewer physical threats while on the streets were coping more actively with street life and had a stronger sense of being in control on the streets, but they were more distrustful. The APA Task Force on War-Related Stress (Hobfoll et al., 1991) concluded that "the fewer coping resources an individual had, the more likely he or she would be overwhelmed by the losses or threats of losses encountered" (p. 848). These studies illustrate that an active and positive coping style is an essential protective factor in buffering war-related trauma. In contrast, negative coping styles such as problem avoidance, blaming others, drug and alcohol abuse, and social isolation do not act as buffers (Hobfoll et al., 1991).

An active coping style or efforts to maintain equilibrium under significant threat by dealing with environmental pressures successfully (Masten et al., 1990) is more adaptive than a passive or avoidant coping style and is positively related to mental health (Schwebel, 1992). An internal locus of control also has been associated with resilience (Masten et al., 1990), although having the flexibility to attribute adverse circumstances to external events when appropriate may be more adaptive.

In Mancilla's (1987) study, Central American youth who had lower psychosocial competence scores had received less social support in El Salvador and were having more coping difficulties after migrating to the United States. They reported feeling hopeless and lacking control over their lives. One-third of all individuals studied agreed with the statement "nothing ever turns out the way I wanted or expected"; 33% agreed with "my worries make me ill"; and 50% agreed with "sometimes I wonder if anything matters anymore."

Cognitive factors. Cognitive factors such as intelligence and problem-solving ability help compensate for trauma (Masten et al., 1990). We examined the relationship between exposure to war violence and the freedom from distractibility index obtained from the WISC-R and found a strong negative relationship ($r = -.35$, $p < .01$) between these two indices. Children who had been more exposed to the violence of war were more easily distractible. This relationship is consistent with Green's (1985) finding that physically abused children spend much of their attention looking for danger signs and Arroyo and Eth's (1985) observation that Central American children who had been exposed to war experience frequent intrusions in thought. These attentional problems have a negative effect on their academic performance. Our finding, that greater exposure to war violence is negatively related to freedom from distractibility, also suggests that attentional problems may be the source of the academic difficulties traumatized children experience. Although a causal relationship has not been established, it seems that exposure to war violence interferes with the intellectual development of some children, much as anxiety or depression interfere with IQ (Sattler, 1982). Intelligence may also serve as a mediator of the impact of violence. We found that there was an interaction between exposure to violence and Verbal IQ in predicting posttraumatic stress disorder symptoms. Under moderate levels of exposure to violence, IQ did not have an effect. Under high levels of exposure to violence, however, children with lower Verbal IQ scores had more PTSD symptoms. A similar but not significant trend suggested that under high levels of exposure to violence, children with lower Performance IQ also had more PTSD symptoms. Therefore, it appears that having a high IQ can provide needed resources that help children cope with extreme stress.

Outcomes

There is little agreement among psychologists about the effects of exposure to war-related violence on children's mental health. According to Punamaki (1982), some researchers, particularly those who conducted their research during World War II, found no evidence of emotional disturbances among children subjected to air raids. Allodi (1989) found that both Salvadoran and Chilean child refugees in Toronto whose parents were victims of persecution and torture were not different in emotional health and social behavior from other Latino immigrant children. He attributes these findings to the buffering effect of parental presence and, as mentioned earlier, to acceptance within the host country. Other researchers, however, have found evidence of anxiety, cognitive delays, posttraumatic stress disorder, and other disturbances among Latin American children who experienced war-related violence (Arroyo & Eth, 1985; Diehl et al., 1994; Hjern et al., 1991; Masser, 1992; Melville & Lykes, 1992).

Negative socialization.   Much of the focus of research has been on psychological effects of war on children—more specifically, on psychological symptoms such as PTSD. For example, Diehl et al. (1994) found that the greater the amount of exposure to war violence, the greater the number of PTSD symptoms the children developed. However, war trauma can have consequences other than psychological symptoms, such as negative socialization, which often go unnoticed. Negative socialization occurs when children have internalized the notion that violence is acceptable, which leads them to dehumanize their opponents and those who are different from themselves, which in turn leads them to place no value on other people's lives. An excellent example of the effect of exposure to violence on socialization of children was given by Martín-Baró (1989). In discussing Leahy's study of the formation of the concept of social class in El Salvador, Martín-Baró (1989) wrote:

> More than two hundred children of various ages, belonging to various social sectors, were interviewed. One of the questions asked was: "What would have to happen in order for there to be no poor people?" Several of the children from the higher socioeconomic sectors gave this response: "Kill them all."
>
> Of course, this piece of data can be interpreted in various ways, and the study is still unfinished. But the studies carried out in the United States have never reported this kind of answer. It should be added that some sectors of Salvadoran society propose as a solution to the civil war the elimination of "all the subversives," in the style of the 1932 mass killing that took place in the country in order to "win this way another fifty years of peace." (p. 6)

Martín-Baró (1989) further described tactics or situations that lead to the development of a lack of sensitivity for the suffering of others as "criminalization of children's minds" (p. 14). Punamaki (1982) contends that it is impossible to teach children norms such as "do not kill" or "respect other's dignity" when exactly the opposite is being valued in their surroundings. Some of the socialization problem behaviors Central American youth who have been exposed to war violence are currently manifesting in the United States (such as delinquency) include involvement in delinquent and gang-related activities (Gutiérrez, 1994). It has been suggested that, among other factors, the manifestations of delinquency may in part be a consequence of these children's earlier socialization to war violence (Garbarino, Kostelny, & Dubrow, 1991).

Posttraumatic stress disorder.   One of the most widely discussed psychological outcomes of exposure to violence, PTSD involves reexperiencing of the traumatic incident, recurrent distressing dreams of the event, flashbacks, and intense psychological distress at exposure to circumstances that resemble or symbolize the traumatic experience. Cristina, the young Salvadoran woman mentioned earlier, described reaching a point where she was numb. She no longer felt anything when she saw the atrocities carried out by the army in San Salvador. Her experiences are similar to those of the children interviewed by Arroyo and Eth (1985). For instance, they described one Central American child as having to avoid experiencing any emotion in order not to bring any attention to himself. This "painful state of forced silence," caused by frequent death threats, forced this child to avoid admitting to others that he could identify some of the many corpses found in the street (Arroyo & Eth, 1985, p. 114).

Espino et al. (1987) developed a scale based on the DSM-III-R to assess PTSD in Central American children. They found that the greater the extent of exposure to violence the children experienced, the greater the number of PTSD symptoms they showed. These findings are consistent with those of Malmquist (1986), who found PTSD symptoms in North American children who had witnessed parental murder, and those of Masser (1992), who found that 11 out of 15 Central American children who had been exposed to war violence presented PTSD symptoms, whereas only two out of 16 who had *not* been exposed to violence had PTSD symptoms.

In a study by Cervantes et al. (1989), Central American young adults manifested higher rates of PTSD than Mexicans and Mexican Americans. The authors initially assumed that self-report of the reason for leaving the country would be an indicator of exposure to war. Although 44 of the Central American participants reported migrating because of the war and 76 for other reasons, it is likely that both groups were exposed to a substantial amount of war violence. This could explain the lack of differences in PTSD symptoms between those Central Americans migrating because of the war (52%) and those Central Americans migrating for other reasons (49%). The two Central American groups contrast with the significantly smaller percentage of Mexican immigrants presenting PTSD symptoms (25%). These findings suggest that asking people why they migrated is too indirect a measure of exposure to war; they may downplay their experiences by saying they migrated for other reasons. War has a pervasive impact on a country (e.g., infrastructure, economic well-being), and reasons for migrating can be attributed to the indirect consequences of war, such as joblessness, poverty, or joining friends and relatives who migrated earlier. Thus, in a survey, it could be difficult to get the respondents to admit that they migrated because of the war, particularly if they fear being associated with political activity in their country, which could jeopardize their stay in the United States.

Psychological symptoms.   In addition to PTSD, we have described other psychological symptoms that seem to appear as a consequence of the trauma associated with experiencing war-related violence: cognitive delays (Diehl et al., 1994; Espino et al., 1987); school difficulties (Malmquist, 1986); concentration difficulties (Cervantes et al., 1989); and anxiety, depression, and regressive behaviors (Chimienti, Nasr, & Khalifeh, 1989; Mancilla, 1987).

Additional studies support the previous findings about the negative impact of war-related violence on children and adults. For instance, Chimienti et al. (1989) studied 1,039 Lebanese children between the ages of 3 and 9. Thirty percent of these children had experienced war trauma such as witnessing death, forced displacement of family, the death of a family member, or destruction of their home. These children were more likely to exhibit symptoms of fear and anxiety and behavior problems such as aggressiveness than those children who did not experience war trauma.

In addition to psychological symptoms, there are other feelings and fears that exceed the realm of daily experiences. When Melville and Lykes (1992) asked Guatemalan children who were living in a refugee camp to describe the feelings they had during an experience of violence which they had reported, *susto* (sudden fear) was described as the strongest emotion experienced by the children (91%), followed by sadness (88%). These are powerful emotions that many of these children will remember for the rest of their lives, and that, under normal circumstances, we try to protect children from experiencing.

Summary

In this chapter we have discussed some of the special circumstances in the lives of Central American children and youth who have migrated to the United States because of the war. Unfortunately, the sequelae of the trauma to which they have been exposed seem to be long term, and the lack of services offered to this specific community worsens the situation. Outreach efforts through the public school system, health providers, the church, and the neighborhoods are examples of culturally appropriate interventions for Central American youth. Training of professionals and paraprofessionals in psychology and related fields who provide services to immigrant populations should include information about war-related stress. Although peace may be obtained in one place, violence is likely to appear elsewhere in the Americas and the rest of the world, bringing thousands of refugees with mental health needs that we must be prepared to address.

We have proposed a model for research that includes risk and protective factors that mediate the trauma of war violence, which we hope will contribute to a more encompassing conceptualization of the research in this area. Because political violence is not a controlled experiment, it is difficult to meet the rigorous guidelines for publishing research findings in this field. Yet it is imperative that we further study the harmful consequences of exposure to violence, because there are no conclusive findings about the best way to prevent and treat some of the psychological problems that surface as a consequence of the terrifying experiences to which children are exposed. Researchers have a contribution to make to the communities that receive war refugees by helping them better understand, protect, and help the children. Practitioners need to be informed by empirical research in order to plan effective treatments and interventions for war refugees, as well as to plan interventions in collaboration with the school systems that receive these young innocent victims.

References

Allodi, F. (1989). The children of victims of political persecution and torture: A psychological study of a Latin American refugee community. *International Journal of Mental Health, 18*(2), 3–15.

Aron, A. (1990). Problemas psicologicos de los refugiados Salvadoreños en California. En I. Martín-Baró (Ed.), *Psicologia social de la guerra: Trauma y terapia*. San Salvador: UCA.

Arroyo, F., & Eth, S. (1985). Children traumatized by Central American warfare. In S. Eth & R. S. Pynoos (Eds.), *Post-traumatic stress disorder in children* (pp. 101–120). Washington, DC: American Psychiatric Press.

Barrera, M., Jr., Sandler, I. M., & Ramsay, T. B. (1981). Preliminary development of a scale of social support: Studies on college students. *American Journal of Community Psychology, 9,* 435–447.

Benjamin, M. P., & Morgan, P. C. (1989). *Refugee children traumatized by war and violence: The challenge offered to the service delivery system*. Washington, DC: CASSP Technical Assistance Center, Georgetown University Child Development Center.

Berry, J. W. (1990). Acculturation and adaptation: A general framework. In W. H. Holtzman & T. H. Bornemann (Eds.), *Mental health of immigrants and refugees*. Austin: University of Texas.

Caplan, G. (1974). *Support systems and community mental health: Lectures on concept development.* New York: Behavioral Publications.

Caplan, G. (1976). The family as a support system. In G. Caplan & M. Killelea (Eds.), *Support systems and mutual help*. New York: Grune & Stratton.

Cervantes, R. C., Salgado de Snyder, V. N., & Padilla, A. M. (1989). Posttraumatic stress in immigrants from Central America and Mexico. *Hospital and Community Psychiatry, 40,* 615–619.

Chimienti, G., Nasr, J. A., & Khalifeh, I. (1989). Children's reactions to war-related stress: Affective symptoms and behaviour problems. *Social Psychiatry and Psychiatric Epidemiology, 24,* 282–287.

Cobb, J. (1976). Social support as a moderator of life stress. *Psychosomatic Medicine, 38,* 300–314.

Cohen, S., & McKay G. (1984). Social support, stress and the buffering hypothesis: A theoretical analysis. In A. Baum, S.E. Taylor, & J.E. Singer (Eds.), *Handbook of psychology and health* (Vol. 4). Hillsdale, NJ: Lawrence Erlbaum Associates.

Cohen, S., & Wills, T. A. (1985). Stress, social support, and the buffering hypothesis. *Psychological Bulletin, 98,* 310–357.

Diehl, V. A., Zea, M. C., & Espino, C. M. (1994). Exposure to war violence, separation from parents, post-traumatic stress, and cognitive functioning in Hispanic children. *Interamerican Journal of Psychology, 28,* 25–41.

Espino, C., Sanguinetti, P., Moreno, F., Diehl, V., & Zea, M. C. (1987, August). Testing of Central American children: Effects of war violence. In

L. Comas-Díaz (Chair), *Psychological testing with Hispanics: New research findings.* Symposium for the 95th Annual Convention of the American Psychological Association, New York.

Eth, S., & Pynoos, R. S. (1985) Interaction of trauma and grief in childhood. In S. Eth & R. S. Pynoos (Eds.), *Post-traumatic stress disorder in children.* Washington, DC: American Psychiatric Press.

Fitzpatrick, K. M. (1993). Exposure to violence and presence of depression among low-income African-American youth. *Journal of Consulting and Clinical Psychology, 61,* 528–531.

Freud, A., & Burlingham, D. T. (1943). *War and children.* New York: Medical War Books, Ernest Willard.

Garbarino, J., Dubrow, N., Kostelny, K., & Pardo, C. (1992). *Children in danger: Coping with the consequences of community violence.* San Francisco: Jossey-Bass.

Garbarino, J., Kostelny, K., & Dubrow, N. (1991). What children can tell us about living in danger. *American Psychologist, 46,* 376–383.

García, M. O., & Rodríguez, P. F. (1989). Psychological effects of political repression in Argentina and El Salvador. In D. R. Koslow & E. P. Salett (Eds.), *Crossing cultures in mental health.* Washington, DC: Sietar International.

Green, A. H. (1985). Children traumatized by physical abuse. In S. Eth & R. Pynoos (Eds.), *Post-traumatic stress disorder in children.* Washington, DC: American Psychiatric Press.

Gutiérrez, B. (1994, September 2). La vida loca de las pandillas Latinas de Washington. *El Tiempo Latino,* p. B1.

Hjern, A., Angel, B., & Höjer, B. (1991). Persecution and behavior: A report of refugee children from Chile. *Child Abuse and Neglect, 15,* 239–248.

Hobfoll, S. E., Spielberger, C. D., Breznitz, S., Figley, C., Folkman, S., Lepper-Green, B., Meichenbaum, D., Milgram, N. A., Sandler, I., Sarason, I., & van der Kolk, B. (1991). War-related stress: Addressing the stress of war and other traumatic events. *American Psychologist, 46,* 848–855.

Holahan, C. J., & Moos, R. H. (1981). Social support and psychological distress: A longitudinal analysis. *Journal of Abnormal Psychology, 90,* 365–370.

Kinzie, J. D., Sack, W. H., Angell, R. H., Manson, S., & Rath, B. (1986). The psychiatric effects of massive trauma on Cambodian children: The children. *Journal of the American Academy of Child Psychiatry, 25,* 370–376.

Lakey, B., & Heller, K. (1988). Social support from a friend, perceived support, and social problem solving. *American Journal of Community Psychology, 16,* 811–824.

Malmquist, C. P. (1986). Children who witness parental murder: Post-traumatic aspects. *Journal of the American Academy of Child Psychiatry, 25,* 320–325.

Mancilla, Y. E. (1987). *Exposure to war-related violence and psychosocial competence of adolescent males from El Salvador.* Unpublished manuscript.

Martín-Baró, I. (1989). Political violence and war as causes of psychosocial trauma in El Salvador. *International Journal of Mental Health, 18*(1), 3–20.

Martín-Baró, I. (1990a). Guerra y trauma psicosocial del niño Salvadoreño. In I. Martín-Baró. (Ed). *Psicologia social de la guerra: Trauma y terapia.* San Salvador: UCA.

Martín-Baró, I. (1990b). Religion as an instrument of psychological warfare. *Journal of Social Issues, 46,* 93–107.

Masser, D. S. (1992). Psychosocial functioning of Central American refugee children. *Child Welfare, 71,* 439–456.

Masten, A., Best, K. M., & Garmezy, N. (1990). Resilience and development: Contributions from the study of children who overcome adversity. *Development and Psychopathology, 2,* 425–444.

Melville, M. B., & Lykes, M. B. (1992). Guatemalan Indian children and the sociocultural effects of government-sponsored terrorism. *Social Science and Medicine, 34,* 533–548.

Mollica, R. F., Caspi-Yavin, Y., Bollini, P., Truong, T., Tor, S., & Lavelle, J. (1992). The Harvard Trauma Questionnaire: Validating a cross-cultural instrument for measuring torture, trauma, and posttraumatic stress disorder in Indochinese refugees. *Journal of Nervous and Mental Disease, 180,* 111–116.

Montes, S. & García, J. J. (1988). *Salvadoran migration to the United States: An exploratory study.* Washington, DC: Center for Immigration Policy.and Refugee Assistance, Georgetown University.

Punamaki, R. L. (1982). Childhood in the shadow of war: A psychological study of attitudes and emotional life of Israeli and Palestinian children. *Current Research on Peace and Violence, 5*(1), 26–41.

Pynoos, R. S., & Eth, S. (1986). Witness to violence: The child interview. *Journal of the American Academy of Child Psychiatry, 25,* 306–319.

Radloff, L. S. (1977). The CES-D Scale: A self-report depression scale for research in the general population. *Applied Psychological Measurement, 1,* 385–401.

Ronstrom, A. (1989). Children in Central America: Victims of war. *Child Welfare, 68,* 145–153.

Sattler, J. M. (1982). *Assessment of children's intelligence and special abilities.* Boston: Allyn and Bacon.

Schwebel, M. (1992). Making a dangerous world more tolerable for children: Implications of research on reactions to nuclear war threat, war, and disaster. In G. W. Albee, L. A. Bond, & T. V. Cook Monsey (Eds.), *Improving children's lives: Global perspectives on prevention* (pp. 107–128). Newbury Park, CA: Sage Publications.

Tyler, F. B. (1978). Individual psychosocial competence: A personality configuration. *Educational and Psychological Measurement, 38,* 309–323.

Tyler, F. B., Brome, D. R., & Williams, J. (1991). *Ecology, ethnic validity and psychotherapy: A psychosocial competence approach.* New York: Plenum Press.

Tyler, F. B., Tyler, S. L. Echeverry, J. J., & Zea, M. C. (1992). Making it on the streets in Bogota: A psychosocial study of street youth. *Genetic, Social, and General Psychology Monographs, 117,* 395–417.

Vonberger, W. (Ed.). (1986). *Fire from the sky: Salvadoran children drawings.* New York: Writers and Readers.

Zea, M. C., Jarama, S. L., & Bianchi, F. (1995). Social support and psychosocial competence: Explaining the adaptation to college of ethnically diverse students. *American Journal of Community Psychology, 23,* 509–531.

Ziv, A., & Israeli, R. (1973). Effects of bombardment on the manifest anxiety level of children living in kibbutzim. *Journal of Consulting and Clinical Psychology, 40,* 287–291.

Chapter 4

A Sociocultural Context for Understanding Gang Involvement among Mexican-American Male Youth

JERALD BELITZ
DIANA M. VALDEZ
University of New Mexico

Youth gangs are becoming more prevalent in the urban communities in which Mexican-American children live. These gangs threaten the physical and psychological health of the youths who either belong to gangs or are exposed to violence related to gang activities. Gang involvement also reflects disruption in the psychosocial and cultural developmental course of the participating members.

Recent analyses of Mexican-American gang members indicate that these youths seem to seek out the support and protection of gangs because their families, communities, and other social systems have failed to meet their developmental needs (Belitz & Valdez, 1994; Morales, 1992; Vigil, 1988a). Generally, researchers have focused on the more alienated and disturbed gang youths, who typically experience serious family, social, cultural, psychological, academic, and legal problems.

This chapter examines the psychosocial and cultural variables associated with youth gang affiliation among a larger spectrum of Mexican-American males. More

The authors refer to research participants in the masculine form because this review does not include females.

specifically, this chapter delineates cultural-familial factors and personal and cultural identity factors that are pertinent to the conceptualization and assessment of gang-involved youth. Incorporated into the text are discussions about youths whose families experience varying levels of acculturation stress and utilize varying acculturation strategies. This includes dysfunctional families who have marginal cultural identities, recently immigrated families in the process of adapting to a new culture, and assimilated families who have variable levels of identification with their Mexican-American culture.

Treatment issues are presented within the context of cultural-familial and cultural identity development models. Multimodal interventions are proposed with particular emphases on family systems, group therapy, and an integration of community programs and resources. Finally, the roles and responsibilities of the mental health professionals in this process are defined. Many of the perspectives and observations presented in this chapter are derived from the authors' work in community mental health and juvenile justice settings.

Sociocultural Context

Acculturation and Parent–Child Conflict

Acculturation has been mentioned as one factor in a myriad of factors that place Mexican-American youth at risk for gang involvement. The impact of acculturation on the functioning of immigrant and successive generation Mexican-American families has been extensively documented (Falicov, 1983; Montalvo & Gutierrez, 1989; Ramirez, 1984; Rueschenberg & Buriel, 1989; Szapocznik, Kurtines, & Fernandez, 1980).

The relationship between parent–child cultural conflict and the risk for gang involvement, however, requires further exploration. Familial contexts include severely dysfunctional families and families in which sociocultural pressures negatively affect parenting styles. A decreased focus on ethnic-cultural practices among more assimilated families may motivate youths to "claim" a cultural identity through gang affiliation (Belitz & Valdez, 1994).

Any discussion about cultural familial patterns must take into account the regional, generational, and socioeconomic familial variations found among Mexican-American families. Falicov (1983) writes, "Both public (cultural) and private (idiosyncratic) norms govern family relationships and combine to make every family unique." (p. 137).

Transcultural Family Conflict

Gang-involved youth are described as coming from families in which there is a considerable amount of domestic violence, exposure to an abusive male, physical and/or sexual abuse, and substance abuse (Belitz & Valdez, 1994). This pattern of severe family dysfunction, however, can be viewed as being caused by "transcultural dysfunctional patterns" (Falicov, 1983). These are patterns that transcend culture and reflect characteristics of dysfunctional family systems such as poverty, inadequate housing, and insufficient community resources (Adler, Ovando, & Hocevar, 1984). According to Falicov, problems associated with transcultural variables may be further aggravated by the stress associated with cultural adaptation or cultural dissolution.

These dysfunctional family systems are often characteristic of the more aggressive, psychologically disturbed *vato loco* or *crazy guy* described by Belitz and Valdez (1994). For many of these youths, an aggressive father figure may play a negative role in the youth's psychosocial development. Many of these youths have been physically abused by this male adult and/or have witnessed their mothers and siblings being battered. This paternal figure, through the use of force and intimidation, brandishes the most power and control in the family system. As a result of their own experience of victimization by male figures, the mothers feel powerless to protect themselves or their children from this violence. Confused by the mother's inability to maintain a safe home, the youths may develop ambivalent feelings and behavior toward their mothers. In an effort to defend themselves psychologically against pervasive feelings of helplessness and vulnerability, and to contain their rage, the boys ultimately may identify with the aggressor—the abusive father (Belitz & Valdez, 1994). As the boys approach adolescence, the family becomes less capable of providing for their emotional needs. These youngsters can become increasingly marginalized and isolated from their families, their culture, and the social system in which they are involved. According to these authors, as parental supervisory control deteriorates, the youths may eventually discover replacement "families" on the street to fulfill their dependency needs.

Morales (1992) observes that the street gang may function as a youth's surrogate family, providing for his psychosocial needs. Gang members regularly identify their gang as *mi familia* and openly express their loyalty and commitment to their *carnales* or *homeboys*.

Immigrant Families

Families who emigrate to the United States face multiple problems created by the process of migration. These families often move into impoverished, high-risk neighborhoods where drugs and gangs are present. In addition, because of the parents' inability to speak English, the children may be assigned the role of language and social mediators for their parents, thus creating an imbalance in the relationship between parent and child (Falicov, 1983). This alteration in the hierarchy becomes intensified when these children enter the school or the legal system and are put in the position of negotiating these systems for their parents. Through this process, the parents become disempowered, which in turn gives the children an increased sense of responsibility and authority. Additionally, the youths experience anxiety because they may view their parents as being unable to intervene on their behalf. In particular, these youths may view their parents as being unable to protect them from the threats of their neighborhood. As indicated by Vigil (1983, 1988a), these younger adolescents may perceive the youth gang and the older gang peers as the most powerful agents of acculturation in an urban environment in which they feel vulnerable.

As immigrant families reorganize and adapt to a new environment, normal developmental stress can become more problematic for their children (Falicov, 1983). Through this process, adolescents become susceptible to gang involvement if the family system is viewed as being too rigid. The adolescents may eventually associate with a "gang family" to defy what they perceive to be a static, authoritarian family structure. Although strict child-rearing practices may be attributed to their immigrant status or to a traditional cultural orientation, such practices are often an attempt by the parents to protect their children from the dangers of high-risk neighborhoods. For example, parents may severely restrict their children's activities, utilize punitive forms of discipline, and forbid neighborhood friendships. These child-rearing strategies are similar to those used by parents who raise their children in environments characterized by high community violence (Garbarino, Kostelny, & Dubrow, 1991). Although such adaptations are well intentioned, the development of age-appropriate adolescent behavior or positive parent–child interactions may be disrupted.

Youths also view their parents as potentially obstructing their process of acculturation and their struggle to achieve mastery and control in their new environments. Children often acculturate at a faster rate than their parents, creating a dissonance in values that may intensify a parent–child conflict, putting the child at risk of dealing with cultural adaptation negatively and becoming a gang member (Falicov, 1983; Montalvo & Gutierrez, 1989).

Successive-Generation Families

Although there has been some upward mobility among Latinos in the past two decades, successive generations continue to confront socioeconomic problems disproportionate to their percentage of the population. As indicated in Chapter 1, Latinos, particularly Mexican-American youths, have the highest high school dropout rate of any major group in the United States, live in poverty, and typically live in inner-city environments (García & Montgomery, 1991; Soriano, 1994). Additionally, these youths are exposed to institutional discrimination and disrespect for their culture (Goldstein & Soriano, 1994). The impact of poverty, discrimination, and low educational attainment increases the adolescents' awareness of the disparity between their aspirations for achievement and the actual opportunities that exist (Knight, Kagan, Nelson, & Gumbiner, 1978). This is likely to lead to lower self-esteem and social alienation. These youths are more likely to seek alternative, albeit delinquent, means of securing prestige and economic success. Gangs provide a mechanism for these adolescents to achieve financial gain and status in their communities (Moore, García, García, Cerda, & Valencia, 1978; Vigil, 1983).

For successive generations of Mexican-American youth, there exists a trend for greater separation from the core values and norms that characterize traditional Mexican culture (Buriel, Calzada, & Vasquez, 1982). A study by Kaplan and Marks (1990) showed that psychological distress increased in Mexican-American young adults in concordance with increased acculturation. As Mexican Americans become further removed from the influence of their culture, they may internalize the negative stereotypes of their group held by the dominant culture and act out these stereotypes. Buriel et al. (1982) concluded that a strong cultural orientation may foster healthier psychological adjustment and could offset pressure toward delinquent behavior. Likewise, minority youth who possess strong ethnic identities have higher levels of self-esteem (Phinney, 1992; Phinney, DuPont, Espinosa, Revill, & Sander, 1994).

For some families, their efforts to assimilate to the dominant culture have resulted in providing less attention to the teaching of language, cultural knowledge, and behaviors that are prerequisites for a strong cultural identity. Parents expect that assimilation will protect their children from negative societal attitudes and from the enduring effects of racism and discrimination. When the child enters adolescence, however, issues of personal cultural identity become important developmental tasks (Phinney et al., 1994). Without parental cultural socialization, they may adopt stereotypic views of a cultural identity, which may include gang affiliation.

Adolescent Identity Development

Adolescence is the period in which youths strive to develop an independent personal identity. This requires adolescents to become less dependent on parents, develop a sexual identity, develop peer relationships and obtain security from an increasing mastery of the self and the environment (Erikson, 1968; Slaff, 1979). For minority youths, their ethnicity is a core component of their identity. These adolescents face the complex developmental task of integrating their ethnic identity with their personal identity (Phinney, 1992; Phinney et al., 1994; Bernal, Saenz, & Knight, 1995).

Ethnic identity is a multidimensional construct which incorporates such key elements as self-identification as a group member, sense of belonging and attachment to the group, familiarity with the group's history and culture, and behavioral and emotional participation in the group's practices (Phinney, 1991, 1992; Phinney et al., 1994). Phinney (1991, 1992) conceptualizes that ethnic identity formation results from an active personal exploration of the meaning of one's ethnicity. Only after this exploration occurs can the individual achieve a commitment to a secure ethnic identity. Complicating this process is the task of negotiating the meaning and conflict related to their membership or identification with their own cultural group vis-à-vis their interactions with the dominant culture.

Issues of identity are particularly salient for gang-involved youth. A large majority of Mexican-American gang members may experience alienation both from their traditional cultural group and from the dominant cultural group. Because of their disorganized family environment, these youths' psychosocial cultural developmental needs, including those centering on identity formation, have been neglected or inadequately assuaged (Belitz & Valdez, 1994). There is little involvement of community resources (e.g., church activities, community centers) and when involvement does exist, the youths typically experience themselves as failures (e.g., in school). They also are perceived by adults and peers as failures within these systems. Interactions with members of institutions of the dominant culture often leave the adolescents feeling invalidated at both the personal and cultural levels (Vigil, 1983).

Vigil observes that Mexican-American youths who are attracted to gangs are experiencing "multiple marginality" due to the effects of low socioeconomic status, cultural conflicts, discrimination, and family problems. Vigil concludes that the "gang subculture is very attractive to young Mexican-Americans who objectively reflect a dual heritage, but ironically, subjectively reject both ..." (p. 67). This results in diminished self-esteem, psychological problems, substance abuse, and confusion about one's personal cultural identity.

Research indicates that minority youths who have an absence of parental or other adult role models are at higher risk for gang involvement or delinquent behavior (Buriel et al., 1982; Oyserman, 1993; Wang, 1994). These youths have minimal contact with adults who function as either masculine or culturally integrated role models. Instead they are exposed to street life at an early age and are subsequently socialized and acculturated to the streets (Vigil, 1988a). *Veteranos*, the older, more powerful gang members, are the dominant males in the streets and serve as masculine role models for the latency-age preadolescent youths. As the youths mature into adolescence, they internalize the behaviors and values of these *veteranos*. Gang members, who tend to have remarkably similar life histories, validate and legitimatize each other's experientially and culturally determined concepts of masculinity based on an identification with aggressive role models. Gang members define masculinity as a demonstration of power, bravado, aggression, and dominance (Belitz & Valdez, 1994; Vigil, 1988a). In the extreme, this tough masculine posture is referred to as *locura* or "craziness," and it seems to help adolescents manage their anxieties, fears, and anger (Moore, 1988; Vigil, 1988a, 1988b).

Membership in the gang enables adolescents to construct a personal identity, cultural identity, and social identity derived from the explicit and implicit norms of the gang subculture. In their effort to minimize their sense of marginality, these adolescents accept an identity that is determined largely by the external ethnic and cultural labels projected onto them by their communities, and by the institutions of the dominant culture. The gang reinforces certain cultural aspects, such as a negative distortion of *machismo*, that ensure survival of the individual and the gang on the streets. Other indicators of their efforts to identify with their Mexican-American heritage include frequently using Spanish idioms and words in their dialogues and wearing clothing adorned with religious symbols. Rather than personally and actively exploring the meaning of their ethnicity or identity, the youths adopt the gang's narrow construct of what it means to be Chicano or Mejicano (Belitz & Valdez, 1994).

A more recent observation is the phenomenon whereby gangs provide a cultural identity to a growing number of Mexican-American youths whose families have assimilated with the dominant culture (Belitz & Valdez, 1994). These youths grow up with diminished identification or association with their traditional Mexican-American culture. Few have contact with adults who embody what are termed bicultural identities (Berry, 1980; Ramírez, 1984). This means the youths lack role models who possess strong ethnic identities while demonstrating membership and/or competency in the majority culture.

A distinctive subgroup of gang members are youths whose families recently immigrated from Mexico. As noted earlier, many of these immigrant families live in urban neighborhoods characterized by substandard housing and community services, lack of economic opportunity, high crime rates, and discrimination from the majority culture. These youths are experiencing alienation not only from the dominant culture but also from the Mexican-American culture in their new communities. Vigil (1983) observes that street gangs are part of the dangerous *barrio* environment to which recently immigrated youth must acculturate.

In summarizing this section on identity development and gang involvement, newly arrived youths often join a neighborhood gang in an effort to develop a Mexican-American identity—that is, to acculturate to their new environment. Many ally with their *barrio* gang, but many others join gangs that are largely made up of Mejicanos. This enables them to adapt to the streets while maintaining their already established ethnic identity. For these youths, gang membership also serves to minimize the effects of marginalization in their new community.

Assessment Issues

Because many gang youth are involved in the juvenile justice system, psychological evaluations generally occur within a forensic or legal setting. These evaluations are requested to assist the court in making preadjudicatory decisions or dispositional recommendations. Gang-involved youth are evaluated for a range of problems including shoplifting, aggravated battery, domestic violence, substance abuse, drug trafficking, drive-by shootings, and homicide. Typically, these youths are evaluated during their placement in detention. Because these evaluations are court-ordered, the youths are generally cooperative with the test process; any resistance to the process could have a negative impact on them in court.

Several issues are important when evaluating Mexican-American gang youth. First, concerns regarding the administration of standardized psychological tests with minority children must be considered. Whereas past research has examined test bias in intelligence testing with minority children (e.g., García, 1984), the study of cultural bias in the use of personality measures and clinical diagnosis has received less attention (Esquivel, 1992). It is crucial that test findings be interpreted within a cultural context, particularly when Latinos were not included in the normative sample (Cervantes & Arroyo, 1994). Second, language dominance needs to be determined before the evaluation is conducted. Because a high percentage of these youth have significant learning disabilities, a youth's ability to read and understand the test materials must be adequately assessed in order for the testing to be valid. Clinicians should use alternative means of test administration, such as audio tapes. Third, collateral information from family, friends, employers, social service workers, or teachers must be included in order to provide a more comprehensive view of the child. This is essential when the validity of standardized test results is questionable. This allows the evaluator to understand the complexities that go beyond the adolescent's stereotypic presentation as a gang member. Fourth, it is important that evaluators have adequate training in the assessment of minority group children (American Psychological Association, 1993; López & Hernández, 1987; Ramírez, Wassef, Paniagua, Linskey, & O'Boyle, 1994).

Another issue in the assessment of Mexican-American gang youth is the risk of overdiagnosing an adolescent's problems because of his gang affiliation. López & Hernández (1987) state that when one considers cultural issues in the assessment of Mexican-American clients, a clinical error can be made in terms of either overdiagnosing or underdiagnosing certain problems. Often, gang-involved youth are perceived to be entrenched in a delinquent criminal lifestyle that is sanctioned by a negative peer group. Given this view, the youth's problems are seen as being ingrained, with little hope for change toward a more prosocial lifestyle. Serious mental health disorders such as depression, anxiety, and posttraumatic stress may be underdiagnosed if the behavioral problems are solely attributed to the youth's gang involvement. For many, an underlying neurobiological disorder may be present, and further neurological, psychiatric, or neuropsychological evaluations are indicated (Lewis, Shanok, Pincus, & Glaser, 1979).

Additionally, it is important for the evaluator to have some knowledge of the gang culture in the local community as well as knowledge of the sociocultural stressors that affect minority youth. Jacobsen (1988) stresses the need to obtain a comprehensive account of the client's ethnocultural background in order to develop a contextual framework for the client's subjective experience. He proposes a model that takes into account the family's perception of its identity, the history of the family's relocation to the United States and its impact on family unity and cohesiveness, and the client's feelings regarding his or her sense of ethnic integration. Because parents of these youths feel disempowered by the various systems in which their children are involved, they should be apprised of the test results and the evaluator's recommendations. Although these youth have a history of emotional and behavioral problems, this is typically the family's initial encounter with a mental health professional. This provides an opportunity to inform the family about the child's mental health issues and treatment needs.

Within the juvenile justice system, mental health professionals can advocate strongly for the mental health needs of these youths. Forensic psychological evaluators can provide a context for the gang-related behaviors and provide appropriate referrals to mental health or other social service systems.

Treatment Interventions

In clinical work with ethnic minority families, the emphasis on the sociocultural context is critical in the development of culturally appropriate formulations and interventions. Falicov (1983) maintains that knowledge of the family's cultural norms and sociocultural context is crucial in defining the family's problems and defining the therapist's role. Accordingly, family therapy involves the interaction between two sets of cultural values, those of the therapist and those of the family.

Martínez (1994) contends that it is the responsibility of the therapist to maintain an "informed perspective that balances a broadly defined cultural sensitivity that includes an awareness of sociocultural and spiritual issues with sound clinical judgment based on well founded family therapy principles" (p. 79). Martínez (1994) states that a culturally sensitive approach should address issues of intrafamilial dynamics, poverty, discrimination, cultural dissolution, and acculturation.

Treatment of Transcultural Family Conflict

Treatment of the more alienated and marginalized youths requires an integration of individual, family, and group psychotherapies, as well as coordination of services among community agencies and resources (Belitz & Valdez, 1994). These youths, referred to as *vatos locos*, are experiencing significant psychosocial and cultural problems and are typically referred to treatment via the juvenile justice system. It is not uncommon for these adolescents to have had multiple legal contacts and several abortive attempts with therapy.

Within the framework of individual therapy, the youth can explore his history and experience of trauma related to living in his family system and his community. Through the therapeutic relationship, the adolescent processes his conflicted feelings toward his mother and father figures. Maladaptive behaviors can be reframed as the youth's effort to survive, psychologically and physically, in a dangerous world. Therapy provides the adolescent with a cognitive framework and language by which to identify, understand, and manage affective states and to differentiate between emotions and behavior. The therapy process also enables the youth to develop a larger repertoire of effective problem-solving strategies (Belitz & Valdez, 1994).

A cardinal component of therapy involves recognizing and exploring the adolescent's normative and psychosocial cultural developmental needs. Belitz and Valdez also indicated that gang involvement provides the youth with a sense of belonging to a family type system, a sense of being fully accepted and validated, a sense of competency and mastery, an accepted means of managing psychological distress, and a sense of a personal cultural identity. Because the gang is so integral to the youth's existence, the therapeutic work entails facilitating the youth's separation and individuation from the gang rather than from his family. Within the therapeutic context the youth begins to expand his personal, cultural, and masculine identity as a Mexican American beyond that of a gang member. This allows the youth to develop more culturally adaptive means of meeting his psychosocial needs.

Much of the family therapy focuses on resolving the family's dysfunction. Without placing blame on the parents or the culture, the therapist provides an arena in which all family members can process and validate their own traumatic experiences. This enables the family to understand the youth's gang involvement and for the adolescent to comprehend the family's inability to protect him or provide for his developmental needs.

Family therapy can effectively redefine the youth's role in the family system. An essential goal is to reintegrate the youth into his family while maintaining the adolescent's proficiency in developing an independent identity. Parental authority and power can be established, and the youth can function in a more age-appropriate manner. Often this involves helping the parental system effectively access and interact with other community agencies. The therapist may need to function as an advocate or case manager, or assign a community-based paraprofessional to function in that capacity. It is often useful to include extended family members in the treatment who can provide additional support to the adolescent in a surrogate parental role. Family members with secure Mexican-American identities can encourage the youth and family to identify their cultural strengths and integrate them into more positive individual and family identities (Belitz & Valdez, 1994).

If the youth is incapable of functioning within the family system or if the family is incapable of providing for the youth's needs, the therapist helps secure an out-of-home placement. Ideally this decision is processed in family therapy so that the youth does not feel rejected or abandoned. Such a decision results from the intent of maintaining the youth's well-being and providing him with the safest and most appropriate environment (Belitz & Valdez, 1994).

Treatment of Immigrant Families

Parent–child conflict issues that require therapeutic intervention include (1) overprotective parental styles that develop in order to protect the child from the dangers of high-risk neighborhoods; (2) disempowerment of the parent(s) by various institutions as a result of immigrant status, language barriers, and lower socioeconomic status; (3) the child's empowerment due to his intermediary role in negotiating systems for the parent(s), which creates a hierarchical imbalance in the family; (4) uneven levels of acculturation, where children acculturate faster than the parents, creating a dissonance in parent–child values (Falicov, 1983; Montalvo & Gutierrez, 1989; Szapocznik, Kurtines, & Fernandez, 1980). Child issues that also require therapeutic attention include helping the youths manage feelings of anxiety and vulnerability and exploring identity issues with an emphasis on developing alternative models of cultural adaptation. Parents sometimes feel helpless to confront the influence of the gang because of the situational stress caused by poverty, social isolation, and cultural conflict between the family and the school. The family's employment patterns and absence of extended family may also compromise their ability to provide the parental control that is essential in high-risk neighborhoods (Belitz & Valdez, 1994).

In family therapy with immigrant families, acculturation pressures that affect parent–child relationships are explored in terms of their meaning to both the parental and child subsystems. Frequently, youths complain that their parents are trying to raise them as if they still lived in Mexico. Parents perceive their children as adopting American ways at the expense of their family and cultural responsibilities (Belitz & Valdez, 1994). If the therapist exclusively interprets this conflict as part of the normal separation and individuation process that occurs when a child attempts to develop an ethnocultural identity apart from that of the parents, both the parents' perspective and the acculturation stress will be ignored. The therapeutic task is to restore the hierarchical balance in the family by validating the parents' efforts to maintain their family's cultural integrity. Concurrently, therapy focuses on increasing the parents' ability to tolerate and allow their child's exploration of alternative identities.

An important goal of treatment is to release the youth from the responsibility of negotiating the family's needs within their community. Restoring power to the parents and structural balance to the family allows the parents to provide support and protection in more culturally congruent and adaptive ways. This requires the therapist to assume the role of intermediary between the family and other social systems until other intermediaries, such as school counselors, case managers, or church volunteers, can be incorporated into the process. It also involves securing an interpreter for the parents so the youth is not their only connection to the English-speaking world. Community resources and youth programs can simultaneously empower the parents to negotiate or mediate for themselves, while providing the youths with new methods of culturally adjusting to their new environment (Belitz & Valdez, 1994).

Treatment of Successive-Generation Family Systems

Gang-involved youths whose families are characterized as assimilated are not, typically, as psychologically or behaviorally impaired as the *vatos locos* coming from dysfunctional families. These youths have little contact with the juvenile justice system and rarely have prior histories of mental health treatment. They are as likely to be referred by their families or teachers as by the legal system. Their developmental histories are more parallel to the normative processes conceptualized by Erikson (1968). As indicated earlier, their gang affiliation is often related to the adolescent issues of personal and cultural identity development rather than to family dysfunction.

Both individual and family therapy focuses on the adolescent's effort to define his identity, with a particular emphasis on ethnicity and culture. Issues of separation and individuation are as germane as any family structural imbalances. Therapy serves to facilitate the youth's and family's exploration of their Mexican/ Chicano heritage. This may include increasing their knowledge of their ethnicity and culture, participating in ethnic behaviors and practices, and reappraising their attitudes and values toward their group (Phinney, 1992). The goal is for the adolescent to achieve commitment and a sense of belonging to his Mexican-American group and to integrate cultural with personal identity. Participation by parents in this process validates its importance and provides an antidote to the negative cultural stereotypes to which the adolescent is exposed. Phinney and Chavira (1995) reason that ethnic minority parents are challenged to socialize their children to their own culture, to the dominant culture, and to the effects of prejudice and discrimination. This socialization facilitates the child's development of an ethnic identity and ability to function in the dominant culture. In the absence of such parental support, the youth is likely to internalize and incorporate negative paradigms in lieu of achieving a positive and stable Mexican-American identity. Parental involvement ensures the parents' primary role in assisting their children through this difficult and confusing developmental period.

Therapy with other successive-generation Mexican-American families needs to address the sociocultural variables, such as low socioeconomic status and ethnic discrimination, that result in a sense of familial social disempowerment (Martínez, 1994). The therapeutic process allows for the exploration of the dissonance in cultural values that exists between the parent(s) and the child. This involves examining both the parents' and the youth's definitions of achievement and status and their expectations for the youth's realization of that status. As communication improves and values become more explicit, the parents can function as more appropriate role models and advocates for their children. For instance, parents can collaborate with the school system to ensure that the youth's education needs are being answered.

Group Therapy and Identity Development

Group therapy is a powerful agent of change for gang-involved adolescents (Belitz & Valdez, 1994). Members of rival gangs from different socioeconomic and acculturation levels can participate as long as they commit to adhere to the group rules. An all-male group permits the adolescents to explore more honestly issues related to trauma, sexuality, self-esteem, and identity development. A successful group provides the youths with an alternative reference group and an alternative means of problem solving and of managing one's emotions and behaviors.

The principal theme is the exploration, development, and integration of their masculine, cultural, and personal identities. Identity issues are continually processed within a sociocultural context. Through the use of discussions, artwork, storytelling, listening to music, watching videos, and reproducing traditional rituals, the youths examine their sociocultural, family, and individual histories. The adolescents begin to discern what they learned about themselves and their masculinity from their interactions with their parent figures and other significant role models. As their critical-thinking skills increase, the boys examine the messages and images they received about their personal and their cultural selves from their families, churches, schools, neighborhood, media, and representatives of the various institutions of the majority culture. Members explore how gang affiliation has reflected, defined, and reinforced their Mexican-American identities.

Youths engage in the process of differentiating the positive and negative messages they internalized about their ethnicity. They begin to locate other role models who have secure Mexican-American identities. Through this active exploration they increase their knowledge of, identification with, and positive feelings about being a Mexican American/Chicano. Each adolescent strives to construct a cultural and personal identity that synthesizes his own unique experiences. Although being gang members will most likely remain a part of their identity, its centrality and importance recedes as these adolescents develop a more complex and integrated Mexican-American identity.

Concurrently, the adolescents evaluate their attitudes and feelings toward the dominant culture. By acknowledging and recognizing the discrimination and obstacles they confront, the youths can begin to develop more adaptive strategies in their interactions with individuals and systems of the dominant culture. The group process enables the youths to practice and learn new social skills, problem-solving skills, planning skills, and goal attainment skills that will help them adapt to the dominant culture. This process involves both identity exploration and building a larger repertoire of behavioral skills.

Role of the Therapist

For the therapeutic process to be meaningful and effective for the adolescent, the therapist must be cognizant of transference and countertransference issues (Belitz & Valdez, 1994; Morales, 1992). When working with the more disturbed adolescents, the therapist can expect to be the recipient of their negative transferential feelings. Because of their trauma histories, the adolescents mistrust adults, particularly adults who are perceived to occupy positions of authority. Therapists are often viewed as extensions of the justice system, with the power to determine the legal fate of the adolescents. Further, therapists are perceived to be part of an impersonal institution that replicates the punitive role of their often abusive father figures or the immobilized role of their mothers. The capacity to tolerate the youth's negative, hostile feelings is a fundamental prerequisite. Also, it is crucial to establish a therapeutic alliance before engaging in the therapeutic work. The issue of trust is central to the youth's psychosocial level of functioning and ability to engage in the therapeutic process.

Morales (1992) suggests that mental health professionals need to examine their attitudes, values, and biases toward Mexican Americans and other ethnic minority groups, gang members, socioeconomic status, and the saliency of culture and acculturation vis-à-vis identity development. An effective clinician sees a complex adolescent who is struggling with multiple developmental, familial, cultural, and socioeconomic issues behind the gang persona. Similarly, it is important to assess each youth accurately and not to minimize the negative behaviors and psychological disturbances as a justifiable adaptation to the youth's ecological environment. Morales lists several countertransferential beliefs that impede the therapeutic process, including (1) the belief that gang members are antisocial and thus untreatable; (2) the belief that gang members, because of their lack of education or lower socioeconomic status, are incapable of having insight; (3) a "do-gooder" attitude that assumes that all gang members are treatable; and (4) a "police mentality" that attempts to catch the youth in a lie. Other countertransferential issues that could be added to this list include difficulty tolerating the expression or exhibition of intense negative emotions; a vicarious gratification from hearing graphic descriptions of violence leading to inappropriate encouragement of clients to detail their gang activities; and an overidentification with either the rebellious adolescent or rigid institutional systems.

Familiarity with the gang culture and the communities in which the youths live is essential (Belitz & Valdez, 1994). For example, gang members are never asked to "rank out" of the gang. Apart from the psychological consequences, it is physically dangerous. The youth endures a physical assault by fellow gang members and then is left vulnerable and unprotected in an environment populated by hostile rival gang members. Therefore, treatment interventions need to emphasize the development of comparable support systems that may prevent the deterioration of the youth's level of functioning, which is likely to happen in the case of gang disaffiliation.

Frequently, several professionals and/or systems are intervening with the youth and the family. The mental health clinician is in a pivotal position to facilitate collaboration among many professionals. This often involves advocating for the mental health needs of the youth and providing a psychosocial cultural context in which other service providers can develop more appropriate interventions. For example, the clinician may attend a school meeting to assist in the development of the youth's individualized education plan. The therapist may also consult with the juvenile justice system to help create probation stipulations that account for the youth's multiple needs, such as attending school, gaining vocational training, receiving treatment for substance abuse, participating in community service programs that allow for positive contributions to their *barrios,* or participating in a mentoring program (Belitz & Valdez, 1994).

Belitz and Valdez also addressed issues of confidentiality that require special attention. Before any communication with other providers is effected, release of information forms must be obtained and the purpose of the communications made explicit. The limits of confidentiality are fully explained to the youth. Not only does this enable the clinician to practice ethically and in the best interest of the youth; it also models direct and honest communication. Only relevant information is to be shared with other professionals. The clinician's relationship with the juvenile justice system is the most difficult to manage. Although the youth may be court-ordered to treatment, the mental health professional functions as the youth's psychotherapist, and not as an officer of the legal system. Each clinician must balance the necessity of maintaining confidentiality and the therapeutic alliance with the responsibility of apprising the juvenile probation officer of the youth's progress. It is reasonable to inform the probation officer regularly of the youth's attendance, level of participation, and level of progress. Therapeutic issues, however, should be maintained as confidential. When the youth discloses he has violated the terms of probation, this information becomes part of the therapeutic discussion concerning the youth's motivation to change. However, when the youth engages in behavior that represents a risk to himself or others, the therapist should collaborate with the family and the probation officer to provide protection for the youth and/or others. This collaboration should occur only after therapeutic efforts to resolve the risk are unsuccessful. For example, if a youth discloses he is abusing drugs, the juvenile probation officer can be encouraged to enforce random drug screens.

Summary

The seminal works of Vigil (1983, 1988a) and Morales (1992) have been significant in describing the psychosocial and cultural contexts of Mexican-American youth involved in gangs. The more recent work of Belitz and Valdez (1994) addressed the treatment issues of Mexican-American gang youth who are seen in clinical and forensic settings, with particular focus on the family systems dynamics and adolescent development variables that motivate gang participation.

The present chapter has attempted to provide a broader clinical description of these Mexican-American gang youth in terms of acculturation stress, parent–child conflict, and cultural identity development. The impact of acculturation and stress can be detrimental to the parent–child relationship and can result in parenting styles that interfere with normal family and adolescent developmental processes. Families who are at varying levels on the acculturation continuum face difficult challenges in their attempts to maintain a sense of familial integrity and cohesiveness. For families who live in high-risk neighborhoods, certain levels of overcontrol and overprotection are necessary to confront the dangers of the streets. With successive-generation Mexican-American families, parent and ethnic socialization plays an important role in facilitating an adolescent's cultural identity and strategies for coping with discrimination stereotypes.

In the assessment of Mexican-American gang-involved youth, issues of potential cultural bias must be addressed. The role of various moderator variables, such as language proficiency or dominance, level of acculturation, and socioeconomic status, must be considered (Velasquez & Callahan, 1992). In both the assessment and the treatment of Mexican-American gang youth, clinical errors can be made when an adolescent's mental health problems are attributed mostly to his gang affiliation. More serious emotional problems may be underdiagnosed if the youth is identified solely as a conduct problem. On the other hand, these youths may be viewed as less amenable to treatment because they are perceived to be entrenched in a delinquent lifestyle that is supported by the gang. The complex psychological profiles that are revealed by psychological testing often stand in contradiction to the sensationalized stereotypic images of gang members.

The emphasis on the sociocultural lens through which to view the dynamics of gang-involved youth is critical in the development of culturally appropriate formulations and interventions. Issues of intrafamilial dynamics, poverty, discrimination, cultural dissolution, and acculturation are integral to a culturally responsive approach.

Mental health professionals must continue to advocate for the needs of gang-involved youth in both legal and mental health settings. A position of advocacy is one that recognizes the integration of the sociocultural, psychological, and political contexts in which gang behavior occurs. An examination of such contexts is critical in order to understand the characteristics of gang youth that go beyond stereotypes. Advocacy and education on behalf of these youth can help deter their criminalization and can provide them with culturally responsive mental treatment so that the emotional, social, and spiritual quality of their lives is improved.

References

American Psychological Association. (1993). Guidelines for providers of psychological services to ethnic, linguistic, culturally diverse populations. *American Psychologist, 48*, 45–48.

Adler, P., Ovando, C., & Hocevar, D. (1984). Familiar correlates of gang membership: An exploratory study of Mexican-American youth. *Hispanic Journal of Behavioral Sciences, 6*, 65–67.

Belitz, J., & Valdez, D. (1994). Clinical issues in the treatment of Chicano male gang youth. *Hispanic Journal of Behavioral Sciences, 16*, 57–74.

Bernal, M. D., Saenz, D. S., & Knight, G. P. (1995). Ethnic identity and adaptation of Mexican-American youths in school settings. In A. M. Padilla (Ed.), *Hispanic psychology: Critical issues in theory research* (pp. 71–88). Thousand Oaks, CA: Sage Publications.

Berry, J. W. (1980). Acculturation as varieties of adaptation. In A. M. Padilla (Ed.), *Acculturation: Theory, models and some new findings* (pp. 9–25). Boulder, CO: Westview.

Buriel, R., Calzada, S., & Vasquez, R. (1982). The relationship of a traditional Mexican-American culture to adjustment and delinquency among three generations of Mexican-American male adolescents. *Hispanic Journal of Behavioral Sciences, 4*, 41–45.

Cervantes, R. C., & Arroyo, W. (1994). DSM-IV: Implications for Hispanic children and adolescents. *Hispanic Journal of Behavioral Sciences, 16*, 8–27.

Erikson, E. (1968). *Identity, youth and crisis.* New York: Norton.

Esquivel, G. (1992). Some needed research on the assessment of Hispanics in clinical settings. In K. F. Geisinger (Ed.), *Psychological testing of Hispanics* (pp. 267–269). Washington, DC: American Psychological Association.

Falicov, C. J. (1983). Mexican families. In M. McGoldrick, J. K. Pearce, & J. Giordano (Eds.), *Ethnicity family therapy* (pp. 134–163). New York: Guilford Press.

Garbarino, J., Kostelny, K., & Dubrow, N. (1991). *No place to be a child: Growing up in a war zone.* Lexington, MA: Lexington Books.

García, J. (1984). The logic and limits of mental aptitude testing. In J. L. Martínez, Jr., & R. H. Mendoza (Eds.), *Chicano psychology* (pp. 41–58). New York: Academic Press.

García, J. M., & Montgomery, P. A. (1991). *The Hispanic population in the United States* (Series P-20, No. 455). Washington, DC: U.S. Government Printing Office.

Goldstein, A. P., & Soriano, F. I. (1994). Juvenile gangs. In L. D. Eron, J. H. Gentry, & P. Schlegel (Eds.), *Reason to hope: A psychosocial perspective on violence and youth* (pp. 315–333). Washington, DC: American Psychological Association.

Jacobsen, F. M. (1988). Ethnocultural assessment. In L. Comas Díaz & E. E. H. Griffith (Eds.), *Clinical guidelines in cross-cultural mental health* (pp. 135–147). New York: Wiley.

Kaplan, M. S., & Marks, G. (1990). Adverse effects on acculturation: Psychological distress among Mexican-American young adults. *Social Science Medicine, 31*, 1313–1319.

Knight, G. P., Kagan, S., Nelson, W., & Gumbiner, J. (1978). Acculturation of second- and third-generation Mexican American children: Field independence, locus of control, self-esteem, and school achievement. *Journal of Cross-Cultural Psychology, 9*, 87–97.

Lewis, D. O., Shanok, S. S., Pincus, J. H., & Glaser, G. H. (1979). Violent juvenile delinquents: Psychiatric, neurological, psychological and abuse factors. *Journal of the American Academy of Child Psychiatry, 18*, 307–319.

López, S., & Hernández, P. (1987). When culture is considered in the evaluation and treatment of Hispanic patients. *Psychotherapy, 24*, 120–126.

Martínez, K. J. (1994). Cultural sensitivity in family therapy gone awry. *Hispanic Journal of Behavioral Sciences, 16,* 75–89.

Montalvo, B., & Gutiérrez, M. J. (1989). Nine assumptions for work with ethnic minority families. In G. S. Saba, B. M. Karrer, & K. V. Hardy (Eds.), *Minorities and family therapy* (pp. 35–52). Binghamton, NY: Haworth Press.

Moore, J. W. (1988). Variations in violence among Hispanic gangs. In J. F. Kraus, S. B. Sorenson, & P. D. Juárez (Eds.), *Research conference on violence and homicide in Hispanic communities* (pp. 215–230). Los Angeles: UCLA Publication Services.

Moore, J. W., García, R., García, C., Cerda, L., & Valencia, F. (1978). *Homeboys, gangs, drugs, and prison in the barrios of Los Angeles.* Philadelphia: Temple University Press.

Morales, A. T. (1992). Latino youth gangs: Causes and clinical intervention. In L. A. Vargas & J. Koss-Chioino (Eds.), *Working with culture: Psychotherapeutic intervention with ethnic minority children and adolescents* (pp. 129–154). San Francisco: Jossey-Bass.

Oyserman, D. (1993). Adolescent identity and delinquency in interpersonal context. *Child Psychiatry and Human Development, 23,* 203–214.

Phinney, J. S. (1991). Ethnic identity and self esteem: A review and integration. Special issue: Ethnic identity and psychological adaptation. *Hispanic Journal of Behavioral Sciences, 13,* 193–208.

Phinney, J. S. (1992). The multigroup and ethnic identity measure: A new scale for use with diverse groups. *Journal of Adolescent, 7,* 156–176.

Phinney, J. S., & Chavira, V. (1995). Parental ethnic socialization and adolescent coping with problems related to ethnicity. *Journal of Research on Adolescence, 5,* 31–35.

Phinney J. S., DuPont, S., Espinosa, C., Revill, J., & Sander, K. (1994). Ethnic identity and American identification among ethnic minority youths. In A. M. Bouvy, F. J. R. von de Vijus, P. Boski, & P. Schmitz (Eds.), *Journeys into cross-cultural psychology* (pp. 167–183). Amsterdam: Swets and Zeitlinger.

Ramírez, M. (1984). Assessing and understanding biculturalism-multiculturalism in Mexican-American adults. In J. Martínez & R. Mendoza (Eds.), *Chicano psychology* (pp. 77–94). Orlando, FL: Academic Press.

Ramírez, S. Z., Wassef, A., Paniagua, F. A., Linskey, A. O., & O'Boyle, M. (1994). Perceptions of mental health providers concerning cultural factors in the evaluation of Hispanic children and adolescents. *Hispanic Journal of Behavioral Sciences, 16,* 28–42.

Rueschenberg, E. J., & Buriel, R. (1989). Mexican-American family functioning and acculturation: A family systems perspective. *Hispanic Journal of Behavioral Sciences, 11,* 232–244.

Slaff, B. (1979). Adolescents. In J. Noshpitz (Ed.), *Basic handbook of child psychiatry* (Vol. 3, pp. 504–518). New York: Basic Books.

Soriano, F. I. (1994). U.S. Latinos. In L. D. Eron, J. H. Gentry, & P. Schlegel (Eds.), *Reason to hope: A psychosocial perspective on violence and youth* (pp. 119–132). Washington, DC: American Psychological Association.

Szapocznik, J., Kurtines, W., & Fernández, T. (1980). Biculturalism, involvement, and adjustment in Hispanic American youth. *International Journal of Intercultural Relations, 4,* 353–365.

Velásquez, R. J., & Callahan, W. J. (1992). Psychological testing of Hispanic Americans in clinical settings: Overview issues. In K. F. Geisinger (Ed.), *Psychological testing of Hispanics* (pp. 253–265). Washington, DC: American Psychological Association.

Vigil, J. D. (1983). Chicano gangs: One response to Mexican urban adaptation in the Los Angeles area. *Urban Anthropology, 12,* 45–75.

Vigil, J. D. (1988a). Group processes and street identity: Adolescent Chicago gang members. *Ethos, 16,* 421–445.

Vigil, J. D. (1988b). Street socialization, locura behavior, and violence among Chicano gang members. In J. F. Kraus, S. B. Sorenson, & P. D. Juárez (Eds.), *Research conference on violence and homicide in Hispanic communities* (pp. 231–241). Los Angeles: UCLA Publication Services.

Wang, A. Y. (1994). Pride and prejudice in high school gang members. *Adolescence, 29,* 279–291.

Chapter *5*

Latino Culture and Sex: Implications for HIV Prevention

BARBARA VanOSS MARÍN
CYNTHIA A. GÓMEZ
UCSF Center for AIDS Prevention Studies
University of California, San Francisco

Until recently, sexual attitudes and sexual behaviors have been largely misunderstood and poorly studied in most populations. The HIV (human immunodeficiency virus) epidemic has finally forced a serious look at sex. Our reticence to investigate sexuality seriously maintains our sense of sexual behavior as a mysterious, unspoken activity. Although we admit that sex occurs, few of us are willing to address sex among adolescents, homosexuality, or a myriad of other difficult or stigmatized sexual issues to the depth needed in order to achieve prevention of HIV. In fact, much of the research on sexual behavior has been atheoretical (Fisher & Fisher, 1992), and the current theories available (Bandura, 1986; Fishbein & Ajzen, 1975; Fisher & Fisher, 1992) are based largely on cognitive models of behavior. Sexual behavior, being emotional, physical, and dyadic much more than cognitive, may not be well understood using these models. Sexual behaviors also occur within a cultural and political context, as evidenced by elaborate ceremonies like those found in Inca history or sexual restrictions such as the sodomy laws cur-

This chapter was supported in part by grants from the National Institute of Mental Health, Nos. MH46777 and MH46789.

rently found in the United States. The influence of cultural norms and values is not sufficiently acknowledged when sexual behavior is examined.

Our purpose in this chapter is to suggest a number of factors that may influence sexual behavior in the context of HIV prevention. We will emphasize condom use, as most work in this area has done, although nonpenetrative sex and use of dental dams are also important and frequently recommended prevention measures. In this chapter, we will first survey the current situation regarding cases of AIDS (acquired immune deficiency syndrome) and HIV infection among Latinos. Next we will outline a set of behaviors that have been proposed (Fisher, 1990) as necessary for successful HIV prevention, indicating those Latino cultural factors that may make each skill or behavior more difficult or easier. Finally, we will discuss how various aspects of Latino culture might be incorporated in order to deal in a health-promoting way with the HIV challenge to the Latino community.

Distribution of AIDS in Latinos in the United States

According to the Centers for Disease Control and Prevention (CDC), Latinos account for 18% of the total AIDS cases reported through June 1995 (Centers for Disease Control and Prevention, 1995), despite representing only 10% of the U.S. population. Latinos account for 17% of adult male cases, 20% of adult female cases, and 27% of pediatric cases. Of all racial/ethnic groups, Latino women have the second highest proportion (44% versus 56% in Asians) of exposure to AIDS through heterosexual transmission. HIV infection is the eighth leading cause of death among all Latinos, the second leading cause of death among Latinos ages 25 through 44. The latest reports indicate that Latinos accounted for an even greater proportion of AIDS cases in 1994 and 1995 than in previous years (Centers for Disease Control and Prevention, 1994).

Geographic and Ethnic Subgroup Distribution of AIDS among Latinos

The Latino population in the United States is more geographically concentrated than the total population, with 87% residing in ten states: California, Texas, New York, Florida, Illinois, New Jersey, Arizona, New Mexico, Colorado, and Massachusetts. Unfortunately, 55% of Latinos in the United States live in the top five U.S. AIDS epicenters, and those living in Puerto Rico are living in the area of highest concentration of AIDS cases after Washington, D.C., and New York.

Of the 18,625 AIDS cases among Latinos reported in 1993, 37% were born in the United States, 28% were born in Puerto Rico, and 8% were born in Mexico. Persons born in Central or South America and in Cuba each represented 5% of all cases, and the remaining 17% were persons born in locations other than those listed by the CDC, such as persons born in the Dominican Republic or Spain.

These data are consistent with the high concentration of HIV among Latinos in the northeastern region of the United States, which is residence for Latinos from Puerto Rico and the Dominican Republic predominantly. Lower incidence rates are reported for Latinos of the western and southwestern regions of the United States, where Latinos are predominantly of Mexican and Central or South American origin (Selik, Castro, & Pappaioanou, 1988). These regional differences have been attributed primarily to the higher injection drug use pattern among those residing in the Northeast versus the West or Southwest, combined with some differences in sexual behaviors, such as higher numbers of sexual partners and more male-to-male sex (Marín, Gómez, & Hearst, 1993; Díaz, Buehler, Castro, & Ward, 1993).

It is likely that some AIDS cases in Latinos living in the Southwest are underreported because of the current immigration policy of excluding HIV-infected persons from entry and residency in the United States, complicated further by the negative climate created by passage of Proposition 187 in California. This is not an issue for Puerto Ricans, who are U.S. citizens and have no restrictions regarding travel to and from the island of Puerto Rico regardless of HIV status. Latino cases also have been underreported in health departments, where they are often mistakenly identified as non-Latino white (Lindan et al., 1990). In addition, health care access in general continues to be an issue for this population, which may mean identification of cases later in the disease process.

Distribution of AIDS Cases by Transmission Category among Latinos

Although the United States is considered a pattern I country (groups most affected are homosexual men and intravenous drug users) in terms of epidemiological patterns of HIV infections as described by the World Health Organization (Mann, Chin, Piot, & Quinn, 1988), the countries of origin of most Latinos (the Caribbean and Latin America) are considered pattern II areas, where most HIV infections are in sexually active heterosexuals. These sexual patterns of transmission are likely to remain consistent when Latinos migrate to the United States. Although Puerto Ricans in the United States and on the island already seem to have a pattern II distribution of the epidemic, current case reports suggest that Mexican Americans in the Southwest may still be predominantly pattern I.

It is important to note that for both Latino men and women living in the United States, sexual behavior accounts for more than 50% of all transmission, and this form of transmission is likely to be even higher given the hierarchical transmission categorization used by CDC. The possibility of the legalization of needle exchange brings great hope in decreasing the amount of HIV transmission through injection drug use, which is disproportionately affecting our Puerto Rican population (54%). Even if we stopped transmission through injection drug use, however, changing sexual behavior will still be a monumental task, as evidenced by our century-old epidemic of sexually transmitted diseases. HIV is an STD that will kill.

Sexual Behavior among Latinos

Frequency of Multiple Partners and Homosexual Behavior

Because a large proportion of HIV infection is sexually acquired, it is important to examine in detail what is currently known about sexual behaviors and condom use in Latinos. In the spring of 1991 we conducted a telephone survey that employed a sampling technique that allowed us to generate a stratified random sample of Latino households in nine states with concentrations of Latinos ranging from 5% to 38% in the northeastern (New York, New Jersey, Massachusetts, and Connecticut) and southwestern United States (California, Arizona, Colorado, New Mexico, and Texas). Latinos in these states represented 77% of all U.S. Latinos. Latinos in the Northeast were oversampled because Latinos in this region have been disproportionately affected by the AIDS epidemic. A random subset of non-Latino white respondents also were interviewed at both stages of sampling. These individuals do not necessarily represent non-Latino whites in these nine states but, rather, represent non-Latino whites living in areas where Latinos are found. A total of 1,592 Latinos and 692 non-Latino whites between 18 and 49 years of age were interviewed for this survey, and the response rate was 58%. Details of the sampling technique are available in Marín, Gómez, and Hearst (1993).

Respondents were interviewed in the language of their choice. The instrument was developed from extensive focus groups and pretesting and was assessed through closed-ended questions about both sexual behaviors and various psychosocial predictors of those behaviors. The final instrument was completed in an average of 24 minutes per interview, and variables were measured on four- or five-level response scales.

With regard to multiple sexual partners, Latino men were much more likely than Latino women to report more than one sex partner in the prior 12 months (Marín, Gómez, & Hearst, 1993). Other surveys confirm this pattern (Sabogal, Pierce, Pollack, Faigeles, & Catania, 1993). Whereas 60% of unmarried Latino men reported multiple sexual partners, 18% of Latino married men did so, as compared to only 9% of their non-Latino white counterparts (Marín, Gómez, & Hearst, 1993). Whereas only about 3% of married Latino women reported multiple partners, 15% of unmarried Latino women did so. In addition, about 2% of Latino adult men reported same-gender sexual behavior in the past 12 months (Marín, Gómez, & Hearst, 1993). Interestingly, in-depth analysis of a more recent national data set suggests that those men who reported same-sex behavior are far more likely to be over 25 years old and highly acculturated than the sample as a whole, suggesting that there is a strong reporting bias (González & Marín, manuscript under review).

Condom Use

With regard to condom use, among those with multiple partners, Latino men and women are as likely as non-Latino white men and women to report condom use with a secondary partner. In fact, about half of Latinos and non-Latino white adults reported "always" using condoms with secondary partners in the past 12 months (Marín, Gómez, & Hearst, 1993). As with other ethnic groups, however, those with multiple partners are far less likely to use condoms consistently with a *primary* partner (Marín, Gómez, & Hearst, 1993; Sabogal et al., 1993). The dynamics of condom use with primary and secondary partners may be quite different. At least one study (Catania, Coates, & Kegeles, 1994) has found that norms are unimportant in predicting condom use with a primary partner, even though they are very important for predicting condom use with secondary partners.

In general, Latinos are no less likely than other groups to use condoms (Marín, Gómez, & Hearst, 1993; Tanfer, Grady, Klepinger, & Billy, 1993), with the possible exception of Latino gay men (Díaz, Stall, Hoff, Daigle, & Coates, in press; Richwald, Kyle, Gerber, Morisky, Kristal, & Friedland, 1988). A study in Latin America suggests that men there perceive condoms as more appropriate outside of marriage (Bailey, López-Escobar, & Estrada, 1973), which may help to explain these high levels of condom use among Latino men with secondary partners and their lower rates of use with primary partners.

Anal Intercourse

These relatively high levels of condom use represent the good news, but there are other issues. Only recently have national surveys begun to provide information about specific sexual behaviors, such as anal intercourse. Because of its very high risk, anal sex is of particular interest when discussing HIV transmission. Data from several studies suggest that anal intercourse may occur at higher frequencies among Latinos than other ethnic groups. In a national sample of 20- to 39-year-old men, 23% of Latinos, 21% of African Americans, and 9% of non-Latino whites reported anal intercourse in the past 4 months (Billy, Tanfer, Grady, & Klepinger, 1993). In a sample from high-risk cities (i.e., cities with the highest rates of HIV) of the National AIDS Behavior Survey, 31% of non-Latino whites, 17% of African Americans, and 33% of Latinos reported ever having anal intercourse, and 18% of Latinos compared to 10% of non-Latino whites and 9% of African Americans reported anal intercourse in the last 6 months (Catania, personal communication).

Sexual Activity in Adolescents

High rates of HIV, STD, and pregnancy also have been reported among Latino adolescents, and are caused in part by earlier onset of sexual activity (Centers for Disease Control [CDC], 1988; Holmes, Karon, & Kreiss, 1990). Although reliable national estimates of sexual activity for children as young as sixth grade are unavailable, one study reported 8% of 162 11- and 12-year-old Latino youth had ever had intercourse (DiClemente et al., 1992). In another study of 3,810 sixth to eighth graders in a large, urban multiethnic school district in northern California, 18% of the sample and 24% of the Latinos had ever had sex (J. Fetro, personal communication). These numbers are consistent with national data on older teens, showing that 33% of Latino males aged 15 had ever had sex (Sonenstein, Pleck, & Ku, 1989), and 17% of Latino high school students had had four or more sexual partners during their lifetime (CDC, 1990). Studies demonstrating trends in sexual activity among adolescents show a striking increase in sexual activity during the last 30 years, particularly among younger adolescents (Newcomer & Baldwin, 1992).

Unfortunately, condom use among Latino adolescents is far from consistent. Data from the most recent national sample of adolescent males indicates that about 47% of 15- to 19-year-old Latino males did not use condoms the last time they had sex (Sonenstein et al., 1989). DiClemente et al. (1992) reported that only 37% of 12- to 16-year-olds who had ever had sex consistently used condoms. Latino youth represent a particularly important group for yet another reason: they are the fastest growing ethnic group in the United States. By 2030, the Latino youth population will grow by 80%, whereas the white youth population will decline by 10% (Brindis, 1992).

In summary, levels of condom use often are as high among Latinos as in other groups, although there is certainly room for improvement. Anal intercourse, a particularly risky behavior, seems to be higher among Latinos, and in some subgroups, like married men, there are higher levels of multiple sexual partners than for non-Latino whites. Early onset of sexual activity may be a particular risk factor for Latino male adolescents. The rest of this chapter will present a framework for thinking about condom use behavior and some of the particular reasons that it might be difficult for some Latinos.

Behaviors and Skills Necessary for Successful Condom Use

One of the serious problems of much of the sexual research currently being done is that models and variables being considered tend to be rational or cognitive in nature. The theory of reasoned action, the health belief model, social learning theory, and the like all offer a cognitive approach to behavior. Sexual behavior, however, is physical, emotional, cultural, and social in nature and may be cognitive to a much smaller degree than other behaviors that have been studied previously. To provide a better understanding of sexual behavior among Latinos, we will present one cognitive-behavioral approach that has been offered for thinking about condom use and then indicate how the cultural, emotional, and social aspects of sexual behavior, particularly for Latinos, also need to be addressed in order to fully understand sexual behavior.

William Fisher (1990; Fisher, Fisher, Williams, & Malloy, 1994) proposes a set of behaviors or skills that are assumed to be necessary for an individual to use condoms successfully on a consistent basis: (1) self-acceptance of sexuality; (2) acquisition of behaviorally relevant information; (3) negotiation of AIDS prevention with a partner; (4) public prevention acts; and (5) consistent AIDS prevention. Each of these behaviors and the ways in which they interact with Latino cultural values will be discussed next.

In the following section, we will refer repeatedly to our study of unmarried Latino adults. This random-digit dial telephone survey was conducted in 1993 and involved a representative sample of 1,600 Latinos, aged 18 to 49, from ten states in the Northeast and Southwest, representing 87% of Latinos in the United States. Half-hour telephone interviews provided us with detailed data not only on the sexual behavior of these respondents but on their beliefs and attitudes about condoms and sex as well. This survey was designed to provide more in-depth information about the segment of the Latino population with greater likelihood of reporting multiple sexual partners in the 12 months prior to the interview and, therefore, greater potential for HIV risk.

Self-Acceptance of Sexuality

Sexual comfort.   At the most basic level of prevention, a person must realize that he or she has sexual desires and a physical body that requires care. Implicit in this is the idea that a person can be comfortable enough with his or her own sexual desires and activities to perform needed prevention. Note that this comfort with oneself as a sexual being is an emotional aspect of sexuality, one that often is not discussed in models of sexual behavior. Unfortunately, comfort with sexuality is not universal in Latino culture or elsewhere. In our study of Latino unmarried adults, 31% of Latino unmarried adult men and 55% of unmarried women reported that they would be uncomfortable having sex with the lights on. It is very difficult to put on a condom or to use a dental dam in the dark, so sexual comfort is an important prerequisite to safe sex. Another way that sexual discomfort interferes with safer sex is in attitudes toward masturbation. Among Latinos, masturbation is often seen as harmful (almost half of this same sample of unmarried adults indicated that masturbation could be physically or mentally harmful, and a quarter believed it to be a sin), yet mutual masturbation is a safer form of sexual release than condom use.

Latino women may be particularly prone to difficulties in acknowledging themselves as sexual beings. A number of authors have indicated that in traditional Latino culture, the "good" woman is not supposed to know about sex, so it is inappropriate and may be seen as disrespectful for her to bring up subjects like AIDS and condoms (Burgos & Díaz-Pérez, 1986; Pavich, 1986). In our most recent survey, 25% of the sample indicated that a man shows less respect for a woman if he talks to her about sex, and 20% believed it was dangerous for a woman to know as much or more about sex as a man.

Homophobia.   Latino men and women with homosexual desires also may have particular difficulty acknowledging these desires. Latino culture includes a fairly powerful homophobic component (Carrier, 1985, 1989), not unlike other groups in the United States. There does not exist any nonpejorative Spanish equivalent for the word *gay*, except *de ambiente*, which is used by gays in some Latin American countries to describe themselves. In our survey, less than 20% of the sample agreed "sex between men is acceptable" and almost two-thirds believed "homosexuality is distasteful." Homosexual men and women must often choose between their culture and their sexuality. Some turn to the mainstream gay/lesbian community for support, thus losing their Latino identity. Others, those who remain immersed in a culture that views their behavior as reprehensible, often hide their sexual orientation from family and friends (Carballo-Dieguez, 1988). Internalized homophobia may contribute to a negative self-concept and ultimately to risky sexual behavior for many homosexual Latinos (Díaz et al., 1993; Carballo-Dieguez, 1988).

Up to now, very little data on Latino gay men and lesbians has been available, and what is available is not as useful as it might be. Two types of studies have been done so far with Latino gay men (Díaz et al., 1993). One group includes studies of Latino gay men that have described AIDS knowledge, beliefs, and behaviors without trying to predict behavior. Studies in the other group have reported on data from multiethnic samples, indicating that being Latino is a predictor of risky behavior. Neither of these approaches helps us to understand clearly what puts Latino gay men at risk or how to intervene. Studies of the meanings of and barriers to safe sex among Latino gay men and lesbians are urgently needed.

Religiosity.   There is debate in the literature about the extent to which religion or religiosity may play a role in Latino sexuality. Many authors have assumed that Catholicism or a deeper religiosity would predict less use of contraception among Latinos. Although religiosity was associated with less contraception among U.S.-born Latinos, (Sabagh & López, 1980) and among Catholic Latinos (Goldscheider & Mosher, 1991), other investigators have not found an association between religion or religiosity and contraceptive use (Amaro, 1988; Mikawa et al., 1992). In our own work, religiosity had no effect on condom use among Latino men with multiple sexual partners (Marín, Gómez, & Tschann, 1993).

Acquisition of Behaviorally Relevant Information

Information about AIDS and sex.   According to Fisher (1990), an additional important skill is knowing how to inform oneself about protection. A number of studies have indicated that Latinos, particularly less educated and less acculturated individuals, are at some disadvantage in terms of sexual and AIDS-related information (Dawson, Cynamon, & Fitti, 1987; Forrest, Austin, Valdes, Fuentes, & Wilson, 1993; Marín & Marín, 1990; Padilla & O'Grady, 1987; Villas, Bouvet, & Bernal, 1992). Misconceptions commonly reported include the belief that one can tell by looking whether someone has HIV, which is apparently also a common belief of college students (Fisher et al., 1994). Latino women are less knowledgeable of their own sexual anatomy than non-Latino women (Scrimshaw, Carballo, Ramos, & Blair, 1991). In focus groups we have conducted, Latino women often report that the first person to explain anything about sex to them was their spouse. One man, asking what "oral sex" (*sexo oral*) was, suggested it might mean "sex by the hour" (*sexo por hora*). Men in focus groups report that lemon and other substances may be applied to the penis after intercourse to avoid STDs (Forrest et al., 1993).

This lack of information has detrimental effects. Low levels of education and lack of instructions in Spanish may impede understanding of the instructions for condom use (Richwald, Schneider-Muños, & Valdez, 1989). Pregnant Latino adolescents differed from their nonpregnant counterparts in having received less information about sex from their parents (Baumeister, Flores, & Marín, 1995).

Messages children receive about sex. Deficits in information about sex can be traced in part to a lack of communication about sexual issues between parents and children. In an optimal environment, children will receive positive messages and thorough answers to their questions about sexuality, but in many Latino families this is not the case. In our study, almost half of the unmarried Latino men and women responded that their parents had never talked to them about sex. Despite a strong emphasis on family interactions, Latinos are currently less likely than other groups to provide their children with vital information about sex and AIDS (CDC, 1991). Of course, the basic embarrassment about sexuality that was discussed earlier also will interfere with seeking and obtaining accurate information. Thus, if children are told anything about sex, it may be difficult to understand exactly what is meant. A common admonition to young men and women, for example, is to "be careful"—not a very explicit message.

On the positive side, Latinos may have at least one source of protective information that is less common in other groups. Forrest and colleagues found that Latino men in focus groups often indicated that older men who were members of their family or close family friends would take younger men aside and very explicitly indicate that they should use condoms. In our unmarried adult sample, we have found that 45% of men and 66% of women had such a *condom mentor*.

Negotiating AIDS Prevention with a Partner

Discussing condoms. Before having sex, Fisher (1990) suggests, it is also necessary for partners to discuss condom use or other behaviors. In fact, Latinos report to us that condoms may not be discussed even when they are used: "I just pull it out of my pocket, she sees it and doesn't object, so I put it on." Among unmarried Latino adults, 73% of those who used a condom in their most recent sexual encounter had discussed condoms prior to use, and 26% of those who discussed condoms before having sex did not use them. So discussing condoms is highly associated with actual use.

Sexual silence. Latino culture (among others) supports what Díaz calls "sexual silence"—that is, a failure to acknowledge verbally many of the realities of sexual behavior. For a gay man or a lesbian to discuss his or her sexual orientation with family members would be considered disrespectful. Similarly, a man may have an affair, but his wife should not find out, and if she suspects something, the norm of sexual silence may inhibit her from saying anything. Latino married men are significantly more likely to report multiple sexual partners in the past 12 months, compared to non-Latino white married men (Marín, Gómez, & Hearst, 1993). In fact, one-fourth of our sample thought it might be all right for a man who wanted different sexual activities than the ones he has with his partner to look for them elsewhere. In one focus group, when asked what they would most like to communicate to their husbands, women reported that they would like to tell them to use condoms with their other partners.

Sexual ambivalence.   Latino culture also may make it particularly difficult for heterosexual partners to discuss their intentions prior to sex. Men report that women in sexual encounters may be ambivalent about whether actually to have sex. Certainly, cultural messages to women are that a *good* woman does not engage in sexual behavior except with her husband, so a woman entering a casual relationship risks loss of her reputation and her self-esteem. In our survey, half of the sample believed it was important for women to be virgins at marriage and believed that a decent woman refuses to take part in certain sexual activities. Men in focus groups report that if they stopped to look for a condom, the woman might change her mind. In fact, stopping to look for a condom is one of the most difficult items on our index of self-efficacy to use condoms.

Passion.   It is likely that the *script* for sexual encounters in Latino culture (and probably others as well) is that sexual partners should be "swept off their feet." Negotiation of condom use usually requires conversation, but passion may be constructed or scripted in many cultures with little conversation except words of love. If sex is a *surprise*, the needed preparations for safe encounters are less likely to take place. In our most recent survey, over half of the respondents thought that men could not control their sexual desires as easily as women, and 42% thought it would be harmful for men to be sexually excited without ejaculating. These strong beliefs that men's sexual desires are uncontrollable are as common in women as in men. So sex is seen as passionate, emotional, a difficult-to-control drive, rather than something to be discussed or negotiated calmly.

Sexual coercion.   On the other hand, the power differential between Latino men and women and the belief that passion is uncontrollable may lead to sexual coercion. We have recently conducted another random-digit dial telephone survey of 1,600 unmarried Latino adults. In addition to questions about condom use and sexual partners, we asked about coercive sexual behaviors and traditional gender-role beliefs. In our study, 73% of sexually active women reported that a male partner had insisted on having sex when they were not interested in the past year, and an even higher percentage (92%) of the men indicated that they had insisted on sex when their partner was not interested. In our previous study, Latino women who fear their partner will be angry if condom use is requested report using condoms less (Gómez & Marín, in press). Latino men with more traditional gender-role beliefs also report greater likelihood of insisting on sex when their partner is not interested and of lying to obtain sex (Gómez, Marín, & Grinstead, 1994).

In our most recent survey, we asked women whether they had ever been raped or sexually abused. Interestingly, the less acculturated were less likely to report rape or sexual abuse than the more highly acculturated women. Although it is unlikely that the less acculturated actually experience less rape or abuse, it is probable that they are more uncomfortable about reporting it or that their perceptions of what constitutes rape or sexual abuse are different from those of the more highly acculturated women. It may be that less acculturated women perceive rape only when force is involved or that they are more reticent to discuss it because of cultural victim-blaming or fear of hurting their families. Sexual abuse is also a documented problem among Latino gay men and men who have sex with men. In one study of 182 Puerto Rican gay or bisexual men, 18% of the men reported forced sex before the age of 13 with a person at least 4 years older, and another 18% reported willing sex at this early age with someone older. When these groups were compared to men who had not had an older partner at an early age, the *abused* group reported significantly more unprotected anal intercourse than the *no-older-partner* group, and the *willing* group fell somewhere between the two (Carballo-Dieguez & Dolezal, 1995). In a sample of 110 Latino gay men in San Francisco, R. Díaz (unpublished data) found that 49% reported sexual experience under the age of 16 with someone 5 or more years older, and, of these, half reported that the sexual activity was coerced. Half of those reporting early sexual activity with someone significantly older reported that the abuse had occurred 10 times or more, whereas 71% of the men categorized as high behavioral risk for HIV due to unprotected anal intercourse had experienced this. Although these data necessarily come from convenience samples, they suggest an alarming pattern. Various studies in non-Latino samples indicate that sexual abuse is not uncommon in males and that it is much more frequently reported by homosexual and bisexual men than by heterosexual men (Cunningham, Stiffman, Dore, & Earls, 1994; Cameron & Proctor, 1986; Johnson & Shrier, 1985; Veiel, 1995).

Sexual abuse, sexual coercion, and rape are important experiences both because they are traumatic at the time of occurrence and because they can have lasting effects, including earlier sexual experimentation and more HIV risk behavior. Unequal power and the possibility of violence in sexual relationships are often realities in the Latino community and elsewhere, realities that must be acknowledged by those who wish to promote HIV prevention.

Power in sexual relationships. Serrano-García and López-Sánchez (1991) have proposed a framework for understanding sexual behavior in Latinos. They suggest that one must begin with the reality of unequal levels of power and work with women to help them ask for what they want. Specifically, they suggest four levels of consciousness, based on Ander-egg (1980): (1) submissive consciousness, in which social reality is seen as natural, given, and unchangeable; (2) the precritical level, in which feelings of dissatisfaction begin to arise and people begin to search for solutions; (3) the critical-integrative level, in which people begin to analyze the social-historical roots of situations and initiate change efforts; and (4) the liberating level, in which people come to consider their situation oppressive and demand social transformation. Serrano-García and her colleagues are currently implementing an intervention with sexually active university women in Puerto Rico designed to raise levels of consciousness about the asymmetry of women's situation, particularly regarding condom use, in order to decrease levels of sexual risk behavior in these women.

Latino gay men also see sex as passionate and uncontrollable. Díaz (in press) reports that in focus groups, one man reported, *"Cuando la de abajo se calienta, la de arriba no piensa"* ("When the head of your penis gets hot, your [other] head doesn't think"). Díaz attributes much of the difficulty with safe sex among Latino gay men to the double bind of "It's a great privilege to be male, but you're not really a man until you prove it." It's likely that both heterosexual and homosexual Latino men experience strong normative pressure to prove manhood through penetrative sex.

The ideas that discussing sex is disrespectful, that sex is uncontrollable, and that all men (but only bad women) are highly sexual result in a fairly strong double standard in which men's sexual behavior is encouraged and applauded while women's is restricted and frowned on. Of course, those with higher education and acculturation are almost certainly less likely to endorse such traditional beliefs (Vazquez-Nuttal, Romero, & de Leon, 1987). To the extent that they play a role in people's thinking, however, silence, secrecy, passion, and coercion are apt to interfere with self-protective discussion of sexual behavior. Whether and what kind of discussion is truly necessary to ensure safe sex is still not entirely clear.

Public Prevention Acts

Both Latino men and women report some embarrassment about purchasing condoms, and this embarrassment is predictive of being less likely to carry condoms (Marín & Marín, 1992). Latino women, especially the less acculturated, are much less likely than men to carry condoms (Marín & Marín, 1992). This is not surprising given the messages they often receive about not being sexual beings.

In their last sexual encounter, of those unmarried men and women who carried condoms with them, most (82%) used condoms. Of those not carrying condoms, only 27% used them. Because carrying condoms is so highly predictive of actual use (Marín, Gómez, & Tschann, 1993), the ability to purchase condoms is a crucial one. Anecdotal reports suggest that condoms are the most frequently shoplifted item, suggesting that purchasing may be difficult because of both embarrassment and, in some cases, lack of resources. Indeed, one study showed that individuals at a clinic (not necessarily Latinos) were much more likely to take condoms offered in the restroom than at the counter (Amass & Bickel, 1993).

On the positive side, reports from Latin America (Bailey et al., 1973) suggest that Latino men may view condoms as most appropriate with casual partners. This may explain the finding that the less acculturated men in our samples actually carry condoms more and have a more positive attitude toward use than the highly acculturated men (Marín, Tschann, Gómez, & Kegeles 1993). This suggests that, at a very fundamental level, Latino culture is not negative about condoms, but may still view them as most appropriate outside primary relationships.

Consistent AIDS Prevention

Other forms of contraception as a barrier. Fisher notes that not only must a couple use condoms the first time they have sex, but they must continue to do so. A number of factors work against this consistent use. For one thing, couples turn to other forms of contraception. As mentioned earlier, in Latinos and other groups (MacDonald, Wells, Fisher, Warren, & King, 1990), those who use oral contraceptives or have some reason for not needing to contracept are much less likely to use condoms (Gómez & Marín, in press). People in steady relationships often abandon condom use in favor of other methods of contraception. In fact, less than 20% of Latinos and non-Latino whites with one partner consistently used condoms, compared to about half of those with multiple partners (Marín, Gómez, & Hearst, 1993). Finally, condoms are inappropriate for those who wish to conceive.

Of course, at times individuals with a single partner may still be at risk for HIV infection. Latino women report some concern that their partners may be putting them at risk. It may be necessary for women in these situations to frame condom use as their contraceptive of choice. Support groups may help women increase their sexual assertiveness or to leave a risky or abusive partner (Kelly et al., 1994).

Consistent HIV prevention also means using protection for all types of sexual activities. Little data is currently available on the extent of condom or dental dam use among Latinos for oral and anal intercourse. If condoms are viewed primarily as a contraceptive and anal sex is done in part to avoid procreation, then condoms may be viewed as unnecessary. I. Cunningham (personal communication) has found in large surveys of students at the University of Puerto Rico that those who began having sex at the earliest ages also report the highest levels of anal intercourse. These surveys indicate that Puerto Rican men had anal intercourse primarily for their own pleasure, whereas women participate primarily to please their partner (Cunningham, Díaz-Esteve, Gonzalez-Santiago, & Rodríguez-Sánchez, 1994).

Reinforcement for use. Fisher suggests that condom use will be most consistent if the couple reinforce each other for use. This type of reinforcement might take the form of a person thinking about and even mentioning to a partner how relieved they are that they used a condom last night and avoided multiple risks. To the extent that sexual behavior is surrounded by embarrassment, difficulties in discussion, coercion, use of alcohol, and the like, such reinforcement of condom use is less likely to occur.

Barriers to consistent use. One setting in which safe sex cannot be easily practiced, and which represents a concern for the Latino community, is prisons. Most penal systems do not allow condoms to be distributed, with the idea that sex while in prison is prohibited and therefore does not occur. The reality is that sex in prison is a fact of life and that many of those who are serving time are doing so for drug-related offenses, meaning that exposure to HIV in a prison setting is a serious risk (CDC, 1992). Given the disproportionate number of people of color who spend time in jails and prisons, most of whom eventually return to their communities, current policy is unrealistic and health-endangering.

Thus far, we have seen that the behaviors that may be necessary for successful condom use often are not easy in the context of Latino culture, given the silence, discomfort, power differentials between men and women, and intolerance of homosexuality. Children receive powerful messages, both verbal and nonverbal, that perpetuate these problems. On the positive side, Latinos are just as likely as other groups to be using condoms, and use is fairly high for those with multiple partners. Latinos are deeply concerned about the health of their families, so that approaches intended to enhance family health, even if they involve uncomfortable topics like sexuality, often will be very well received. In the final section we will review some ideas for increasing safer sexual practices in the Latino community.

HIV Prevention in the Context of Latino Culture

Cultural Factors

The cultural factors of sexual gender norms, homophobia, and sexual discomfort contribute to high-risk sexual activity in important ways. These cultural factors can be addressed beginning with the socialization process. Although respect for and understanding of culture are vital to developing effective HIV prevention strategies for the Latino community, these strategies sometimes may need to challenge established cultural norms and ingrained standards.

Acculturation differences.   As men and women from Latin America adjust to life in the United States, they learn English and slowly take on beliefs and customs of the mainstream culture. This process of acculturation can continue for several generations and can have a powerful effect on sexual behavior, particularly for women. Less acculturated Latino women report less frequently carrying and using condoms than the more highly acculturated women (Marín & Marín, 1992; Marín, Tschann, Gómez, & Kegeles, 1993). They also report fewer sexual partners, so the overall sexual risk of women with different levels of acculturation may be difficult to compare. Among adolescent Latino women, the less acculturated have been found to be least likely to have had sex, but if they were sexually active, they were less likely to be using any type of birth control, and if they became pregnant they were more likely to carry their pregnancy to term (Aneshensel, Becerra, Fielder, & Schuler, 1990; Aneshensel, Fielder, & Becerra, 1989). The less acculturated hold more traditional sex-role beliefs and have lower levels of sexual comfort. Less acculturated women are more likely to be coerced sexually, whereas men are more likely to be coercive. These differences are important to consider when developing interventions in English or in Spanish for Latino populations.

Sexual socialization.   To socialize children more appropriately about sexuality, Latino parents must be taught both basic information about sex and methods to communicate with their children about this topic. Proper sex education for par-

ents must go beyond the basic biological facts and focus on the values and attitudes they transmit to their children regarding sex roles and homosexuality, as
well as finding ways to increase children's communication, refusal, and decision-
making skills. Many Latino families are based on a model of respect for authority
mixed with strong love for and emphasis on children. Self-regulation theory suggests that parents must be loving and supportive, while challenging their children
to think through issues and become more competent. In the domain of sexuality,
frank and wide-ranging discussions between parents and children are likely to be
more helpful than lectures where parents always have the last word. Unfortunately, in analyses of taped conversations between 19 parent–child dyads, half of
whom were Latino, regarding sex and chores, the proportion of words the child
spoke decreased dramatically when talking about sex as compared to chores (Hall,
García, & Marín, unpublished data). Homework assignments involving parent–
child discussions of such topics as when someone is *ready* to have sex, or why boys
and girls should or should not have the same chores around the house, could nur-
ture children's sense of competence in the sexual domain and help them be critical
of gender-role stereotypes.

One hopeful sign is that in our most recent survey, over 56% of the respondents reported that a parent or other relative had told them they should use condoms when they were young. Adults (not just parents, but aunts and uncles,
teachers, and family friends as well) could be encouraged to talk to young men and
women about condoms and to explain some of the details about size and how to
put them on. Young men who wish to use them during their first sexual encounter
must practice using them, and although this topic is the ultimate taboo, young men
could be encouraged to use condoms when they masturbate as a way to help them
become more comfortable with condoms and more familiar with how they feel. It
would also help them to associate sexual pleasure with condom use.

Sexual comfort.   Talking about sex and information about sex are crucial
components in the struggle to increase sexual comfort. One man reported that his
mother referred to his penis as *la porquería* ("that disgusting thing"). In more subtle
ways, parents who fail to name sexual body parts but refer instead to "down there"
are giving important messages that sex is not talked about in the same way as other
bodily functions. So parents must be given proper names for sexual parts and functions and told to use them "for the sake of your children." Exercises and games in
which parents are asked to use sexual words can desensitize them.

Sexual gender norms.   Many HIV prevention strategies focus on promoting
condoms with women, often because women are more easily accessible in health
settings than men. However, there are multiple problems with this strategy: Latino
culture defines assertive behavior of women regarding sex as inappropriate; many
Latino women do not see themselves as at risk because they have only one partner;
others are aware of the risk but feel hopeless about changing their partner's behavior; and some Latino men may become angry and even violent when their partner
suggests condom use. In our survey, 20% of women were afraid that their partner

might yell at them, hit them, or harm them in some other way during sex. Because of these problems and high levels of sexual discomfort in some Latino women, work with women regarding sexuality often will proceed more slowly than work with men. Women not only will require support and skills building in how to suggest condoms, but in some cases also will need support to leave an abusive relationship. When providers wish to promote condom use among Latino women, they should include the male partner as an additional target of the intervention.

Although men are difficult to reach, their greater openness to sexual messages and the fact that they are the ones who actually use the condom make them an ideal target for condom promotion and for changing sexual norms to support condom use. To change sexual gender norms, men must be reminded of the positive aspects of sexual gender norms, such as protecting women and providing for the family; these values, along with protecting their "manhood," should be used to promote safer sexual behaviors. Programs such as date rape prevention could be created to address coercion in Latino heterosexual relationships. Men should be directly involved in the development and implementation of such programs.

Homophobia. A more appropriate understanding of homosexuality, one that sees it as a natural variation of human sexuality, must be promoted in Latino communities. Currently, levels of homophobia mean that Latino young people with homosexual feelings and fantasies feel fearful and rejected by their peers and family. In open-ended interviews we conducted, Latino adolescent boys reported strong rejection of any peer who might be homosexual. Consequently, a number of Latino adolescents with homosexual desires may experience severe depression leading to suicidal ideation or attempts, or they may engage in risky behaviors such as drug and alcohol use and anonymous sexual encounters (Rotheram-Borus et al., 1992). Latino parents should be informed of the high levels of adolescent gay suicide and risky sex in the hope that they will process some of their fears and misunderstanding and provide their children with more openness and support. Currently, even in loving Latino families, homosexual adults often report that their sexuality cannot be openly discussed, but remains the "family secret."

Psychological Constructs

In addition to the cultural factors already addressed, there are a number of psychological constructs that are also related to HIV prevention. These have an important place in prevention campaigns with Latinos.

Self-efficacy. The belief that someone can perform the behavior of using condoms even under difficult circumstances is strongly associated with actual use. In our most recent survey of unmarried Latino adults, we found that those who reported higher self-efficacy to use condoms also reported significantly more condom use. The most difficult aspects of using condoms were being able to introduce them into an ongoing relationship, to use them if the respondent is "in love" or if their partner objects, to look for them if already aroused, to use them if under the influence of alcohol, and to use them without spoiling the mood. These are clearly areas where those at risk may need help to build their condom use skills, and role playing and other individual and small-group interventions may be very helpful. In small groups or individual sessions, men should be asked to work out solutions when condoms are not readily available, when a partner objects, or when they have been drinking or using drugs. Given the strong association of carrying condoms with actual use, health care providers should encourage patients to carry condoms and encourage men to practice using them.

Norms. For Latinos, personally knowing someone with HIV or AIDS predicts both more carrying of condoms and more use of condoms with a secondary partner (Marín, Gómez, & Tschann, 1993). To take advantage of this effect of perceived susceptibility, health care providers should assess and emphasize the Latino's personal vulnerability to HIV due to personal sexual risk behaviors and previous sexually transmitted diseases. Community programs should continue to utilize Latino persons with HIV to reach and motivate the community.

Having friends who carry condoms and use them with secondary partners are circumstances predictive of both carrying and using condoms for Latino men (Marín, Gómez, & Tschann, 1993). Therefore, mass media, social marketing, and community-level approaches should be explored as a way to promote condom use among Latino men. Increased availability of condoms in vending machines could reduce the embarrassment associated with buying a condom and increase the perception that "everybody" uses condoms.

For Latino gay and bisexual men, promoting a norm of condom use and a social environment that is accepting of homosexuality will each be important. Programs to reach these Latino men may be the most difficult because of the very underground and taboo nature of their activities (Peterson & Marín, 1988). For the Latino man having sex with men, it may be necessary to use gay-identified outreach workers or those who have sex with men of various sexual identifications. Outreach workers should be educated about AIDS and taught how to make contacts effectively with men in places where anonymous sex takes place and talk to them about AIDS. Educational material like posters and condoms might also be provided in places such as restrooms. Latino gay-identified men may benefit from programs designed to help them explore homophobia and support each other in the search for safer sexual practices and a greater sense of empowerment around their sexuality (see the program being developed by R. Díaz, called *Luna y Sol*).

Behavioral Skills

Ultimately, condom promotion must include practice of behavioral skills needed to enact the intention to use condoms, including purchasing, carrying, and negotiating condom use.

Carrying and purchasing condoms.　Given the vital importance of carrying and purchasing condoms, those wishing to promote condoms should place considerable emphasis on these activities and should encourage people actually to carry them out. Sex education programs for adolescents sometimes include the activity of finding condoms in a store and learning their price. Desensitization should include actually purchasing them, although parents may object to this activity.

Negotiating condom use.　Some work is now being done to help Latino women to negotiate condom use (Kelly et al., 1994; Serrano-García and colleagues, personal communication). These programs provide consciousness-raising activities, emotional support, and behavioral skills training to help Latino women talk to their partners about condom use, eroticize condom use with a partner, and leave abusive relationships as necessary. Surprisingly little has been done to train Latino men to negotiate with a partner, even though Latino men report that a partner who does not want to use condoms is an important barrier to use (Marín, unpublished data).

Summary

Cultural beliefs about sex among Latinos are closely tied to sexual attitudes and behaviors, often contributing to lower levels of comfort with one's own body and sexual activities, more risk behaviors, and coercive attitudes and behaviors toward women. Current models of behavior that have been used to study condom use have not taken these cultural components of sexual behavior into account. Interventions that attempt to challenge the prevailing cultural *wisdom* must take into account the power of beliefs about sexual gender norms and sexual discomfort. But Latino culture is not monolithic. Much variation exists in levels of beliefs about appropriate sexual activity. The HIV epidemic, though tragic in its consequences, is nonetheless contributing to a movement in the Latino community to abandon sexual silence and seek information and discussion about sex.

References

Amaro, H. (1988). Women in the Mexican-American community: Religion, culture, and reproductive attitudes and experiences. *Journal of Community Psychology, 16,* 6–20.

Amass, L., & Bickel, W. (1993). The taking of free condoms in a drug abuse treatment clinic: The effects of location and posters. *American Journal of Public Health, 83,* 1466–1468.

Ander-egg, E. (1980). *Metodología del desarrollo de comunidad.* Madrid, Spain: UNIEUROP.

Aneshensel, C., Becerra, R., Fielder, E., & Schuler, R. (1990). Onset of fertility-related events during adolescence: A prospective comparison of Mexican American and non-Hispanic white females. *American Journal of Public Health, 80*(8), 959–963.

Aneshensel, C., Fielder, E., & Becerra, R. (1989). Fertility and fertility-related behavior among Mexican-American and non-Hispanic white female adolescents. *Journal of Health and Social Behavior, 30,* 56–76.

Bailey, J., López-Escobar, G., & Estrada, A. (1973). A Colombian view of the condom. *Studies in Family Planning, 4,* 60–64.

Bandura, A. (1986). *Social foundations of thought and action.* Englewood Cliffs, NJ: Prentice-Hall.

Baumeister, L., Flores, E., & Marín, B. (1995). Sex information given to Latina adolescents by parents. *Health Education Research, 10,* pp. 233–239.

Billy, J., Tanfer, K., Grady, W., & Klepinger, D. (1993). The sexual behavior of men in the United States. *Family Planning Perspectives, 25,* 52–60.

Brindis, C. (1992). Adolescent pregnancy prevention for Hispanic youth: The role of schools, families, and communities. *Journal of School Health, 62,* 345–351.

Burgos, N. M., & Díaz-Pérez, Y. I. (1986). An exploration of human sexuality and the Puerto Rican culture. *Journal of Social Work and Human Sexuality, 4,* 135–150.

Cameron, P., & Proctor, K. (1986). Child molestation and homosexuality. *Psychological Reports, 58*(1), 327–337.

Carballo-Dieguez, A. (1988). Hispanic culture, gay male culture, and AIDS: Counseling implications. *Journal of Counseling and Development, 68,* 26–30.

Carballo-Dieguez, A., & Dolesal, C. (1995). Association between history of childhood sexual abuse and adult HIV risk sexual behavior in Puerto Rican men who have sex with men. *Child Abuse and Neglect, 19,* 595–605.

Carrier, J. (1985). *Mexican male bisexuality.* In F. Klein & T. Wolf (Eds.), Bisexualities: Theory and research (pp. 75–85). New York: Haworth Press.

Carrier, J. (1989). Sexual behavior and spread of AIDS in Mexico. *Medical Anthropology, 10,* 129–142.

Catania, J., Coates, T., & Kegeles, S. (1994). A test of the AIDS risk reduction model: Psychosocial correlates of condom use in the AMEN cohort study. *Health Psychology, 13*(6), 548–555.

Centers for Disease Control. (1988). Continuing increase in infectious syphilis–United States.

Morbidity and Mortality Weekly Report, 37, 35–38.

Centers for Disease Control. (1990). Selected behaviors that increase risk for HIV infection among high school students. *Morbidity and Mortality Weekly Report, 41,* 237–240.

Centers for Disease Control. (1991). Characteristics of parents who discuss AIDS with their children—United States 1989. *Morbidity and Mortality Weekly Report, 40,* 789–791.

Centers for Disease Control. (1992). HIV prevention in the U.S. correctional system, 1991. *Morbidity and Mortality Weekly Report, 41,* 389–391.

Centers for Disease Control and Prevention. (1994). *HIV/AIDS Surveillance Report, 6*(1), 1–27.

Cunningham, I., Díaz-Esteve, C. M., González-Santiago, M. I., & Rodríguez-Sánchez, M. H. (1994). University students and AIDS: Some findings from three surveys—1989, 1990 and 1992. In B. Vasquez (Ed.), *Puerto Ricans and AIDS: It's time to act.* Special issue of *Centro, 6*(1 & 2), 44–59. (Published by Centro de Estudios Puertorriqueños, Hunter College, New York, NY 10021).

Cunningham, R. M., Stiffman, A. R., Dore, P., & Earls, F. (1994). The association of physical and sexual abuse with HIV risk behaviors in adolescence and young adulthood: Implications for public health. *Child Abuse and Neglect, 19*(3), 233–245.

Dawson, D., Cynamon, M., & Fitti, J. (1987). *AIDS knowledge and attitudes, provisional data from the National Health Interview Survey: United States.* (Vol. 146). Hyattsville, MD: National Center for Health Statistics.

Díaz, R. (in press). Latino gay men in the AIDS epidemic. In M. Levine, J. Gagnon, & P. Narde (Eds.), *The impact of HIV on the lesbian and gay community.* Chicago: University of Chicago Press.

Díaz, R., Stall, R., Hoff, C., Daigle, D., & Coates, T. (in press). HIV risk among Latino gay men in the Southwestern United States. *AIDS Education and Prevention.*

Díaz, T., Buehler, J., Castro, K., & Ward, J. (1993). AIDS trends among Hispanics in the United States. *American Journal of Public Health, 83*(4), 504–509.

DiClemente, R., Durbin, M., Siegel, D., Krasnovsky, F., Lazarus, N., & Comacho, T. (1992). Determinants of condom use among junior high school students in a minority, inner-city school district. *Pediatrics, 89,* 197–202.

Fishbein, M., & Ajzen, I. (1975). *Belief, attitude, intention and behavior: An introduction to theory and research.* Menlo Park, CA: Addison-Wesley.

Fisher, J., & Fisher, W. (1992). Changing AIDS risk behavior. *Psychological Bulletin, 111,* 455–474.

Fisher, J., Fisher, W., Williams, S., & Malloy, T. (1994). Empirical Tests of an information-motivation-behavioral skills model of AIDS-preventive behavior with gay men and heterosexual university students. *Health Psychology, 13*(3), 238–250.

Fisher, W. A. (1990). Understanding and preventing adolescent pregnancy. In L. Heath & E. J. Posavac (Eds.), *Social influence processes and prevention. Social psychological applications to social issues* (Vol. 1, pp. 71–101) New York: Plenum Press.

Forrest, K., Austin, D., Valdes, M., Fuentes, E., & Wilson, S. (1993). Exploring norms and beliefs related to AIDS prevention among California Hispanic men. *Family Planning Perspectives, 25,* 111–117.

Goldscheider, C., & Mosher, W. D. (1991). Patterns of contraceptive use in the United States: The importance of religious factors. *Studies in Family Planning, 22,* 102–115.

Gómez, C., & Marín, B. (in press). Gender, culture, and power: Barriers to HIV prevention strategies for women. *Journal of Sex Research.*

Gómez, C., Marín, B. V., & Grinstead, O. (1994). *Sexual coercion in the face of AIDS: Will Latino men and women challenge it?* Tenth International Conference on AIDS. Yokohama, Japan.

Gonzalez, F., & Marín, B. V. (Manuscript under review). *Same-sex behavior among Latinos: Results of a national survey.*

Holmes, K. K., Karon, J. M., Kreiss, J. (1990). The increasing frequency of heterosexually acquired AIDS in the United States, 1983–88. *American Journal of Public Health, 80,* 858–862.

Johnson, R. L., & Shrier, D. K. (1985). Sexual victimization of boys. *Journal of Adolescent Health Care, 6,* 372–374.

Kelly, J., Murphy, D., Washington, C., Wilson, T., Kobb, J., Davis, D., Ledezma, G., & Davantes, B. (1994). The effects of HIV/AIDS intervention groups for high-risk women in urban clinics. *American Journal of Public Health, 84,* 1918–1922.

Lindan, C., Hearst, N., Singleton, J., Trachtenberg, A., Riordan, N., Tokagawa, D., & Chu, G. (1990). Underreporting of minority AIDS deaths in San Francisco Bay area, 1985–86. *Public Health Reports, 105*(4), 400–404.

MacDonald, N. E., Wells, G. A., Fisher, W. A., Warren, W., & King, M. (1990). High-risk STD/HIV behavior among college students. *Journal of the American Medical Association, 263,* 3155–3159.

Mann, J., Chin, J., Piot, P., & Quinn, T. (1988). The international epidemiology of AIDS. *Science American, 256,* 82–89.

Marín, B. V., Gómez, C. A., & Hearst, N. (1993). Multiple heterosexual partners and condom use among Hispanics and non-Hispanic whites. *Family Planning Perspectives, 25,* 170–174.

Marín, B., Gómez, C., & Tschann, J. (1993). Condom use with casual partners with secondary female sexual partners. *Public Health Reports, 108,* 742–750.

Marín, B., Tschann, J., Gómez, C., & Kegeles, S. (1993). Acculturation and gender differences in sexual attitudes and behaviors: A comparison of Hispanic and non-Hispanic white single adults. *American Journal of Public Health, 83,* 1759–1761.

Marín, B. V., & Marín, G. (1990). Effects of acculturation on knowledge of AIDS and HIV among Hispanics. *Hispanic Journal of Behavior Sciences, 12,* 110–121.

Marín, B. V., & Marín, G. (1992). Predictors of condom accessibility among Hispanics in San Francisco. *American Journal of Public Health, 82,* 592–595.

Mikawa, J., Morones, P., Gómez, A., Case, H., Olsen, D., & Gonzalez, M. (1992). Cultural practices of Hispanics: Implications for the prevention of AIDS. *Hispanic Journal of Behavioral Sciences, 14,* 421–433.

Newcomer, S., & Baldwin, W. (1992). Demographics of adolescent sexual behavior, contraception, pregnancy and STDs. *Journal of School Health, 62,* 265–270.

Padilla, E. R., & O'Grady, K. E. (1987). Sexuality among Mexican Americans: A case of sexual stereotyping. *Journal of Personality and Social Psychology, 52,* 5–10.

Pavich, E. G. (1986). A Chicano perspective on Mexican culture and sexuality. *Journal of Social Work and Human Sexuality, 4,* 47–65.

Peterson, J., & Marín, G. (1988). Issues in the prevention of AIDS among black and Hispanic men. *American Psychology, 43,* 871–877.

Richwald, G., Kyle, G., Gerber, M., Morisky, D., Kristal, A., & Friedland, J. (1988). Sexual activities in bathhouses in Los Angeles County: Implications for AIDS prevention education. *Journal of Sex Research, 25,* 169–180.

Richwald, G., Schneider-Muñoz, M., & Valdez, R. (1989). Are condom instructions in Spanish readable? Implications for AIDS prevention activities for Hispanics. *Hispanic Journal of Behavioral Sciences, 11,* 70–82.

Rotheram-Borus, M., Meyer-Bahlburg, H., Rosario, M., Koopman, C., Haignere, C., Exner, T., Matthieu, M., Henderson, R., & Gruen, R. (1992). Lifetime sexual behaviors among predominantly minority male runaways and gay/bisexual adolescents in New York City. *AIDS Education and Prevention,* Suppl., pp. 34–42.

Sabagh, G., & López, D. (1980). Religiosity and fertility: The case of Chicanas. *Social Forces, 59* (2), 431–439.

Sabogal, F., Pierce, R., Pollack, L., Faigeles, B., & Catania, J. (1993). Multiple partners among Hispanics in the United States: The national AIDS behavioral surveys. *Family Planning Perspectives, 25,* 257–262.

Scrimshaw, S., Carballo, M., Ramos, L., & Blair, B. (1991). The AIDS rapid anthropological procedures: A tool for health education planning and evaluation. *Health Education Quarterly, 18,* 111–123.

Selik, R. M., Castro, K. G., & Pappaioanou, M. (1988). Racial/ethnic differences in risk of AIDS. *American Journal of Public Health, 78,* 1539–1545.

Serrano-García, I. & López-Sánchez, G. (1991). *Un enfoque diferente del poder y el cambio social para la psicología social-comunitaria.* Invited address at the Interamerican Congress of Psychology, San José, Costa Rica.

Sonenstein, F., Pleck, J., & Ku, L. (1989). Sexual activity, condom use and AIDS awareness among adolescent males. *Family Plannning Perspectives, 21,* 152–158.

Tanfer, K., Grady, W., Klepinger, D., & Billy, J. (1993). Condom use among men. *Family Planning Perspectives, 25,* 61–66.

Vázquez-Nuttal, E., Romero, I., & de Leon, B. (1987). Sex roles and perceptions of femininity and masculinity of Hispanic women. *Psychology of Women Quarterly, 11,* 409–425.

Veiel, H. O. F. (1995). *Childhood abuse and HIV infection in homosexual men: A review of the literature.* Prepared for AIDS Care and Treatment Unit, Preventive Health Services Division, Health Canada. Available from HV Psychological and Health Research Consultants, Inc., 1315–750 West Broadway, Vancouver, B.C. V5Z 1H5.

Villas, P., Bouvet, M., & Bernal, P. (1992, January–February–March). Acculturation and HIV/AIDS knowledge among Hispanos: Findings from southern New Mexico. *Border Health, 7* (1), 10–17.

Chapter 6

Treatment Barriers: Accessing and Accepting Professional Help

JOHN J. ECHEVERRY
The George Washington University

Two of the most difficult issues confronting the provision of mental health care to the Latino communities of the United States are the extent to which these services are available and accessible to those in need, and the degree to which those in need seek and accept professional help (Woodward, Dwinell, & Arons, 1992). This chapter is an overview that examines some of the most salient factors involved in this problem, taking into account client variables, client–therapist variables, and organizational or structural variables that may contribute to the creation and maintenance of barriers to treatment.

The first section of this chapter focuses on client variables that may constitute factors in the pattern or nature of help-seeking. The second section focuses on organizational or systemic variables. The third and final section offers some ideas for the remediation of barriers to mental health treatment.

This approach is consonant with the findings of Woodward, Dwinell, and Arons (1992), who in their review of the literature on barriers to mental health care to Latinos found that most research has concluded that the most important barriers include both financial variables, such as cost of services and access to health insurance, and nonfinancial demographic and cultural variables (see Figure 6.1).

As pointed out in Chapter 1 by García and Marotta, the Latino population of the United States is extremely complex because of its intragroup diversity. This diversity is reflected along racial, ethnic, and cultural lines; historical differences

Client Variables

Demographic characteristics:
  Age
  Gender
  Educational level
  Legal status in the United States

Cultural factors:
  Religious beliefs
  Degree of acculturation
  National origin
  English proficiency level
  Resource preference
  Beliefs about mental illness and treatment

Individual factors:
  Presenting problem(s)
  Personality variables

Client–Therapist Variables
  Confidentiality concerns
  Socialization with clients

Organizational/Structural Variables
  Geographic location of mental health services
  Cost of evaluation and treatment
  Schedule of services
  Type of services offered
  Spanish-speaking or bilingual personnel

**FIGURE 6.1   Factors That May Influence Access to and
Acceptance of Professional Help by Latinos
in the United States**

regarding residence in the United States; legal status in the country; and socioeconomic status. This complexity makes it very difficult, if not inappropriate, to speak of Latinos as if they were a monolithic group. For the sake of simplifying our arguments, however, we will talk about Latinos in general, but particularly those who are in the early phases of the acculturation process or whose financial situation limits their access to mental health services in some way.

Client Variables

These variables include *demographic characteristics* such as age, gender, level of education, and legal status in the United States. Other client variables are *cultural factors* such as religious beliefs, degree of acculturation, national origin, level of proficiency in the English language, resource preference, and beliefs about mental illness and treatment (Comas-Díaz, 1993; Padgett, Patrick, Burns, & Schlesinger, 1994). Moreover, this category includes *individual factors,* such as presenting problem, and personality variables. It is fundamental to remember that each client is different, and that therefore there is no specific pattern or order of importance of the factors listed above. What may constitute a barrier to treatment for one individual may not be an impediment for another person, even if that person is from the same country or shares similar life circumstances.

Demographic Characteristics

Age. Differential availability of mental health services to the various age groups constitutes a barrier to treatment. For Latino communities this is particularly troublesome, because in general the Latino population of this country tends to be relatively young when compared to other ethnic groups (U.S. Bureau of the Census, 1985). Moreover, children and youths may present with multiple needs and problems, including developmental, family, peer, health, vocational, academic, and behavioral issues (Young Rivers, & Morrow, 1995). A similar situation occurs at the other end of the spectrum. Latino elderly constitute a much smaller proportion of the Latino population at large as compared with other groups (Espino, Neufeld, Mulvihill, & Libow, 1988), but also present with unique problems that merit attention, such as poverty, health problems, dementia, depression, substance abuse, and the social problems inherent in being a member of a minority group (Baker & Lightfoot, 1993; Grant, 1995). However, there seem to be very few programs to address their needs, as well as very few social workers, psychologists, psychiatrists, and other mental health professionals trained on providing culturally relevant and age-specialized services for them.

Gender. This is another barrier to mental health care for Latinos. This problem is particularly salient because of the need for more alcohol and substance abuse treatment programs, where a majority of those Latinos in need may be male. Another way gender may be a problem is the apparent reticence of Latino men to seek mental health services because of cultural influences. There appears to be a notion among many Latino men that it is emasculating to seek mental health help (Casas, Wagenheim, Banchero, & Mendoza-Romero, 1994). Therefore, unless a program already exists and makes a concerted effort to engage Latino men into treatment, whether as individual clients or as part of a family or a couple, Latino men may have even lower rates of mental health service utilization than Latinas. A study of the utilization of a substance abuse treatment program on the part of arrestees suggests that Latino males may be significantly more likely to refuse treatment, in part because of the belief that "I can quit on my own" (Longshore, Hsieh, Anglin, & Annon, 1992).

Latinas also have specific and unique issues that need to be addressed by mental health professionals. Epidemiological and other types of data are beginning to show that Latinas are at great risk of mental health problems (Espin, 1993; Napholz, 1994; Vásquez, 1994).

Educational level. This may be a factor in help-seeking as it may be correlated with income, knowledge of available resources, degree of acculturation, and level of English proficiency. Having some understanding of mental health treatment may be related to level of education, which, if low, further impedes seeking or accessing mental health services (Aponte & Crouch, 1995). Unfortunately, Latinos have the lowest educational levels of all ethnic groups in the United States. Only 51% of Latinos complete high school, and far fewer than half of Latinos enter college (O'Brien, 1993; Zea, Jarama, & Trotta Bianchi, 1995). Retention rates for Latinos who enter college have been estimated to be as low as 20% (Solberg, Valdez, & Villarreal, 1994).

Legal status in the United States. This is one of the most important barriers to treatment because it has implications for the availability of services and for the perception on part of the community of whether or not the services would be available to them. Some undocumented immigrants fear seeking services in a government-sponsored clinic because they assume that there will be a direct conduit between the clinic and the Immigration and Naturalization Service (INS) and that they will be deported immediately if their legal status in the country is reported. Carballo-Dieguez (1989) suggests that this belief prevents many undocumented gay Latinos from seeking AIDS-related health care or counseling. However, not many places ask potential clients on intake about their legal status, even if their funding comes from the federal government. In the state of Maryland and the District of Columbia, for example, questions about the client's immigration status are not supposed to be asked. However, the impact of this fear is difficult to measure, since potential clients—that is, any Latino in need of mental health services—may not even place a call to a clinic to find out what services are available, let alone get to the intake stage. Even after an undocumented client enters the system, the fear of being reported and deported persists and surfaces through questions such as: "Does the government know I come here?" "Do you report my name to the police?" "Will you call *la migra*" [the immigration authorities]? Constant reassurances are needed in those instances.

Aside from legal status in the United States, the mere experience of migration, as immigrants, refugees, or sojourners (Berry & Kim, 1988), increases the likelihood of the development of psychological problems (Aponte & Barnes, 1995).

Cultural Factors

Religious beliefs. These may constitute a barrier to treatment among those whose belief system dictates that life's difficulties, such as a physical illness or disability, are entirely God's will (Smart & Smart, 1991) and that only God may solve a problem or illness, as this may impede them from seeking services even after other options have been tried unsuccessfully. Consultations with clergy may be helpful in some instances—for example, when help is needed regarding a moral or spiritual problem or when support or a good listener is all that is needed. But unless the member of the clergy is trained in pastoral counseling or in another mental health profession, there are clear limits to the effectiveness of the help he or she can provide.

Those who tend to rely on alternative approaches to deal with physical and mental health problems may not seek help from a more traditional practitioner or mental health clinic, especially at the early stages of the problem. The usual pattern is that those in need may have tried to resolve their difficulties within the nuclear or extended family, by going to a trusted friend or *compadre*, by consulting a folk healer, or *santero, curandero,* or *espiritista* (Koss-Chioino, 1995), and, if none of those resources provides any alleviation of the problem, the person may finally go to an emergency room or to a mental health professional when the situation reaches crisis proportions (Wallen, 1992).

Degree of acculturation.   Research findings suggest that a low level of acculturation is associated with low utilization rates (Wells, Golding, & Hough, 1989), and, conversely, that the more acculturated the person, the more likely he or she is to seek mental health services (Wells et al., 1989), presumably because of greater understanding about mental health treatment and greater knowledge of the available resources. The more acculturated also may be more willing to depart from alternative interventions (e.g., folk remedies) and may have a greater knowledge of the nature of mental health treatment. This does not mean, however, that a more acculturated client will necessarily be a *better* patient (i.e., more intelligent, verbal, and insightful) or will benefit more from psychotherapeutic interventions. Conversely, independent of degree of acculturation, the provision of culturally sensitive services to Latinos may increase their service utilization rates and treatment effectiveness (Curtis, 1990; Rogler, Malgady, Costantino, & Blumenthal, 1987).

National origin.   This could be a barrier to help-seeking in instances in which a potential client is a minority within his own ethnic group. This may occur, for example, when a Central American client refuses to participate in a therapy group because virtually everyone else in the group is from a Caribbean country, and the person assumes he or she would not fit in. Also, if a clinic is identified with a particular national group (e.g., Mexican, Puerto Rican), people from other Spanish-speaking countries may choose not to seek services there, as they may believe that services would not be available to them or that their unique problems would not be understood or addressed.

Level of English proficiency.   This is one of the client variables most often thought of as a barrier to the accessibility to mental health services (see Chapter 13 by Preciado and Henry), as well as to treatment outcome (Marcos, 1976). The most obvious reason is that English is this country's language and most mental health services are, of course, provided in English. Even those with some ability to understand and speak the language know beforehand—or find out shortly after entering the mental health system—that a knowledge of English adequate for their daily lives and their work is not sufficient to allow them to talk in English about intimate personal matters that may be laden with emotion and with subtle cultural nuances.

For those Spanish-monolingual clients who, because of a crisis, have to be cared for by a clinician who does not speak Spanish, there are possible harmful consequences, including misdiagnosis and hence inappropriate treatment (Bamford, 1991; Malgady, Rogler, & Costantino, 1987). Mental health experts advocate the use of bilingual clinicians rather than interpreters when providing services to monolingual Latinos (Comas-Díaz, 1993).

Resource preference. This has to do with the individual's choice of whom to consult in case of need of emotional support for a problem. This seems to be a highly individualized choice (Marín, 1993). Some people would never trust a friend, even a close friend, with a personal problem; others would never go to a therapist or counselor because "How can one tell a complete stranger about personal problems?" This may be a barrier to treatment because some people who might otherwise benefit from psychological intervention fall through the cracks, particularly if they do not have a solid support system to see them through a crisis. Many times over the years I have found clients who, when in need of mental health care, would go only to a priest, a *compadre*, a homeopath, or a palm reader, or to a *botánica* for some remedy. Only when it was clear that no amelioration of symptoms was evident would the person go to a mental health clinician.

In general, research has shown that Latinos, like other racial or ethnic minorities, have consistently lower rates of utilization of outpatient mental health services (Wu & Windle, 1980), and this phenomenon may be due in part to their use of other types of resources, such as those enumerated earlier.

Beliefs about mental illness and treatment. More specifically, this refers to people's understanding of mental processes, emotions, the body–mind connection, and the causes of mental or emotional problems (Cohen, 1979). For many Latinos, emotional or mental problems are a sign of weakness, lack of strength or character, bad luck, the result of a spell or a similar supernatural event, or simply God's will. Going to a therapist or other clinician is therefore seen as admission of a weakness one cannot resolve on one's own. Alternatively, if someone suggests visiting a psychologist or psychiatrist, it must mean that one is crazy. The underlying message is that mentally healthy people do not need consultation with a mental health professional; only the insane or unstable do. These beliefs may constitute some of the strongest barriers to access to mental health care, even when services are available to the person in his or her community.

Besides the various demographic and cultural variables listed here, there exist other potential barriers that have to do with the relationship between the client and the therapist.

Client–Therapist Variables

The variables related to the relationship between the therapist and the client may be numerous and complex, and an in-depth discussion of them is beyond the scope of this chapter. However, some examples may be helpful to illustrate this point. One of the most common complaints from potential or actual clients is their fear that information about them or their disclosures in therapy will become, somehow, part of public record and that their families, neighbors, or the community at large will know about their personal life. Unfortunately, partial reporting of patients' disclosures is sometimes unavoidable. The clinician is obligated to report cases of abuse, neglect, or exploitation, or the threat of potential harm to self or others. Losses often result from that reporting, such as the incarceration of an abusive spouse who was the only breadwinner in the family, or the placement in foster care of a child because of an accusation of neglect. Information about such cases seems to spread very rapidly, and members of the community may believe that any information given to a mental health professional is disclosable, with negative consequences to the client. This issue of *confidentiality* may affect the seeking of mental health care, as those in need of treatment may resort to other sources of help, which may or may not be appropriate or even helpful to the individual.

Even after a person has actually become a client, the issue of confidentiality may surface, as in the formation of groups. Typically, when offered therapy in the form of group work, the client will immediately say, "I don't want to be in a group," or, "I don't do well in groups," or, "How will hearing about everybody else's problems help me?" Upon probing, their main concern is revealed to be that they might be in the same room with other members of the community, even neighbors, and they fear that their problems or intimate circumstances will then be known by others in their community.

For many, if not most, clients who typically visit a community mental health center, knowledge about mental health treatment is limited; that is, they are what some of us call "not psychologically minded." Some aspects of this phenomenon may create barriers to treatment, especially if the client's expectations of the role of the therapist are not clear from the outset. Latino clients may discontinue therapy early because their therapist would not accept their invitations to socialize with them and their families, or would not do for them things that were not within the realm of the therapist's professional responsibility, which would be only to provide case management and/or psychotherapeutic services. As therapists gain more experience and develop a greater understanding of these cultural nuances, they may be able to clarify to incoming clients what can and cannot be done for them, in order to avoid unfulfilled expectations, misunderstandings, and potential ethical violations on the therapist's part. This change may lead to a decrease in the frequency of clients stopping therapy early.

Organizational/Structural Variables

Another set of variables that may constitute barriers to the access and acceptance of mental health services has to do with institutional or structural elements of the organizations that provide mental health services.

These variables include the geographic location of the mental health service, the cost of evaluation and treatment, the schedule of services, and the type of services offered, as well as the availability of Spanish-speaking personnel or, in the case of acculturated Latinos (those who presumably speak English), personnel who are bicultural or at least familiar with the cultural norms of the group(s) being served.

Geographic location. This is of paramount importance for many clients, especially those with limited funds (because of the cost of transportation), age (e.g., children or the infirm elderly), and those who live in rural areas. Having to take public transportation is sometimes a burden to those with children, who are expected to attend family therapy sessions. Besides the time and effort involved, if the family does not own a car it must have enough funds to pay round-trip fares for several people. Having to use public transportation can also be a potential source of embarrassment to those transporting a family member to therapy who may be visibly disturbed or difficult to manage. Another common complaint is that although the services may be available at a place reachable by bus or subway, it is located in a neighborhood away from Latino enclaves. The notion that mental health services should be located within the communities they are supposed to serve is an important one because it takes into account the importance of community (or *barrio*).

Cost. This has been found to be one of the major barriers to access to mental health services (Woodward et al., 1992). A substantial segment of the Latino population has either limited insurance, which covers health but not mental health services, or no coverage at all. Another segment may be covered only by Medicaid or Medicare, whose coverage may be limited to inpatient mental health care. Given these circumstances, the person may have to pay out of pocket for mental health services, or pay a co-payment that in many cases may be a financial burden.

Another aspect of cost that should be considered is what it costs a system to provide services to Latinos. Hu, Snowden, and Jerrell (1992) suggest that Latinos, along with African Americans, incur fewer costs—that is, they are not expensive-to-serve clients—and that actually, if they were provided with comprehensive services (psychological interventions and case management), savings could result from their decreased likelihood of using inpatient hospitalization.

Schedule of services. Many Latinos do not have the luxury of being able to take time off during the day, even during their lunch hour, to attend a therapy session, and may have to rely on services that are open evenings or Saturdays. Potential clients may have two jobs, a family to take care of, no car, and no way to be able to take sick leave for treatment. Typically, community mental health agencies in the Washington, D.C., area do open at least one evening a week to accommodate working clients and families with school-age children. However, clients often have to forego pay to be able to attend a therapy session; they usually miss two hours of work, one for the session and one for round-trip transportation.

Availability of bilingual/bicultural services. This is perhaps the most important organizational barrier to access to mental health services for Latinos (see Chapter 13 by Preciado & Henry). This variable affects primarily those Latinos who are monolingual in Spanish or would prefer services in Spanish. Highly acculturated, middle-class, and well-educated Latinos may prefer to seek services with bilingual/bicultural professionals. Often they will say they feel more comfortable and better understood by a fellow Latino even if their English is impeccable and they could be seen by any other English-speaking clinician.

Availability of Spanish-speaking personnel. This includes intake evaluation and treatment support staff with whom the client has the first contact. Often, just being able to speak in Spanish with the receptionist who answers the phone may make the difference between giving up on seeking services and continuing to pursue assistance.

The cases discussed next are the result of my observations and experiences while working with Latinos in two very distinct settings, a county government-sponsored program in the state of Maryland serving Latinos and other racial and ethnic minorities, and a department of psychiatry at a teaching hospital, where inpatient and outpatient mental health services are provided through a health maintenance organization (HMO). The population served by the county mental health center is primarily working class, uninsured, with limited education, and quite diverse in terms of national origin and presenting problem. Perhaps half of the clients at this clinic are undocumented immigrants. By contrast, the population served by the hospital outpatient psychiatry service is entirely covered by some sort of health insurance policy, middle class, able to work legally in this country, and relatively well educated. Both populations were similar in terms of diversity of national origin and variety of presenting problems.

Case Illustration I

A 30-year-old male Spanish monolingual construction worker was referred for counseling to the Multicultural Program of a county-sponsored mental health clinic. He had been stopped for driving under the influence of alcohol, and arrested for allegedly attacking the police officer who stopped him on the road. No explanation was given on the referral form about what counseling meant, what the focus was, or for how long the treatment had to take place. However, judging from past experience with this type of referral, the client would be in serious trouble if he could not document for his probation officer regular meetings with a therapist. The client lost his driver's license and had to rely on a co-worker to get to his job site nearly 25 miles away. He was torn between complying with court-mandated counseling and keeping his regular work hours (7:30 A.M. to 6:30 P.M.). After his second session at the clinic, which took place in the latest possible slot of 7 P.M., he was given notice at work that if he left early again, for whatever reason, he would be dismissed.

The patient started driving without a license so he could use his own car to make it to the sessions, but soon he stopped attending regularly because of his lack of understanding why he had been ordered to receive mental health treatment and his resistance to treatment as it added to his transportation problems. He refused alcohol abuse treatment, denied the existence of a problem, and began articulating worries that he might be deported if this government clinic were to report him to the authorities. His worry soon became anger against the clinic and the therapist/case manager, and he dropped out by the third session.

In this case, the three sessions were devoted to gathering some basic data from the patient in the form of an official intake, and much time was spent dealing with the patient's anger and frustration about a legal obligation he did not understand and in trying to find a way to enable the patient to find appropriate transportation to the clinic or a referral to a mental health center closer to his work site. There was no time to discuss many issues, including the confidentiality limitations posed by the involvement of a third party, the referring probation officer. Subsequent referrals of this type were not accepted unless there was direct communication with the probation officer regarding the reasons for the referral and the court's expectations about treatment: type, focus, and duration. That enabled clinicians to formulate a better treatment plan and to be clear with the patient about confidentiality issues and the relationship between the clinician and the client and the clinician and the referral source, in this case a probation or parole officer.

Case Illustration II

A 45-year-old South American woman, who was a high-level employee of an international organization, sought couples therapy at an HMO because of serious conflicts in her one-year marriage to a European-born fellow professional. She spoke little English despite her five years in the United States, because she did not have to use English in her job. Her husband spoke both English and Spanish equally well, but all sessions were conducted in Spanish to accommodate her monolingualism. The couple had requested a bilingual and bicultural therapist, and one was available. However, when the woman had to be seen for a medication evaluation, the session had to include an interpreter because the attending psychiatrist was monolingual in English.

These two cases help illustrate the types of clients who may be seen in a mental health center. In Case I, the client came to the clinic against his will and did not understand why he had to be in therapy. He denied that his apparent alcohol abuse was a problem and did not find it necessary to get help for a "nonproblem." Moreover, even if he had sought services willingly, there were some clear barriers to his compliance with and success in treatment. These included demographic variables such as his limited educational level and his undocumented status in the United States. Cultural variables that constituted barriers to treatment included his inability to speak English, which required that he be seen at an agency that provided services in Spanish. He was also greatly concerned about confidentiality. The organizational/structural barriers that he encountered were the clinic's location and its schedule of services, which made it almost impossible for him to receive treatment.

In Case II, the barriers to treatment were less numerous and perhaps even less serious, but important to note nevertheless. The patient was fortunate to have found a Spanish- speaking therapist with available time. Typically, Spanish-speaking therapists are the only ones within their organization who are assigned all Spanish-speaking clients, at times in addition to their regular clients. They also may be called on to assist in interpreting, translation, and crisis intervention, to the point of their being overwhelmed by work demands. If this patient's request for a bilingual/bicultural clinician had not been granted, it is likely that she would have desisted from seeking treatment or gotten only marginal interventions, given the presence of a language barrier. The psychopharmacological evaluation turned out to be lengthier and more expensive than a typical assessment of that type because two clinicians were needed, one to conduct the evaluation and another to serve as interpreter.

Conclusions

The variables that constitute potential barriers to access to mental health services for Latinos in this country are multiple in number, vary in degree of seriousness, and do not lend themselves to easy solutions. The complexity of the issue lies in part on the roots of the problem, particularly those that are systemic or organizational, but also some that have to do with deeply ingrained cultural beliefs. Some seem more situational or temporal, such as legal status in the United States. Others, like degree of acculturation, ability to speak English, resource preference, or beliefs about mental illness and treatment, may respond more readily to education and prevention efforts.

The political climate in the mid-1990s and the substantial changes taking place in the provision of health services in this country are also becoming barriers to the accessibility of care. In many places, managed care and the political climate contribute to decreased financial resources to provide mental health services—particularly to those with few resources—which further complicates the picture. The solution is complex because it must involve the government at the federal, state, and local levels, policymakers, third-party payers, providers, and consumers. Unless advocates from each of these groups engage in the struggle for greater availability of resources for mental health programs, the situation will further deteriorate at the organizational/structural level discussed earlier, and the consumer will suffer the most.

To address client demographic characteristics that may be barriers to access to mental health care, advocacy is needed to ensure that at least basic services are provided to all age groups and to both men and women equally. Each group presents with specific needs, and programs and clinicians should be aware of what those particular needs are (Sue, Fugino, & Hu, 1991). This may apply to the provision of primary and secondary prevention interventions to youth regarding alcohol and substance abuse, and specialized services to women and the elderly. As more Latinos become legal residents of the United States or naturalized U.S. citizens, their access to mental health care will likely improve. The current movement to encourage Latinos to legalize their status in this country is a positive step to eliminate legal barriers and anti-immigrant sentiment.

In terms of the cultural factors that present barriers to mental health care, the solutions may be more elusive. The point is not to *Americanize* Latinos, but to respect their culture and world view and to provide them with culturally sensitive services that take into consideration diversity among Latinos, their place in the acculturation continuum, and their traditional beliefs. This, of course, demands that service providers educate themselves in order to be cognizant of cultural differences; respectful of Latinos regardless of their socioeconomic background, skin color, or national origin; and trustful of Latinos' ability to adapt to different ways of behaving and thinking. In this regard, training programs have the obligation to train more culturally sensitive psychologists and other mental health professionals who can work directly serving the mental health needs of clients, and also as researchers, policymakers, and teachers of future generations of service providers and academicians (Bernal, 1990).

As far as client–therapist factors are concerned, mental health providers have the responsibility to ensure to all clients the confidentiality of their sessions and to address promptly and directly client concerns about confidentiality. Failure to ensure confidentiality may lead to early termination from therapy or may impair the therapist–client relationship. The mental health professionals need to help Latinos understand that there are limits to socializing with clients outside of the therapeutic environment because of ethical and transferential considerations. This must also be made clear to clients at the onset of a therapeutic relationship.

However, the provision of services that are geographically accessible, affordable, and available on days and times when clients are most likely to be able to use them is not an impossibility. Of particular importance is the provision of mental health services to Latinos by bilingual and bicultural staff, from receptionists and intake workers to psychologists and psychiatrists. This would require the commitment and support of funding sources, be it a hospital, community mental health center, or other organization that would provide mental health services to Latinos, who may be part of the population they serve (Rodriguez, Lessinger, & Guarnaccia, 1992).

In these rapidly changing times, much is unknown about the increasing need for mental health services for Latinos. Therefore, encouraging researchers to look into the myriad of unexplored issues and concerns of this expanding group is both necessary and exciting (Rogler et al., 1987).

References

Aponte, J. F., & Barnes, J. M. (1995). Impact of acculturation and moderator variables on the intervention and treatment of ethnic groups. In J. F. Aponte, R. Young Rivers, & J. Wohl (Eds.), *Psychological interventions and cultural diversity* (pp. 19–39). Boston: Allyn and Bacon.

Aponte, J. F., & Crouch, R. T. (1995). The changing ethnic profile of the United States. In J. F. Aponte, R. Young Rivers, & J. Wohl (Eds.),

Psychological interventions and cultural diversity (pp. 1–18). Boston: Allyn and Bacon.

Baker, F. M., & Lightfoot, O. B. (1993). Psychiatric care of ethnic elders. In A. C. Gaw (Ed.), *Culture, ethnicity, and mental illness* (pp. 516–552). Washington, DC: American Psychiatric Press.

Bamford, K. W. (1991). Bilingual issues in mental health assessment and treatment. *Hispanic Journal of Behavioral Sciences, 13*(4), 377–390.

Bernal, M. E. (1990). Ethnic minority mental health training. In F. C. Serafica, A. I. Schwebel, R. K. Russell, P. D. Isaac, & L. B. Myers (Eds.), *Mental health of ethnic minorities* (pp. 249–274). New York: Praeger.

Berry, J. W., & Kim, U. (1988). Acculturation and mental health. In P. R. Dasen, J. W. Berry, & N. Sartorius (Eds.), *Health and cross-cultural psychology: Toward applications* (pp. 207–236). Newbury Park, CA: Sage.

Carballo-Dieguez, A. (1989). Hispanic culture, gay male culture, and AIDS: Counseling implications. *Journal of Counseling and Development, 68*, 26–30.

Casas, J. M., Wagenheim, B. R., Banchero, R., & Mendoza-Romero, J. (1994). Hispanic masculinity: Myth or psychological schema meriting clinical consideration. *Hispanic Journal of Behavioral Sciences, 16*(3), 315–331.

Cohen, L. M. (1979). *Culture, disease, and stress among Latino immigrants.* Washington, DC: Smithsonian Institution.

Comas-Díaz, L. (1993). Hispanic Latino communities: Psychological implications. In D. R. Atkinson, G. Morten, & D. W. Sue (Eds.), *Counseling American minorities: A cross-cultural perspective* (pp. 245–263). Madison, WI: Brown & Benchmark.

Curtis, P. A. (1990). The consequences of acculturation to service delivery and research with Hispanic families. *Child and Adolescent Social Work, 7*(2), 147–160.

Espín, O. M. (1993). Psychological impact of migration on Latinas: Implications for psychotherapeutic practice. In D. R. Atkinson, G. Morten, & D. W. Sue (Eds.), *Counseling American minorities: A cross-cultural perspective* (pp. 165–171). Madison, WI: Brown & Benchmark.

Espino, D. V., Neufeld, R. R., Mulvihill, M., & Libow, L. S. (1988). Hispanic and non-Hispanic elderly on admission to the nursing home: A pilot study. *The Gerontologist, 28*(6), 821–824.

Grant, R. W. (1995). Interventions with ethnic minority elderly. In J. F. Aponte, R. Young Rivers, & J. Wohl (Eds.), *Psychological interventions and cultural diversity* (pp. 199–214). Boston: Allyn and Bacon.

Hu, T., Snowden, L. R., & Jerrell, J. M. (1992). Costs and use of public mental health services by ethnicity. *Journal of Mental Health Administration, 19*(3), 278–287.

Koss-Chioino, J. D. (1995). Traditional and folk approaches among ethnic minorities. In J. F. Aponte, R. Young Rivers, & J. Wohl (Eds.), *Psychological interventions and cultural diversity* (pp. 145–163). Boston: Allyn and Bacon.

Longshore, D., Hsieh, S., Anglin, M. D., & Annon, T. A. (1992). Ethnic patterns in drug abuse treatment utilization. *Journal of Mental Health Administration, 19*(3), 268–277.

Malgady, R. G., Rogler, L. H., & Costantino, G. (1987). Ethnocultural and linguistic bias in mental health evaluation of Hispanics. *American Psychologist, 42*(3), 228–234.

Marcos, L. R. (1976). Bilinguals in psychotherapy: Language as an emotional barrier. *American Journal of Psychotherapy, 30*, 552–560.

Marín, G. (1993). Defining culturally appropriate community interventions: Hispanics as a case study. *Journal of Community Psychology, 21*, 149–161.

Napholz, L. (1994, November). Dysphoria among Hispanic working women: A research note. *Hispanic Journal of Behavioral Sciences, 16*(4), 500–509.

O'Brien, E. M. (1993). Latinos in higher education. *Research Briefs, 4*(4), 1–15.

Padgett, D. K., Patrick, C., Burns, B. J., & Schlesinger, H. J. (1994). Ethnicity and the use of outpatient mental health services in a national insured population. *American Journal of Public Health, 84*(2), 222–226.

Rodríguez, O., Lessinger, J., & Guarnaccia, P. (1992). The societal and organizational contexts of culturally sensitive mental health services: Findings from an evaluation of bilingual/bicultural psychiatric programs.

Journal of Mental Health Administration, 19(3), 213–223.

Rogler, L. H., Malgady, R. G., Costantino, G., & Blumenthal, R. (1987). What do culturally sensitive mental health services mean? A case of Hispanics. *American Psychologist, 42*(6), 565–570.

Smart, J. F., & Smart, D. W. (1991). Acceptance of disability and the Mexican American culture. *Rehabilitation Counseling Bulletin, 34*(4), 357–367.

Solberg, V. S., Valdez, J., & Villarreal, P. (1994). Social support, stress, and Hispanic college adjustment: Test of a diathesis–stress model. *Hispanic Journal of Behavioral Sciences, 16,* 230–239.

Sue, S., Fugino, D., & Hu, L. (1991). Community mental health services for ethnic minority groups: A test of the cultural responsiveness hypothesis. *Journal of Consulting and Clinical Psychology, 59,* 533–540.

U.S. Bureau of the Census, U.S. Department of Commerce. (1985, March). Persons of Spanish origin in the United States. *Current Population Reports,* Series P-20, No. 403. Washington, DC: U.S. Government Printing Office.

Vásquez, M. J. T. (1994). Latinas. In L. Comas-Díaz & B. Greene (Eds.), *Women of color: Integrating ethnic and gender identities in psychotherapy.* New York: Guilford Press.

Wallen, J. (1992). Providing culturally appropriate mental health services for minorities. *Journal of Mental Health Administration, 19*(3), 288–295.

Wells, K. B., Golding, J. M., & Hough, R. L. (1989). Acculturation and the probability of use of health services by Mexican Americans. *Health Services Research, 24,* 237–257.

Woodward, A. M., Dwinell, A. D., & Arons, B. S. (1992). Barriers to mental health care for Hispanic Americans: A literature review and discussion. *Journal of Mental Health Administration, 19*(3), 224–236.

Wu, I., & Windle, C. (1980). Ethnic specificity in the relationship of minority use and staffing of community mental health centers. *Community Mental Health Journal, 16,* 156–168.

Young Rivers, R., & Morrow, C. A. (1995). Understanding and treating ethnic minority youth. In J. F. Aponte, R. Young Rivers, & J. Wohl (Eds.), *Psychological interventions and cultural diversity.* Boston: Allyn and Bacon.

Zea, M. C., Jarama, S. L., & Trotta Bianchi, F. (1995). Social support and psychosocial competence: Explaining the adaptation to college of ethnically diverse students. *American Journal of Community Psychology, 23,* 509–531.

Chapter 7

A Conceptual Framework for Conducting Psychotherapy with Mexican-American College Students

AUGUSTINE (GUS) BARÓN
The University of Texas at Austin

MADONNA G. CONSTANTINE
Temple University

According to the 1990 census, the Mexican-American/Chicano(a)[1] population increased from 2.1 million in 1960 to 13.3 million 30 years later. The overall representation of Chicanos in the U.S. population rose from 1.2% in 1960 to 5.4% in 1990. These numbers are part of larger demographic changes occurring in the United States, where it is predicted that by the year 2000, one-third of the population will be non-White minorities (Aguirre & Martínez, 1993; Griffith, Frase, & Ralph, 1989; National Council of La Raza, 1990).

Mexican Americans are a burgeoning group poised to make major social, political, and economic contributions to U.S. society well into the twenty-first century. Unfortunately, educational attainment data indicate a poor prognosis for the advancement of this group. Although gains have been made over the last 15 years, the proportion of Chicanos completing four or more years of high school is still less than half (30.9% in 1975 vs. 44.1% in 1990). This is much lower than the percentage of Cubans (64.5%) and Puerto Ricans (55%) completing four or more years of high

---

[1] In this chapter, the terms *Mexican American* and *Chicano(a)* will be used interchangeably, although there are connotational meanings for each that have important psychological implications as will be discussed in a later section.

school (1990). Regarding completion rates for four or more years of college, Mexican Americans continue to lag in comparison to other Latino groups—20.2% for Cubans, 9.7% for Puerto Ricans, and 5.4% for Mexican Americans. In comparison, the rates for four or more years of college completion are 39.9% for Asians, 28.5% for Whites, and 11.4% for African Americans (Aguirre & Martínez, 1993; U.S. Bureau of the Census, 1991). So although the Mexican-American population is one of the fastest growing Hispanic subgroups, it is also one of the least well educated subgroups in the United States.

College enrollment data for the fall of 1992 (*Chronicle of Higher Education*, 1994) indicated that there were 954,000 Latino students, representing 6.5% of the total U.S. college population. Although exact figures for Chicanos are difficult to ascertain because of the collapsing of data across all Latino subgroups, researchers have assumed that Chicanos generally represent about 60% of total Latino enrollment (Astin, 1982; U.S. Bureau of the Census, 1991).

The data on completion of four years or more of college clearly show that successfully navigating the challenges of higher education is a major accomplishment for Chicanos. While there have been many studies attempting to ascertain academic predictors of success for Mexican-American college students (e.g., Durán, 1983; Humphreys, 1988; Lunneborg & Lunneborg, 1986; Willie, 1987), the literature suggests that personal, nonacademic factors are often better predictors of persistence in college than are scores on standardized tests. Such factors include positive self-esteem, leadership ability, community involvement, ability to conduct a realistic self-appraisal, an understanding and effective way of dealing with racism, development of long-range goals rather than reliance on short-term ones, and availability of a strong support person (Arbona & Novy, 1990; Pennock-Roman, 1988; Sedlacek, 1987; Sedlacek & Brooks, 1976; Tracey & Sedlacek, 1984, 1985, 1987; Young, 1992).

Studies of Chicanos who pursue post-baccalaureate degrees also indicate that psychological factors are strong predictors for success. Among these are parents' work ethic, strong emotional support from one's family, strong maternal role model (for female students), and demonstration of gratitude for one's family by working hard and achieving a degree (Aguirre & Martínez, 1993; Cortese, 1992; Fiske, 1988; Gandara, 1982; Madrid, 1988).

Given the salience of these psychosocial and cultural factors, the role of college psychological services seems particularly important for retaining and successfully graduating Chicanos. With their emphasis on primary, secondary, and tertiary interventions, many college counseling centers are involved in a variety of service modalities that are ultimately designed to assist students in maintaining academic persistence. Because the largest component of a counseling center is its individual and group therapy services, this chapter concentrates on some of the knowledge and skills needed for assessing and intervening with Mexican-American college students presenting for treatment. Three core psychosocial/cultural concepts we have found useful in conceptualizing treatment planning will be discussed, along with assessment methods and a case example illustrating the concepts and strategies.

Core Psychosocial/Cultural Constructs

In our work with Chicano college students, we have found three constructs of special relevance in addressing their mental health concerns: acculturation, ethnic/racial identity development, and gender-role socialization. More broadly defined, these constructs are directly applicable to psychotherapy with any ethnic minority individual, although they do not constitute an exclusive list nor are they always the most relevant in individual cases. The constructs are presented here as useful tools for determining what themes in the client's life might be appropriate to address and for regulating the types of interventions that might prove most effective. A clinician with a good basic understanding of cross-cultural listening and helping skills (e.g., Sue & Sue, 1990) can use these three constructs to refine treatment planning further for ethnic minorities in general and Chicanos in particular.

Acculturation

As the literature on cross-cultural psychotherapy has grown, so too has the importance of acculturation as an explanatory variable (Bernal & Knight, 1993; Bernal, Saenz, & Knight, 1991; Birman, 1994). Rogler, Malgady, and Rodríguez (1989) define acculturation as a complex process whereby the attitudes, values, beliefs, customs, and behaviors of a minority group change toward those of the majority group through continuing exposure to the dominant culture. This process is complex because it can be bidirectional (Casas & Vásquez, 1989). That is to say, it can be reversed; and the rate of acculturation can be halted, slowed down, or accelerated depending on a variety of factors.

Perhaps the model that best captures the complexity of acculturation outcomes and processes is that of Mendoza and Martínez (1981). Their model attempts to show changes that may occur across the primary modalities of cognitions (e.g., thoughts, beliefs), affect (e.g., emotional reactions), and behavior (e.g., customs, habits). They describe four core acculturation processes:

1. *Cultural resistance*, whereby there may be active and/or passive resistance to incorporating dominant cultural patterns (i.e., lack of acculturation in one or more modalities)
2. *Cultural shift*, which is the substitution of one set of patterns for those of the dominant culture (i.e., replacing new cognitions, affects, and/or behaviors while extinguishing the prior ones)
3. *Cultural incorporation*, which is the adaptation of patterns representative of both one's own culture and the dominant culture (i.e., retaining both cultures at once)
4. *Cultural transmutation*, the alteration of certain elements from both cultures to create a third, unique, hybrid pattern (e.g., religious practices that fuse Christian and indigenous spiritual practices)

Acculturation is a critical variable in issues related to psychotherapy, such as client dropout rates (Miranda, Andujo, Caballero, Guerrero, & Ramos, 1976), content and extent of self-disclosure (Castro, 1977), willingness to seek professional help (Ruíz, Casas, & Padilla, 1977), overall success of therapy (Miranda & Castro, 1977), preferences for an ethnically similar therapist (Sánchez & Atkinson, 1983), and likelihood of seeking particular mental health services (Atkinson, Casas, & Abreu, 1992; López, López, & Fong, 1991; Ponce & Atkinson, 1989).

Acculturation has been researched using mainly paper-and-pencil instruments. Among the more notable measures are the Measure of Acculturation for Chicano Adolescents (Olmedo, Martínez, & Martínez, 1978), the Bilingualism/Multiculturalism Experience Inventory (Ramírez, 1991), the Acculturation Rating Scale for Mexican Americans (Cuellar, Harris, & Jasso, 1980), the Behavioral Acculturation Scale (Szapocznik, Scoppeta, & Tillman, 1979), and the African American Acculturation Scale (Landrine & Klonoff, 1994, 1995).

These instruments can be useful in clinical practice, and any one of them can fit well within a screening battery. Such measures are designed to assess degree of acculturation, typically along a dimension ranging from traditional/unacculturated to balanced/bicultural to acculturated/assimilated. Research has shown that unacculturated individuals, for example, will often prefer ethnically similar therapists; bicultural individuals may not have a strong preference; and acculturated individuals tend to favor therapists of the dominant culture (Atkinson, Casas, & Abreu, 1992; Ponce & Atkinson, 1989). Such preferences are further influenced by a client's ethnic/racial identity development, a discussion of which follows.

Acculturation status, then, has its most profound implications in the area of client expectations regarding such aspects as background of the therapist, length of treatment, and acceptability of certain interventions. The assessment of acculturation is best used to make decisions about assigning a client to a psychotherapist and setting appropriate treatment goals and interventions. For example, research has found that less acculturated individuals expect very few sessions of therapy (fewer than three), provided by a directive, active therapist, to produce clear, concrete outcomes. A more acculturated individual may be more likely to expect and appreciate longer term treatment by a less directive therapist, with goals focused on broad personal developmental criteria (Atkinson et al., 1992; Ponce & Atkinson, 1989).

Ethnic/racial identity development. Along with acculturation, there has been a significant increase in the number of theoretical models that attempt to conceptualize developmental processes related to ethnic/racial identity. Cross-cultural researchers recognize that ethnic minorities have their ethnicity/race and minority status underscored in many overt and covert ways by the dominant society. How each ethnic minority individual internalizes the identity components of ethnicity/race and sense of difference (i.e., minority status) has been found to have psychological importance. Such identity development status plays a role in successful client–therapist matching (Parham & Helms, 1981; Helms & Carter, 1991), degree of self-regard, self-esteem, and self-actualization (Parham & Helms, 1985a, 1985b), and degree of felt anxiety (Parham & Helms, 1985b).

Whereas acculturation is broadly concerned with the degree to which dominant cultural norms are accepted, rejected, and/or transformed by ethnic minorities, ethnic/racial identity development usually refers to one's attitudes, beliefs, and feelings about one's own group vis-à-vis the dominant culture (Keefe & Padilla, 1987; Phinney, 1990). It is a barometer of how ethnic minority individuals perceive their group relative to that of the prevailing culture. Increasingly researchers have begun to note that acculturation and ethnic identity development are distinct, though related, processes. Keefe and Padilla (1987) have discussed a model that describes cultural orientation among Mexican Americans in terms of two distinct yet related domains: cultural awareness (largely synonymous with level of acculturation) and ethnic loyalty (corresponding to the concept of ethnic identity). Their research on Chicanos of varying generational levels indicates that these two constructs are independent. Recently, Arbona, Flores, and Novy (1995) presented data on a survey of Mexican-American college students, using Keefe and Padilla's (1987) model and instruments, which further support the notion of acculturation status and ethnic identity development as independent factors.

Many models of ethnic/racial identity development have emerged from work conducted mostly with African Americans (e.g., Cross, 1971, 1991; Helms, 1985, 1990, 1994; Thomas, 1971), and applied in a generic manner to other ethnic/racial groups (Atkinson, Morten, & Sue, 1979; Christensen, 1986). Table 7.1 summarizes several of these models.

The commonalities across most of the models include hypothesized stages or phases that minorities can experience as they confront issues of diversity. Usually this entails a shedding of negative stereotypes about one's own group in order to arrive at a healthy state of self-esteem and pride. Along the way, the person may move from a state of being unaware of differences toward a stage of total exclusion (typically hostile) of others. The ideal outcome is to develop an appreciation of diversity as manifest by all people, not just one's own group.

Although the stage or phase nature of the models has been criticized as restrictive and not always valid, certain components are worth noting for clinical practice. College is a time when many students question and revise some long-held beliefs and attitudes. It is a time of experimentation and encounters with differences, particularly on large campuses. In our practice, we often note a shifting in attitudes as a Chicano student studies the history of his or her group for the first time in an in-depth manner. Becoming angry over the injustices that are discovered through such study propels the student through some of the phases that the identity development models are intended to capture. One of the changes may be in the ethnic labels a student uses. Terms such as *Hispanic* or *Mexican American* often indicate a beginning stage of awareness. As the student progresses, he or she may take on labels that have an ideological valence such as *Chicano(a)*, *Latino(a)*, or *Hispano(a)* as a way of asserting a new awareness of group identity (Barón, 1991).

Using the Atkinson et al. model (1979) as an example, a student who has moved from a conforming stage into dissonance, resistance, and immersion is

TABLE 7.1   Examples of Status and Phases from Key Ethnic/Racial Identity Development Models

Thomas (1971)	Cross (1971, 1991); Helms (1985, 1990, 1994)	Atkinson, Morton, & Sue (1979)	Christensen (1986)
Withdrawal	Preencounter	Conformity	Unawareness
Testify	Encounter	Dissonance	Beginning awareness
Processing of information	Immersion/Emersion	Resistance and Immersion	Conscious awareness
Actively work through	Internalization	Introspection	Consolidated awareness
Transcendental	Internalization/ Commitment (Cross) or integrative awareness (Helms) Introspection	Synergetic articulation and awareness	Transcendental awareness

likely to search out an ethnically similar therapist in the belief that only he or she can fully understand the experiences of Chicanos. This also may be a statement of exclusivity, where the student wishes to immerse himself or herself into *all things Chicano*. From a developmental perspective, such behavior becomes understandable and workable within a therapy context (Atkinson et al., 1992; Ponce & Atkinson, 1989).

The identity development models have given therapists useful "road maps" for understanding where an ethnic minority group member may be "coming from" and where he or she may be headed. The models provide ways of interpreting thoughts, feelings, and actions that lead toward empowering individuals rather than relying only on pathological perspectives. In highlighting the broader social context in which ethnic/racial minorities exist, a fuller appreciation of the interplay between internal and external forces can be gained.

Gender-role socialization.   Much has been made of Latino culture's overemphasis on the status of men and the resulting double standard. From the Spanish language comes the word that we now use almost universally to capture a kind of hypermasculinity: *machismo*. The term is often used synonymously with male chauvinism. In Latino culture, however, *machismo* has several positive connotations that have been lost in the translation. As one Mexican-American psychologist (Ruíz, 1981, pp. 191–192) states:

It [*machismo*] connotes physical strength, sexual attractiveness, virtue, and potency. In this sense, the label "macho" has many of the same connotations it has in English…. At a more subtle level of analysis, "real" masculinity among Latinos involves dignity in personal conduct, respect for others, love for the family, and affection for children. When applied by non-Latinos to Latino males, however, "macho" often is defined in terms of physical aggression, sexual promiscuity, dominance of women, and excessive use of alcohol. In reaction to this abuse, Latino women are assumed to be submissive, nurturant, and virtuous, thereby maintaining the unity of the Latino family despite all the disruption from their fathers, husbands, and sons.

Thus, what is lost in the translation are the elements of chivalry, gallantry, courtesy, and charity. Because of generational differences, many younger Mexican Americans do not know about these other aspects of the term. However, the confusion around the notion of *machismo* reflects a broader social process taking place concerning gender roles and socialization processes. To the extent that a Chicano student has grown up with conservative, traditional views of male–female relationships, then these are likely to be tested in the crucible of academe—particularly if the social climate is significantly nontraditional.

A variety of therapy-related questions arise in the arena of gender-role socialization. What does it mean to be a Chicano man or woman? And by whose cultural standards will this be judged? What aspirations, career and otherwise, are legitimate to have? Is it O.K. to date outside one's ethnic group? How will one deal with adverse consequences from peers? Can one be gay, lesbian, or bisexual and still be considered "manly" or "womanly"? How assertive can one be without violating one's cultural norms? Our Mexican-American clients grapple with these and many other questions. The struggle is twofold. First, clients must deal with the social discourse going on more broadly about male-female differences. Second, the debate is further complicated by culturally based beliefs about appropriate gender-role behavior. Because the college years are typically critical for exploring and establishing ongoing romantic relationships and career goals, we find that gender-role issues arise quite readily in our therapy work. Skill in addressing these thorny issues becomes crucial in the psychotherapeutic process. The use of gender-role measures such as the Bem Sex-Role Inventory (Bem, 1974) and the Personal Attributes Questionnaire (Spence, Helmreich, & Stapp, 1974) may provide useful data to ascertain inter- and intracultural conflicts about female/male attitudes and beliefs.

Interactive culture strain.   When individuals attempt integration, the existence of differences in the levels of awareness and development across all the dimensions of the three psychosocial/cultural constructs may result in emotional distress or conflict, which we have labeled interactive culture strain. We believe this definition captures the psychological/developmental demands faced by a Chicano college student or, indeed, by any minority student. At any given point in time, the acculturation processes of resistance, shift, transmutation, and incorporation (Mendoza & Martínez, 1981) can be occurring across cognitions, emotions, and behaviors associated with ethnic/racial identity development and gender-role socialization. There is an inherent interactive strain because development, or lack thereof, in any one dimension influences other areas. Thus, a student may often be juggling a variety of psychological changes, both conscious and unconscious, across the core psychosocial/cultural domains. These changes produce a concomitant stress. Much of our therapy work focuses on the management of this resulting interactive culture strain.

Assessing the Core Psychosocial/Cultural Constructs through the Clinical Interview

For mental health professionals to become competent and successful within the context of their therapy work, it is important to develop culturally appropriate clinical assessment and intervention procedures (American Psychological Association, 1993). This is especially relevant when dealing with the core constructs of acculturation, ethnic/racial identity development, and gender-role socialization. Although there are many ways to assess these core constructs (e.g., through the use of acculturation scales, ethnic/racial identity development scales, and sex-role inventories), many counseling center therapists may not have such measures at their immediate disposal. An added dilemma may lie in attempting to administer and score paper-and-pencil instruments to Chicano clients early in the psychotherapy relationship, particularly before an adequate level of rapport is established. This is why psychotherapists have to rely for the most part on the clinical interview to assess these variables.

A standard clinical interview often will be the one vital assessment mechanism through which therapists may obtain information about the core constructs, in addition to gleaning information about other critical information in the lives of their Chicano clients. Most clinical or diagnostic interviews consist of several basic elements, which may include, but are not limited to, a history and assessment of the presenting problem(s); family, social, and occupational/academic histories; information about previous ways that clients may have coped (successfully and unsuccessfully) in attempting to address the presenting concern(s); clients' resources for addressing presenting issues (e.g., personal characteristics, familial and peer relationships, social functioning, economic standing); and goals for treatment. The authors have developed a conceptual framework to assess the core cultural concepts of acculturation, ethnic/racial identity, and gender-role socialization for Chicano college students in the context of this type of interview.

This framework lists the three core psychosocial/cultural concepts, along with inquiry dimensions that may give clinicians access to the assessment of cognitions, emotions, and behaviors associated with each cultural construct. This framework has not been empirically validated. On the basis of our collective clinical experiences with Chicano college students (and other minorities), we have extracted these three key constructs because they appear to arise consistently across a variety of students. Each of these constructs has been discussed extensively in the literature and has received varying degrees of empirical validation. We have coalesced the three into an inclusive concept labeled *interactive culture strain*. Our contribution, then, is an attempt to join together the three constructs under this concept to assist in conceptualizing the mental health needs of Chicano college students and other similar minorities.

Many of these dimensions can be integrated into a standard clinical interview and may be assessed in any order deemed appropriate by the clinician. The purpose of this type of assessment is to determine whether clients may be experiencing difficulties related to the constructs presented earlier, and to ascertain their effect on clients' presenting problems. The incorporation of this type of framework within a clinical interview may also lead to a more open dialogue between therapists and their clients about cultural differences (e.g., race/ethnicity, gender), and the potential impact of these on the psychotherapy relationship. Table 7.2 illustrates this assessment framework.

In addition to having significant utility as a clinical assessment tool, this framework has important implications for treatment planning and intervention. By fully evaluating and understanding the psychological impact of each of the core psychosocial/cultural constructs, mental health professionals treating Chicano students

TABLE 7.2   Examples of Assessment Dimensions Across the Three Psychosocial/Cultural Constructs

Core Cultural Constructs	Examples of Assessment Dimensions
Acculturation (e.g., first or second generation)	1. Generational status in the United States 2. Primary language spoken to communicate with others 3. Degree of affiliation with majority culture (e.g., composition of peer network, Anglicization of name) 4. Role conflicts with regard to familial expectations 5. Value systems, customs, and orientations (particularly with regard to religion, political affiliation, etc.) 6. Level of involvement in cultural traditions or activities
Ethnic/racial identity	1. Ethnic group label used when asked about own ethnicity 2. Ways ethnicity has affected life 3. Ethnicities or races of members of peer support system 4. Affiliations with clubs or organizations that reflect own ethnic group representation and/or ideology 5. Awareness of Chicano(a) history and heritage 6. Ability to recognize and confront racial or ethnic oppression 7. Other internalized issues of oppression or racism related to ethnic identity (e.g., feeling shame about having an accent, being "too dark-skinned")
Gender-role socialization	1. Gender-role definitions within family of origin 2. Gender-role expectations within family of origin 3. Socialization with regard to gender-role affiliation (i.e., androgyny vs. specific sex role) 4. View of male–female relationships (e.g., romantic, work, social, etc.) 5. Awareness of gender-based differences in relationships (e.g., communication styles) 6. Impact of gender-role socialization on choice of academic major or career

will have vital information that may significantly increase the likelihood of achieving successful therapy outcomes. The framework is also intended to assess the various areas of interactive culture strain that may be operative in a client's life. The case study described next illustrates the use of this framework with a Chicana college student during an initial clinical interview and over the course of a psychotherapy relationship.

The Constructs in Practice: A Case Study

Bonita (a pseudonym) was a 22-year-old Mexican-American college senior majoring in elementary education at a large southwestern university. She lived in one of the campus residence halls with an Anglo female roommate. Bonita came to the university counseling center for an intake appointment to address feelings of anxiety and depression related to her upcoming graduation in four months and her chronic interpersonal difficulties, which spanned the course of her college career. On the intake form, Bonita listed her ethnic/racial affiliation as Chicana. Her family had lived in Mexico until they immigrated to Laredo, Texas, when Bonita and her two younger male siblings were in high school (about eight years previously). Bonita's family lived about four hours away from the university by car. She was the first member of her immediate family to attend college.

During the intake session, Bonita expressed a great deal of ambivalence about having come to the counseling center because she was not sure the therapist would really understand her. Initially she appeared uncomfortable during the session; she fidgeted in her seat and smiled nervously, but as the session progressed she seemed to relax. She stated that she had "never done anything like this before," and claimed that her "traditional" parents did not believe in going to mental health counselors for help with "private problems." Bonita also stated that she was unsure why she was feeling anxious and depressed, particularly since she felt as though she would soon have "everything I could ever want in life—a college degree and a husband." She claimed that her fiancé, whom she identified as "a Mexican guy who never went to college," still lived in Laredo and was planning to marry her within a year of her graduation from college.

Assessing the Core Psychosocial/Cultural Constructs During the Intake Session

In addition to sharing specific information about her anxiety and depression related to her upcoming graduation and her interpersonal difficulties with college peers through a semi-structured clinical interview, Bonita was also queried about her level of acculturation, her primary ethnic identity, and her family-of-origin socialization with regard to gender-role issues. In responding to such questions, she discussed some initial and ongoing adjustment difficulties she had experienced at the university related to feeling like an outsider. More specifically, Bonita believed that many of her difficulties in this arena were related to discriminatory and racist attitudes of some students on campus because she was a "dark-skinned" Chicana with a "heavy accent," descriptions of herself about which she seemed very proud. Bonita stated that her ethnic group affiliation had always served as a source of pride for her, and she shared her frustration that for this reason she was not accepted or affirmed by many other students on campus. Bonita also claimed that she and her Chicano friends frequently spoke Spanish when conversing with one another and that, on several occasions, some students who overhead them had yelled, "You're in the United States. Speak English!" In addition, she asserted that many of the students, including her roommate, referred to her as "Bonnie" at times, although she did not feel comfortable being called by that name. Bonita claimed she felt emotionally supported by her parents regarding some of her difficulties related to these issues, but also believed her parents did not fully understand her experience of going to college in a predominantly Anglo environment. She stated that their support consisted primarily of encouraging her to "hurry up and graduate so that you can come back home and get married."

Bonita also shared her feelings of ambivalence and anger related to her "love–hate relationship with this racist university." She also claimed that while she was pleased to be receiving a college degree soon, she was not excited about the prospect of teaching elementary-aged schoolchildren. She stated that her strongest interest was in medicine. In particular, Bonita discussed her desire to become a physician, but said that she felt her parents would not support her in this goal because they feared she would not be able to marry anyone because she would be "much more educated than her potential husband." Bonita claimed her parents also believed that "no man would want to marry a woman who made more money than himself." She asserted that the primary reason she chose to major in elementary education was because of her parents' advice and influence concerning this decision. Near the end of the intake session, Bonita and her therapist agreed to spend time during her psychotherapy sessions dealing with concerns related to her presenting problems, and with issues related to the core cultural constructs which, in many ways, were closely tied to her presenting concerns.

Impact of the Assessment on Subsequent Sessions

Over the next several therapy sessions, Bonita explored how her level of acculturation, ethnic/racial identity development, and gender-role socialization played critical roles in her presenting problems, including her choice of an academic major and her interpersonal interactions. She processed with her therapist the familial and peer conflicts she experienced with regard to her acculturation level. She often spoke of feeling torn between "keeping the values and beliefs of my family and culture alive and well" and changing her beliefs about some of her more traditional Chicano values because "I think about some of those things a lot differently now than I did a few years ago." Bonita expressed some difficulties she encountered in balancing the values, norms, and expectations of both the Anglo and Chicano cultures, but stated that by exploring these struggles during her therapy sessions, she began to see herself as a "bilingual, bicultural" individual who could successfully navigate between "both Anglo and Mexican cultures."

In terms of her ethnic/racial identity development, Bonita claimed she felt very comfortable with her ethnic identification. She stated that her peer support network consisted primarily of Chicano, African-American, and some Anglo college students. Bonita was an active member of several campus Chicano organizations, and she asserted that she felt supported to a large degree by her fellow Chicano and African-American peers as they, too, struggled with acculturation and ethnic/racial identity issues. Through therapy, she was able to express anger about the ways she had been treated by several Anglo students on the campus; and she explored how she might potentially confront and challenge some of their racist and stereotypical remarks in ways that felt comfortable to her. Bonita discussed one confrontation she had experienced with the roommate who called her "Bonnie." She shared with her roommate her feelings about being referred to by this "nickname," and her roommate "really understood my point and agreed never to call me by that name again."

As therapy progressed, Bonita also began to experience a greater awareness of her feelings of sadness and frustration around the gender-related messages she received from her parents to be a "more traditional" Chicana, particularly with regard to her career choice. That is, on the basis of the ways her parents viewed and defined gender roles and expectations within the context of her family of origin and culture, Bonita had consciously limited her potential career options by choosing only careers that would decrease the likelihood of "earning more money than my future husband and would not serve as a threat to him." She explored her feelings about this insight, brainstormed a list of alternatives to her current academic major, and, toward the end of therapy, decided to remain as an undergraduate for an additional two years to pursue a degree in premedicine. After role playing with her therapist some hypothetical conversations she might have with her parents and her fiancé to discuss her decision with them, Bonita was able to inform them of her plans to pursue a medical degree. In general, they agreed to support her decision. Bonita stated that although her fiancé was not "completely happy" with her decision to remain in school and thus delay their marriage, he was supportive of her goal of becoming a physician.

Summary of the Case

Bonita's case is an example of a Chicana college student who presented with different levels of awareness and development in terms of the core psychosocial/cultural constructs of acculturation, ethnic/racial identity, and gender-role socialization. As noted earlier, when an individual attempts integration, the existence of differences in the levels of awareness and development across the three psychosocial/cultural constructs may result in interactive culture strain. This phenomenon appears to be particularly salient in this case. Although it is not uncommon for Chicano college students who seek psychotherapy to present with varying levels of awareness and development with regard to each of these constructs, mental health professionals may, at times, make significant errors or may experience confusion if they attempt to generalize their assessment of one of these constructs to one or both of the others.

In terms of the construct of acculturation, Bonita's level was labeled by her therapist as moderate (as opposed to either low or high), as evidenced by a combination of several acculturation dimensions. First, Bonita's family had moved to the United States less than a decade ago, making Bonita a first-generation U.S. college student. Bonita claimed she communicated fairly regularly in both Spanish and English. Although Bonita did experience some role and value conflicts with regard to familial and cultural expectations, she was also quite involved with Chicano student organizations on her campus. She seemed somewhat affiliated with the Anglo culture in terms of her friendships with Anglo peers and some of her changing values and beliefs, but not to a degree that contributed to significant interactive culture strain. She also seemed willing, by the end of therapy, to take steps toward behaving more assertively with regard to cultural and ethnic issues, for example by confronting her roommate about her name.

Bonita appeared to have been at an advanced stage of awareness of her ethnic identity. She proudly acknowledged her Mexican-American heritage and demonstrated an awareness of the ways in which her ethnicity had affected her life. Bonita's peer network consisted of an ethnically and racially diverse group of individuals, and she seemed to take pride in this fact. She showed little or no evidence of internalized issues of oppression, as she took pride in being a "dark-skinned" Chicana with a heavy accent and in having a strong Chicana identity. In addition, she was eventually able to acknowledge the importance of being flexible in interacting with both the Anglo and Chicano(a) cultures so as to ensure her personal and professional success. At the beginning of therapy, Bonita's gender-role identity matched that of a more traditional feminine role orientation. The result of this level of identification was that her gender-role identity seemed somewhat constrictive and limiting to her as opposed to being more open and androgynous. Her gender-role socialization in her family of origin clearly reflected the idea that there were stereotypical roles for both men and women with regard to career, marriage, and financial issues.

With the help of psychotherapy, Bonita was able to identify the impact of her parents' gender-role expectations and her gender-role socialization on her choice of an academic major and her subsequent career aspirations. Through the exploration of some of these issues, she was eventually able to pinpoint more congruent career and personal options for herself, and she emerged with a greater sense of her beliefs and values regarding her gender role identity. Table 7.3 presents a profile of Bonita's interactive culture strain by providing examples of clinical interview data across cognitive, affective, and behavioral domains and referenced against the three psychosocial/cultural constructs.

TABLE 7.3   Bonita's Interactive Culture Strain Profile: Examples from Clinical Interview Data

Domain/ Construct	Cognitive	Affective	Behavioral
Acculturation Level Moving from more monocultural to more bicultural as a function of her college experiences	Cultural values and beliefs are important to her (e.g., keeping close family ties).	She feels conflicted about changing some "traditional" beliefs.	She moved away from home to attend college.
Ethnic Identity Development Immersion evolving to Internalization	She has a positive attitude about her Mexican heritage.	She feels proud to be Mexican.	She asserts the Spanish form of her name rather than use an Anglicized nickname (i.e., "Bonita" vs. "Bonnie").
Gender Role Socialization Traditional female developing into androgynous orientation	Her belief, instilled by parents, is that Latinas should pursue more traditional female careers, but challenges this belief as therapy progresses.	She expresses sadness and frustration over her parents' beliefs about women's career options.	Historically, she limited her career options to conform to traditional male/ female roles but considers being a physician as she challenges her parents' beliefs about careers for women.

Summary

This chapter has attempted to illustrate the importance of acculturation, ethnic/ racial identity development, and gender-role socialization in the developmental challenges faced by Chicano(a) college students. The existence of differences in the levels of awareness and development across all the facets of these three psychosocial/cultural constructs may result in emotional distress or conflict when integration is attempted by an individual. This distress is what we have labeled interactive culture strain, a unifying concept that is intended to capture the dynamic interplay of the three psychosocial/cultural constructs. Acculturation processes can be occurring simultaneously across cognitions, emotions, and behaviors associated with ethnic/racial identity development and gender-role socialization. There is an inherent interactive strain because development, or lack thereof, in any one dimension influences development in the other dimensions. Thus, a student often may be juggling a variety of psychological changes, both conscious and unconscious, across the core psychosocial/cultural constructs. This variety of changes produces stress and confusion, which may motivate a student to seek counseling. Much of our therapy work focuses on the management of this resulting strain. In working with Chicano(a) college students, it is important that clinicians assess the impact of acculturation level, ethnic/racial identity development, and gender-role socialization issues on the presenting concerns. Such assessment may be an important process in the development of treatment plans, including the focus of therapeutic interventions, and the type and intensity of services required. Suggestions for conducting efficient assessment of these phenomena through the clinical interview were also discussed.

References

Aguirre, A., Jr., & Martínez, R. (1993). *Chicanos in higher education: Issues and dilemmas for the 21st century.* ASHE-ERIC Higher Education Report No. 3. Washington, DC: The George Washington University, School of Education and Human Development.

Almanac issue. (1994). *Chronicle of Higher Education, 41.*

American Psychological Association. (1993). Guidelines for providers of psychological services to ethnic, linguistic, and culturally diverse populations. *American Psychologist, 48,* 45–48.

Arbona, C., Flores, C. L., & Novy, D. M. (1995). Cultural awareness and ethnic loyalty: Dimensions of cultural variability among Mexican American college students. *Journal of Counseling and Development, 73,* 610–614.

Arbona, C., & Novy, D. (1990). Noncognitive dimensions as predictors of college success among Black, Mexican American, and White students. *Journal of College Student Development, 31,* 415–422.

Astin, A. W. (1982). *Minorities in higher education.* San Francisco: Jossey-Bass.

Atkinson, D. R., Casas, J. M., & Abreu, J. (1992). Mexican American acculturation, counselor ethnicity and cultural sensitivity, and perceived counselor competence. *Journal of Counseling Psychology, 39,* 515–520.

Atkinson, D. R., Morten, G., & Sue, D. W. (1979). *Counseling American minorities: A cross-cultural perspective.* Dubuque, IA: W. C. Brown.

Barón, A., Jr. (1991). Counseling Chicano college students. In C. C. Lee & B. L. Richardson (Eds.), *Multicultural issues in counseling: New approaches to diversity* (pp. 171–184). Alexandria, VA: American Association for Counseling and Development.

Bem, S. L. (1974). The measurement of psychological androgyny. *Journal of Consulting and Clinical Psychology, 42,* 155–162.

Bernal, M. E., & Knight, G. P. (Eds.). (1993). *Ethnic identity: Formation and transmission among Hispanics and other minorities.* Albany: State University of New York Press.

Bernal, M. E., Saenz, D. S., & Knight, G. P. (1991). Ethnic identity and adaptation of Mexican American youth in school settings. *Hispanic Journal of Behavioral Sciences, 13,* 135–154.

Birman, D. (1994). Acculturation and human diversity in a multicultural society. In E. J. Trickett, R. Watts, & D. Birman (Eds.), *Human diversity: Perspectives on people in context* (pp. 261–284). San Francisco: Jossey-Bass.

Casas, J. M., & Vasquez, M. J. T. (1989). Counseling the Hispanic client: A theoretical and applied perspective. In P. Pedersen, J. G. Draguns, W. J. Lonner, & J. E. Trimble (Eds.), *Counseling across cultures* (3rd ed.), (pp. 153–175). Honolulu: University of Hawaii Press.

Castro, F. G. (1977). *Level of acculturation and related considerations in psychotherapy with Spanish speaking/surnamed clients* (Occasional Paper No. 3). Spanish Speaking Mental Health Research Center, University of California, Los Angeles.

Christensen, C. (1986). *Cultural boundaries.* Toronto: University of Toronto Press.

Cortese, A. (1992). Academic achievement in Mexican Americans: Sociolegal and cultural factors. *Latino Studies Journal, 3,* 31–47.

Cross, W. E. (1971). The Negro-to-Black conversion experience: Toward a psychology of Black liberation. *Black World, 20,* 13–27.

Cross, W. E. (1991). *Shades of Black.* Philadelphia: Temple University Press.

Cuellar, I., Harris, L. C., & Jasso, R. (1980). An acculturation rating scale for Mexican-American normal and clinical populations. *Hispanic Journal of Behavioral Sciences, 2,* 199–217.

Durán, R. (1983). *Hispanics' education and background.* New York: College Entrance Examination Board.

Fiske, E. (1988). The undergraduate Hispanic experience: A case of juggling two cultures. *Change, 20,* 29–33.

Gandara, P. (1982). Passing through the eye of the needle: High-achieving Chicanas. *Hispanic Journal of Behavioral Sciences, 4,* 167–180.

Griffith, J., Frase, M., & Ralph, J. (1989). American education: The challenge of change. *Population Bulletin, 44*(4).

Helms, J. E. (1985). Toward a theoretical explanation of the effects of race on counseling: A Black and White model. *The Counseling Psychologist, 12,* 153–165.

Helms, J. E. (1990). *Black and White racial identity: Theory, research, and practice.* New York: Greenwood Press.

Helms, J. E. (1994). Racial identity and career assessment. *Journal of Career Assessment, 2,* 199–209.

Helms, J. E., & Carter, R. T. (1991). Relationships of White and Black racial identity attitudes and demographic similarity to counselor preferences. *Journal of Counseling Psychology, 38,* 446–457.

Humphreys, L. (1988). Trends in levels of academic achievement of Blacks and other minorities. *Intelligence, 12,* 231–260.

Keefe, S. E., & Padilla, A. M. (1987). *Chicano ethnicity.* Albuquerque: University of New Mexico Press.

Landrine, H., & Klonoff, E. A. (1994). The African American Acculturation Scale: Development, reliability, and validity. *Journal of Black Psychology, 20,* 104–127.

Landrine, H., & Klonoff, E. A. (1995). The African American Acculturation Scale II: Cross-validation and short form. *Journal of Black Psychology, 21,* 124–152.

López, S. R., López, A. A., & Fong, K. T. (1991). Mexican Americans' initial preferences for counselors: The role of ethnic factors. *Journal of Counseling Psychology, 38,* 487–496.

Lunneborg, C., & Lunneborg, P. (1986). Beyond prediction: The challenge of minority achievement in higher education. *Journal of Multicultural Counseling and Development, 14,* 77–84.

Madrid, A. (1988). Missing people and others. *Change, 20,* 55–59.

Mendoza, R. H., & Martínez, J. L. (1981). The measurement of acculturation. In A. Barón, Jr. (Ed.), *Explorations in Chicano psychology.* New York: Praeger.

Miranda, M. R., Andujo, E., Caballero, I. L., Guerrero, C., & Ramos, R. A. (1976). Mexican American dropouts in psychotherapy as related to level of acculturation. In M. R. Miranda (Ed.), *Psychotherapy with the Spanish-speaking: Issues in research and service delivery.* Spanish Speaking Mental Health Research Center, University of California, Los Angeles.

Miranda, M. R., & Castro F. G. (1977). Culture distance and success in psychotherapy with Spanish-speaking clients. In J. L. Martínez (Ed.), *Chicano psychology* (pp. 249–262). New York: Academic Press.

National Council of La Raza. (1990). *Hispanic education: A statistical portrait 1990.* Washington, DC: Author.

Olmedo, E. L., Martínez, J. L., & Martínez, S. R. (1978). Measure of acculturation for Chicano adolescents. *Psychological Reports, 42,* 159–170.

Parham, T. A., & Helms, J. E. (1981). The influence of Black students' racial attitudes on preferences for counselor's race. *Journal of Counseling Psychology, 28,* 250–257.

Parham, T. A., & Helms, J. E. (1985a). Attitudes of racial identity and self-esteem of black students: An exploratory investigation. *Journal of College Student Personnel, 26,* 143–147.

Parham, T. A., & Helms, J. E. (1985b). Relation of racial identity attitudes to self-actualization and affective states of black students. *Journal of Counseling Psychology, 32,* 431–440.

Pennock-Roman, M. (1988). *The status of research on the Scholastic Aptitude Test (SAT) and Hispanic students in postsecondary education.* Princeton, NJ: Educational Testing Service.

Phinney, J. S. (1990). Ethnic identity in adolescents and adults: A review of research. *Psychological Bulletin, 3,* 499–514.

Ponce, F. Q., & Atkinson, D. R. (1989). Mexican American acculturation, counselor ethnicity, counseling style, and perceived counselor credibility. *Journal of Counseling Psychology, 36,* 203–208.

Ramírez, M. (1991). *Psychology of the Americas: Multicultural perspectives in personality and mental health.* New York: Pergamon Press.

Rogler, L. H., Malgady, R. G., & Rodríguez, O. (1989). *Hispanics and mental health: A framework for research.* Malabar, FL: Krieger.

Ruíz, R. A. (1981). Cultural and historical perspective in counseling Hispanics. In D. W. Sue (Ed.), *Counseling the culturally different: Theory and practice* (pp. 186–214). New York: Wiley.

Ruíz, R. A., Casas, J. M., & Padilla, A. M. (1977). *Culturally relevant behavioristic counseling.* Spanish Speaking Mental Health Research Center, University of California, Los Angeles.

Sánchez, A. R., & Atkinson, D. R. (1983). Mexican-American cultural commitment preference for counselor ethnicity, and willingness to use counseling. *Journal of Counseling Psychology, 30,* 215–220.

Sedlacek, W. E. (1987). Black students on white campuses: Twenty years of research. *Journal of College Student Personnel, 28,* 484–495.

Sedlacek, W. E., & Brooks, G. C., Jr. (1976). *Racism in American education: A model for change.* Chicago: Nelson-Hall.

Spence, J. T., Helmreich, R. L., & Stapp, J. (1974). The Personal Attributes Questionnaire: A measure of sex-role stereotypes and masculinity–femininity. *JSAS Catalogue of Selected Documents in Psychology, 4,* 127.

Sue, D. W., & Sue, D. (1990). *Counseling the culturally different: Theory and practice.* New York: Wiley.

Szapocznik, J., Scopetta, M. A., & Tillman, W. (1979). What changes, what stays the same and what affects acculturative change? In J. Szapocznik & M. C. Herrera (Eds.), *Cuban Americans: Acculturation, adjustment and the family.* Washington, DC: COSSMHO.

Thomas, C. W. (1971). *Boys no more.* Beverly Hills, CA: Glencoe Press.

Tracey, T. J., & Sedlacek, W. E. (1984). Noncognitive variables in predicting academic success by race. *Measurement and Evaluation in Guidance, 16,* 172–178.

Tracey, T. J., & Sedlacek, W. E. (1985). The relationship of noncognitive variables to academic success: A longitudinal comparison by race. *Journal of College Student Personnel, 26,* 405–410.

Tracey, T. J., & Sedlacek. W. E. (1987). Prediction of college graduation using noncognitive variables by race. *Measurement and Evaluation in Counseling and Development, 19,* 177–184.

U.S. Bureau of the Census. (1991). *The Hispanic population in the United States, March, 1990.* Washington, DC: U.S. Government Printing Office.

Willie, C. (1987). On excellence and equity in higher education. *Journal of Negro Education, 56,* 485–492.

Young, G. (1992). Chicana college students on the Texas–Mexico border: Transition and transformation. *Hispanic Journal of Behavioral Sciences, 14,* 341–352.

Anger, Ataques de Nervios, *and* la Mujer Puertorriqueña: *Sociocultural Considerations and Treatment Implications*

MIGDALIA RIVERA-ARZOLA
Saint Joseph College

JULIA RAMOS-GRENIER
Grenier Associates
Hartford, Connecticut

Anger as an emotion has been interpreted in the light of various theories, including the psychodynamic, the constructivist, and the feminist. Despite the vast array of literature on this topic, however, there has been no in-depth analysis of anger in relation to somatization, and particularly *ataques de nervios*,[1] among Puerto Rican women. This chapter offers an analysis, paying particular attention to the constructivist and feminist perspectives, and concludes with recommendations for clinical treatment from both intrapsychic and the psychosocial perspectives.

Women in Puerto Rican Culture

Like other Puerto Ricans and Spanish-speaking peoples in the United States, Puerto Rican women suffer stress due to emigration, acculturation, and the language barrier (Padilla & Ruíz, 1973). They grapple with prejudice, discrimination, rejection,

[1.] The words *ataque* and *nervios* mean *attack* and *nerves*, respectively. Many Puerto Ricans use the term *ataque* to refer to other ailments like *ataque del corazón* (heart attack) or *ataque epiléptico* (epileptic attack), but most frequent is *ataque de nervios*. The *ataque* is also known as *nervios, mal de pelea* (fighting sickness), the *Puerto Rican syndrome*, hyperkinetic seizure, and hysterical psychosis.

and alienation because they differ from mainstream Americans and, even more fundamentally, because of their gender, class, and color (Comas-Díaz, 1989, Miranda-King, 1974). Nevertheless, despite long-standing social, political, and economic oppression, many of these women play a central role in their family and community.

Macro-level forces have changed the roles and socioeconomic status of Puerto Rican women over time (Zavala-Martínez, 1988). The statistics are sobering. Women now head 44% of Puerto Rican households and live in grave social and economic distress (U.S. Census, 1988; Zavala-Martínez, 1988; González, Rodríguez-Fraticelli, Torres, Torres, & Vazquez, 1989).[2] These heads of household have a mean annual income of $11,327. Sixty-five percent live in poverty, a higher rate than for any other ethnic subgroup in America (Barreto, 1986; González et al., 1989), and 14.6% are unemployed, as compared with the U.S. average of 7.15% (Barreto, 1986). Only 44% of Puerto Rican women over the age of 25 have completed high school, compared with 70% of White women and 51% of Black women (National Congress for Puerto Rican Rights, 1989; Rodríguez, 1989).

The adversity with which Puerto Rican women routinely cope places them at greater risk for health and mental health problems than the general population. Although recent epidemiological studies conducted both on the island and on the mainland have found that most psychiatric disorders are no more prevalent among Puerto Ricans than among Euro-Americans, somatization appears to be an exception, particularly for women (Angel & Guarnaccia, 1989; Canino, Rubio-Stipec, Shrout, Bravo, Stolberg, & Bird, 1987). Many women communicate distress symbolically, through their bodies, rather than assertively (López-Garriga, 1980). These women exhibit depression (Canino et al., 1987; Comas-Díaz & Duncan, 1985); suicidal fits (Trautman, 1961; Zayas, 1989); and *ataques de nervios* (De La Cancela, Guarnaccia, & Carrillo, 1986; Guarnaccia, Rubio-Stipec, & Canino, 1989; Zavala-Martínez, 1981). As a possible cultural idiom, *ataques de nervios* are of particular interest. Should they be regarded as a purely pathological phenomenon or, rather, as a prevalent, culturally accepted distress signal?

Ataques de Nervios among Puerto Rican Women

The clinical entity labeled *ataques de nervios*, or *nervios*, has been defined as a physical manifestation of strong emotions that occurs under particularly stressful psychological and social conditions (De La Cancela et al., 1986; Guarnaccia, 1993). The physiological reactions associated with this entity were first observed clinically by psychiatrists attending Puerto Rican male military personnel in the 1950s (Fernández-Marina, 1961; Rothenberg, 1964; Rubio, Urdaneta, & Doyle, 1955). Symptoms

---

[2.] Puerto Ricans are the second largest Latina/Latino subgroup in this country and the second fastest growing (Rodríguez, 1989: Vásquez-Hernandez, 1991) and, like other ethnic groups in this country, suffer from poverty, high unemployment, low educational attainment, poor housing, and other social problems (Pérez & Martínez, 1993).

include trembling, heart palpitations, numbness, loss of consciousness, difficulty in breathing, and a transient hyperkinetic state. The entity's essential feature is the transient hyperkinetic state, which mirrors that seen in conditions such as schizophrenia, epilepsy, psychosis, and other behavioral and personality disorders. During an episode, an individual may shout, swear, cry, or strike out at others (see Appendix A).

Diagnostically speaking, the *ataque de nervios* is an anomaly. Davis and Guarnaccia (1989) argue that it cannot be assigned to any one DSM-III [DSM-IV] category because its symptoms span several and because prevailing diagnostic categories overlook its cultural construction and significance. According to Guarnaccia et al. (1989), the higher prevalence of somatization in Puerto Ricans, and especially in women, may reflect culture-specific ways of expressing psychosocial distress rather than a greater incidence of psychiatric disorders (Guarnaccia, Canino, Rubio-Stipec, & Bravo, 1993). Some writers maintain that Puerto Ricans both on the island and on the mainland perceive *ataques de nervios* as a "normal" reaction to a stressful situation (De La Cancela et al., 1986; Grace, 1959; Guarnaccia et al., 1989).

Although it cannot be said that *ataques de nervios* elicit social approbation, they are "expected from women when they do not get their own way [self-realization] or when they are faced with an act of aggression they cannot otherwise stop" (Harwood, 1981, p. 419). Thus, *ataques de nervios* are a "culturally recognized, acceptable cry to help or an admission of inability to cope, and family and friends are required by norms of good behavior to rally to the aid of the *ataque* victim [survivor] and relieve the intolerable stress [for women]" (Garrison, 1977, p. 389).

For Puerto Rican women, anger and stress seem to be related. According to various authors (Serra-Deliz, 1989; Soto & Shaver, 1982; Torres-Matrullo, 1976), women, both in Puerto Rico and on the mainland, routinely cope with high levels of stress associated with their inferior position in society. One consequence may well be the need to repress anger within the family and in the broader community. Comas-Díaz (1982) suggests that some Puerto Rican women have no option under certain circumstances but to release their bottled-up anger through *ataques de nervios*. That is, possibly because Puerto Rican women lack the cultural scripts that would foster widespread, direct expression of anger, their bodies often become the arenas in which external and internal conflicts of emotional pain and anger are played out.

Women who experience *ataques*, however, distinguish between anger and aggression and describe them as developing gradually. One subject reported: "Much of the time I do not have problems letting people know that something is bothering me [anger] but other times I get so outraged (*me dá un coraje tan grande*) that I think I am going to explode (*creo que voy a explotar*). My heart begins to pound as if it is going to jump out of my chest. I get so angry that I lose sight of everything." The same woman stated that her first *ataque de nervios* had been precipitated by the death of her son when she was 18 years old. Ever since, whenever she has been under a great deal of stress, has become enraged, or has experienced the loss of a loved one, she has responded with an *ataque de nervios*.

The psychiatric literature on *ataques de nervios* in the 1950s reflected mainly clinical observations of males, but more recent studies have reported on women (Harwood, 1981). During the 1970s, *ataques de nervios* were discussed in the literature as occurring only among women (Abad, Ramos, & Boyce, 1977; Garrison, 1977). In the clinical settings where men and women received treatment for the condition in the 1980s, the number of female patients seeking services was disproportionately large (Harwood, 1981; McCormick, 1986). Recent cross-cultural studies have also found that women are more susceptible than men (Davis, 1989; Dunk, 1989; Finerman, 1988; Nations, Camino, & Walker, 1988; Van Schaik, 1989). Although empirical data are lacking, several analyses, including one that was epidemiological (Guarnaccia et al., 1989), suggest that stressful socioeconomic conditions that have an impact particularly on women, both on the island and on the mainland, may account for the different experience of the sexes (Davison, Rivera, Singer, & Scanlon, 1989).

Cayleff (1988) suggests that *nervios* have historically been one response to gender ideologies that attempt to devalue and suppress women's power. If so, the meaning of *ataques* should be sought at least partly in their social and cultural context—a setting with power and patriarchy among its principal features. Conceivably, too, *ataques de nervios* may serve in some social situations as a vehicle to communicate deep pain, helplessness, powerlessness, or anger (Comas-Díaz, 1987; Zavala-Martínez, 1981).

When a Puerto Rican woman with a history of *ataques de nervios* confronts an insensitive, authoritarian gynecologist, for example, she may show her feelings and her sense of helplessness by having an *ataque*. *Ataques de nervios* may also occur at times of intense grief (such as funerals), when one has witnessed or learned of a shocking event involving a family member, or when one is experiencing diffuse anger or extreme frustration. The daily life of Puerto Rican women provides many occasions when a reaction to extreme stress would seem warranted.

Some studies indicate that sufferers of *ataques de nervios* are likely to be middle-aged women of low socioeconomic status. Such women are among the least acculturated in U.S. society (McCormick 1986; Rivera-Arzola, 1992). Women with *ataques de nervios* reportedly also have rural backgrounds and exhibit a high prevalence of somatization and psychological distress (Rivera-Arzola, 1992; Rothenberg, 1964; Rubio-Stipec, Shrout, Bird, Canino, & Bravo, 1989).

According to one study (Rivera-Arzola, 1992), women with a history of *ataques de nervios* report high rates of traumatic life events—incidents of physical and sexual abuse, the witnessing of violent death, abandonment by a parent, and near-death experiences as a child and as an adult. One out of four divorced Puerto Rican women reportedly suffers physical abuse and/or emotional abuse prior to getting divorced (Muñoz-Vásquez, 1980).[3] A review of the literature on emotions and anger as experienced by women affords a theoretical basis for assessing the significance of *ataques de nervios*.

Theoretical Views

The Constructivist View of Emotions

Early in the development of anthropology and psychology, emotions were rarely mentioned. Not until later did they emerge as a prominent area of concern in personality development research. The study of emotions initially found its niche within the framework of psychodynamic theory (Levine, 1973), which paid particular attention to potentially dangerous, unrestrained displays of anger and rage and to their displacement or softening through ritualized forms of expression (DeVos & Hippler, 1969). *Ataques de nervios* are arguably one such ritualized expression of anger.

Subsequent theories placed emotions in a sociocultural perspective (Lock, 1989; Strongman, 1987). Lock states, for instance, that the cultural construction of emotions "focus[es] on how the indigenous concepts of the person, selfhood, and associated symbolism work to create the manner in which people experience and understand themselves" (1989, p. 81). The detailed ethnographic analyses of Rosaldo indicate that both feelings and conceptions of the self relate to specific forms of social and political relationships and that cultural idioms "provide the images in terms of which our subjectives are formed" (1984, p. 510). According to Rosaldo, dualities such as thought/action, which are present in all cultures, derive from Western philosophy. Thought and affect constitute one such duality: "just as thought does not exist in isolation from affective life, so affect is culturally ordered and does not exist apart from thought" (Rosaldo, 1984, p. 137). If Rosaldo's statement is correct, *ataques de nervios* have a cultural component.

Averill defines emotions as "socially constituted syndromes (transitory social roles) which include an individual's appraisal of the situation, and which are interpreted as passions rather than action" (1982, p. 6). He suggests that psychologists should be examining social etiology and the current functions of emotions rather than their biological basis. According to Averill, anger is a conflictive emotion—a reaction with specific symbolic meanings that arises when society's demands encounter "incompatible biological or psychological impulses" (1982, p. 318). Averill's interpretation of anger parallels the Freudian theory of hysterical (conversion) reactions. As a conflictive emotion, anger is, "on the biological level, ... related to aggressive systems and, even more important, to the capacities for cooperative social living, symbolization, and reflective self-awareness; ... on the psychological level, [it] is aimed at the correction of some appraised wrong; and ..., on

---

[3.] High rates of violence have been documented in New York and other cities. In one study, conducted in Hartford, Connecticut, preliminary results of interviews with Puerto Rican women indicated a high frequency of abusive relationships and a history of abuse as young women (Flores, Davison, Rivera, Torres, & Castillo, 1989). The subjects reported low self-esteem, depression, feelings of isolation, anxiety, and *nervios.* Many, especially those who had been born or raised on the mainland, felt inept and incompetent, had weak social support networks, and were uncritical of the negative stereotypes they had been conditioned to accept. They seemed confused about their cultural identity and were almost totally uninformed, both regarding Puerto Rico's history and regarding their own personal and legal rights.

the sociocultural level, [it] functions to uphold accepted standards of conduct" (Averill, 1982, p. 317).

The constructivist view thus focuses on the psychological and sociocultural variables associated with anger and other emotions. From a constructivist perspective, Puerto Rican women may be said to experience and deal with their anger by registering it (at the psychological level) and responding with acceptable standards of conduct (at the sociocultural level). If so, *ataques de nervios* may well constitute a response to conflicting emotional or emotional and social demands.

The Feminist View of Anger

Feminist scholars assert that all women's lives have been informed by the norms and values devised by a patriarchal society to further its agenda. Accordingly, most feminist writers situate female anger in the broader context of women's oppression and inferior status (Kaplan, Brook, McComb, Shapiro, & Sodano, 1983; Miller, 1976). The hypothesis that the sexes express anger in different ways accords with the constructivist view that distinctive features of any group's sociocultural situation necessarily affect norms governing members' expression of emotion (Averill, 1982; Stoner & Spencer, 1987).

Miller (1983) argues that anger is a different emotion for men and women because of gender differences in child-rearing practices, in the socialization process, and in socioeconomic status. Furthermore, she suggests that sociocultural definitions of such concepts as relationships, power, and conflict create differences between men and women, promote male supremacy, and contribute to the direct expression of anger under certain circumstances (Baker-Miller, 1988; Baker-Miller & Surrey, 1990).

Bernardez-Bonesatti (1978), a feminist psychologist, describes the intrapsychic and cultural variables that are specifically related to women's difficulties with anger and aggression. In her discussion, she stresses the ways in which sex differences in child rearing and the socialization process encourage men to display anger and aggression. Bernardez-Bonesatti also notes that women's anger is viewed as a destructive emotion in conflict with the feminine ideal in any particular culture (Bernardez, 1988).

Lerner (1985) describes anger as the voice of women's pains, needs, and desires. She observes that women have been discouraged from acknowledging and expressing anger directly, especially to men, because to do so would be *unladylike*, unfeminine, not maternal, and sexually unattractive; strident speech is also considered at variance with behavioral norms. Women who express their anger may be denounced as shrews, witches, bitches, hags, man-haters, and castrators, words that connote not only a lack of femininity but also evil and destructiveness.

According to Lerner (1985), unexpressed anger can feed into a cycle of self-defeating and self-perpetuating behaviors that produce feelings of helplessness, powerlessness, and loss of control. Other concomitants of unexpressed anger include loss of dignity and a decrease in self-esteem. Such feelings—and particularly the sense of a loss of control—have been reported by Puerto Rican women who experience *ataques de nervios* (Lerner, 1985). The sense of being out of control seems particularly noteworthy in cultures that equate control with the suppression of emotion.

Various feminist scholars have linked suppression of anger to the relational self (Gilligan, 1982; Jordan, Kaplan, & Surrey, 1982). They view relationships as important for women's self-esteem and sense of identity; they maintain that women need to feel connected and in a relationship. These writers see women as developing in a relational matrix—that is, in the context of relationships rather than in isolation, as presumed by mainstream psychology (Jordan, 1989).

In line with this view, Bernardez (1979) writes that some women do not express anger directly because they fear (and are vulnerable to) the relational consequences—specifically, the threat of abandonment, isolation, and disconnection. If women regard a relationship with another person as a way of being, they will find the loss of the relationship at least potentially threatening to the self (Baker-Miller, 1988). Furthermore, because social acceptance is an important component of a woman's sense of self-worth, there is a fear of being ostracized.

Jordan (1989) writes that shame is a silencing mechanism, a means of making women sublimate their anger, a feeling of worthlessness when one is not connected, and "a deep sense of unlovability [unloveliness], with on-going awareness of how very much one wants to connect with others" (p. 6). Jordan considers women particularly vulnerable to shame because they want to be connected and because they fear loss. Furthermore, she states that "while shame involves extreme self-consciousness, it also signals powerful relational longings and awareness of the other's response" (p. 6).

Some women feel shame when they experience themselves as defective, out of control, betrayed, awkward, or somehow different from others. Block-Lewis (1986) contends that women are more susceptible to shame than men. Jordan (1989) and Block-Lewis (1986) agree that patriarchy promotes the shaming and silencing of women's reality. Gender socialization is laden with shaming, particularly in those cultures in which shame is a culturally admired construct. When we view women's development in the context of relationships and sociocultural expectations, then, it becomes clear that many Puerto Rican women find themselves with few sanctioned outlets for their thoughts and feelings.

Feminist scholars continue to examine anger among women. The argument that patriarchal societies take as their main goal the protection of men's privileged roles offers grounds for believing that gender differences in the expression of anger are culturally entrenched. The feminist perspective thus offers insights into the dynamics of Puerto Rican women's anger and *ataques de nervios* as well.

Anger in Puerto Rican Culture

Literature on anger in Puerto Rican culture is scarce. A few writers mention anger in connection with other issues (Soto & Shaver, 1982). Cultural values—transmitted through child-rearing and societal norms—discourage displays of anger and assertiveness by Puerto Rican women (Comas-Díaz & Duncan, 1985). In particular, child-rearing practices in Puerto Rico have been found to inhibit aggression and auton-omy (Wolf, 1952). Nieves-Falcon (1972), for instance, states that parents teach sons from a very early age to be aggressive toward the opposite sex while teaching daughters to be passive and dependent.[4]

Some of the cultural values that discourage the expression of anger, assertive-ness, and aggression include *respeto* (respect), *familiarismo* (familism), *humildad* (humility), and *vergüenza* (shame) (Comas-Díaz, 1985; Díaz-Royo, 1976; Lauria, 1964). *Respeto* is expected toward family members generally and particularly toward males. Many women regard the expression of anger as inconsistent with respect; a woman who vents is likely to be identified as a *malcriada* (someone who is disrespectful and who lacks manners). The Puerto Rican cultural value of *vergüenza* (shame), viewed from a feminist perspective, promotes the repression of anger and women's submission to male control, with rejection as the penalty for insubordination.

Puerto Rican culture embraces three other concepts that condition the relation-ship between men and women and influence their expression of feelings, includ-ing anger. *Marianismo, hembrismo,* and *machismo* all prescribe gender-specific roles with corresponding ways of expressing anger (Comas-Días, 1982). The *marianista* concept, which exemplifies a passive ideal of femininity, may discourage women from asserting themselves in oppressive situations. A *marianista* woman, for exam-ple, is likely to remain in an abusive relationship for the sake of her children. True to a martyrlike ideal of motherhood, she will submit willingly to a life of abuse and pain. On the other hand, *hembrista* behavior, which can inspire Puerto Rican women to exert power and influence within their families and communities, may also lead to abuse. *Hembrista* women are usually considered aggressive and lack-ing in femininity. They are regarded as angry women and will often be avoided, exploited, or deserted by men. *Marianismo* and *hembrismo* both complement *machismo,* which applies to the behavior of Puerto Rican men; all three serve and sustain the patriarchy.

Religious tradition, shaped in part by Puerto Rico's history of colonization, has produced another cultural factor that has contributed to the way in which Puerto Rican woman deal with anger. This factor is fatalism, apparent in the adage *uno debe aceptar lo que Dios manda* ("One should accept what God decrees"). Fatalism prompts women to accept adversity while suppressing any anger that they feel. In the short run this is clearly an adaptive survival mechanism for some women.

The cultural perpetuation of women's dependency, the ideal of female coop-eration and compliance, and the lack of importance accorded women's education reflect a long-standing traditional interpretation of sex roles (Vásquez-Nuttal & Romero, 1989). Rivera (1990) has identified 25 culturally loaded linguistic terms and adages that can be invoked to manifest emotional states of anger (see Appen-dix 8B). The expressions connote different levels of anger that individuals can feel in different situations, depending on the person toward whom the anger is directed. The phrases range from mild to strong, with the majority falling toward the strong end. Socioeconomic status, lifestyle, degree of acculturation, and accep-

---

[4.] The situations that evoke shame in many Puerto Ricans are comparable to situations that arouse guilt in many middle-class Euro-Americans (Rivera-Ramos, 1984).

tance of socially sanctioned sex roles and behavioral norms influence individual use of these terms and adages.

Local newspaper coverage of Puerto Rican women works to inculcate public acceptance of violence against them (the *Vocero,* for example, presents violence against women as normative behavior) (Maldonado, 1989). Oral tradition also promotes ideology and socialization (Serra-Deliz, 1989), imparting values that include behavioral norms. In one analysis of colloquial speech in Puerto Rican society (Serra-Deliz, 1989), proverbs were found to reflect the subordination, condemnation, and exploitation of women and conveyed the message that women should suppress certain feelings. Such proverbs include *jode mas que una mujer preñá'* ("She is more trouble than a pregnant woman"), *las mujeres estan hechas para violarlas como las leyes,* ("Women, like laws, are made to be violated"), *todas las mujeres pelean* ("All women fight or nag"), and *las nenas no muerden, los que muerden son los perros* ("Dogs bite, not girls"). By the same token, *piropos* (flirtatious verbal compliments) and the lyrics of popular salsa music (Afro-Latin tunes) often disparage women and thereby help keep them subordinate.

In an investigation of Puerto Rican women in Hartford, Rivera-Arzola (1992) found a complex, multiphasic relationship between *ataques de nervios* and anger. Her descriptive study used a convenience sample ($N = 106$) of women with and without a history of *ataques de nervios.* The study sought to identify characteristics distinguishing sufferers from nonsufferers: patterns of anger expression, psychological and physiological symptoms, sex-role traditionalism, history of traumatic events, lack of acculturation, and an absence of social supports. It was hypothesized that repressed anger would have the greatest predictive value. Scales were administered to obtain ratings on anger, sex roles, traditionalism, acculturation, and exposure to traumatic events.

Contrary to her hypothesis, Rivera-Arzola (1992) found that the key factors in predicting *ataques de nervios* were psychological distress and modulation of anger. Only partial support was found for the literature arguing that *ataques de nervios* reflect repressed anger (Abad et al., 1977; De La Cancela et al., 1986; Rothenberg, 1964); women with a history of *ataques de nervios* scored higher on both repressed and expressed anger.

The critical factor distinguishing sufferers was the ability to control or modulate anger. Specifically, women who experience *ataques de nervios* have difficulty in modulating their anger, whether it is repressed or expressed outwardly toward others. This finding suggests that the relationship between anger and *ataques de nervios* is complex and that episodes reflect more than repressed anger or lack of assertiveness (see, e.g., Comas-Díaz, 1985). Rivera-Arzola's (1992) result is consonant with the constructivist and feminist views of anger, however, in that modulation is influenced by cultural forces as well as by intrapsychic ones. Simply stated, women suffering from *ataques de nervios* need both to recognize the sources of their anger and to learn how to manage it so that it does not overwhelm them.

Implications for Clinical Work with Puerto Rican Women

As we have indicated, the available research suggests that *ataques de nervios*, whether regarded as deviant or merely as culture-specific, have both a psychological and a sociocultural aspect. To be truly effective, then, clinical interventions must address the woman's psychosocial development and her place in the surrounding community.

Treatment Modality

A group model is the preferred mode of intervention for women suffering from *ataques de nervios* because it is culturally congruent, promotes affirmation of ethnic and feminist identity, decreases feelings of isolation, and increases social support. The program may include music, drama, poetry, oral histories, short stories, vignettes, and videos, all of which have been found to be effective with Puerto Ricans (Ramos-McKay, Comas-Díaz, & Rivera, 1988). The group modality may also use liberating action techniques, such as community service projects, and political consciousness-raising activities such as marches and rallies. Although a therapist may act as facilitator, the benefits of collective process and contact necessarily come from the women themselves.

To be effective, the intervention needs to include strategies for coping with traumatic life events, which seem to contribute to the high levels of distress associated with *ataques de nervios*. Two other elements also should be incorporated into the intervention. First, as indicated by the literature on posttraumatic stress, individuals should be encouraged to process and retell their trauma so that they can master it and thereby increase their capacity for self-love and empathy. Second, developmental consciousness therapy (Ivey, 1986) should be used to assist women who experienced trauma before they had reached a developmental stage that would allow them to process events accurately.

Because there is evidence that Puerto Rican women with *ataques de nervios* modulate or control anger poorly, one key component in any intervention should be assertiveness training within a cultural context (see, e.g., Comas-Díaz & Duncan, 1985). Assertiveness training should focus on helping women with a history of *ataques de nervios* avoid repressing their anger, avoid expressing anger aggressively, and avoid losing control.

The treatment group functions importantly to help the Puerto Rican women experience their pain psychologically, emotionally, and physically and to help them learn how they use their bodies to construct and share their inner selves and personal experiences. The group modality also can promote collective awareness of oppressive conditions. The leader, for example, can help members identify forms of resistance (survival skills that women use in their daily lives). The leader and the individual members alike need to appreciate the ways in which Puerto Rican women have withstood adversity.

Case Management

Emigration, industrialization, poverty, and divorce all may have undermined traditional support systems, thereby increasing vulnerability in times of stress. Techniques to draw on outside sources of support should be incorporated into any intervention. Possible new supports include churches, women's collectives, and social service agencies.

In addition, educational and occupational training needs must be incorporated into any intervention (Rivera, 1990). Low socioeconomic status is known to be related to mental health and behavioral problems (Dohrenwend & Dohrenwend, 1974; Hollingshead & Redlich, 1958; Inclán, 1983). Other basic needs of women include transportation, child care, housing, and medical care, some of which may require attention before women can participate in treatment.

Cultural Interventions

On the psychocultural level, the authors recommend using something on the order of Paulo Freire's model of *critical consciousness* to help Puerto Rican women critically understand the historical, political, and social problems that interact with their own interpersonal issues and relationships.

A psychocultural intervention also should incorporate feminist psychology. The object is not to make the participants into feminists but to encourage them to be more self-critical, self-reflective, and self-determined. Ideally, the intervention should engender a more androgynous sex role and lifestyle, broaden members' view of behavioral norms for both sexes, and illuminate power/domination relationships in the patriarchal system and in traditional Puerto Rican culture.

Finally, any intervention model developed for use with Puerto Ricans, and specifically with women with *ataques de nervios,* should address problems of acculturation and ethnic identity. The aim should be to sensitize women to their level of acculturation, their behavior, their values, and their beliefs. By increasing their knowledge of Puerto Rican and other cultures, women can improve their overall functioning and can adapt more readily to mainland society. The acculturation process should produce not only greater self-awareness and a stronger sense of cultural identity, but also a clearer grasp of the impact of racism, colonialism, and human oppression.

Conclusion

Cultural values, traditions, and language all influence the ways in which Puerto Rican women learn to express their feelings. Puerto Rican society discourages assertive expressions of emotions among women, although some courageous women flout the norm despite reprisals. Anger, stress, and generalized distress all appear to be implicated in *ataques de nervios* among Puerto Rican women. Feminist theoretical paradigms and perspectives, and the constructivist view, afford useful insights and suggest ways in which *ataques de nervios* may reflect sociocultural forces as well as psychodynamic ones. Further research is needed, however, because the relationship between these forces and *ataques de nervios* appears to be complex and is not satisfactorily explained by the available literature.

References

Abad, V., Ramos, J., & Boyce, E. (1977). Clinical issues in the psychiatric treatment of Puerto Ricans. In E. R. Padilla & A. M. Padilla (Eds.), *Transcultural psychiatry; An Hispanic perspective*, Monograph 4, Spanish Mental Health Research Center, University of California, Los Angeles.

Angel, R., & Guarnaccia, P. J. (1989). Mind, body, and culture: Somatization among Hispanics. *Social Science Medicine, 28*(12), 1229–1238.

Averill, J. R. (1982). *Anger and aggression.* New York: Springer-Verlag.

Baker-Miller, J. (1988). Women and power. In M. Braude (Ed.), *Women, power and therapy* (pp. 1–11). New York: Harrington Park.

Baker-Miller, J. B., & Surrey J. (1990). Revisioning women's anger: The personal and the global. *Work in Progress, 43.* Wellesley, MA: Stone Center Working Paper Series.

Barreto, J. (1986). *Puerto Ricans: Growing problems for a growing population.* Washington, DC: The National Puerto Rican Forum.

Bernardez, T. (1979). *Observations on the sociology of anger and its implications for treatment for women.* Paper presented at the American Academy of Psychoanalysis, New York.

Bernardez, T. (1988). Women and anger: Cultural prohibitions and the feminine ideal. *Work in Progress, 31.* Wellesley, MA: Stone Center Working Paper Series.

Bernardez-Bonesatti, T. (1978). Women and anger: Conflicts with aggression in contemporary women. *Journal of the American Medical Association, 33*, 215–219.

Block-Lewis, H. (1986). Is Freud an enemy of women's liberation? Some historical considerations. In T. Bernay & D. W. Cantor (Eds.), *The psychology of today's women: New psychoanalytic visions.* (pp. 7–36). Cambridge, MA: Harvard University Press.

Canino, G. J., Rubio-Stipec, M., Shrout, P., Bravo, M., Stolberg, R., & Bird, H. (1987). Sex differences and depression in Puerto Rico. *Psychology of Women Quarterly, 11*, 443–459.

Cayleff, S. E. (1988). Prisoners of their own feebleness: Women, nerves and Western medicine—A historical overview. *Social Science Medicine, 26*(12), 1199–1208.

Comas-Díaz, L. (1982). Mental health needs of Puerto Rican women in the United States. In R. Zambrana (Ed.), *Work, family and health: Latina women in transition* (pp. 1–10). New York: Hispanic Research Center, Fordham University.

Comas-Díaz, L. (1985). Cognitive and behavioral group therapy with Puerto Rican women: A comparison of content themes. *Hispanic Journal of Behavioral Sciences, 7*(3), 273–283.

Comas-Díaz, L. (1987). Feminist therapy with mainland Puerto Rican women. Special issue: Hispanic women and mental health. *Psychology of Women Quarterly, 11*(4), 461–474.

Comas-Díaz, L. (1989). Puerto Rican women's cross-cultural transitions: Developmental and clinical implications. In C. García-Coll & L. Mattei (Eds.), *The psychosocial development of Puerto Rican women* (pp. 166–199). New York: Praeger.

Comas-Díaz, L., & Duncan, J. W. (1985). The cultural context: A factor in assertiveness training with mainland Puerto Rican women. *Psychology of Women Quarterly, 9*, 463–476.

Davis, D. L. (1989). The variable character of nerves in a Newfoundland fishing village. *Medical Anthropology 11*, 63–78.

Davis, D. L., & Guarnaccia, P. J. (Eds.). (1989). Health, culture, and the nature of nerves. *Medical Anthropology: Cross-Cultural Studies in Health and Illness, 11*(1), 1–13.

Davison, L., Rivera, M., Singer, M., & Scanlon, K. (1989). *Puertorriqueñas: Sociodemographics, health and reproductive issues among Puerto Rican women in the U.S.* Hartford, Connecticut: Hispanic Health Council.

De La Cancela, V., Guarnaccia, P., & Carrillo, E. (1986). Psychosocial distress among Latinos: A critical analysis of *ataques de nervios. Humanity and Society, 10,* 431–447.

DeVos, G., & Hippler, A. (1969). Culture psychology: Comparative studies of human behavior. In L. Gardner (Ed.), *The handbook of social psychology* (pp. 323–417). Reading, MA: Addison-Wesley.

Díaz-Royo. (1976). *Respeto y dignidad: Dos temas centrales en la cultura puertorriqueña (Respect and dignity: Two central themes in the Puerto Rican culture).* Unpublished mimeograph.

Dohrenwend, B., & Dohrenwend, B. (1974). Social and cultural influences on psychopathology. *Annual Review of Psycholology, 25,* 417–451.

Dunk, P. (1989). Greek women and broken nerves in Montreal. *Medical Anthropology, 11,* 29–46.

Fernández-Marina, R. (1961). The Puerto Rican syndrome: Its dynamics and cultural determinants. *Psychiatry, 24,* 79–82.

Finerman, R. D. (1988). The price of power: Gender roles and stress-induced depression in Andean Ecuador. In P. Whelan (Ed.), *Women and health: Cross-cultural perspectives* (pp. 153–169). Granby, MA: Bergin & Garvey.

Flores, C., Davison, L., Rivera, M., Torres, M. I., & Castillo, Z. (1989). *Gender, life experience, and reproductive illness among Puerto Rican women in Hartford, Connecticut.* Paper presented at El Primer Congreso Puertorriqueño, Mujer y Salud, San Juan, Puerto Rico.

Garrison, V. (1977). The "Puerto Rican syndrome" in psychiatry and *espiritismo.* In V. Crapanzano & V. Garrison (Eds.), *Case studies in spirit possession* (pp. 383–447). New York: Wiley.

Gilligan, C. (1982). *In a different voice: Psychological theory, and women's development.* Cambridge, MA: Harvard University Press.

González, J., Rodríguez-Fraticelli, C., Torres, A., Torres, Z., Vázquez, B. (1989). *The status of Puerto Ricans in the United States.* Unpublished manuscript, National Congress for Puerto Rican Rights.

Grace, W. J. (1959). *"Ataque." New York Medicine, 15,* 12–13.

Guarnaccia, P. J. (1993). Ataques de nervios in Puerto Rico: Culture-bound syndrome or popular illness? *Medical Anthropology, 15,* 157–170.

Guarnaccia, P. J., Canino, G., Rubio-Stipec, M., & Bravo, M. (1993). The prevalence of *ataques de nervios* in the Puerto Rico disaster study. *Journal of Nervous and Mental Disease, 181*(3), 157–165.

Guarnaccia, P. J., Rubio-Stipec, M., & Canino, G. (1989). *Ataques de nervios* in the Puerto Rico Diagnostic Interview Schedule: The impact of cultural categories on psychiatric epidemiology. *Culture Medicine Psychiatry, 13,* 275–295.

Harwood, A. (1981). *Ethnicity and medical care.* Cambridge, MA: Harvard University Press.

Hollingshead, A. B., & Redlich, J. J. (1958). *Social class and mental illness: A community study.* New York: Wiley.

Inclán, J. E. (1983). Psychological symptomatology in second generation Puerto Rican women of three socioeconomic groups. *Journal of Psychology, 11,* 79–90.

Ivey, A. E. (1986). *Developmental therapy.* California: Josey-Bass.

Jordan, J. (1989). Relational development: Therapeutic implications of empathy and shame. *Work in Progress, 39.* Wellesley, MA: Stone Center Working Papers Series.

Jordan, J., Kaplan, A., & Surrey, J. (1982). Women and empathy. *Work in Progress, 14.* Wellesley, MA: Stone Center Working Papers Series.

Kaplan, A. G., Brook, B., McComb, A. L., Shapiro, E. R., & Sodano, A. S. (1983). Women and anger in psychotherapy. In J. H. Robbins & R. J. Siegal (Eds.), *Women changing therapy: New assessments values, and strategies in feminist therapy* (pp. 29–40). New York: Haworth Press.

Lauria, A. (1964). *Respeto, relajo,* and interpersonal relations in Puerto Rico. *Anthropological Quarterly, 37*(2), 53–67.

Lerner, H. G. (1985). *The dance of anger.* New York: Harper & Row.

Levine, I. (1973). *Culture, behavior and personality.* Chicago: Aldine.

Lock, M. (1989). Words of fear, words of power: Nerves and the awakening of political consciousness. *Medical Anthropology, 11,* 79–90.

López-Garriga, M. (1980). Estratégias de autoafirmación en mujeres puertorriqueñas. In E. Acosta-Belén (Ed.), *La mujer en la sociedad Puertorriqueña* (pp. 183–210). Rio Piedras: Edición Huracán.

Maldonado, M. A. (1989). *Violencia contra la mujer: Mitos y estereotipos perpetuados en el Vocero.* [Violence against women: Myths and stereotypes perpetrated by the Vocero]. Presented at El Primer Congreso Puertorriqueño: Mujer y Salud. Puerto Rico: University of Puerto Rico.

McCormick, R. J. (1986). *Personality concomitants of the Puerto Rican syndrome as reflected in the Minnesota Multiphasic Personality Inventory.* Rutgers University: University Microfilms.

Miller, J. B. (1976). *Towards a new psychology of women.* Boston: Beacon.

Miller, J. B. (1983). The construction of anger in women and men. *Work in Progress, 4.* Wellesley, MA: Stone Center Working Paper Series.

Miranda-King, L. (1974). Puertorriqueñas in the United States: The impact of double discrimination. *Civil Rights Digest, 6*(3), 20–28.

Muñoz-Vázquez, M. (1980). The effects of role expectations of the marital status of urban Puerto Rican women. In E. Acosta-Belén (Ed.), *The Puerto Rican woman* (pp. 110–120). New York: Praeger.

National Congress for Puerto Rican Rights. (1989). *The Status of Puerto Ricans in the United States.* Presented at the Third National Puerto Rican Convention, June 1, Philadelphia.

Nations, M. K., Camino, L. A., & Walker, F. B. (1988). Nerves: Folk idiom for anxiety and depression. *Social Science Medicine, 26*(12), 1245–1259.

Nieves-Falcón, L. (1972). *Diagnóstico de Puerto Rico.* [A diagnosis of Puerto Rico]. Rio Piedras: Editorial Edit.

Padilla, A. M., & Ruíz, R. A. (1973). *Latino mental health: A review of the literature.* Washington, DC: U.S. Government Printing Office.

Ramos-McKay, J. M., Comas-Díaz, L., & Rivera, L. A. (1988). Puerto Ricans. In L. Comas-Díaz & E. E. H. Griffith (Eds.), *Clinical guidelines in cross-cultural mental health* (pp. 204–232). New York: Wiley.

Rivera, M. (1990). *Toward an understanding of ataques de nervios with special attention on anger.* Unpublished manuscript, University of Massachusetts, Amherst.

Rivera-Arzola, M. (1992). *Differences between Puerto Rican women in the United States with and without history of ataques de nervios.* Unpublished Ph.D. dissertation, University of Massachusetts, Amherst.

Rodríguez, C. (1989). *Puerto Ricans born in the U.S.A.* Winchester, MA: Unwin Hyman.

Rosaldo, M. (1984). Toward an anthropology of self and feeling. In R. Shweder & R. Levine (Eds.), *Culture theory* (pp. 137–157). Cambridge, MA: Cambridge University Press.

Rothenberg, A. (1964). Puerto Rico and aggression. *Journal of Psychiatry, 6,* 1767–1772.

Rubio, M., Urdaneta, M., & Doyle, J. L. (1955). Psychopathologic reaction patterns in the Antilles Command. *U.S. Armed Forces Medical Journal, 6,* 1767–1772.

Rubio-Stipec, M., Shrout, P. E., Bird, H., Canino, G. J., & Bravo, M. (1989). Symptom scales of the Diagnostic Interview Schedule: Factor results in Hispanic and Anglo samples. *Psychological Assessments, 1,* 30–34.

Serra-Deliz, W. (1989). La construcción social de la imagen de la mujer en el refraneo Puertorriqueño [The construction of women's images in Puerto Rican popular slang]. *Caribbean Studies, 22,* 1–2.

Soto, E., & Shaver, P. (1982). Sex-role traditionalism assertiveness, and symptomatology among Puerto Rican women living in the United States. *Hispanic Journal of Behavioral Sciences, 4*(1), 1–20.

Stoner, S. B., & Spencer, W. B. (1987). Age differences on the State Trait Personality Inventory. *Psychological Reports, 4*(3), 1315–1319.

Strongman, K. T. (1987). *The psychology of emotion.* Chichester: John Wiley and Sons.

Torres-Matrullo, C. (1976). Acculturation and psychopathology among Puerto Rican women in mainland United States. *American Journal of Orthopsychiatry, 46*(4), 710–719.

Trautman, E. C. (1961). The suicidal fit. *Archives of General Psychiatry, 5,* 76–83.

U.S. Department of Commerce, Bureau of the Census (1988). *The Hispanic population in the United States: March,* Series P-20, No. 431.

Van Schaik, E. (1989). Paradigms underlying the study of nerves as a popular illness term in Eastern Kentucky. *Medical Anthropology, 11,* 15–28.

Vázquez-Hernández, V. (1991). *The status of Puerto Ricans in the United States.* Philadelphia: National Congress for Puerto Rican Rights.

Vázquez-Nuttal, E., & Romero, I. (1989). From home to school: Puerto Rican girls learn the American student role. In C. Garcia-Coll & L. Mattei (Eds.), *The psychosocial development of Puerto Rican women* (pp. 60–83). New York: Praeger.

Wolf, K. K. (1952). Growing up and its price in three Puerto Rican subcultures. *Journal of Psychiatry, 15,* 401–433.

Zavala-Martínez, I. (1981). *Mental health and the Puerto Rican In the United States: A critical literature review and comprehensive bibliography.* A Preliminary Comprehensive Examination Project.

Zavala-Martínez, I. (1988). *En la lucha*: The economic and socioemotional struggles of Puerto Rican women. In L. Fulani (Ed.), *The psychopathology of everyday: Racism and sexism* (pp. 3–25). New York: Harrington Park.

Zayas, L. H. (1989). A retrospective on "the suicidal fit" in mainland Puerto Ricans: Research issues. *Hispanic Journal of Behavioral Sciences, 11*(1), 46–57.

Appendix 8A: Essential Manifestation in a Definition of Ataques de Nervios

Essential Manifestations

Nervousness as a precursor
Transient hyperkinetic state
Feeling out of control
Sense of loss of oneself
Loss of muscle tone
Aggression against self and others
Amnesic episodes
Manipulative features with secondary gains
Display of affect
Signs of anxiety
Loss of consciousness
Tremors
Heart palpitations
Sense of heat rising to the head
Numbness
Histrionic characteristic
Involuntary disturbance or alteration of
  physical functioning

Population

Latinos (Puerto Rican and Central and South Americans) and other ethnic groups: Greek, African Americans, Canadians

Duration

Five to ten minutes (usually), but also 30 minutes to 24 hours in some reported cases

Predisposing Factors

Psychological or socioeconomic problems
Frustrating events
Death of loved person
Witnessing accidents
Family conflicts
Abrupt occurrence after an associated distressful event (usually)

Situations that create powerlessness, helplessness, feeling of inferiority and nonbeing

Sex Ratio

Reported to be more common among females than males

Familial Pattern

No information

Age of Onset

Although first episode has been reported as early as childhood, the more typical onset is seen in adulthood.

Prevalence

Apparently found among a variety of ethnic groups, but common particularly among Latin Americans

Associated Factors

Physiological:
Illness
"Nervous system"

Psychological:
Generalized or directed anger
Poorly suppressed anger
Internal conflict about a distressful temporary or terminal event
Volatile temperament
Fear of external forces
Painful feelings per separation/ abandonment
Mental suffering/stress
Child abuse

Feelings of failure as a woman, daughter, and/or wife
Sexual abuse/physical abuse
Impact of stressful life
Grief reaction due to loss of a loved person
Fear of harm to loved one
Sexual disturbances

Socioeconomic:
Genocide tactics
Inadequate housing and high mobility
Issues of power at the micro level
Industrialization
Rapid urbanization
High rate of unemployment
Forced migration
High rate of criminality
Economic disruptions
Unsuccessful marriages
Conflictual family relationship
Dependency on welfare system
Discrimination and racism
Sexist practices

Cultural:
Acculturation/assimilation
Acculturative stress
Intergenerational conflict
Power struggles among family members
Disruption of cultural modes of behavior
Religious beliefs
Breakdown of family support system
Disruption in cultural ego ideals

Historical:
Colonization under Spain and the United States
Forced citizenship
Forced migration
Forced military participation

Appendix 8B: Definitions of Terms and Adages in the Puerto Rican Language

Spanish Usage	English Usage

Terms:

estoy nerviosa	I am nervous; angry
tengo coraje	I have courage; spirit; anger
estoy molesta/o	I am annoyed; uncomfortable
estoy irritada/o	I am irate; irritated
estoy brava/o	I am ill-tempered; angry
estoy enojada/o	I am annoyed; troubled
tengo rabia/estoy rabiosa/o	I have rage; fury
estoy encojonada/o	*slang:* I have rage*
estoy encabronada/o	*slang:* I have rage*
tengo cólera	I have anger; wrath
estoy enfogonada/o	*slang:* I am enraged*
estoy ensangrentada/o	I am stained with blood; rage*
estoy enfurecida/o	I am enraged; infuriated
estoy frenética/o	*slang:* I am enraged*
estoy iracunda/o	I am ireful; wrathful
estoy furiosa/o	I am furious

Adages (proverbs):

estoy que hecho humo	I am so angry that I could smoke
estoy calientita	I am very hot (angry)
se me sube la bilis	My bile will go up (very angry)
estoy hirviendo	I am boiling (very angry)
estoy como agua pa chocolate	I am like hot water for chocolate (very angry)
si me pican no suelto sangre	If cut I will not bleed (very angry)
estoy envenená'	I am poisoned (very angry)
estoy que no hay quien me beba el caldo	No one can drink my broth (very angry)
estoy prendida/o en candela	I am set on fire (very angry)

*These words were not defined in the dictionary. They are words that are colloquially used by Puerto Ricans.

Chapter **9**

Mental Health Needs of Latinos with Professional Status

LILLIAN COMAS-DÍAZ
Transcultural Mental Health Institute

Like other people of color, Latinos tend to view education as a means of survival and progress within the mainstream society (Ho, 1987; McGoldrick, Pearce, & Giordano, 1982). Many Latino parents envision education as an aspiring value for their offspring (Ford Foundation, 1984; McGoldrick et al., 1982). Indeed, Latinos have focused on work and education as a tool for the development of their communities. For example, according to a report on Hispanic education prepared by ASPIRA (1994), Latino high school students aged 16 to 24 are generally more likely than African-American students but less likely than Whites to be working while enrolled in school. However, Latinos are more likely than other high school students to work 35 hours a week or more. Furthermore, more Latinos are enrolling in college after high school. Between 1989 and 1991, the college participation rate of Hispanic high school graduates ages 18 to 24 increased from 29.9% to 34.4%, while the participation of Whites also increased from 32.5% to 41.1% (ASPIRA, 1994).

The value of education may facilitate Latinos' presence in the professional arena. Notwithstanding Latinos' emphasis on education, they tend to be proportionately underrepresented in the professional arena. Indeed, education, ranging

The author wishes to gratefully acknowledge the comments made by Julia Ramos Grenier, Ph.D. on an earlier version of this work.

from preschool through graduate training levels, represents the most serious gap in achievement between Latinos and other ethnic groups, resulting in significantly lower representation in higher education institutions (Ford Foundation, 1984). Latinos are the only major ethnic group to be more likely to attend two-year rather than four-year colleges (ASPIRA, 1994). Moreover, Latinos' underrepresentation in many public and private-sector organizations has led to a call for intensified targeted recruiting of this ethnic group (Edwards, Rosenfeld, Thomas, & Thomas, 1993). The increasing presence of Latinos in professional settings is further aided by federal legislation and affirmative action policies forbidding discrimination in employment practices on the basis of race, color, sex, religion, or national origin (Romero & Garza, 1986).

Latinos with professional status often represent a source of pride and joy for their families and communities. Frequently, they are identified as role models within the Latino population, particularly for children and adolescents. However, many Latinos with professional status face a stressful reality in the workplace—environmental barriers, ethnocultural conflicts, and lack of support. The fatigue created by coping with a significant amount of ethnocultural occupational stress in a non-supportive environment tends to increase Latinos' distress and vulnerability to health and mental health problems.

In this chapter, I address the mental health needs of Latinos with professional status, with attention to the interface of individual, ethnocultural, organizational, and sociopolitical dynamics. Although there is a wide diversity among Latinos with professional status, I concentrate on those factors that appear to be common to most Latinos who work within mainstream professional environments. Treatment implications for these populations are presented. Identifying data have been altered to protect confidentiality.

Mosaico Latino: Latinos' Heterogeneity

As presented in the first chapter of this book, there is a significant heterogeneity among Latinos. Latinos comprise a multiethnic and multiracial mosaic. This mosaic is woven with threads of age, gender, acculturation level, class, sexual orientation, nativity (native or foreign-born status), generational status, nationality, color, and religion, among many others.

Latinos' presence and experience in the professional and managerial arena reflect a combination of cultural features, majority–minority relations, and within-group diversity (Ferdman, 1992). Additionally, color and racial differences between Latinos constitute central factors bearing significant implications in the workplace. Indeed, color differences are one of the most disturbing issues within Latino communities (Comas-Díaz, 1994). The individual and institutionalized racism prevalent in the United States often encourages a racial division among many Latinos. For example, in our racially polarized (Black/White) society, light-skinned Latinos may face less racism in the workplace than their darker skinned *hermanos* (siblings). Darker Latinos confront specific problems due to their combined ethnic and racial status. Comas-Díaz (1994) has coined the term *LatiNegros* to identify those African Latinos who are perceived beyond any doubt as Black by both the North American and the Latino communities. Many LatiNegros in the professional workplace encounter ethnoracial-specific issues that require special attention during their mental health treatment.

Latinos' heterogeneity is also manifested through their type of immigration to the United States—documented or undocumented—and their subsequent entry into the workplace. Many immigrant Latinos may experience alienation, poverty, prejudice, uprooting, and ethnocultural conflict. The immigrant state of mind often reinforces a sense of disadvantage (Wheeler, 1971), which paradoxically can provide an impetus for some immigrants to succeed within the host culture through work and formal education. Other Latinos may experience the migrant mentality, which frequently involves maintaining the dream of return to the homeland and which is facilitated by the circularity of the process due to migration and reverse migration. For example, as U.S. citizens, many Puerto Ricans with educational and professional skills migrate to the continent in search of employment, specialized education, and/or career advancement. Many, however, return to Puerto Rico, initiating a cycle of circular migration.

Some exiled Latino professionals may be actively involved in the reconstruction of their homeland and, by re-creating the lifestyle left behind, may achieve professional advancement in the host country. Some Cubans in Miami appear to be an illustration of this type of exile mentality. They have recreated Little Havana in Miami and, in the process, have helped to make Miami a commercial pathway between North and South America. Of course, there is also significant heterogeneity among Cubans in their adaptation and financial struggles in the United States. Furthermore, the heterogeneity among Cubans is often related to class and color differences.

Another type of exiled Latinos may cope with a complicated adjustment to the United States. For example, some Central American immigrants are more likely to suffer from posttraumatic stress disorder than are Mexican immigrants (Cervantes, Salgado de Snyder, & Padilla, 1989).

Many Salvadorans in the United States cope with specific concerns such as political status and war-related trauma, which may interfere with their occupational functioning (Vargas, 1984) and advancement. Immigration status tends to interact with level of acculturation and socioeconomic class in Latinos' adaptation process to the host country's society and workplace. However, regardless of Latinos' immigrant status, their traditional ethnocultural values often promote paradoxes in the professional workplace.

Ethnocultural Values: Paradoxes in the Professional Arena

The traditional Latino culture embraces values that tend to both facilitate and hinder Latinos' presence in the professional workplace. Latinos' level of acculturation, socioeconomic class, plus family and gender roles affect their adherence to traditional values and their behavior within an organization. For example, Saldaña

(1994) empirically found that acculturation provided information about minority-status stress reported by Latino college students in a predominantly White institution, but it was less relevant in terms of their psychological distress. She found that students with stronger ethnic identity reported higher levels of minority-status stresses.

Latinos' collective orientation may be divergent and conflictive with the individualistic orientation prevalent among the dominant group culture. Latinos in the United States have been described as being more collectivistic than Whites, such that the group is emphasized over the individual, the need for consensus is greater, and interpersonal behavior is stressed over task achievement (Triandis, Marín, Lisansky, & Betancourt, 1984). Although individual achievement is not particularly emphasized (Falicov, 1982), Latino high achievers usually become a source of pride for the Latino community because their individual achievement is perceived as a collective one.

The concept of family is also central to many Latinos with traditional cultural values. Similarly, being a member of a community is part of the ethos of Latino culture. This sense of community can affect many Latinos' view of work-related behavior. As an illustration, in a survey comparing the willingness to relocate for employment, Edwards and colleagues (1993) found that even highly educated Latinos may place more restrictions on relocation than Anglos and African Americans. The researchers found that Latinos were more willing to relocate if the new employment had high incentives and if the geographical areas had high Latino concentrations. The preference for areas of high Latino concentration appears to suggest the importance of family and community among many employed Latinos.

The centrality of family and community is related to the traditional cultural value of familism. *Familism* refers to the tendency to extend kinship relationships beyond the nuclear family boundaries, leading to emotional proximity, affective resonance, interpersonal involvement, and cohesiveness (Falicov, 1982). A paradoxical cultural value within the mainstream workplace, familism may conflict in the professional workplace where norms of "dog eat dog," "sink or swim," "you're on your own," "take it or leave it," and other similar corporate dynamics may prevail. On the other hand, because familism emphasizes interdependence over independence, affiliation over confrontation, and cooperation over competition (Falicov, 1982), it may enhance Latinos' interpersonal relationships at work in companies that value such traits as talking the company line and playing the game.

Another traditional Latino cultural value is *personalismo*. *Personalismo* (personalism) is the Latino tendency to prefer personal contacts over impersonal or institutional ones (Comas-Díaz, 1989). Hispanics tend to rely more on their own personal estimation of a person rather than on the person's economic position, status, or achievements. Because of *personalismo*, many Latinos tend to develop personal affiliations at work, as opposed to relating to an abstract institutional affiliation. This style of interaction, though personal, is not informal. Further, the traditional Latino value of *simpatía* can potentially interfere with Latinos' ability to make decisions, disagree with co-workers, and play power games in a professional workplace. *Simpatía* is an interpersonal style that emphasizes maintaining a pleasant demeanor, aimed at lowering conflict and promoting agreement. It values dignity and respect in interpersonal relations and emphasizes positive and de-emphasizes negative behaviors (Triandis et al., 1984). In a professional situation, Latinos' *simpatía* can make them popular colleagues but may lead to unassertiveness and indirect behavioral expressions. The collective orientation, familism, personalism, and *simpatía* can therefore be at odds with the individualistic, assertive, autonomous, and decisive behavior that may be required to be successful in a mainstream professional arena.

To examine professionals' adherence to traditional cultural values in the workplace, Ferdman and Cortés (1992) studied a sample of Latino managers in an Anglo business context. These researchers found that their sample of Latino managers experienced their styles as contrasting with the styles of their White co-workers. Latino managers endorsed an orientation to people, a direct approach to conflict resolution, and a flexible attitude toward hierarchy. Their attention to other people and to interpersonal relationships at work (*personalismo*) appeared to be combined with a strong belief in respect for oneself and others, and a value to attending to the feelings of others (allocentrism). Somewhat contrary to the *simpático* conflict avoidance style, these Latino managers' direct approach to conflict resolution was related to self-respect, professionalism, and commitment to work. Their flexible attitude toward hierarchy was associated with the importance attributed to accomplishing the job and maintaining positive relationships rather than following "proper" channels, and with a preference for autonomy in their work. Ferdman and Cortés's (1992) findings can be explained as resulting from a combination of *personalismo* and *familismo*, with a need for autonomy due to the managers' minority status in the context of a majority-group organization.

Latinos in the Workplace: The Interface of External and Internal Dynamics

Person–Environment Transaction

Latinos' experiences in the professional workplace can be examined through the lens of the person–environment context. This concept involves analyzing the interface of such environmental factors as sociopolitical context, organizational dynamics, and membership in an ethnic minority group, interacting with ethnocultural and individual behavior. Similarly, Prillerman, Myers, and Smedley (1989) propose a person–environment transaction as a more appropriate model for an accurate understanding of the functioning of college students of color on White campuses. They argue that this contextual model is more relevant than the traditional emphasis on an intellectual and academic paradigm of success and failure.

Many professionals of color usually have to overcome significant socioeconomic and cultural barriers even before achieving their professional status. Most students of color often lack the kinds of supportive infrastructure that White middle-class students typically have (Romero Ramos, 1990). For example, many students of color juggle getting a degree with helping to support their poor or dysfunctional family, others live at home for financial and cultural reasons, while others have difficulties fitting into predominantly White institutions (Moses, 1991). As previously indicated, Latino high school students are more likely than other high school students to work 35 hours a week or more.

Those Latinos who come from middle- and upper-class backgrounds also cope with specific ethnocultural issues. As an illustration, in describing his experiences as a Chicano in Harvard, Navarrette (1993) struggles with his ethnic identity, racial politics, and the fear of emotional and intellectual separation from his family and community. According to him, his odyssey culminates in becoming a Harvard Man, or being taught well by being pushed to test his limits.

Although many Latinos share commonalities with other professionals and with professionals of color in general, they also face unique situations due to their ethnocultural context. Some of the unique concerns involve different ethnocultural values, loneliness, being outsiders, and a commitment to work toward helping other Latinos and people of color. There is often a clear and explicit expectation that those Latinos who have some measure of success need to help bring others along. This may further impinge on financial and emotional resources in a way that it does not for mainstream professionals.

The demands from the Latino community are related to professionals' commitment to the welfare of their ethnic group as well as the group's expectation that they will fulfill such commitment. Latinos with professional status are frequently asked to participate in numerous community activities—volunteering in schools or churches, serving on the boards of nonprofit organizations that help the Latino community, organizing community events, and countless others. Many Latinos with professional status identify with the needs of the Latino community as an extension of themselves and of their own families (Anders, 1993).

As members of the professional class, Latinos tend to represent the elite of the society's work force. They share with other professionals in general the usual steps in the occupational journey, such as obtaining degrees, meeting professional standards, and fulfilling licensing requirements in systems and institutions. Unlike their Anglo counterparts, however, Latinos are often unwelcome in such institutions. Many Latino professionals carry the burden of needing to prove that their achievement is more than the result of affirmative action policies. Some grow to resent these policies because of the negative stereotypes that they engender. Moreover, for their academic and professional success, many Latinos pay a high emotional cost in the form of personal sacrifices and strained interpersonal relationships with families and significant others (Romero Ramos, 1990). Similarly, as a consequence of feeling that they have to fight negative ethnic stereotypes, some Latino professionals experience difficulty in articulating positive and differentiated visions of what it means to be Hispanic (Ferdman & Cortés, 1992).

Like other professionals of color, many Latinos do not enjoy the advantages of a professional status to the same extent as their Anglo counterparts do, because they face ethnic and racial discrimination in hiring and professional advancement (Leggon, 1980). Additionally, professional status can be experienced differently by those Latinos who are pigeonholed as affirmative action quotas, tokens, or "professional Latinos." The exclusion from the club that many professionals of color experience often results in low expectations, shattered hopes, self-censorship, and identity troubles (Cose, 1993).

Latinas also share gender-specific problems common to other professional women, such as sexual harassment, problems obtaining maternity leave, issues of equal pay for equal work, the reality that traditionally male professions are designed and structured to accommodate the traditional responsibilities of men rather than those of women (Spence, Deaux, & Helmreich, 1983), and the so-called mommy track—the creation of separate and unequal tracks, one for exclusively career-oriented women, the other for those who seek to blend career and parenting, balancing career and family (Schwartz, 1989). However, the *mami* track may be perceived differently by Latinas due to the cultural emphasis on mothering (Anders, 1993). Moreover, like other women of color with professional status, Latinas often experience the second burden of racism in addition to sexism in the workplace, and the additive effects of both (Comas-Díaz & Greene, 1994).

Obtaining a formal education, achieving a professional status, and embarking on an occupational journey is not the end of a professional career for a person of color. Attaining and maintaining a professional position may involve more than being socialized into the dominant-group culture and learning the rules of the corporate and professional culture. To survive and advance in the business and professional worlds, women and minorities need to be socialized into the organizational culture. This socialization includes mastering the corporate gamesmanship, or the games and rules of business that have been designed by and for White men (Harragan, 1977). Corporate gamesmanship not only includes learning the "games your mother never taught you" (Harragan, 1977), but also "swimming with the sharks without being eaten alive" (strategies for succeeding in business) (Mackay, 1988), and learning the "secrets of a corporate headhunter" (strategies for upper management advancement) (Wareham, 1983), among many others. It is very unlikely that many Latino parents, even those who are professionals, have taught their offspring much about corporate gamesmanship. Even if Latinos are willing and able to commit to a professional career, become socialized into the organizational culture, and master corporate gamesmanship, many find themselves located in subsidiary positions within prestigious professions or in positions that do not accord them the autonomy, prestige, or pay customarily associated with successful professional status.

Latinos' membership in an ethnic minority group, their role as classic outsiders, and their subsequent otherness can further interfere with their professional career success. Goal setting, planning, and problem solving are professional skills that can be acquired and formally learned, but their usefulness and effectiveness depend on the professional's working relationships with others (Hennig & Jardim, 1977). Furthermore, career advancement and success often depend on how well professionals fit into the culture of the organization (Cose, 1993) and on how others perceive them (or accept them). Let us consider an example of a transition to a higher step on the career advancement ladder. Within this context, there is a critical difference between supervision and upper management. Supervision requires technical or professional expertise, short-term goal setting and planning, and self-reliance, whereas upper management requires working knowledge of different functional areas, broader long-term goals, a learning base that is informal and behaviorally oriented, and reliance on others (Hennig & Jardim, 1977). Thus, the successful transition from supervision to upper management depends on becoming a member of the informal organizational system, which in turn depends on the acceptance of superiors, colleagues, and subordinates (Hennig & Jardim, 1977). As ethnic minorities, many Latinos are considered outsiders and thus will often experience difficulties being accepted by others. Moreover, in order to be included in the organizational higher echelon, Latinos are required to absolutely fit in. This ability to fit in the upper management structure is frequently translated into being "one of us" (Wareham, 1983) or becoming like the members of the higher echelon. Therefore, because Latinos are ethnoculturally different from the members of the ruling professional class, their inability to be "one of us" can seriously compromise their professional advancement.

Even if Latinos become socialized into the organizational culture and become adept at corporate and professional games, their behaviors may be misinterpreted, and institutional barriers can prevent them from becoming successful players in the game of professional advancement. Like other professionals of color, many Latinos face significant institutional barriers such as the questioning of their qualifications, the glass ceiling, and tokenism.

Institutional Barriers

The ongoing influx of White women and people of color into managerial and other professional ranks traditionally dominated by White males is changing the dynamics of the North American workplace. It is estimated that by the year 2000, the majority of the American labor force will be made up of White women plus men and women of color (Henry, 1990). Similarly, market changes are pressing corporations and companies to accommodate to the diversification of the North American society in order to remain viable.

Many organizations are beginning to examine more intensely the question of how best to incorporate and manage diversity in the workplace (Cox, 1991; Ferdman, 1992; Jackson, 1992; Morrison & Von Glinow, 1990). In contending with the process of incorporating increasing numbers of ethnic minorities and culturally diverse individuals, organizations are also faced with dilemmas regarding the proper ways to handle such differences (Ferdman, 1992). Because these organizations are challenged to manage work force diversity (Jackson, 1992), many engage in inefficient and counterproductive attempts. These attempts often collude with institutional barriers against Latinos with professional status.

Latinos can also experience multiple jeopardy within mainstream organizations. For example, Pettigrew and Martin (1987) describe the triple jeopardy that African Americans face as they are recruited, enter, and seek promotion in organizations. These barriers include negative stereotypes, being the only person of color in a work group, and tokenism. Although Latinos may or may not experience

direct blatant discrimination on the job, there is a tendency to question their qualifications by presuming that their ethnicity and not their merit got them the position or gives them an advantage. Because of social powerlessness, the person of
color typically will be identified in group terms, whereas members of the dominant group will be more likely to see themselves and to be seen by others in individual terms or as not being part of a group (Deschamps, 1982). For instance, many
majority-group members often attribute people of color's success to luck or other
situational factors, while attributing failures to laziness, stupidity, or other internal
factors (Weitz & Gordon, 1993). As Carter (1991) asserts, some individuals suspect
that all people of color with professional status achieved such status because of
affirmative action policies and not because of their merit. He terms this suspicion
the "qualification question."

The glass ceiling phenomenon is another institutional barrier that can be dev-
astating to Latinos with professional status. The "glass ceiling" is a barrier so subtle that it is transparent, yet so strong that it prevents women and people of color
from moving up in the management hierarchy (Morrison & Von Glinow, 1990).
Thus, the glass ceiling is a real institutional barrier that limits Latinos' advancement toward upper management in organizations in the United States. Latinas and
LatiNegros often confront a double-paneled glass ceiling, with ethnicity and gender as one panel and ethnicity and race as the second panel. Similarly, LatiNegras
confront a triple-paneled glass ceiling, composed of ethnicity, race, and gender.
Likewise, gay Latinos frequently encounter a double-paneled glass ceiling due to
their ethnicity and sexual orientation, whereas Latino lesbians encounter a triple-
paneled glass ceiling composed of ethnicity, gender, and sexual orientation.

Tokenism: Professional Latinos or Latino Professionals?

Tokenism is an overwhelming institutional barrier as well as a dysfunctional organizational dynamic. It can be present throughout the different stages of Latinos'
professional career development. Being the only Latino (or one of the very few) in
professional settings often may mean becoming a token, a symbol of how-Latinos-
can-do. A token position is often designed to give affirmative action credibility to
the organization. The fact that overt discrimination is illegal in the United States
offers professionals of color options for legal recourse against discrimination.
However, the sociopolitical and economic contexts further enforce the attribution
of tokenism to many Latinos with professional status. In an era of declining support for affirmative action policies such as reverse discrimination lawsuits, financial constraints, and budgetary cutbacks, suspicion appears to emerge as to why
and how Latinos and other people of color have advanced professionally (Romero
& Garza, 1986). Similarly, whenever people are losing their jobs and socioeconomic decline is visible, it is often easier to blame the troubles on racial minorities—especially those who have made some advancement—than to confront the
political leaders who are responsible (Greider, 1991). This double discrimination in

the professional domain reinforces tokenism, with its dynamics of visibility (invisibility), pressure to perform, and peer resentment.

Tokenism can impart high visibility. By being different, Latinos may be highly visible in a system where success is tied to becoming known in particular ways. Although tokenism may afford an initial access to professional positions, being perceived as a token entails a denial of the Latino's capabilities. Therefore, tokenism is a form of racism because it implies that the Latino is not qualified for his or her professional position, thus reinforcing the qualification question. Although the token does not have to work hard to be noticed, paradoxically, professionals of color have to work extra hard to have their achievements noticed (Comas-Díaz & Greene, 1994).

The token visibility makes Latinos public figures and thus, undermines their individuality and privacy. A token's individual characteristics tend to be distorted to fit stereotypes or familiar generalizations about a person's type (Kanter, 1977) or ethnicity. Because their lives are in the limelight, tokens' work and behavior are scrutinized more closely than those of the members of the dominant group (Comas-Díaz & Greene, 1994). Within this context, problematic situations in the workplace tend to be blamed on the category of membership of the token (Kanter, 1977). The extended symbolic consequences of being a token place added pressure on Latinos who feel that their performance could affect the prospects for other Latinos in the professional setting. The collective orientation within the Latino culture further emphasizes the role of being the gate opener for other Latinos in professional settings. Indeed, the existence of successful ethnic minority role models can help to counteract racist assumptions that people of color cannot succeed (Williams, 1990).

Tokenism entails artificial power or a semblance of power. In discussing corporate female tokenism, Kanter (1977) observes that it is rarity and scarcity, rather than femaleness per se, that bred the dynamics of tokenism. Furthermore, she states that tokenism, like powerlessness, sets in motion self-perpetuating cycles that reinforce the low numbers of women and keep them in the position of tokens. Kanter further argues that members of the dominant group become more aware of their commonality and their differences from the token and, to preserve their commonality, try to keep the token slightly outside. This process often creates psychological resistance or heightened emotional energy toward the outsider's presence.

Tokenism can result in being assigned nonessential tasks or those below one's capacity, bearing minimal responsibilities without autonomy and any real decision-making authority (Comas-Díaz & Greene, 1994; Melia & Lyttle, 1986). In discussing female tokens and their lack of real power, Melia and Lyttle (1986) argue that tokens: (1) extend the males' power by following their dictates; (2) give other women in the organization the perception of female inclusion at the top; (3) experiment with new ideas and policies that may backfire, thus protecting male supremacy; and (4) create an expendable executive who can be scapegoated (by being an asset today and disposable tomorrow).

Tokenism also can generate detrimental consequences for the token, such as self-doubts, loneliness, and alienation, as in the following example.

Nancy, a Chicana, was hired by the federal government as an engineer. After she began working, she realized that her sole responsibility was to develop a newsletter for the office. Although Nancy had no previous experience in developing newsletters, her supervisors did not address her concerns about the assignment. After a year at her position, Nancy entered therapy at the request of her close friends, who were worried about her well-being. Her main complaints were: "I feel useless and inadequate" and "I never had emotional problems before I got this position." The precipitating event was that during an agency activity Nancy was asked to sing and entertain her co-workers. Thus, Nancy realized that not only was she being placed in the position of token by not being used as an engineer, but she was also the ethnic token who entertains. Nancy's predicament was an example of Hill's (Wiltz, 1991) assertion that being a token in a predominantly White environment, with minimal support, can take a profound emotional toll.

The heightened awareness of hiring Latinos who are professionals can, paradoxically, result in making them invisible. In investigating tokens' invisibility, Castro (1990) found that White women and people of color suffer from the invisibility syndrome, whereby White male managers commonly tend to ignore them in meetings and thus overlook their contributions. Here is an example:

Olga, a Mexican-American woman with a master's degree in business administration from an Ivy league university, complained of not being acknowledged when she spoke during staff meetings. She became upset because most of her ideas were used by the organization without acknowledging Olga's authorship. Moreover, they were attributed to a fellow White male colleague. Olga stated: "Not only am I invisible, but I am being plagiarized as well."

Paradoxically, if tokens become too successful, they encounter peer resentment and run the risk of being penalized. This penalization can be translated into retaliation by the members of the dominant group. Kanter (1977) argues that when tokens do well enough to outperform members of the dominant group, it cannot be kept a secret, because the tokens' behaviors are public, and therefore it is more difficult to avoid public humiliation of a colleague from the dominant group. On the other hand, their success may be kept conspicuously secret. This paradox creates a pressure for Latinos who need to maintain a delicate balance between doing well and doing too well, thus generating peer resentment and retaliation. Consider the following example.

María, a Mexican-American psychiatric social worker in an academic setting, was repeatedly advised to publish in order to get promoted. Because María was recognized as a seasoned clinician, particularly in the area of couples therapy, her immediate supervisor suggested that she publish on this topic. She followed his advice, and her book became so popular that it made her the most famous person in the academic institution. Her supervisors, who had previously expressed pleasure at her training skills, appeared to be threatened by her instant national reputation. Soon after the publication of her book, her supervisors and co-workers began to feel resentful and to retaliate by severely criticizing the students under her supervision. By attacking her trainees' work, they were in effect attacking María's work, albeit indirectly, thus minimizing her influence and power in the training institution.

Ethnocultural Occupational Shock, Stress, and Distress

Ethnocultural and sociopolitical factors affect Latinos' entry, adjustment, performance, and advancement in the mainstream professional workplace. Regardless of competence, Latinos with professional status often encounter ethnocultural conflicts within their occupational experience. The Latino with professional status may have to cope with multigenerational guilt and resultant conflict. Individuals who experience privileges and challenges that separate them from their ethnic and gender traditions in the past tend to develop multigenerational guilt (Lerner, 1988). Multigenerational guilt is often associated with a vague sense of hardship, deprivation, and unfulfilled longing for previous generations in their families. The multigenerational guilt can be compounded among Latinos with professional status who cope with the immigrant experience during a multigenerational history of disadvantage.

Latinos' ethnocultural conflicts also extend to their adaptation to the professional and organizational cultures. Organizational cultures frequently reflect the culture of the dominant group. For example, corporate executives are expected to commit to cultural values embracing the Puritan ethic (Wareham, 1983). The ethnocultural conflicts faced by many Latinos often get translated into occupational shock, stress, and distress.

The occupational shock involves the conflicts created by the workplace demands from the dominant cultural values of assertiveness, competition, and individual striving in contrast to the ethnocultural values of personalism, familism, cooperation, and collective orientation. Latinos' occupational stress emerges out of coping with ethnocultural value conflicts, institutional barriers, and dysfunctional organizational dynamics. The occupational distress results from the ethnocultural occupational shock and continuous stress in the professional workplace.

The occupational shock and stress often parallel the cultural shock and bicultural stress that many Latinos experience within the dominant society. As with other ethnic minorities, Latinos' management of cultural demands from the majority culture and the ethnic minority culture may result in bicultural stress (Bell, 1990). Membership in an ethnic minority group requires a constant adjustment between the duality of being both a North American and a Latino within an ethnocentric and racist society. Additionally, membership, identification, and participation in a profession imply complex involvements supporting the norms and values of the dominant society (Gilkes, 1982).

As an illustration, professionals are expected to support and behave according to the needs and values of the mainstream society (Rueschemeyer, 1972). Meeting these expectations may be paradoxical, conflictive, and distressful for many Latinos. The social sharing of systematic experiences shaped by immigration (generational and or individual), ethnocultural conflicts, minority group membership, and by the ethnocentric and racist North American society tends to create an ethnocultural and minority identity tied to the sense of community with other Latinos. Therefore, for some Latinos with professional status, the implied political sensitivity of a multiple and an ethnic minority identity may not be conducive to a full commitment to the values of the dominant society (Comas-Díaz & Greene, 1994).

Occupational Socialization Failure

All newcomers into organizations go through a socialization process (Van Maanen, 1976), and this experience is exacerbated for those whose culture is different from the majority's (Ferdman & Cortés, 1992). As indicated previously, many Latinos have not been socialized into the organizational and professional culture. Thus, a major feature of ethnocultural occupational shock, stress, and distress is socialization failure. Socialization failure is the process whereby severe consequences arise when new members do not get properly socialized into the culture of the host group (Schein, 1987). Therefore, occupational socialization failure occurs when Latinos are not effectively socialized into the dominant-group professional workplace. The occupational socialization failure often results in Latinos' marginalization and accentuation of their experiences as outsiders.

Occupational socialization failure can be pervasive throughout all developmental stages of a professional career. At the entry level, however, occupational socialization failure often results in occupational shock, which frequently involves the following: (1) the qualification question; (2) ambiguous information about the Latino's professional position and its relationship to the organizational power structure; (3) lack of support and respect; (4) negative unconscious assumptions (e.g., Latinos will not have the same level of success as Anglos); (5) ignorance and/or misunderstanding of the organizational culture; (6) exclusionary practices such as inadequate introductions to colleagues and personnel; (7) inadequate corporate gamesmanship skills; and (8) other related dysfunctional dynamics that compel Latinos, regardless of competence, to expend excessive resources on organizational dynamics, with a negative effect on their productivity. Consider the following example illustrative of occupational socialization failure and shock.

Miguel, a Latino with a master's degree in public health, worked as an administrator in a White-dominated professional association agency. He was recruited in another state and was told that his professional experience matched the vacancy. When Miguel requested the organization chart, however, he could not locate his position and was not given information about his role even after repeated inquiries. When he asked a colleague, he was informed that the organization needed a Latino to satisfy a constituency group. The colleague confided that because Miguel was hired for political reasons, he would not be given any substantive work. Miguel became angry and confronted his supervisor during a staff meeting. The supervisor denied any hidden agenda in Miguel's recruitment and, furthermore, denied having any questions regarding Miguel's professional qualification for the position.

Miguel's previous career record had been exemplary, but he had now experienced occupational shock due to socialization failure. He began to feel inadequate as a professional. Miguel experienced a pressure to act like a member of the dominant group while simultaneously representing a Latino constituency group. Paradoxically, he felt like a lone voice in a wilderness while discussing racial and ethnic issues. Although Miguel could not identify any direct discrimination at work, he felt a pressure to emphasize his commonalities with his co-workers and minimize his differences. He began to feel irritable toward his White colleagues. Miguel felt that his accommodating dance to his occupational situation required too much energy and was causing significant emotional strain. He decided to leave the agency to work in a more racially mixed institution.

Occupational Stress and Distress

Occupational socialization failure can become internalized by the Latino with professional status and thus generate occupational stress. Indeed, occupational stress is pervasive for many Latinos with professional status. Similarly, Cose (1993) has identified coping fatigue among professionals of color who confront racial politics in the workplace. Continued experience of racism can produce chronic stress among professionals of color (Byars & Hackett, 1994). The continuous occupational stress can transform itself into distress, which then further compromises Latinos' occupational performance. The organizational dynamics that generate occupational stress and distress often include: (1) tokenism; (2) lack of understanding and support for Latinos' ethnocultural occupational conflicts (e.g., *simpatía* vs. assertiveness); (3) absence of role models and mentoring; (4) deficient communication and/or information-sharing channels; (5) lack of institutional buffers and appropriate responses against group or individual ethnic and gender discriminatory behavior; (6) blaming-the-victim dynamics; (7) unclear evaluation criteria and feedback about the Latino's performance, including mixed messages about success; and (8) glass ceiling limitations. The following vignette illustrates an organization's dysfunctional dynamics of lack of institutional buffers and appropriate responses to discriminatory behavior, blaming the victim, and tokenism.

Carlos, a Puerto Rican lawyer, complained to his supervisor that a White male co-worker had made racist remarks. Carlos was very upset by the incident, and when he discussed it with his supervisor he had an agitated tone. Instead of providing a fair examination of the incident, his supervisor, a White male, criticized Carlos for "being excessively aggressive" and labeled him as having a chip on his shoulder due to his ethnicity.

Another dysfunctional reaction to occupational stress is the internalization of the token image (Ramos-Grenier, personal communication, August 1994). Here the Latino professional becomes nonproductive and accepts the token role, thus fulfilling the stereotype of the Latino professional as incompetent and lazy. Such internalization results in a self-fulfilling prophecy and in a vicious cycle.

Latinos and Latinas: Gender Differences at Work

The combination of ethnicity and gender creates specific ethno-gender results in the professional workplace. These ethno-gender-specific factors significantly affect Latinos differently from Latinas. During mental health treatment, it is important to recognize and address the ethno-gender-specific factors with which Latinos with professional status cope.

Latinos with professional status often face ethnocultural demands due to their gender-role expectations. Within their male roles as providers, many Latinos are expected to assume financial responsibility for elderly parents, younger siblings, grandparents, and extended family members such as aunts, uncles, nephews, and nieces. Thus, because they have an earning potential, Latino professionals are frequently expected to help out their extended families financially. Because of their professional status, which grants them a good education (*una buena educación*), regardless of their financial situation, Latinos are often presumed to "know better," and thus, are considered capable of assuming such financial responsibility. If these ethno-gender-specific expectations are not met, intergenerational conflicts are likely to occur.

These ethno-gender-specific expectations add pressure to Latinos in the workplace. Financial demands from families of origin, extended families, and significant others may hinder Latinos' responses to direct or indirect discrimination at work. They may fear losing employment while being financially responsible for a larger family group. Thus, for many Latinos it may be difficult to negotiate when the stakes are as high as losing their jobs because they begin to concentrate on what they can lose and not on the actual negotiation. For instance, Melia and Lyttle (1986) state that women and other low-power opponents (like most Latinos) are unprepared by training and experience to operate beyond the "penny ante" game. Thus, if during negotiation the suggestion is made to eliminate the Latino's job, this tactic can eliminate his focus on his original goal and prevent him from calling the bluff. On the contrary, those Latinos who take a stand against discrimination and dysfunctional organizational dynamics may find themselves penalized by not receiving promotions, having dead-end jobs, and/or losing employment, which then affects their capacity to take care of their families. The high costs of taking a stand could be interpreted as consequences of Latino professionals' individual selfishness and of not thinking in collective terms about the welfare of their families.

Although Latinos' gender may qualify them for entrance into the "good old boys" professional club, such a club is primarily a White male establishment (Melia & Lyttle, 1986). An illustration of this assertion is the existence of discrepancies between the salaries of Latinos and Whites. In 1992 the median income of

Latino men was 44% of that of White men, while the median income of Latinas was 77% of that of White women (ASPIRA, 1994). As members of an ethnic minority group, Latinos are not full members of the White male establishment. They can be accepted as males but rejected as Latinos. Therefore, many Latinos may receive mixed messages (due to their gender and ethnicity) about their entrance into the club, which can further augment their occupational stress.

Latinas with professional status also confront specific ethno-gender stressors at work. Like other professional women of color, many Latinas encounter racism and sexism in the workplace (Comas-Díaz & Greene, 1994). They experience role conflict, ambiguity, and overload in addition to unrealistic demands and pressures. Latinas cope with the negative impact of sex-role stereotypes and of situational and contextual factors that affect women in a male-dominated arena (Kanter, 1977). Many working Latinas experience the pressure of "having it all." Emerging from a *machista* culture that celebrates the man as chief provider and encases the woman in the role of self-sacrificing mother and homemaker, most Latinas are still forced to define themselves in relationship to the family (Anders, 1993). Thus, when they balance the scale between career and family, the scale seems to be pretipped toward family (Anders, 1993), creating unrealistic expectations and adding stress to professional Latinas.

Although some Latinas may find support from their family and significant others, balancing their multiple roles with conflicting demands can cause more stress. For example, Latina single mothers face serious difficulties in balancing work and family. Even though many of them may have some family support systems for raising their children, they also confront the realities of financial concerns, the immediate need to be both mother and father to their children at times, and numerous other realities (Comas-Díaz & Greene, 1994). As Melia and Lyttle (1986) assert, women simply cannot have it all.

Todos Somos Hermanos? *Gender and Ethnic Dilemmas in the Workplace*

Latinos and Latinas may confront conflicting gender and ethnic loyalties that lead to dilemmas in the workplace. Latinas share common goals with Latinos because their issues are bonded by strong ethnic ties. However, the solidarity among Latinos may be divided across gender lines in the workplace (Comas-Díaz & Greene, 1994). Many men of color may proclaim their sexism in their effort to enhance male power or may appear to ignore gender differences in determining the experience of people of color (Reid, 1988). For example, in discussing male and female power issues within an organizational setting, Melia and Lyttle (1986) assert that not only men join ranks against a woman when male identity is on the line, but that Black men will join ranks with White men against Black women. This ethno-gender dynamic may be shared by some Latinos.

Some Latinos in the professional arena may feel resentful at Latinas' perceived advantage of being a double minority (Comas-Díaz & Greene, 1994). Work institutions seem to encourage this dynamic by often placing women of color in competition against men of color (Comas-Díaz & Greene, 1994). For example, because of the qualification question, a Latina may be perceived as a more "qualified" candidate, given appropriate credentials, in addition to being both a woman and a person of color, and thus able to fill two affirmative actions seats with a single person.

Despite this practice, conflict in loyalties among women of color often result in racial and ethnic factors transcending gender issues (Painton, 1991). Many women of color experience racism as a greater barrier to opportunity in their lives (Almquist, 1989). Moreover, some women of color may feel they are betraying their ethnic group by revealing secrets of men of color's sexism against them (Comas-Díaz & Greene, 1994). Within this context, many women of color have been taught that personal disclosure outside their ethnic and cultural community is treason (Boyd, 1990). Due to the frustration with a racist society, many Latinas may have difficulties holding men responsible for their sexist behavior, sustaining Latinos' *machismo* and their generally privileged role in the family.

Latinas' solidarity with Latinos may be related to their commitment to their families and communities. For Latinas with professional status, interpersonal relationships, including romantic liaisons, appear to be central to their lives and sense of well-being. In research on Latino professional women's well-being, Amaro, Russo, and Johnson (1987) found that although marital status was not associated with psychological distress, it was associated with personal life satisfaction. In other words, professional Latinas with a romantic partner were more satisfied with their personal lives than those who did not have a romantic partner. For a comprehensive analysis of the issues regarding women of color with professional status, the reader is advised to see Comas-Díaz and Greene (1994).

Mental Health Treatment

Tokenism can affect individuals' mental status. The inconsistent occupational status that accompanies the token position can yield unsatisfactory social relationships, unstable self-images, frustration from dealing with contradictory demands (from self and others), and insecurity (Kanter, 1977). Latinos, like many other professionals of color, encounter specific circumstances that must require negotiation on an ongoing basis. For instance, the perpetual weighing of responses to racism and discrimination or the need to monitor one's responses constantly can strain the professional of color (Wiltz, 1991).

Being in a token position tends to reinforce a feeling of powerlessness. The use of coping behaviors characteristic of powerless individuals, such as passive aggression, manipulation, and dependency, means that the professional of color is *reacting* instead of *acting* and therefore cannot consistently make decisions, assume responsibility, or exert leadership in the workplace (Pinderhughes, 1983). Even adaptive coping behaviors can claim a high price among Latinos with professional status. The ethnocultural occupational shock, stress, and distress can deteriorate into mental health problems. Some of the most common mental health problems that Latinos with professional status experience are depression, stress reactions, anxiety, psychosomatic disorders, and addiction.

Several psychotherapeutic approaches can be helpful for this special population. For example, psychodynamic approaches recognize the importance of understanding Latinos' internal and personal experiences, cognitive-behavioral approaches are efficacious in reducing dysfunctional symptoms, and family/ group therapy approaches are highly congruent with Latinos' collectivism. Regardless of theoretical orientation, however, treatment needs to reinforce and restore professionals' sense of competence, self-reliance, and balanced functioning (Comas-Díaz & Greene, 1994). This is crucial because students and professionals of color who become successful tend to have determination, persistence, self-sufficiency, and effective interpersonal skills (Moses, 1991). Therefore, techniques that restore Latinos' previous functioning while acknowledging the importance of family and work contexts are culturally relevant. With its emphasis on contextual factors, interpersonal psychotherapy (Klerman, Weissman, Rounsaville, & Chevron, 1984) can address the person–occupational environment transaction. As an illustration, interpersonal psychotherapy techniques such as inventories, decision analysis, and communication analysis can be particularly effective in dealing with work-related problems (Comas-Díaz & Greene, 1994).

Clinicians working with Latinos with professional status also need to be familiar with alcohol and substance abuse prevention and treatment. Some professional contexts promote alcohol use as a means of conducting business, making it difficult for some individuals to avoid alcohol use (Comas-Díaz & Greene, 1994). In fact, for Latinos there might be a relationship between professional status and alcohol use or abuse. For example, although Latinas report being either abstainers or light drinkers (Caetano, 1989), those with higher income and education are more likely to use alcohol (National Coalition of Hispanic Health and Human Services Organizations, 1988). Consequently, culturally relevant assessment and treatment interventions of alcohol and addictive behaviors among Latino professionals need to be included in their mental health treatment. An example of such interventions is the *future past* technique developed by Comas-Díaz (1989) for the treatment of alcoholic Latinas. In this technique, older Latinas demonstrate to younger Latinas the effects of alcoholism and substance abuse by describing, through their own history, the younger women's potential future if they continue drinking—thus, the "future past." This technique could be used in a group format with professional Latinas, where older women mentor younger ones, modeling functional coping behaviors and discussing dysfunctional ones such as substance abuse.

Occupational Component in Mental Health Treatment

The occupational component acknowledges the person–environment transaction, thus recognizing the organizational and societal contexts of Latinos' occupational lives. Treatment needs to address the management of the ethnocultural occupational stress and distress. This management requires the clinician's awareness and sensitivity to occupational conditions (Jenkins, 1985), organizational dynamics, and ethnocultural conflicts faced by Latinos in the professional arena. More specifically, the occupational component involves the building of skills to deal with ethnocultural conflicts, occupational socialization failure, and dysfunctional organizational dynamics such as the qualification question, glass ceiling, and tokenism.

The occupational socialization failure is an area that requires special attention. Its management specifically involves addressing the client's occupational coping skills for survival and advancement in the professional workplace. As an illustration, LaFromboise (1989) developed a professional skills training manual for decreasing American Indian women's socialization failure and increasing their occupational skills. The manual includes comprehensive workshops on self-esteem, assertiveness, career planning, financial management, and other areas designed to help women develop the skills necessary to succeed in the White professional world. This approach can be modified to be used with Latinos. For example, the clinician can discuss Latino ethnocultural values that have paradoxical effects on the workplace.

Psychoeducation on the interface between organizational issues, personal dynamics, and membership in one or multiple minority groups can be of help in understanding Latinos' complex occupational situation. Moreover, the clinician needs to address issues of tokenism and the glass ceiling actively. As an illustration, several strategies for surviving the glass ceiling range from developing more realistic professional expectations to maintaining emotional and spiritual balance (Wiltz, 1991). Furthermore, exploration and working though of these issues need to be tailored to the particular client. For example, a LatiNegro's experiences with tokenism and the glass ceiling may be different from those of a lesbian Latina.

Psychoeducation can address the management of anger in occupational settings. Coping strategies against racism in the workplace often include self-censorship, silence, mendacity, or lies about the United States' approach to race and ethnicity (Cose, 1993), as well as anger. Ethnoracial rage is the cumulative result of ethnic and racial assaults, traumas, oppression, exclusion and humiliation. The management of anger and rage based on racial inequities is an essential issue for Latinos with professional status. Dealing with discrimination in the workplace further promotes feelings of powerlessness, preventing professionals of color from adopting a creative, problem-solving mind set (Wiltz, 1991). Indeed, problems with anger relate to oppressed individuals' difficulties in creative pursuits (Bernardez-Bonesatti, 1978). In studying the lives of accomplished African Americans, Lawrence-Lightfoot (1994) found that as they age, they experience a stronger racial identification and a deeper sense of racial rage. She suggests that African Americans with professional status can creatively channel their racial rage into their occupations. Within this context, the management of ethnoracial anger in a non-self-defeating way becomes a therapeutic goal. Teaching culturally assertive responses (Comas-Díaz & Duncan, 1985) and conflict management skills and encouraging clients to seek appropriate support systems (Vásquez, 1994) are essential for dealing with racial anger and rage.

Bibliotherapy can be an excellent tool in the ethnocultural occupational treatment approach. Books on organizational dynamics faced by professionals of color are not only effective but also highly congruent with this population's need for achievement, self-reliance, and collective orientation. If clinicians are not familiar with these readings, they may want to review the references in this chapter and/ or contact the different professional associations (American Medical Association, American Bar Association, American Association for the Advancement of Science, American Psychological Association, and others) for recommendations.

The clinician can refer clients to a support group for Latino professionals. If the geographical area where clients live does not have a critical mass of Latinos with professional status, the clinician can encourage them to develop a network at a state or national level. Professional and trade organizations can facilitate the identification of potential support (Comas-Díaz & Greene, 1994). National Latino organizations also can provide potential support for Latinos. Those clinicians who do not have the ethnocultural occupational expertise may need to refer their clients to appropriate professionals for conjoint treatment.

Ethnocultural Occupational Inventory

An occupational inventory aims to facilitate clients' knowledge, development, and enhancement of occupational skills during previous and current work (both paid and pro bono). This inventory examines the history of occupational success and failure, including a reality-based analysis of clients' previous and current occupational coping skills. The inventory examines the presence of ethnic and racial discrimination in the workplace in combination with the interaction of gender, color, class, and sexual orientation. The presence and management of racial anger and rage is addressed.

The occupational inventory additionally entails an evaluation of fears, fantasies, family scripts, and wishes, which are examined in order to expand the context of the clients' occupational experiences. Similarly, the presence and internalization of occupational socialization failure is assessed, addressed, and cognitively challenged. Irrational and dysfunctional belief systems about work are identified and challenged through cognitive-behavioral techniques. Using a systemic approach, the occupational inventory examines the projection of the client's family, career, and personal goals within the development of attainable objectives. This process can help Latinos to assess their occupational professional status realistically. The occupational inventory can be used as both a diagnostic tool and a therapeutic intervention. Table 9.1 summarizes some of the areas to be assessed during an occupational inventory.

Conclusion

Latinos' experiences in the professional workplace accentuate the interface of environmental factors, such as sociopolitical context, organizational dynamics, and membership in an ethnic minority group, with ethnocultural and individual behavior. Many Latinos with professional status face a stressful reality in the

---

TABLE 9.1   Ethnocultural Occupational Inventory

1. Previous and current work (paid and pro bono)
2. Occupational success and failure
3. Occupational socialization failure
4. Discrimination as a professional of color
5. Racial and/or ethnocultural anger and rage
6. Interaction of ethnicity, gender, color, and sexual orientation
7. Previous and current occupational coping skills (functional and dysfunctional)
8. Occupational fears, fantasies, family scripts, and wishes
9. Identification and challenge of irrational and dysfunctional belief systems about work
10. Projection of family, personal, and career goals

---

workplace, including environmental barriers, ethnocultural conflicts, occupational shock, stress, and distress. This reality can lead to mental health problems like depression, stress reactions, anxiety, psychosomatic disorders, and addiction. In order to be effective, relevant, and ethical, mental health treatment needs to include an ethnocultural occupational component.

The ethnocultural occupational component includes the management of the ethnocultural occupational stress and distress, socialization failure, and ethnocultural rage. This systemic component uses psychoeducation, bibliotherapy, and the development of occupational support systems. This chapter has introduced the ethnocultural occupational inventory, a tool for examining and enhancing Latinos' behavior within a person–environment confluence of individual and family dynamics, organizational culture, membership in a minority group, and power dynamics in the workplace.

References

Almquist, E. (1989). The experience of minority women in the United States. In J. Freeman (Ed.), *Women: A feminist perspective* (4th ed.) (pp. 414–445). Mountain View, CA: Mayfield.

Amaro, H., Russo, N. F., & Johnson, J. (1987). Family and work predictors of psychological well-being among Hispanic women professionals. *Psychology of Women Quarterly, 11*(4), 505–521.

Anders, G. (1993, July). The *mami* track. *Hispanic Magazine,* 14–19.

ASPIRA (1994, Summer). *The state of Hispanic education 1994.* Washington, DC: Author.

Bell, E. (1990). The bicultural life experience of career-oriented black women. *Journal of Organizational Behavior, 11,* 459–477.

Bernardez-Bonesatti, T. (1978). Women and anger: Conflicts with aggression in contemporary women. *Journal of American Medical Woman's Association, 33,* 215–219.

Boyd, J. (1990). Ethnic and cultural diversity: Keys to power. In L. S. Brown & M. P. P. Root (Eds.), *Diversity and complexity in feminist therapy* (pp. 151–167). New York: Harworth.

Byars, A. M., & Hackett, L. (1994, August). *Career self-efficacy and women of color.* Paper presented at the annual meeting of the American Psychological Association, Los Angeles.

Caetano, R. (1989). Drinking patterns and alcohol problems in a national survey of U.S. Hispanics. In D. Spiegel, D. Tate, S. Aiken, & C. Christian (Eds.), *Alcohol use among U.S. minor-*

ities. National Institute on Alcohol and Alcoholism. Research Monograph No. 18. Washington, DC: U.S. Government Printing Office.

Carter, S. T. (1991). *Reflections of an affirmative action baby.* New York: Basic Books.

Castro, J. (1990, Fall). Get set: Here they come! *Time, Special Issue: Women: The road ahead, 136,* 50–52.

Cervantes, R. C., Salgado de Snyder, V. N., & Padilla, A. M. (1989). Posttraumatic stress disorder among immigrants from Central America and Mexico. *Hospital and Community Psychiatry, 40,* 615–619.

Comas-Díaz, L. (1989). Culturally relevant issues and treatment implications for Hispanics. In D. R. Koslow & E. Salett (Eds.), *Crossing cultures in mental health* (pp. 31–48). Washington, DC: Society for International Education Training and Research (SIETAR).

Comas-Díaz, L. (1994). LatiNegra: Mental health issues of African Latinas. *Journal of Feminist Family Therapy, 5,* 35–74.

Comas-Díaz, L., & Duncan, J. W. (1985). The cultural context: A factor in assertiveness training with mainland Puerto Rican women. *Psychology of Women Quarterly, 9,* 463–475.

Comas-Díaz, L., & Greene, B. (1994). Women of color with professional status. In L. Comas-Díaz & B. Greene (Eds.). *Women of color: Integrating ethnic and gender identities in psychotherapy.* (pp. 347–388). New York: Guilford Press.

Cose, E. (1993). *The rage of a privileged class.* New York: HarperCollins.

Cox, T. (1991). The multicultural organization. *Academy of Management Executive, 5*(2), 34–47.

Deschamps, J.-C. (1982). Social identity and relations of power between groups. In H. Tajfel (Ed.), *Social identity and intergroup relations* (pp. 85–98). Cambridge: Cambridge University Press.

Edwards, J. E., Rosenfeld, P., Thomas, P. J., & Thomas, M. D. (1993). Willingness to relocate for employment: A survey of Hispanics, non-Hispanic Whites, and Blacks. *Hispanic Journal of Behavioral Sciences, 15,* 121–133.

Falicov, C. J. (1982). Mexican families. In M. McGoldrick, J. K. Pearce, & J. Giordano (Eds.),

Ethnicity and family therapy (pp. 134–163). New York: Guilford Press.

Ferdman, B. M. (1992). The dynamics of ethnic diversity in organizations: Toward integrative models. In K. Kelly (Ed.), *Issues, theory, and research in industrial/organizational psychology* (pp. 339–384). Amsterdam: Elsevier Science Publishers.

Ferdman, B. M., & Cortés, A. C. (1992). Culture and identity among Hispanic managers in an Anglo business. In S. Knouse, P. Rosenfeld, & A. Culbertson (Eds.), *Hispanics in the workplace* (pp. 246–277). Newbury Park, CA: Sage.

Ford Foundation. (1984, June). *Hispanics: Challenges and opportunities.* New York: Ford Foundation. Available from the Ford Foundation, Office of Reports, 320 East 43rd Street, New York, NY 10017.

Gilkes, C. T. (1982). Successful rebellious professionals: The Black woman's professional identity and community commitment. *Psychology of Women Quarterly, 6,* 289–311.

Greider, W. (1991, September 5). The politics of diversion: Blame it on the Blacks. *Rolling Stone,* 32–33, 96.

Harragan, B. L. (1977). *Games mother never taught you: Corporate gamemanship for women.* New York: Warner Books.

Hennig, M., & Jardim, A. (1977). *The managerial woman: Survival manual for women in business.* New York: Pocket Books.

Henry, W. A. (1990, April 9). Beyond the melting pot. *Time, 135*(15), 28–31.

Ho, M. H. (1987). *Family therapy with ethnic minorities.* Newbury Park, CA: Sage Publications.

Jackson, S. E. (1992). *Diversity in the workplace: Human resources initiatives.* New York: Guilford Press.

Jenkins, I. M. (1985). The integration of psychotherapy-vocational interventions: Relevance for Black women. *Psychotherapy, 22,* 394–397.

Kanter, E. R. (1977). *Men and women of the corporation.* New York: Basic Books.

Klerman, G. L., Weissman, M. M., Rounsaville, B. J., & Chevron, E. S. (1984). *Interpersonal psychotherapy of depression.* New York: Basic Books.

LaFromboise, T. D. (1989). *Circles of women: Professional skills training with American Indian women*. Newton, MA: Women's Educational Equity Act Publishing Center.

Lawrence-Lightfoot, S. (1994). *I've known rivers: Lives of loss and liberation*. Reading, MA: Addison-Wesley.

Leggon, C. B. (1980). Black female professionals: Dilemmas and contradictions of status. In L. Rodgers-Rose (Ed.), *The Black woman*. Beverly Hills, CA: Sage Publications.

Lerner, H. G. (1988). *Women in therapy*. New York: Harper & Row.

Mackay, H. (1988). *Swim with the sharks without being eaten alive*. New York: Ivy Books.

McGoldrick, M., Pearce, J. K., & Giordano, J. (Eds.). (1982). *Ethnicity and family therapy*. New York: Guilford Press.

Melia, J., & Lyttle, P. (1986). *Why Jenny can't lead: Understanding the male dominant system*. Saguache, CO: Operational Politics, Inc.

Morrison, A. M., & Von Glinow, M. A. (1990). Women and minorities in management. *American Psychologist, 45*, 200–208.

Moses, L. (1991, July). Ties that bind can limit minority valedictorians. *APA Monitor, 22*, 47.

National Coalition of Hispanic Health and Human Services Organizations. (1988). *Delivering preventive health care to Hispanics: A manual for providers*. Washington, DC: Author.

Navarrette, R. (1993). *A darker shade of crimson: Odyssey of a Harvard Chicano*. New York: Bantam.

Painton, P. (1991, October 28). Women power. *Time, 138*(17), 24–26.

Pettigrew, T. F., & Martin, J. (1987). Shaping the organizational context for Black American inclusion. *Journal of Social Issues, 43*, 41–78.

Pinderhughes, E. (1983). Empowerment of our clients and for ourselves. *Social Casework, 64*, 331–338.

Prillerman, S. L., Myers, H. F., & Smedley, B. D. (1989). Psychosocial stress, academic achievement and psychological well-being of Afro-American college students. In G. L. Berry & J. K. Asamen (Eds.), *Black students: Psychological issues and academic achievement* (pp. 159–217). Newbury Park, CA: Sage Publications.

Reid, P. T. (1988). Racism and sexism: Comparisons and conflicts. In P. A. Katz & D. A. Taylor (Eds.), *Eliminating racism* (pp. 203–221). New York: Plenum Press.

Romero, G. J., & Garza, R. T. (1986). Attributions for the occupational success/failure of ethnic minority and nonminority women. *Sex Roles, 14*, 445–452.

Romero Ramos, G. (1990, November). *From Bushwick to Harvard: The educational experience of urban low-income African Americans and Latinos at selective colleges*. Cambridge MA: Harvard–Radcliffe College, Department of Social Studies.

Rueschemeyer, D. (1972). Doctors and lawyers: A comment on the theory of professions. In E. Friedson & J. Lorber (Eds.), *Medical men and their work*. Chicago: Aldine-Atherton.

Saldaña. D. (1994). Acculturative stress: Minority status and distress. *Hispanic Journal of Behavioral Sciences, 16*, 116–128.

Schein, E. H. (1987). Organizational socialization and the profession of management. In D. A. Kolb, I. M. Rubin, & J. M. McIntyre (Eds.)., *Organizational psychology*. Englewood Cliffs, NJ: Prentice-Hall.

Schwartz, F. N. (1989). Management women and the new facts of life. *Harvard Business Review, 89*, 65–76.

Spence, J. T., Deaux, K., & Helmreich, R. L. (1983). Sex related attitudes and personal characteristics in the United States. *International Journal of Psychology, 18*, 111–123.

Triandis, H. C., Marín, G., Lisansky, J., & Betancourt, H. (1984). Simpatía as a cultural script of Hispanics. *Journal of Personality and Social Psychology, 47*, 1363–1375.

Van Maanen, J. (1976). Breaking in: Socialization to work. In R. Dubin (Ed.), *Handbook of work, organization, and society* (pp. 67–130). Chicago: Rand McNally.

Vargas, G. (1984, Autumn). Recently arrived Central American immigrants: Mental health needs. *Research Bulletin* (pp. 1–3). Los Angeles: Spanish-Speaking Mental Health Research Center.

Vásquez, M. (1994). Latinas. In L. Comas-Díaz & B. Greene (Eds.), *Women of color: Integrating ethnic and gender identities in psychotherapy* (pp. 114–138). New York: Guilford Press.

Wareham, J. (1983). *Secrets of a corporate headhunter.* New York: Jove Publications.

Weitz, R., & Gordon, L. (1993). Images of Black women among Anglo college students. *Sex Roles, 28,* 19–34.

Wheeler, T. C. (Ed.). (1971). *The immigrant experience: The anguish of becoming American.* New York: Penguin Books.

Williams, L. E. (1990). The challenges before Black women in higher education. *Journal of the National Association for Women Deans, Administrators, and Counselors, 53,* 1–2.

Wiltz, T. (1991, May). Glass-ceiling survival. *Essence, 35,* 37.

Chapter *10*

The Evolution of Structural Ecosystemic Theory for Working with Latino Families

JOSÉ SZAPOCZNIK[1]
WILLIAM KURTINES[1,2]
DANIEL A. SANTISTEBAN[1]
HILDA PANTÍN[1]
MERCEDES SCOPETTA[1]

YOLANDA MANCILLA[1]
SERGIO AISENBERG[1]
SCOTT McINTOSH[1]
ANGEL PÉREZ-VIDAL[1]
J. DOUGLAS COATSWORTH[1]

[1]*Spanish Family Guidance Center, Center for Family Studies, Department of Psychiatry and Behavioral Sciences, University of Miami School of Medicine*
[2]*Department of Psychology, Florida International University*

This work was funded in part by National Institute on Drug Abuse Grants #1 RO1 DAO 5334 and 1 P50 DA 07697, Center for Substance Abuse Prevention Grants #1 H86 SPO 2350, and 1 H86 SPO 4927, Center for Substance Abuse Treatment Grant #1 HD7 TIOO47, and Administration for Children and Families Grant No. 90 CL 1111.

This chapter is a revised and updated version of an article by J. Szapocznik, W. M. Kurtines, D. A. Santisteban, & A. T. Río (1990). Interplay of advances between theory, research, & application in treatment interventions aimed at behavior problem children and adolescents, *Journal of Consulting and Clinical Psychology, 1990, Vol. 58*, pp. 696–703. Copyright © 1990 by the American Psychological Association. Adapted with permission.

Correspondence regarding this chapter should be addressed to José Szapocznik, Ph.D., Department of Psychiatry, University of Miami, 1425 N.W. 10 Ave, Suite 302, Miami FL 33136, (305) 243-4592.

This chapter describes the evolution of a structural ecosystems theory for working with Latino families. It also describes how our work began with a structural systems approach to family therapy and gradually evolved into a more ecosystemic, family-focused, structural approach that offers a more complete representation of the complexity of a contextualist perspective in that it targets not only the family but also other systems that have an impact on the child and the family.

The structural ecosystemic theory evolved as part of more than two decades of research at the Spanish Family Guidance Center at the University of Miami. The development of this approach involved a continuous interplay among theory, research, and application at several levels. With respect to theory, the structural orientation of our approach draws from both the structural (Minuchin, 1974; Minuchin & Fishman, 1981; Minuchin, Rosman, & Baker, 1978) and strategic (Haley, 1976; Madanes, 1981) traditions in family systems theory, whereas the ecosystemic orientation of our approach draws from the social ecological theory of Bronfenbrenner (1977, 1979, 1986). With respect to application, our work has focused on developing prevention and treatment interventions for what has emerged as a recurrent clinical problem, vis-á-vis behavior problems and drug abuse among Latino children and adolescents. This has involved the investigation of the cultural characteristics of the Latino population (primarily Cuban American but increasingly Nicaraguan, Colombian, Puerto Rican, Peruvian, and Salvadoran), the role that cultural factors may play in the process of prevention and treatment, and the role that cultural factors may play in determining differential outcomes. This structural ecosystemic, family-focused approach to working with Latino families is a direct outgrowth of our efforts to develop and investigate novel, theoretically based, and culturally appropriate interventions that can be used in the prevention and treatment of behavior problems and drug abuse among Latino youth and families.

Elsewhere we have described our approach as multisystemic and structural, and this is a reasonably accurate description of the basic thrust of our work. Our approach, however, is itself embedded in a larger perspective, one that is usually called *contextualism*. Looking back over the past two decades, it is clear that our work and thinking has always been profoundly contextualist in nature, although we have come to recognize and articulate more fully our contextualistic roots in our recent works (cf. Szapocznik & Kurtines, 1993).

Contextualism refers to the view that behavior cannot be understood outside of the context in which it occurs. Contextualism is concerned with the interaction between the organism and its environment—explaining and understanding the individual in a changing world. Our work began with a focus on the family as the basic context for child functioning. Subsequently, we defined family functioning in terms of the repetitive patterns of interactions that occur within a family, and adopted a structural family therapy approach. More recently, as we widened our contextual focus, we became more directly concerned with the impact of other systems on the child (e.g., school, peers, community), and on the relationship between these systems. Finally, we recognized that a tool for understanding within- and between-systems interactions is found in our prior structural work. This means that our interventions should focus on the repetitive patterns of interactions that occur within and between systems. Hence, our latest development, which is presented as the end of our evolutionary chain, is ecosystemic, family-focused, and structural. This approach now pervades our work at many levels, ranging from clinical interventions to community and school-based interventions.

This chapter describes six major challenges that we confronted as part of the evolution of our approach. These are summarized as the need to: (1) develop a culturally appropriate intervention for Cuban youths presenting behavioral problems; (2) develop appropriate measures to assess structural family change; (3) develop an intervention focused on one family member instead of the entire family unit; (4) implement an intervention to engage families into treatment; (5) assess the effectiveness of a structural family system intervention as compared to traditional interventions; and (6) develop a structural ecosystemic family intervention.

Culture-Specific Interventions

The 1970s witnessed a tremendous increase in the number of Latino adolescents involved with drugs. In response to this problem, our work began in 1972 in a small storefront location funded by the Office of Economic Opportunity, Department of Health, Education and Welfare. The program was established to provide services to the local Latino community. The program of research that emerged from these activities was thus rooted in a very real and pressing problem.

The first challenge encountered by our clinical program (from 1972 to 1978) was to identify and develop a culturally appropriate treatment intervention for Cuban youths presenting with behavioral problems. In order to define the Cuban culture and to develop a better understanding of how it resembled, and differed from, the mainstream culture, a comprehensive study on value orientations was designed based on the pioneer work on world views by Kluckhohn and Strodtbeck (1961). The major study on value orientation (Szapocznik, Scopetta, Aranalde, & Kurtines, 1978) that ensued determined that a family-oriented approach in which therapists take an active, directive, present-oriented leadership role matched the expectations of the population.

Structural Family Therapy

The study mentioned earlier provided the first indicator that a structural and systemic approach to family therapy was particularly well suited to this population (Szapocznik, Scopetta, & King, 1978). Structural family therapy had been developed a decade earlier by a team of primarily Latino therapists led by Salvador Minuchin and working with inner-city African-American and Latino families in Philadelphia.

A second indicator of the need for a structural systems approach was that in working with Latino families with children or adolescents, the stress of acculturation may cause disruptions within the family that require direct intervention (Sza-pocznik & Kurtines, 1989; Szapocznik, Scopetta, Kurtines, & Aranalde, 1978; Szapocznik, Kurtines, & Fernandez, 1980). More specifically, normal family processes may combine with acculturation processes to exaggerate intergenerational differences and exacerbate intrafamilial conflicts (Szapocznik, Santisteban, Kurtines, Pérez-Vidal, & Hervis, 1984). A prototypical example can sometimes be found in the case of immigrants who find themselves in a bicultural context. In this case, the adolescent's normal striving for independence combines with the adolescent's powerful acculturation to the American cultural value of individualism. The parent's normal tendency to preserve family integrity, on the other hand, combines with the parent's tenacious adherence to the common Latino cultural value of strong family cohesion and parental control. The combination of intergenerational and cultural differences may produce an exacerbated and intensified intrafamilial conflict in which parents and adolescents feel alienated from each other, as depicted in Figure 10.1.

Structural family therapy is particularly well suited to address this type of situation because it is possible to separate content from process. At the content level, the cultural and intergenerational conflicts can be the focus of attention and make this form of therapy particularly well attuned to the Latino family. At the process level, structural family therapy seeks to modify the breakdown in communication

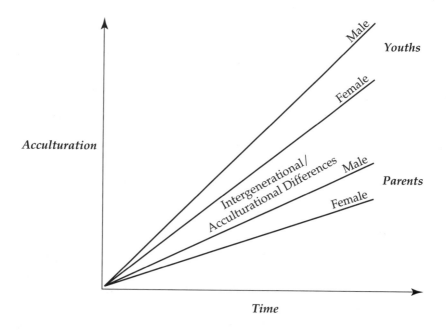

FIGURE 10.1   **The Development of Intergenerational/Acculturation Differences in Nuclear Families as a Function of Time**

Source: Reproduced from J. Szapocznik, M. A. Scopetta, W. Kurtines, & M. A. Aranalde (1978), "Theory and Measurement of Acculturation," *Interamerican Journal of Psychology, 12,* 113–130.

resulting from these intensified cultural and intergenerational conflicts. More specifically, in treating these families, the *content* of therapy may be issues of cultural differences, differences in rates of acculturation, or parent adjustment to changes in their youngster. *Process*-level interventions promote more adaptive communication between family members, thus dissolving barriers to discussing topics like those just mentioned. In this fashion therapy can be tailored to the specific and unique cultural and intergenerational conflicts of Latino families.

To investigate the effectiveness of a family-oriented intervention with Latino families, we conducted a series of pilot research studies (Scopetta, Szapocznik, King, Ladner, Alegre, & Tillman, 1977) in order to compare individual, conjoint family, and family-ecological interventions. These pilot studies provided evidence for the efficacy of family therapy in a conjoint mode. In particular, structural family therapy was found to be compatible with the issues and problems of the Latino population.

Brief Strategic Family Therapy (BSFT)

As a result of these pilot studies, the effectiveness of this modality with behavior problem youths was enhanced by modifying and/or adapting certain components such as making structural family therapy more strategic and time-limited. To distinguish the particular structural family therapy approach that emerged from this phase of our work, we termed it Brief Strategic Family Therapy (BSFT). The evolution of our structural ecosystemic theory thus began with a structural and systemic approach to family therapy. We also began to recognize the profound effect that contextual factors had on Latino families.

More specifically, in utilizing BSFT with recent immigrant Latino families, we realized how profoundly the process of immigration and acculturation could affect the family as a unit as well as each of its individual members. It became evident that these clinical/cultural issues required specifically designed interventions. As a result of this experience, the next step was the development of an intervention that was specifically designed to address the constellation of immigration/acculturation stressors that this population was facing and the clinical problems this constellation of stressors was producing. Our work investigating the clinical impact of exposure to a culturally pluralistic environment best exemplifies the complexity of the embeddedness of contexts, both social and cultural (see, e.g., Szapocznik & Kurtines, 1993).

Bicultural Effectiveness Training (BET)

As a result of this increased understanding of the complex interplay between social and cultural contexts in affecting conduct disorders in youth, we developed an intervention to enhance bicultural skills in all family members, labeled Bicultural Effectiveness Training (BET). BET is an intervention model specifically designed to ameliorate the acculturation-related stresses confronted by two-generation immigrant families. Although BET is based on structural family theory, it is delivered as a psychoeducational modality. BET provides family members with skills for coping effectively with the acculturation stress and conflict that confronts families living at the interface of manifestly conflicting cultural values and behavioral expectations. BET teaches families to feel enriched rather than stressed by the unique opportunities provided them in their daily cross-cultural existence. BET consists in a package of 12 lessons described in more detail in Szapocznik, Santisteban, Kurtines, Pérez-Vidal, and Hervis (1984).

The Bicultural Effectiveness Training study was a clinical trial which we conducted to investigate the relative effectiveness of BET in comparison to structural family therapy (Szapocznik, Santisteban, Rio, Pérez-Vidal, Kurtines, & Hervis, 1986). We utilized an experimental design by randomly assigning 41 Cuban-American families with behavior-problem adolescents to either a Bicultural Effectiveness Training or a Structural Family Therapy condition. Participants were administered a comprehensive battery of tests at the time of intake (pretesting), and at the time of termination (posttesting). Instruments were selected such that outcome could be examined from several perspectives, including the areas of adolescent symptomatology, family functioning, and family acculturation level.

The results indicated that Bicultural Effectiveness Training was as effective as Structural Family Therapy in improving adolescent and family functioning. These findings suggested that BET could accomplish the goals of family therapy while focusing on the cultural content that made this therapy appropriate for Latino families (Szapocznik, Santisteban, Rio, Pérez-Vidal, Kurtines, & Hervis, 1986).

Family Effectiveness Training (FET)

Subsequently, we combined Brief Strategic Family Therapy and Bicultural Effectiveness Training into a package labeled Family Effectiveness Training (Szapocznik, Santisteban, Rio, Pérez-Vidal, & Kurtines, 1986). We conducted a study to investigate the effectiveness of Family Effectiveness Training, a prevention/intervention modality for Latino families with children presenting with emotional and behavioral problems (Szapocznik, Santisteban, Rio, Pérez-Vidal, Santisteban, & Kurtines, 1989). We randomly assigned 79 families and their preadolescent children to either an FET condition or a Minimum Contact Control condition. Families were extensively tested at the time of intake (pretesting), at termination (posttesting), and at two follow-up assessments. The instruments selected measured both child behavior and family functioning.

The results of this study indicated that families in the FET condition showed significantly greater improvement than did control families on independent measures of structural family functioning, on problem behaviors as reported by parents, and on a self-administered measure of child self-concept. Furthermore, the results of the follow-up assessments indicated that the effects of the FET intervention were maintained over time.

More recently, the complexity of our cultural context has changed considerably. When we developed BET and FET in the 1970s, Cuban-born families lived in a culture dominated primarily by Cuban immigrants and mainstream White

Americans. By the 1990s, however, the cultural context of Miami had become a complex melange including Cuban Americans, Cuban immigrants, and mainstream White Americans, as well as Latin Americans from nearly all countries in the Western Hemisphere, African Americans, and Haitian immigrants. Consistent with these contextual changes, we redesigned our BET intervention into a Multicultural Effectiveness Training Program (Mancilla & Szapocznik, 1994) to help non-Cuban Latino parents develop an understanding of the complex cultural context in which they are embedded.

Measurement of Structural Family Change

The second challenge after developing a culture-specific intervention was to construct a clinically appropriate measure to assess structural family change. In attempting to test the effects of interventions that were based on structural family systems theory, we required a valid measure of family functioning.

In undertaking this effort, we borrowed from the work of Minuchin and his colleagues who developed the Wiltwick Family Tasks (Minuchin et al., 1978). These tasks were useful as standard stimuli, but the scoring presented problems of standardization and reliability. For this reason, we reorganized the scoring procedure into broad dimensions of structural family functioning; standardized the administration procedure; developed a detailed manual with anchors and examples to enhance reliability and replicability of the scoring procedure; and obtained validational evidence for the usefulness and nonobtrusiveness of this procedure in family therapy outcome studies (Szapocznik, Rio, Hervis, Mitrani, Kurtines, & Faraci, 1991).

We developed the Structural Family Systems Ratings (SFSR) which (Szapocznik et al., 1991) defines family structure as the family's repetitive patterns of interactions. The SFSR defines family structure in terms of five interrelated dimensions:

1. *Structure* is the basic and most important dimension and is a measure of leadership, subsystem organization, and communication flow.
2. *Resonance* is a measure of the sensitivity of family members toward one another. It focuses on boundaries and emotional distance between family members.
3. *Developmental stage* assesses the extent to which each family member's roles and tasks correspond with the developmental stage of the family and its members.
4. *Identified patienthood* assesses the extent to which the family demonstrates that the primary family problem is the fault of one member who exhibits the symptom.
5. *Conflict resolution* is a measure of the family's ability to express, confront, and negotiate differences of opinion, disagreements, and conflicts.

The psychometric properties of the SFSR have been investigated with over 500 Latino families in treatment (Szapocznik, Rio, Hervis, Mitrani, Kurtines, & Faraci, 1991). Content validity was built into the SFSR by matching the scales with key structural concepts. An extensive examination of construct validity revealed that the SFSR measures changes that can be attributed to structural family therapy and that it discriminates interventions that produce structural family change from interventions that do not produce such structural change (Szapocznik et al., 1991).

The SFSR represents one of the most important advances in our program of research (Kazdin, 1993). It is a theoretically meaningful measure of structural family functioning that has become an essential tool for answering some of the critical questions posed by subsequent steps in our program of research. We have continued to refine the SFSR by extending its use to nonresearch clinical settings (cf. Szapocznik & Kurtines, 1989).

Currently we are working on several adaptations of the SFSR. The SFSR was initially developed to assess family functioning in Cuban-American families with a behavior-problem child or adolescent. Currently, we are striving to adapt this measure to the range of family constellations that occur in our minority communities of the 1990s, including single-parent families and extended kinships. Regarding the measurement of treatment outcomes, it is becoming increasingly difficult to separate the effects of changes in family composition from the effects of the intervention.

One-Person Family Therapy

A national survey sponsored by the National Institute on Drug Abuse revealed that family therapy was widely viewed as a treatment of choice for adolescents experiencing behavioral and drug abuse problems (Coleman, 1976). Unfortunately, the vast majority of counselors who worked with this population reported that they were not able to bring whole families into treatment. Consequently, a third challenge arose consisting in the need to develop a procedure that would achieve the goals of family therapy (changes in maladaptive family interactions) without having to have the whole family present.

To meet this challenge, it was necessary to question some basic theoretical assumptions of conventional family systems practice. Structural family systems theory postulates that drug abuse in youths is a symptom of maladaptive interactional patterns in the family. That is, the family may unwittingly support or encourage the symptomatic behavior, or, alternatively, the family may be incapable of behaving in ways that would eliminate the undesirable behavior. Theoretically, it follows that in order to eliminate problem behaviors, a change to more adaptive family interactions is required. Finally, a basic assumption of conventional family systems theory has been that in order to bring about changes in family interactions, it is necessary to work directly with the conjoint family.

In an effort to meet the requirements of a modality that would change family functioning while focusing on one member only, we developed a modality labeled

One-Person Family Therapy (Szapocznik, Kurtines, Pérez-Vidal, Hervis, & Foote, 1990; Szapocznik & Kurtines, 1989). What made One-Person Family Therapy possible was the novel application of the principle of complementarity (Minuchin & Fishman, 1981). This principle establishes the nature of the interdependency of the behaviors of the members of a system by postulating that a change in the behavior of one family member will require corresponding changes in the behavior of other family members. What is novel about the one-person modality is the deliberate and strategic use of this principle in directing the identified patient in therapy to change her or his behavior in ways that will effect an adjustment in the behavior of other family members toward the identified person experiencing the problem. Several techniques can be used for this purpose, such as role playing by the identified person of several family roles, role playing by the identified person and therapist of complementary roles, using the empty chair technique, and using a blackboard to diagram structural family relationships. These activities allow the therapist to help the person restructure both his or her internalized representation of the family interactional pattern as well as his or her role in maintaining such interactions (Szapocznik, Kurtines, Foote, Pérez-Vidal, & Hervis, 1983).

Having developed a clinical modality based on the assumption that by working strategically with one person it was possible to change family functioning, we designed a rigorous investigation to test these assertions. Such a study was now possible because of the availability of the SFSR to test for changes in family structure. We conducted the Brief Strategic Family Therapy study, a major clinical trials study, which compared the conjoint versus one-person modalities of BSFT (Szapocznik, Kurtines, Foote, Pérez-Vidal, & Hervis, 1983, 1986). This experimental study consisted in randomly assigning 72 Latino-American families with drug-abusing adolescents to either a conjoint or a one-person treatment modality. Both conditions were designed to use exactly the same theoretical framework (BSFT) so that only one variable (conjoint versus one-person) would differ between the conditions. Considerable effort was spent in developing a treatment manual and guidelines for both the one-person condition and the conjoint condition to ensure standardization and replicability of the study (Szapocznik, Hervis, Kurtines, & Spencer, 1984; Szapocznik, Kurtines, Pérez-Vidal, & Foote, 1990; Szapocznik & Kurtines, 1989). Participant families were tested at the time of intake (pretesting), at termination (posttesting), and at a six-month follow-up. The instruments selected measured outcomes of adolescent behavior change and family functioning. The latter was assessed by using the SFSR.

The results indicated that One-Person Family Therapy was as effective as the conjoint modality not only in bringing about significant improvement in behavior problems and drug abuse in the youths, but also in bringing about and maintaining significant improvements in family functioning (Szapocznik, Kurtines, Foote, Pérez-Vidal, & Hervis, 1983, 1986). Consequently, the results of this study demonstrated that it is possible to change family interactions even when the whole family is not present at most sessions, resulting in an important advance in our theoretical understanding of family treatment. As became evident in our later research, however, one-person interventions that do not specifically target family change are not likely to bring about desirable changes in family interactions (Szapocznik, Rio, Murray, Cohen, Scopetta, Rivas-Vásquez, Hervis, Posada, & Kurtines, 1989). This research has shown that it is possible to change maladaptive family interactions while working primarily with one person, but to accomplish these changes it may be necessary to target family interactions strategically as part of the therapeutic process.

Engaging Hard-to-Reach Families

Although our work has established that it is possible to conduct family therapy through one person, getting that one person into treatment has continued to be a problem. For example, in the previous study only 250 clients/families of approximately 650 initial contacts (who met intake criteria on the basis of a phone screen) came for intake. Of this number, only 145 completed the intake procedure and only 72 completed treatment.

The fourth major challenge was to develop a procedure to engage drug abusers and their families in treatment more effectively. The approach that we developed, Strategic Structural Systems Engagement (Szapocznik, Kurtines, Pérez-Vidal, Hervis, & Foote, 1990; Szapocznik & Kurtines, 1989) is based on the premise that resistance to change within the family results from two systems properties. First, the family is a self-regulatory system; that is, the family system tends to maintain structural equilibrium or the status quo, which in the case of drug-abusing or problem-behavior youth can be accomplished by staying out of therapy. Second, while the presenting symptom may be drug abuse, the initial obstacle to change is resistance to coming into treatment. When resistance to coming into treatment is defined as the symptom to be targeted by the intervention, the structural systems model allows for a redefinition of resistance as a manifestation or symptom of the family's current pattern of interaction. Therefore, we have argued that the same systemic and structural principles that apply to the understanding of family functioning and treatment also apply to the understanding and treatment of the family's resistance to engagement (Szapocznik et al., 1990).

Our work on Structural Systems Engagement was made possible by the advances in the theoretical understanding that came out of our earlier research on One-Person Family Therapy. Through this work, we developed a more profound understanding of the power of the principle of complementarity as a mechanism to change family interactions through one person. In developing our specialized engagement procedures we drew from One-Person Family Therapy techniques designed to change family interactions through working with one person. Typically, initial contacts requesting treatment for problem-behavior and drug-abusing youths are made by a parent. In the vast majority of these families, however, either a parent is unwilling to become involved in therapy on a conjoint basis, or, more frequently, the problem youth refuses to come into treatment.

Having defined resistance to treatment as an undesirable problem or symptom to be overcome, the strategic structural model postulates that this symptom of resistance to engagement into treatment is maintained or encouraged by the family's patterns of interactions. Thus, within our framework, the solution to overcoming the undesirable *symptom* of resistance is to restructure the family's pattern of interaction that permits the symptom of resistance to continue to exist. It is here that One-Person Family Therapy techniques become useful because the person making the contact and requesting help becomes our *one person,* through whom we can potentially help restructure the family's pattern of interaction that is maintaining the symptom of resistance. Specific techniques employed to achieve such a goal include role reversal, Gestalt fantasy techniques, and splitting the target person's observant ego. As sufficient intrapersonal change has occurred, the therapist can then engage the person as a therapeutic ally. Having accomplished this first phase of the therapeutic process in which resistance has been overcome and the family, including the *offending* drug-abusing youth, have now agreed to participate in therapy, it becomes possible to shift the focus of the intervention toward the removal of the presenting symptoms of problem behavior and drug abuse.

Our clinical experience suggests that the patterns of interactions that maladaptively permitted the presenting symptom to exist may be the same maladaptive pattern of interactions that keep the family from coming into treatment. Hence, with these so-called hard-to-reach families the therapist typically begins the intervention with the first phone call.

We conducted a major study to test the effectiveness of Structural Systems Engagement in engaging and increasing rates of therapy completion with Latino families (Szapocznik, Pérez Vidal, Brickman, Foote, Santisteban, Hervis, and Kurtines, 1988). This study randomly assigned 108 Latino families with adolescents experiencing behavior problems (who were either suspected of using or observed using drugs) to one of two conditions: Structural Systems Engagement or Engagement as Usual. The Engagement as Usual condition was the control condition. In this control condition, the clients were approached in a way that resembled as closely as possible the kind of engagement that usually takes place in outpatient centers. To define this *Engagement as Usual condition,* we conducted a survey of a representative sample of local outpatient treatment centers using role-playing techniques. In these role plays, a staff member went through a standard protocol on the phone in which the staff member played a mother or father wanting treatment for an adolescent suspected of using drugs who refused to come into treatment at the parents' request. The results of this survey were used to define the parameters for the Engagement as Usual condition. In the experimental condition, client families were engaged using techniques developed specifically for use with families resisting therapy. We developed a manual for the experimental condition and described modality guidelines for both conditions in order to ensure the standardization and replicability of the study (Szapocznik & Kurtines, 1989; Szapocznik, Kurtines, Pérez-Vidal, Hervis, & Foote, 1990).

To monitor treatment integrity, all contacts were logged and all sessions were reviewed and rated by an independent clinical research supervisor who was blind to the conditions of the study. Treatment integrity analyses revealed that interventions in both conditions adhered to guidelines and that the two modalities were clearly distinguishable by the level of engagement effort applied ($F(1,106) = 106.69, p < .001$).

Measurement

The theoretical advances in understanding the nature of resistance to entering treatment, and the concomitant advances in developing strategies for overcoming this type of resistance, required a reconceptualization of our approach to treatment outcome measures. Because the purpose of this study was to increase family engagement in treatment, we had to move beyond the analysis of pre/post outcome measures. Engagement was defined as the rate of treatment completion.

Most studies assess treatment outcomes in individuals who actually complete treatment. Because many studies suggest that there are no differential treatment effects among completers, differential retention/attrition rates may be a critically important measure that distinguishes between different types of interventions (Kazdin, 1986). Therefore, interventions should also be evaluated in terms of their effectiveness on treatment completion rates. Controlling this variable may increase the clinical significance of conventional outcome measures.

Results

Two basic findings can be drawn from our study (Szapocznik et al., 1988). The first had to do with the effectiveness of the Structural Systems Engagement intervention. As Figure 10.2 shows, the effects of the experimental condition were dramatic. Over 57% of the families in the Engagement as Usual condition failed to be engaged into treatment. In contrast, only 7.15% (4 families) in the Structural Systems Engagement condition were lost to treatment ($\chi^2(1,108) = 29.64$, $p < .0001$). Group differences in retention rates were also dramatic. In the Engagement as Usual condition, dropouts represented 41% of the cases that were engaged, whereas dropouts in the Structural Systems Engagement condition represented 17% of the engaged cases. Thus, of the total number of cases initially assigned, 25% in the Engagement as Usual condition and 77% in the Structural Systems Engagement condition were successfully terminated ($\chi^2(1,108) = 26.93$, $p < .0001$). Families completing treatment in both conditions showed significant improvements in adolescent's functioning ($F(1,57) = 39.83$, $p < .0001$), whereas differences across the engagement conditions were not significant. As mentioned earlier, significant between-group differences were found in measures of treatment engagement.

A second major finding of this study was the identification of four distinct types of resistant families and the development of intervention strategies for engaging them in treatment. These four types are listed in order of frequency of occurrence:

Percentage

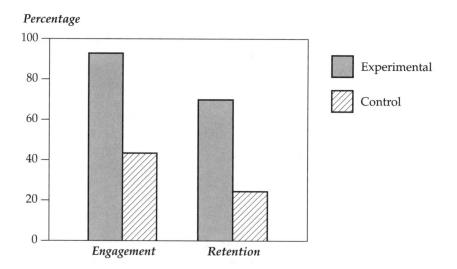

FIGURE 10.2   Differential Engagement and Retention Rates Across the Experimental and Control Conditions

Source: Szapocznik, J., Kurtines, W., Santisteban, D. A., & Río, A. T. (1994). Interplay of advances between theory, research, and application in treatment interventions aimed at behavior problem children and adolescents. *Journal of Consulting and Clinical Psychology, 58*(6), 696–703 [Copyright 1994 by the American Psychological Association, Inc.].

1. The first type of resistant family was characterized by being structured around the target member, who exercises significant power within the family unit. In these families, the Structural Systems Engagement intervention required the establishment of an alliance with the target member in order to engage the family in treatment.

2. The second type of resistant family was characterized by a strong mother–son alliance, while the father was disengaged or distant. In this type of family, the therapist focused on the mother to help her develop a closer relationship with the father in order to increase the probability of his attending the treatment sessions.

3. A third type of resistant family involved the presence of an ambivalent mother. Although she usually initiates a request for help, she is likely to protect the target youth member and shows ambivalence toward involving her husband in family treatment. In these cases, the therapist typically circumvented the mother and dealt directly with the father (upon seeking the mother's approval), who then played the central role in attempting to bring the family for treatment.

4. The fourth type involved one or more members of the family who were concerned about disclosing private family information during treatment. In these

cases, the therapist would attempt to establish a confidentiality agreement delimiting the scope of information to be disclosed in therapy.

We designed a second study to replicate these engagement findings and to begin exploring the mechanisms accounting for the intervention effects (Santisteban, Szapocznik, Pérez-Vidal, Kurtines, Murray, & LePerriere, 1996). This study used a larger and more culturally representative sample, a more stringent criterion for successful engagement, and two control conditions. A statistical analysis of the effects of the specialized engagement interventions showed that they were significantly effective. Highly significant differences were found between the experimental engagement condition and the two control conditions on rate of engagement. In the experimental condition, 81% of the families assigned to this condition (42 of 52) were successfully engaged. In contrast, under the two control conditions, only 60% (84 of 141) of the families assigned were successfully engaged in treatment (χ^2 (1,193) = 7.5, $p < .01$).

When engagement rates of the second study were compared with those of the original study using the original criteria (attending intake), there were no significant differences between the two experimental engagement conditions (first and second studies) (χ^2 (1, $N = 107$) = .57). In the first study, 93% of families assigned to the experimental condition (51 of 55) were successfully engaged in treatment. In comparison, in the second study (using the original criteria) 88% of families assigned to the experimental condition (46 of 52) were successfully engaged.

In addition to investigating the overall efficacy of our specialized engagement intervention, we also investigated whether culture/ethnicity might influence intervention efficacy within our multicultural Latino sample. The data suggested that the differential effectiveness of specialized engagement procedures, as measured by the rate of engagement, were dramatic across different Latino groups. For non-Cuban Latinos, the rate of engagement in treatment was very high (97%). In contrast, for Cuban families assigned to the experimental condition, the rate of treatment engagement was only 64%. The difference between the two groups was significant (χ^2 (1,51) = 9.33, $p < .01$). A more fine-grained case-by-case analysis of these findings suggested that historic differences between these groups may account for the different patterns of resistance to engaging into therapy. These findings allowed us to begin to articulate the mechanisms by which culture/ethnicity and other contextual factors may influence the clinical processes related to treatment engagement (Santisteban et al., 1996; Szapocznik & Kurtines, 1993).

In summary, the results of our second more rigorous study of specialized engagement strategies provided strong support for the effectiveness of these specialized engagement interventions and an indication of the extent to which contextual factors such as cultural/ethnic characteristics and a population's role within a community network can have significant effects on the efficacy of therapeutic processes. Taken together, these results strongly support our belief that therapeutic interventions must be responsive to the constantly evolving population-contextual conditions (Santisteban et al., 1996).

Structural Family Therapy versus Traditional Treatment Modalities

This section focuses on the issue of the relative effectiveness of a structural family systems approach, when compared to other widely used clinical interventions.

Structural Family Therapy versus Individual Psychodynamic Therapy

We conducted a major clinical trials study to investigate the relative effectiveness of structural family therapy against individual psychodynamic child therapy. We decided that psychodynamic therapy was an appropriate comparison approach after conducting a survey study with local child and adolescent therapists. We found that most defined their treatment modality as psychodynamic in nature.

This study also investigated the mechanisms accounting for change under each of the two theoretical/clinical approaches. Both approaches, structural family and child psychodynamic, assume underlying etiologies to symptoms. Both treatment modalities aim at the elimination or reduction of symptoms. However, they postulate different processes as being primarily responsible for symptom resolution. Traditionally, the psychodynamic approach postulates that child psychodynamic functioning is the intervening variable that needs to be modified in order to eliminate the symptoms. Structural family therapy, on the other hand, postulates that what needs to be modified are the family interactions, which account for the behavioral problems. Because of these important differential theoretical predictions, this study explored the effect of each theoretical modality (structural family and child psychodynamic) on measures of family functioning and individual change.

A problem that remained to be solved in this study was controlling for attention placebo effects. For this purpose we called on the experience of others (Strupp & Hadley, 1979; McCardle & Murray, 1974) in designing an intervention that was made up of the kinds of activities that might be carried out by these children "naturally"—that is, when not engaged in therapy. Hence, we designed an attention placebo control condition comprised of recreational activities led by a recreational worker who had no training in psychotherapy.

The basic design used in the study was a mixed experimental design. The between-groups factor was intervention condition with three levels (family structural, child psychodynamic, and control). The within-groups variable was assessment time (pretherapy, post-therapy, and follow-up). Under an experimental design, 69 6- to 12-year-old Latino boys were randomly assigned to one of three conditions: structural family therapy, individual psychodynamic therapy, or a recreational activity control group (Szapocznik et al., 1989). To monitor for treatment integrity, all sessions were videotaped and randomly rated using a checklist. Interjudge reliability on treatment integrity ratings yielded a kappa of .89. Treatment integrity analyses revealed that therapists adhered to guidelines and conducted interventions in a fashion consistent with their respective modes of interventions.

Results. Attrition data were analyzed using chi-squares and outcome data were analyzed using a mixed-design analysis of variance. The results of the analyses revealed several important findings, the first three of which involved treatment outcome and relative effectiveness of the conditions. The fourth finding concerned the articulation of mechanisms that may account for the specific effects of differential treatments.

First, with respect to treatment effects, the control condition was significantly less effective in retaining cases than the two treatment conditions ($\chi^2(2,19) = 13.64$, $p < .01$), with over two-thirds of dropouts occurring in the control condition. These attrition results support our earlier recognition that dropout rates are important outcome measures that may distinguish the effectiveness of different intervention/control conditions. A second finding was that the two treatment conditions, structural family therapy and psychodynamic child therapy, were equally effective in reducing behavioral and emotional problems based on parent and self-reports (time, $p < .001$; time × condition, n.s.).

A third finding involves the greater effectiveness of family therapy over child therapy in protecting family integrity in the long term ($p < .05$ for SFSR total score). In this study, psychodynamic therapy was found to be effective in reducing symptoms and improving child psychodynamic functioning, but it was also found to result in undesirable deterioration of family functioning. These findings provided support for the structural family therapy assumption that treating the whole family is important because it improves the symptoms and protects the family, whereas treating only the child may result in deteriorated family functioning.

The fourth important finding revealed that there is a complex relationship between specific mechanisms (family interaction versus child psychodynamic functioning) and related outcome variables. An examination of the relationship between the putative etiologic factors postulated by the two theoretical/clinical approaches, on the one hand supports some of the underlying assumptions of psychodynamic theory, and on the other does not support some of the underlying assumptions of family therapy, namely that changes in family functioning are necessary for symptom reduction. Hence, there was considerable value to extending the investigation beyond a simple horse race to a study of postulated underlying mechanisms.

Structural Family Therapy versus Group Counseling

We conducted another study to test the effectiveness of structural family therapy in reducing behavior problems and to investigate whether changes in family functioning are mediators of individual behavior change. Structural family therapy was compared with a control condition delivered in a group format. A mixed experimental design was used. The between-groups factor was intervention condition with two levels (structural family therapy and group control) and the within-group variable was time, using a repeated-measures approach with three assessment points (pretherapy, post-therapy, and nine-month follow-up). Seventy-nine Latino families with an adolescent referred by a school counselor or self-referred, and who met criteria for behavior problems in the child (such as violent behavior, conduct problems, or depression/anxiety) or family conflicts (such as frequent arguments/fights in the family) were randomly assigned to one of two treatment conditions: (1) structural family therapy or (2) control group therapy condition.

Results. The outcome data for conduct disorder and socialized aggression from the Revised Behavior Problem Checklist's (Quay & Peterson, 1987) were analyzed using two complementary approaches. The first was the analyses of group means and the second the analyses of clinically significant change as recommended by Jacobson and Traux (1991). The latter method complements the more commonly used analyses of group means by providing a case by case index of change.

Analysis of group means. The effects of treatment on conduct disorder and socialized aggression were analyzed by means of a 2 × 3 repeated-measures multivariate analysis of variance (MANOVA). Multivariate analyses indicated that subjects assigned to the structural family therapy condition showed significantly greater improvement in behavior problems than did subjects assigned to group therapy control. The overall MANOVA revealed a significant time x therapy condition interaction ($F(2,76) = 4.75$, $p < .05$). Follow-up univariate analyses indicated significant time × therapy condition interactions for both conduct disorder ($F(1,77) = 8.37$, $p < .01$), and socialized aggression ($F(1,77) = 7.22$, $p <.01$). Further examination of these interactions revealed that subjects in the structural family therapy condition showed significant preintervention to postintervention improvements in conduct disorder ($t(51) = 3.82$, $p <.001$), and socialized aggression ($t(51) = 3.57$, $p <.001$). Conversely, participants in the group therapy condition showed no significant changes on either conduct disorder ($t(26) = -.74$, n.s.) or socialized aggression ($t(26) = -.65$, n.s.) over time.

Analysis of clinical significance. Clinically significant change in conduct disorder and socialized aggression was assessed using the twofold criterion recommended by Jacobson and Traux (1991). First, a reliable change index was computed to determine whether the magnitude of change for any individual client was statistically reliable. Pre–posttreatment scores exceeding this index indicated reliable change that was not likely to be caused by fluctuations due to imprecise measurement (Christensen & Mendoza, 1986). Second, given reliable change, individuals were categorized into two levels of "clinical significance": (1) improvement, or reliable change, or (2) recovery, change that moved an individual from a clinical level at intake to a nonclinical level at termination. The clinical cutoff points for both conduct disorder and socialized aggression were established based on the Revised Behavior Problem Checklist's published norms for clinical and nonclinical groups (Quay & Peterson, 1987).

The results of the analysis of clinical significance corroborated our previous findings by showing that a substantially larger proportion of family therapy cases demonstrated clinically significant improvement. Of the 52 cases in the structural family therapy condition, 39 (75%) had clinical-level conduct disorder (CD) scores at intake. Of these 39 cases who started therapy at clinical-levels of CD, 17 (44%) made reliable improvement, and 2 (5%) showed reliable deterioration. Further, of the 17 improvers, 10 (26% of the total 39) were classified as recovered. In contrast, within the comparison group, only 2 of the 18 cases with clinical-level intake scores on conduct disorder showed reliable change, and both evidenced deterioration in functioning.

With regard to socialized aggression, 42 cases (81%) from the structural family therapy and 18 cases (72%) from the group therapy control conditions were above clinical levels at intake. Of the clinical cases in the structural family therapy condition, 16 (38%) showed reliable change, whereas only 2 (11%) did so in the comparison condition. Seven cases (17%) from the structural family therapy condition recovered to nonclinical levels, while only one case from the comparison group recovered to nonclinical levels.

A Structural Ecosystemic Approach to Social Ecological Interventions

In response to societal changes, especially declining social conditions in the inner city, which lead to a multiplicity of problems faced by Latino families, we have modified our program of research and intervention. The assumption is that these changes require the development of an articulated structural ecosystemic approach, which became the sixth challenge in our research history.

The theoretical foundations for this extension of our research is the work of Bronfenbrenner (1977, 1979, 1986) and others (Hawkins & Weis, 1985; Henggeler & Borduin, 1990; Henggeler, Melton, & Smith, 1992; Newcomb & Bentler, 1989; Newcomb & Félix-Ortíz, 1992; Newcomb, Maddahian, & Bentler, 1986). Bronfenbrenner was particularly interested in the complexity of contexts, and especially in the complex relationship that exists between various aspects of the context of an individual. He identified and defined four context systems within which families are embedded.

1. *Microsystems* are those systems that have direct contact with the child, such as family, school, and peers.
2. *Mesosystems* are defined as those systems resulting from the interaction of microsystems. One example of this type of system is the interface between parents and school. Another one is the system resulting from the interface between parents and peers (e.g., do parents organize and supervise peer activities?).

3. *Exosystems* are defined as external systems affecting family members, which through their impact on family members have an impact on the child. Examples of exosystems are a mother's place of work or her indigenous support network.
4. *Macrosystems* are cultural blueprints and formal aspects of the social structure that have an impact on the family through regulations and policies. Included among the macrosystems are the government of a country, the laws of the land, cultural traditions, and the international sociohistorical events that shape the lives of Latino families.

In addition to the complexity of contexts mentioned previously, it appears that all social contexts are embedded within a complex set of cultural influences (Szapocznik & Kurtines, 1993). We argued that the concept of culture has been overly simplified because of a lack of understanding of the complexity of the cultural streams that permeate the various aspects of the contexts that affect a family. For example, in reading the literature on Latinos, we found a frequent preoccupation with understanding the culture of origin. However, in our clinical and community work with Latinos in the United States we have rarely encountered Latinos whose only context is their culture of origin. Rather, Latino families are embedded in a complex melange of cultural influences, which includes the culture of origin as it exists in the living memories, values, and behaviors of the older members of the family. However, this cultural melange also includes the hybrid culture in which the children are immersed, both in school and with acculturating peers.

The clash of cultures resulting from interactions at the mesosystems level (e.g., parents and schools) represents another cultural context, one reflecting not the culture of origin but, rather, a clash of cultures. Families also are exposed to the influence of exosystems, those interactions between parents and their own work and support contexts. Some of these contexts are authentically Latino like the networks of support. Others, however, are alien to the Latino culture, such as the characteristics of the parents' workplace. Finally, there are rules that govern the Latino social structure that may be highly personal, whereas in the larger context of U.S. culture, these rules become more impersonal. By incorporating the complexity of contextual interactions faced by Latino families today, our basic structural approach became also ecosystemic.

Three Structural Ecosystemic Programs

The following ongoing studies reflect this complex, structural ecosystemic and contextualist perspective: Shenandoah in Action, Little Havana Parent Leadership, and Human Ecology Treatment. This structural ecosystemic approach extends our basic structural orientation by building on (1) Bronfenbrenner's theory, (2) Hawkins and colleagues' research on drug abuse prevention, and (3) Hengeller and colleagues' drug abuse treatment.

Our approach is compatible with Bronfenbrenner and Hengeller's multisystemic postulates but adds a structural dimension. *Structural*, as in structural family therapy, means that we conceptualize the nature of the interdependency of systems from an interactional perspective. Our approach focuses on repetitive patterns of interactions within and between systems that may lead to maladaptive behaviors.

Shenandoah in Action

This is a school-based study intended to demonstrate that an ecosystemic approach based on Bronfenbrenner's conceptual framework is effective in enhancing adaptive behaviors and reducing risk of drug abuse and antisocial behavior. The interventions are aimed at strengthening adaptive interactions and correcting maladaptive interactions at the microsystem (family, school, and peers), mesosystem (family–school, family–peers), and exosystem levels (parent support networks). The intervention programs address the specific risk and resiliency factors at each systemic level that affect the child's developmental outcomes.

The interventions use structural intervention techniques to attempt to redirect participants out of conflictive or nonsupportive interactions into a supportive network of interactional processes. The Shenandoah in Action programs intervene not only with individual children directly in the microsystems, but also through interventions at the mesosystem level to create a network that will foster positive developmental outcomes.

Little Havana Parent Leadership

This ongoing study in Little Havana, Miami, is investigating the effectiveness of a neighborhood-based, parent-focused approach to prevention of gang involvement in high-risk youth, as compared to existing modes of intervention provided by other community-based programs. This study targets Latino immigrant families with adolescents between 12 and 15 years of age who are experiencing behavioral problems. These youth, referred for services by school counselors, are considered at risk for gang involvement because of factors such as academic failure, chronic truancy, multiple suspensions, and aggressive behavior. One-half of the families were randomly assigned to a control condition, "treatment as usual," and referred to agencies representing the range of professional services usually accessed to address behavioral or family difficulties. The other half of the families were randomly assigned to the experimental condition, the East Little Havana Family Leadership Program (Padres Líderes de la Familia Hispana), a community-based, multifamily, parent-focused prevention intervention. Using concepts derived from strategic structural systems theory, the program is intended: (1) to create a strong social network—a system for change—made up of multiple neighborhood families, that in turn will foster change in the community conditions that lead to gang involvement in youth, and (2) to provide parents with leadership and resource-seeking skills. In the process of designing and implementing a series of supervised activities for their youth, parents have an opportunity to develop and rehearse family and community leadership skills.

This intervention is designed to restructure the social ecology of the family by working at the level of the youth's mesosystems and exosystems. At the mesosystem level, parents become directly involved with their adolescent's peer group as they organize field trips and team sports for youth. At the level of the exosystems, parents develop supportive social networks among themselves and become involved in activities on behalf of the larger community. For example, families are collaborating with the City of Miami Police in activities to promote cross-cultural understanding and prevent crime. The ultimate goal is to restructure the nature of the interactions that occur among the various components of the family's social ecology, in the same manner that structural systems theory restructures interactions among individuals in a family.

Human Ecology Treatment Program

This is a randomized clinical trial investigating the effectiveness of a Human Ecology Treatment as compared against a "treatment as usual" condition, the latter defined by referrals to several community treatment services that offer drug abuse treatment for minority youth. The experimental intervention, Human Ecology Treatment, organizes the life context of adolescent drug abusers using Bronfenbrenner's socioecological conceptual framework. Under this framework, the focus is the relationship between family interactional patterns and the presenting complaint. For example, it targets (1) family organization aspects such as alliance, hierarchy, communication flow, personal and subsystem boundaries; (2) resonance, defined as psychological and emotional distance between family members; (3) developmental issues, defined in terms of the developmental appropriateness of the behavior and responsibilities of each family member; (4) identified patienthood, defined in terms of the extent to which all family problems are blamed on the youth; and (5) conflict resolution style and abilities.

In addition, this intervention examines the interaction patterns between the youth and school authorities, along with examining peer interaction patterns. At the mesosystem level, attention is given to the relationship between parents and the school, parents and peers, and parents and the justice system. A crucial issue is whether the component systems support each other or not. For example, within the parents–school mesosystem interaction, do parents and school support each other? Is there a working alliance, or is there isolation and/or conflict? At the parents–peers mesosystem level, do parents know their children's peers? Do parents organize supervised peer activities? Do parents know the parents of their child's peers? Do parents network with community organizations providing organized, supervised peer activities?

Our experience suggests that it is possible to affect the youth's observable problem behavior syndrome separate from the youth's drug-abusing behavior. It appears that the former requires correction of maladaptive interactional patterns in the microsystem's family and schools and in the mesosystem family–school, whereas the latter requires correction of maladaptive interactions within the microsystem of peers (antisocial versus prosocial peers) and the mesosystem family–peers.

One of the challenges we face is to develop a more effective replicable approach to changing a drug-abusing adolescent's peer system within the natural-life context—that is, while the adolescent continues to live in the same community. We are considering four general strategies. One is to use a One Person Family Therapy approach to help change the youth's interactions with her or his peer system. The second is to create opportunities for bonding the youth with a new peer system. The third is to intervene directly with a youth's peer system in an attempt to bring changes in the nature of his or her activities. The fourth is to empower parents to manage their youth and their youth's peer relations. Selecting one or more of these intervention levels might be strategically dictated by the conditions surrounding each case. This would be based on a theoretical framework emphasizing changes in the interaction patterns within the peer system.

Conclusions

In the line of research that ultimately led us to the development of a structural ecosystemic intervention approach, we have sought to integrate theory, application, and research. Our work began in the 1970s in an effort to address an issue of growing concern: promoting culturally competent therapists and therapies to address behavior and drug abuse problems among Latino youth living in Miami. Since then, structural systems theory has provided the foundation for developing assessment, engagement, treatment, and prevention strategies. Our program of research, in turn, provided a solid foundation from which to pursue new advances and directions. For example, the SFSR enabled us to assess family functioning and, eventually, assessing the effectiveness of structural family therapy and theory. The refinement of structural family theory strategies and goals in the form of BSFT, in turn, enabled us to understand how to modify these strategies to achieve the same goals without having the entire family in therapy, making One-Person Family Therapy possible. Success in changing family interactions by working primarily through one person became the basis for engaging hard-to-reach families in treatment. The finding that changes in family functioning may not be necessary for achieving reduction in symptoms has challenged our most basic postulate regarding the relationship between family interaction and symptom change. Although it appears that family therapy works, our findings raise more questions than answers about the mechanisms through which family therapy brings about change.

Our efforts have also had significant methodological implications. Through the search of theoretically appropriate measures (Kazdin, 1986), we have achieved some of our most important breakthroughs in measuring family interactional functioning. This measure met a number of stringent criteria: It is consistent with the theoretical underpinnings of the theory of pathology and behavior change under investigation; it is clinically relevant and found acceptable by clinicians in each of the theoretical areas under investigation; and it meets psychometric standards. However, there are still challenges ahead regarding the need to develop theoretically relevant measures of mesosystem functioning.

Finally, this work has implications for future directions in supporting Latino families. With changing times and subsequent changing needs of families, interventions should be directed toward addressing the multiplicity of problems that Latino families face today. This means that these efforts will have to continue to focus on the multilayered set of systems that have an impact on Latino families. Current and future efforts operate under the assumption that "it takes a village to raise a child." It is necessary both to create a village that can foster healthy child development and to develop adequate policies and systems for the provision of services to the community. Bronfenbrenner (1979) wrote that "seldom is attention paid to the person's behavior in more than one setting or to the way in which relations between settings can affect what happens within them" (p. 18). He suggested that an individual's social-ecological environment is composed of a complex set of nested structures. As Latino scientists, we cannot help but to be concerned with the broad contextual issues of the social and cultural structures in which Latino families are embedded. This is why we have sought to develop theory, research, and services within the complex of nested structures of the Latino community.

References

Bronfenbrenner, U. (1977). Toward an experimental ecology of human development. *American Psychologist, 32,* 513–531.

Bronfenbrenner, U. (1979). *The ecology of human development.* Cambridge, MA: Harvard University Press.

Bronfenbrenner, U. (1986). Ecology of the family as a context for human development: Research perspectives. *Developmental Psychology, 22*(6), 723–742.

Christensen, L., & Mendoza, J. L. (1986). The moderator–mediator variable distinction in social psychological research: Conceptual, strategic, and statistical considerations. *Journal of Personality and Social Psychology, 51*(6), 1173–1182.

Coleman, A. F. (1976). How to enlist the family as an ally. *American Journal of Drug and Alcohol Abuse, 3,* 167–173.

Haley, J. (1976). *Problem-solving therapy.* San Francisco: Jossey-Bass.

Hawkins, J. D., & Weis, J. G. (1985). The social development model: An integrated approach to delinquency prevention. *Journal of Primary Prevention, 6,* 73–97.

Henggeler, S. W., & Borduin, C. M. (1990). *Family therapy and beyond: A multisystemic approach to treating the behavior problems of children and adolescents.* Pacific Grove, CA: Brooks/Cole.

Henggeler, S. W., Melton, G. B., & Smith, L. A. (1992). Family preservation using multisystemic therapy: An effective alternative to incarcerating serious juvenile offenders. *Journal of Consulting and Clinical Psychology, 60,* 953–961.

Jacobson, N. S., & Traux, T. (1991). Clinical significance: A statistical approach to defining meaningful change in psychotherapy research. *Journal of Consulting and Clinical Psychology, 59*(1), 12–19.

Kazdin, A. E. (1986). Comparative outcome studies of psychotherapy: Methodological issues and strategies. *Journal of Consulting and Clinical Psychology, 54,* 95–105.

Kazdin, A. E. (1993). Adolescent mental health: Prevention and treatment programs. *American Psychologist, 48*(2), 127–141.

Kluckhohn, F. R., & Strodtbeck, F. L. (1961). *Variations in value orientations.* Evanston, IL: Row, Peterson.

Madanes, C. (1981). *Strategic family therapy.* San Francisco: Jossey-Bass.

Mancilla, Y., & Szapocznik, J. (1994). *A manual for a community based, multifamily strategic structural systems intervention for strengthening Hispanic immigrant families of behavior problem adolescents at risk for gang involvement.* [Technical Report, Administration for Children and Families (ACF) Grant No. 9-CL1111]. Miami, FL: University of Miami Spanish Family Guidance Center.

McCardle, J., & Murray, E. J. (1974). Nonspecific factors in weekend encounter groups. *Journal of Consulting and Clinical Psychology, 42,* 337–345.

Minuchin, S. (1974). *Families and family therapy.* Cambridge, MA: Harvard University Press.

Minuchin, S., & Fishman, H. C. (1981). *Family therapy techniques.* Cambridge, MA: Harvard University Press.

Minuchin, S., Rosman, B. L., & Baker, L. (1978). *Psychosomatic families: Anorexia nervosa in context.* Cambridge, MA: Harvard University Press.

Newcomb, M. D., & Bentler, P. (1989). Substance use and abuse among children and teenagers. *American Psychologist* [Special issue on children and their development: Knowledge base, research agenda and social policy application], *44*(2), 242–248.

Newcomb, M. D., & Félix-Ortiz, M. (1992). Multiple protective and risk factors for drug use and abuse: Cross-sectional and prospective findings. *Journal of Personality and Social Psychology, 63*(2), 280–296.

Newcomb, M. D., Maddahian, E., & Bentler, P. M. (1986). Risk factors for drug use among adolescents: Concurrent and longitudinal analyses. *American Journal of Public Health, 76,* 525–531.

Quay, H. C., & Peterson, D. R. (1987). *Manual for the Revised Behavior Problem Checklist.* (Available from H. C. Quay, Department of Psychology, P.O. Box 248185, Coral Gables, FL 33124).

Santisteban, D. A., Szapocznik, J., Pérez-Vidal, A., Kurtines, W. M., Murray, E. J., & LaPerriere, A. (1996). Efficacy of interventions for engaging youth and families into treatment and some variables that may contribute to differential effectiveness. *Journal of Family Psychology, 10,*(1) 35–44.

Scopetta, M. A., Szapocznik, J., King, O. E., Ladner, R., Alegre, C., & Tillman, M. S. (1977). *Final report: The Spanish drug rehabilitation research project* (NIDA Grant #HB1 DA01696). Miami: University of Miami, Spanish Family Guidance Center.

Strupp, H. H., & Hadley, S. W. (1979). Specific vs. nonspecific factors in psychotherapy: A controlled study of outcome. *Archives of General Psychiatry, 36,* 1125–1136.

Szapocznik, J., Hervis, O., Kurtines, W. M., & Spencer, F. (1984). One person family therapy. In B. Lubin & W. A. O'Connor (Eds.), *Ecological approaches to clinical and community psychology* (pp. 335–355). New York: Wiley.

Szapocznik, J., & Kurtines, W. (1989). *Breakthroughs in family treatment.* New York: Springer.

Szapocznik, J., & Kurtines, W. M. (1993). Family psychology and cultural diversity: Opportunities for theory, research and application. *American Psychologist, 48*(4).

Szapocznik, J., Kurtines, W., & Fernandez, T. (1980) Biculturalism and adjustment among Hispanic youths. *International Journal of Intercultural Relations, 4,* 353–375.

Szapocznik, J., Kurtines, W., Foote, F., Pérez-Vidal, A., & Hervis, O. (1983). Conjoint versus one person family therapy: Some evidence for the effectiveness of conducting family therapy through one person. *Journal of Consulting and Clinical Psychology, 51,* 889–899.

Szapocznik, J., Kurtines, W. M., Foote, F., Pérez-Vidal, A., & Hervis, O. (1986). Conjoint versus one person family therapy: Further evidence for the effectiveness of conducting family therapy through one person. *Journal of Consulting and Clinical Psychology, 54,* 395–397.

Szapocznik, J., Kurtines, W., Pérez-Vidal, A., Hervis, O., & Foote, F. (1990). One person family therapy. In R. A. Wells & V. A. Gianetti (Eds.), *Handbook of brief psychotherapies* (pp. 493–510). New York: Plenum Press.

Szapocznik, J., Kurtines, W., Santisteban, D., & Rio, A. T. (1990). The interplay of advances among theory, research and application in treatment interventions aimed at behavior problem children and adolescents. *Journal of Consulting and Clinical Psychology, 58*(6), 696–703.

Szapocznik, J., Pérez-Vidal, A., Brickman, A., Foote, F. H., Santisteban, D., Hervis, O., & Kurtines, W. H. (1988). Engaging adolescent drug abusers and their families into treatment: A Strategic Structural Systems approach. *Journal of Consulting and Clinical Psychology*, 552–557.

Szapocznik, J., Pérez-Vidal, A., Hervis, O., Brickman, A. L., & Kurtines, W. (1990). Innovations in family therapy: Overcoming resistance to treatment. In R. A. Wells & V. A. Gianetti (Eds.), *Handbook of brief psychotherapy* (pp. 93–114). New York: Plenum Press.

Szapocznik, J., Rio, A. T., Hervis, O. E., Mitrani, V. B., Kurtines, W. M., & Faraci, A. M. (1991). Assessing change in family functioning as a result of treatment: The structural family system rating scale (SFSR). *Journal of Marital and Family Therapy, 17*(3), 295–310.

Szapocznik, J., Rio, A., Murray, E., Cohen, R., Scopetta, M., Rivas-Vasquez, A., Hervis, O., Posada, V., & Kurtines, W. (1989). Structural family versus psychodynamic child therapy for problematic Hispanic boys. *Journal of Consulting and Clinical Psychology, 57*, (5) 571–578.

Szapocznik, J., Santisteban, D., Kurtines, W.M., Pérez-Vidal, A., & Hervis, O. (1984). Bicultural Effectiveness Training (BET): A treatment intervention for enhancing intercultural adjustment. *Hispanic Journal of Behavioral Sciences, 6*(4), 317–344.

Szapocznik, J., Santisteban, D., Rio, A., Pérez-Vidal, A., & Kurtines, W. M. (1986). Family Effectiveness Training for Hispanic families: Strategic structural systems intervention for the prevention of drug abuse. In H. P. Lefley & P. B. Pedersen (Eds.), *Cross cultural training for mental health professionals*, Springfield, IL: Charles C Thomas.

Szapocznik, J., Santisteban, D., Rio, A., Pérez-Vidal, A., Kurtines, W., & Hervis, O. (1986). Bicultural effectiveness training (BET): An intervention modality for families experiencing intergenerational/intercultural conflict. *Hispanic Journal of Behavioral Sciences, 8*(4), 303–330.

Szapocznik, J., Santisteban, D., Rio, A., Pérez-Vidal, A., Santisteban, D. A., & Kurtines, W. (1989). Family effectiveness training: An intervention to prevent problem behaviors in Hispanic adolescents. *Hispanic Journal of Behavioral Sciences, 11*, 4–27.

Szapocznik, J., Scopetta, M. A., Aranalde, M. A., & Kurtines, W. (1978). Cuban value structure: Clinical implications. *Journal of Consulting and Clinical Psychology, 46*(5), 961–970.

Szapocznik, J., Scopetta, M. A., & King, O. (1978). Theory and practice in matching treatment to the special characteristics and problems of Cuban immigrants. *Journal of Community Psychology, 6*, 112–122.

Szapocznik, J., Scopetta, M. A., Kurtines, W., & Aranalde, M. A. (1978). Theory and measurement of acculturation. *Interamerican Journal of Psychology, 12*, 113–130.

$Chapter$ 11

Treatment Issues with Latinos Addicted to Cocaine and Heroin

FELIPE G. CASTRO
HELEN M. TAFOYA-BARRAZA
Department of Psychology and Hispanic Research Center, Arizona State University

Background on Illicit Drug Use among Latinos

A Sociocultural Context to Drug Abuse

By the year 2000, Latinos, the fastest growing minority group, are projected to be the largest minority group in the United States (De La Cancela & Guzmán, 1991; Hayes-Bautista, Shink, & Chapa, 1988; Macías, 1977; National Coalition of Hispanic Health and Human Services Organizations, 1988). There are currently more than 22.8 million Latinos in the United States, who constitute 8.9% of the total population and 36% of the ethnic minority population (U.S. Bureau of the Census, 1993). Persistent poverty, unemployment and underemployment, low educational attainment, and acculturation stressors are some of the major factors that adversely affect large portions of the Latino population, particularly Mexican Americans and Puerto Ricans (Enchautegri, 1995). Moreover, these adverse conditions, which induce economic disadvantage and demoralization, are socioeconomic factors that are associated with risks for drug abuse and addiction.

This study was funded by Grant R18-DA05661 from the National Institute on Drug Abuse and R01-CA57140 from the National Cancer Institute. The clerical assistance of Kendra Szabo is warmly appreciated.

For the general population, the National Institute on Drug Abuse (NIDA) (1993), using data from the National Household Survey on Drug Abuse—1991, reported that for people over the age of 35, 6.4% of Anglo-Americans had used cocaine compared with 7.8% of Latinos. For heroin use, 1.4% of Anglo-Americans had tried heroin, compared with 1.6% of Latinos. However, this NIDA report cautions that the prevalence of heroin use is difficult to estimate from telephone surveys and that data from the National Household Survey on Drug Abuse is considered to produce conservative estimates.

In the treatment of cocaine and heroin addictions in Latino populations, various socioeconomic and cultural factors also must be considered. These factors include level of acculturation, income level, level of education, and barriers associated with general health care such as having health insurance, language discrepancies, and access to services (Giachello, 1994; Molina, Zambrana, & Aguirre-Molina, 1994).

Level of acculturation is one important factor to consider when working with any immigrant population. *Acculturation* is a process by which members of an ethnic minority group acquire the majority group's culture while often retaining identification with their mother culture (LaFromboise, Coleman, & Gerton, 1993). Though seldom examined as such, acculturation can be a two-way process. That is, members of the majority group may adopt some of the characteristics of the minority group as well. This is especially likely in communities with high concentrations of ethnic/racial minority residents, such as *barrios* and *colonias*.

Associated with level of acculturation are language fluency, literacy, and preference. In the therapeutic encounter between doctor and patient or therapist and client, language barriers can hinder access to effective services (Pérez-Stable, 1987; Marín, Marín, Padilla, & de la Rocha, 1983). In this interaction, limited communication including idioms in a second language can lead to misunderstandings (Westermeyer, 1985) including misdiagnoses and misattributions regarding the nature and cause of the drug problem and the treatment deemed appropriate. Often treatment programs, available primarily in English, can adversely influence program viability and outcomes in populations that have little or no English fluency and literacy.

In 1993, 28% of Latinos lived below the federal poverty level compared to 11% of Anglo-Americans (U.S. Bureau of the Census, 1993). Socioeconomic factors impede Latinos' access to health care (Ginzberg, 1991; Marín et al., 1983; Pérez-Stable, 1987). Many Latinos, though employed, work at low-paying jobs that provide limited or no medical insurance (Ginzberg, 1991; Pérez-Stable, 1987; U.S. Bureau of the Census, 1993). Thirty-two percent of Latinos in the United States have no health insurance, compared with 13% of Anglo-Americans (U.S. Bureau of the Census, 1993). The lack of health insurance is one of the most serious barriers to access to health services for Latinos, especially for Mexican Americans (Giachello, 1994). Moreover, having the *means* to obtain services is directly related to whether or not one *does* obtain services; that is, access is strongly related to utilization (Solis, Marks, García, & Shelton, 1990). Whereas many drug treatment programs are available only to those with medical insurance that covers drug treatment, other publicly subsidized programs, such as county-supported programs, are available whether or not one has health insurance. In many of these publicly subsidized programs, however, quality of treatment is an issue. And often these programs fail to incorporate socioeconomic and cultural factors as contextual issues that would make drug abuse treatment more relevant for Latinos.

Level of education is another important factor to consider so that intervention/treatment approaches can be tailored to the educational and knowledge needs of the target audience (Balcazar, Castro, & Krull, 1995). That is, if the targeted population has a higher level of education or a need for more advanced knowledge, one would want to design materials at the appropriate reading and educational levels. The same holds true for those with lower education and knowledge needs. It is not appropriate to use an intervention developed at one level of education when the targeted audience includes members with very low levels of education and others with higher levels of education. In such cases, it may be necessary to use multilevel interventions that are targeted and matched to the education and experience levels of various subgroups of recovering addicts.

Issues in Drug Abuse and Need for Treatment

Clients who enter a drug treatment program often are users of multiple drugs and alcohol and often have a history of legal and family problems. These patterns also have been observed among Mexican-American heroin addicts. Maddox and Desmond (1992) have reported on a ten-year longitudinal study of 95 male methadone maintenance clients and a comparison group of 77 male opiate users who were eligible for but not admitted to a methadone maintenance program. The majority of these clients in both groups (over 87%) were Mexican Americans. Among these participants, over 50% had come from broken families, over 33% had disciplinary problems in school, mean years of education completed was 8 years, over 60% had been arrested prior to their first use of opioids, they had over 14 years of opioid use prior to treatment entry, over 67% had a problem with alcohol abuse before admission (or eligibility) to methadone maintenance, their mean age at first admission (or eligibility) to methadone maintenance treatment was 33 to 34 years, and they had been in prior drug treatments an average of three or more times prior to seeking methadone treatment. Clearly, these Mexican-American heroin addicts had a series of social, legal, and other drug problems that preceded or occurred concurrently with their heroin abuse.

Generally, the point at which an illicit drug user realizes that treatment is necessary comes when that person has reached a low point in his or her life (Washton, 1986). An unhealthy *shift* in lifestyle is typically observed among persons who become so addicted to drugs that treatment is necessary (Castro, Barrington, Sharp, Dial, Wang, & Rawson, 1992; Marlatt & Gordon, 1985).

In the 1990s, many of the strategies used to treat cocaine abusers have been adapted from general drug and alcohol treatment programs (Rawson, Obert, McCann, Castro, & Ling, 1991). These strategies include 28-day hospital inpatient programs, which are only minimally modified for cocaine abusers, and outpatient programs. Often both types of programs feature the 12-step philosophy developed by the Alcoholics Anonymous (AA) program. In an extension of these approaches, the treatment of heroin addiction centers on methadone maintenance.

In early work on the efficacy of methadone, Dole and Nyswander (1965) sought a medication that would eliminate a heroin addict's cravings. The strategy was to use a synthetic and prescribed form of heroin to eliminate cravings and lead to a reduction of heroin use and thus to a reduction in the antisocial behavior and crime associated with the need to obtain heroin. Methadone is a long-acting, orally administered, legally available synthetic opiate that satisfies narcotic cravings. It has been demonstrated to be a safe treatment for a large number of heroin addicts (Gearing, 1972). Although the elimination of opiate cravings aids in the avoidance of heroin use, effective treatment for heroin addiction involves more than just methadone dispensing; effective counseling and therapy are also needed.

In one of the few culturally oriented studies of heroin addicts, Jorquez (1984) found that many Mexican-American heroin addicts reject conventional forms of treatment. Jorquez suggests that treatment of Chicano addicts should include a recognition of the difficulties involved in seeking to end the addiction to heroin permanently, thus helping addicts to avoid feeling discouraged at their perceived lack of progress in treatment for heroin addiction. In addition, important psychosocial issues must be addressed in order to provide a more complete and successful program for full drug rehabilitation for these Mexican-American/Chicano heroin users.

The Process of Drug Addiction for Latinos

It is well documented that the development of illicit drug use occurs in various different ways and is influenced by multiple factors. The concept of the *problem behavior syndrome* is now well accepted in the drug literature. This concept refers to the development of illicit drug use in conjunction with many other activities that disrupt normal development in adolescents and young adults (Jessor & Jessor, 1977; Newcomb & Bentler, 1988). By implication, Mexican Americans and other Latinos are also affected by this problem behavior syndrome in a parallel fashion to Anglo-Americans. Among youth, dropping out of school is associated with antisocial and nonconformist attitudes; it is associated with affiliation with deviant peers, including gang involvement; and it is associated with the early use of so-called gateway drugs (alcohol and cigarettes), followed by the use of illicit drugs, including cocaine and heroin. Among Mexican-American adolescents, rates of school dropout are especially high, thus setting the stage for street life and the use of illicit drugs. In some high schools, the dropout rate among Mexican Americans/Chicanos approaches 80%. Nationally, among adults ages 25 and older, only 53.1% of Mexican Americans had a high school diploma, as compared with 84.1% of Anglo-Americans (non-Hispanic whites) (U.S. Bureau of the Census, 1993).

From an integrative theory perspective, important factors that contribute to the development of illicit drug use among Latinos include: (1) community prompts from life in a drug-affected *barrio*; (2) life in a disrupted family system with frequent parental conflict; (3) rebelliousness and nonconformity; (4) the influence of deviant peers who encourage drug use; (5) acculturation stressors; and (6) licit legal/gateway drug use (Castro, Harmon, Coe, & Tafoya-Barraza, 1994).

Offsetting these contributing factors are certain buffering factors that may help to safeguard against the development of illicit drug use among Latinos: (1) family support and bonding; (2) prosocial coping behaviors; (3) cultural identity integration; and (4) culturally relevant health promotion programs that offer culturally meaningful strategies and skills training to avoid drug use (Castro, Sharp, Barrington, Walton, & Rawson, 1991; Oetting & Beauvais, 1991).

Factors such as a disrupted family system, youthful rebelliousness and nonconformity, peer influence, and licit drug use appear to be stable social influences that lead to illicit drug use across several populations. Indeed, these factors seem to lie at the core of the problem behavior syndrome. For Latinos, however, other factors such as acculturation stressors, identity conflicts, economic disillusionment, and unique community or cultural prompts within a *barrio* or neighborhood may impose unique social or environmental influences that also may prompt drug use. Similarly, regarding the buffering factors, the availability of family support and prosocial coping skills provide general ways in which youths from most cultural backgrounds can avoid drugs. In addition, for Latinos, cultural identity integration—that is, a self-concept or self-image as a *non-user* of drugs—and traditional Latino cultural values, along with pride in heritage, would appear to operate as factors that safeguard against drug use (Oetting & Beauvais, 1991). Similarly, the availability of culturally relevant health promotion programs—that is, programs that promote cultural identity and pride as well as certain types of traditionalism, such as family loyalty and social responsibility—may help reduce the risks of illicit drug use among young Latinos.

Once a youth or young adult engages in illicit drug use, three stages of change in personal identity appear to occur in the process of addiction: (1) identity as a *casual* or recreational drug user; (2) identity as an *addict*, which is an imposed identity when the person enters into a drug treatment program; and (3) identity as a *recovering addict*, an achieved identity as the person attempts to return to normality after drug treatment (Castro et al., 1991). Thus, addiction to an illicit drug, such as heroin or cocaine, and subsequent recovery from addiction involve a series of important life changes (changes in lifestyle) and changes in self-identity that include major disruptions and adjustments in life and living.

When a person becomes addicted to heroin and/or to cocaine, life focus narrows such that a large portion of the person's waking hours is focused on procuring heroin or cocaine (Peele & Brodsky, 1991). Both the habitual and the pharmacological effects of heroin and/or cocaine force the person to continue using in order to avoid the discomforts of withdrawal and/or cravings. Criminal behavior involving various illegal acts to procure money to maintain one's drug addiction ultimately becomes a central feature of the person's daily activities. Depending on the type of drug used and the route of administration (e.g., snorting, smoking, or injection), it is now well known that sharing needles also promotes the risk of HIV infection. Although they are knowledgeable of the risks of HIV infection, many addicts (particularly adolescent and young adult addicts) continue to share needles or to use another person's needles without proper cleaning with bleach during runs of drug use in which the desire to get high and to fight off cravings overpowers any concern about the risk of being infected with HIV.

Heroin use has been a stable occurrence in Mexican-American/Chicano communities since the 1940s, although on the national scene heroin use faded in the 1970s and 1980s, while increasing in popularity again in the 1990s (Castro, 1994). Reasons that heroin has been a more enduring drug of choice for many Mexican-American/Chicano *barrio* users, known as *tecatos*, are unclear. However, habitual patterns of use among *cholo* families (Moore, 1990), preferences among *barrio* "homeboys," and the reported pharmacological effects of heroin are likely factors. Pharmacologically, heroin is an opiate that is a fast-acting central nervous system depressant (Platt, 1988). Some Chicano addicts indicate that given economic pressures, discrimination, and multiple chronic stressors experienced in impoverished *barrios*, heroin offers a deep escape, a serene relief that one "falls in love with." This experience of deep escape may offer a powerful reinforcer to many Chicano youth and young adults who live in impoverished communities.

After years of using heroin, which today is often used in conjunction with cocaine, entry into treatment occurs when the individual's significant others or the individual himself or herself realizes that the problem has gotten out of control. At that point, the addicted individual may have lost or compromised work, social relations, and health; thus the need for treatment becomes unavoidable.

Some drug-addicted individuals, however, are unwilling to enter treatment voluntarily and thus are brought in under coercion from the courts or from insistent family members. Entry into treatment under coercion raises questions about the client's preparedness for treatment. Unless convinced by the treatment agency that they must remain in treatment, these unprepared clients often have an antagonistic attitude toward treatment and will not participate actively in the process. Consequently, they are unlikely to recover. Instead, they fall into relapse shortly after release from the treatment program. Such clients appear to have a perceived self-identity as casual users (recreational users), but this is a form of denial and reflects low levels of their preparedness for treatment. In objective reality, they are addicted and in need of treatment (Castro et al., 1991). Such clients often are poor prospects for effective treatment.

For Latinos, little is known about the dynamics of treatment and recovery and how these are similar to or different from the dynamics of recovery for Anglo-American clients. For Mexican-American clients, one possible set of moderators of recovery as well as of addiction is level of acculturation and acculturation-related factors. As the addicted Mexican-American client is culturally different from the mainstream Anglo-American, a unique or culturally appropriate program of treatment would appear to be necessary in order to deliver culturally relevant and thus effective treatment. By contrast, for highly acculturated Latinos, those who do not differ much in cultural orientation from Anglo-Americans, the same type of treatment program as is offered for Anglo-American clients might well be appropriate.

Treatment Issues

General Treatment Approaches

In the 1990s, general treatment approaches for cocaine and heroin addiction typically involved treatment referral to either an inpatient or an outpatient program. Inpatient treatment has typically involved a 28-day program or a portion thereof, depending on extent of insurance coverage. Within an inpatient program, the client or patient is placed in a protective environment and encouraged to participate actively in the process of recovery.

Typical hospital-based inpatient programs have included: (1) an overview of the Alcoholics Anonymous 12-step philosophy, (2) group therapy in which the individual is confronted with psychological issues involved in addiction, (3) brief individual therapy aimed at personalizing issues and developing insight into one's unique process of addiction and recovery, and (4) self-management approaches designed to help the individual recover health and focus on improved patterns of living. Inpatient programs are typically more intense than outpatient programs and are usually more costly.

Early indicators of triage for inpatient versus outpatient treatment have involved general criteria, where indications for inpatient treatment have been: (1) a greater *severity* of addiction (although severity of addiction is difficult to evaluate); (2) the absence of a family support system, necessitating inpatient care; (3) a prior failure at treatment on an outpatient basis; and/or (4) the individual's avowed preference for inpatient treatment.

By contrast, outpatient treatment typically involves sessions offered once a week or more during the early stages of the program. Outpatient treatment typically is less intense or demanding on a day-by-day basis. As with inpatient programs, however, the individual's commitment to the treatment program is essential in order for him or her to benefit from it. A typical outpatient treatment program includes several phases, including an initial month-long phase that involves detoxification if needed, stabilization, assessment, and orientation to treatment, followed by a second-phase of approximately five months, which consists of the core of the treatment program. A third phase may include a follow-up program that focuses on skill building to reduce the risk of relapse and to promote a complete recovery from addiction.

For both inpatient and outpatient treatments, an aftercare phase is typically involved, which seeks to ensure that treatment gains are maintained. Aftercare can include continued outpatient sessions or referral to a residential treatment program in cases where the individual is still unable to return to active recovery in the community. Additionally, continued attendance at Alcoholics Anonymous (AA),

Narcotics Anonymous (NA), and/or Cocaine Anonymous (CA) meetings is a regular feature in many inpatient and outpatient programs.

Need for Culturally Relevant Approaches

How these basic inpatient, outpatient, and aftercare programs should be modified to accommodate the unique needs of Latinos is an interesting and important treatment question in today's contemporary treatment arena. Very few programs nationally include an attention to cultural factors as an integral part of their treatment and recovery program. For example, among less acculturated (low acculturated and bicultural) Latinos, cultural issues such as Latino family dynamics, the importance of ethnic identity in recovery, and culturally relevant strategies to avoid relapse are important areas in which cultural factors may exert a powerful influence. A client's behavior during recovery may well be affected by social obligations to *compañeros* (close friends) or *homeboys*. The value and role of social relations among Latinos as related to the risks of relapse to drug use is an important area that requires further research and clinical work to clarify the unique needs and stressors faced by various Latinos. Highly acculturated Latinos may not require the addition of culturally relevant intervention components, but bilingual/bicultural and especially less acculturated Latinos may greatly require such culturally relevant intervention components in order to ensure enhanced recovery and reduce the risk of relapse.

Latinos and family systems.   As noted, for those Latinos who are bilingual/bicultural or even low in acculturation (those who are Spanish-dominant and/or who are greatly involved in their culture), additional components to a standard treatment program may well be required in order to improve program effectiveness for these clients. For example, conservative Latino cultural traditions and practices exist in many Latino families. Within these families, conservative cultural expectations, values, and attitudes may well influence the way in which the recovering addict is accepted into the family setting and how that individual will be supported in his or her efforts at recovery from heroin or cocaine addiction. A Latino family's history of experience with drug problems may also serve as an important factor that determines how the family system will help or hinder the recovering addict's efforts to remain sober/drug free. For example, among young heroin-addicted Mexican-American females (Chicanas), Moore (1990) has indicated that multigenerational drug-using families develop a system of support that allows the recovering young woman to return and function adaptively in the street and in the family environment. By contrast, for young Mexican-American women from more conservative traditional families that have never before contended with drug problems, their families are less able to provide sufficient support that would foster drug avoidance.

Most recovering addicts feel stigmatized regarding their addiction and are very sensitive to rejection from society and family. A return to a punitive, enmeshed, nonsupportive, rejecting, guilt-inducing family system will set the stage for failure in recovery and to drug relapse (Szapocznik & Kurtines, 1989). By contrast, an overly permissive family system may also set the stage for relapse by not setting appropriate limits and by not fostering a sense of responsibility in the recovering addict. Clearly, a balance in family supportive style is needed to reduce the risk of relapse.

Future drug treatment and recovery research should examine the relative impact of an overly punitive and of an overly permissive Latino family system in the process of recovery of a drug-using family member. Culturally sensitive relapse prevention efforts must consider the supportiveness of the recovering addict's family and other aspects of the preparedness of various Latino families, as this may help their family member avoid relapse.

Gender expectations and roles. A second culturally related issue for Mexican Americans and other Latinos involves differences in gender expectations and roles as these may influence the process of involvement in treatment and the process of recovery from illicit drug use. Whereas in traditional Latino cultures illicit drug use has seldom been seen as acceptable, drug use by males has, in the past, been tolerated and reluctantly accepted as a potential pitfall of male development. By contrast, strong ostracism and rejection appear to be the initial and ongoing reactions within traditional families to a drug-using female. Here again, families not prepared to help their female drug-addicted family member are likely to impose punitive demands that may prompt a return to drug use in the form of relapse. Currently, most treatment programs nationally include little or no information on how these various types of Latino families can be helped in providing the support necessary for their recovering family member to avoid relapse. Further research and clinical work is needed to clarify the ways in which families can provide the necessary support for their drug-using and recovering member.

Treatment and AIDS Risks

In certain parts of the country, primarily inner-city and urban areas, the risk of HIV infection as the result of needle sharing and/or unprotected sex has disproportionately affected African-American and Latino populations (Schilling et al., 1989). It is noteworthy, however, that even in rural, less populated areas and in U.S.–Mexico border cities, the risks of HIV infection, though not as high, may well be increasing given the distribution of illicit drugs including cocaine and heroin into suburban and rural regions of the country. Death rate data for HIV infection by ethnic/racial background for the years 1987 to 1991 have shown increases across this time period for non-Hispanic Whites, African Americans, and Hispanics. During this time period, death rates per 100,000 resident population for males ages 25 to 44 have ranged from 24.4 to 35.1 for Whites, from 76.5 to 104.9 for African Americans, and from 47.3 to 58.2 for Hispanics. Comparable death rate data for females ages 25 to 44 have been 1.6 to 2.4 for non-Hispanic Whites, 15.8 to 23.7 for African Americans, and 7.3 to 9.3 for Hispanics (U.S. Department of Health and Human Services, 1994). Thus, across time, the rates of

HIV deaths among Hispanics have been greater than for non-Hispanic Whites but lower than for African Americans.

Mass media information, such as that presented not only on English-speaking but also on Spanish-speaking television and radio stations, has raised the general Latino public's awareness nationally that the risk of contracting SIDA (the Spanish acronym for AIDS) is a social reality for all Latinos. Nationally, some drug treatment programs have incorporated AIDS information and education as standard components. But less has been done to add cultural sensitivity for Latinos in relation to AIDS issues. Issues such as homosexuality, gender relationships among Latinos, and dynamics within the family and at work have not been introduced into many drug treatment programs, except for specialty programs that are overseen by certain community-based organizations that take an active interest in promoting cultural awareness for Latinos on issues of recovery from drug addiction that include prevention of HIV infection. Further research in the applied clinical setting is needed to clarify those aspects of treatment and prevention that must be modified in order to make drug treatment programs culturally relevant to various Latino populations. In such programs the aim is to introduce content on culture, "the shared values, norms, traditions, customs, arts, history, folklore, and institutions of a group of people," as these relate to the Latino clients' own life situations vis-à-vis recovery from drug addiction (Orlandi, Weston, & Epstein, 1992).

An AIDS Prevention Program Involving Latino and Anglo Heroin Addicts

In a large metropolitan city in the Southwest, an AIDS Prevention Program was developed for working with injection drug users who were addicted to heroin. These individuals, who also used cocaine and methamphetamine, engaged in injection drug use and needle sharing. The target audience, heroin addicts involved with or initiating a regimen of methadone maintenance, included Chicanos/Mexican Americans, other Latinos, and a few clients from other ethnic/racial groups. The purpose of the program was to increase knowledge and to modify high-risk behaviors for HIV infection such as needle sharing and unprotected sex. This fourteen-week program focused on HIV risk reduction, with material presented in three phases. In the early phase (weeks 1–6), the program goal involved establishing rapport and trust with program participants while conveying accurate information about AIDS and HIV testing. This information emphasized reducing the risk of AIDS by avoiding needle sharing and learning ways to engage in safe sex. In addition, some clients entered the program in great medical and psychological distress and in this early phase the program goal was medical and psychological stabilization.

In the middle phase (weeks 7–10), intervention activities included the opportunity to detox (to taper off the dosage and to end use) from methadone, orientation to job seeking, and exploration of feelings about recovery from addiction to heroin and other drugs. Speakers from other drug treatment programs, from NA, and from vocational counseling programs were invited to make presentations to the program participants. For some clients, individual therapy or counseling sessions were used to address specific issues that could not be examined in group. The opportunity for volunteer detoxification from methadone was offered as an option, but all clients were allowed to choose whether or not they wanted to seek detoxification from methadone.

In the late phase (weeks 11–14), the AIDS Prevention Program counselors explored options and plans for self-sufficiency. Goals included skills in handling and saving money, getting a job, paying for one's own methadone, pursuing a residential treatment or vocational training program, or choosing naltrexone treatment, and so on. Program staff referred clients to social service and job placement agencies, although the staff noted that most clients from this population were inconsistent about following through with such referrals. Some clients, however, dropped out before reaching this final phase.

Methods

An evaluation of this AIDS Prevention Program was conducted by comparing the activities of this program against a standard Methadone Only comparison group. This group, who received almost no AIDS counseling, was drawn from a local methadone maintenance dispensary. Participating clients in the AIDS Prevention Program were interviewed at intake (week 1), week 7, and week 16. Week 16 constituted the end of their participation in the AIDS Prevention Program. Important program outcomes included: (1) appropriate changes (a reduction) in drug use, such as a reduction in the use of heroin, cocaine, and other illicit drugs as well as alcohol; (2) a reduction in criminal behavior or illegal activities for profit; (3) an increase in self-efficacy to avoid relapse; and (4) an increased capacity to elicit social support from significant others who discourage drug use. The participating sample consisted originally of 63 participants in the AIDS Prevention Program and 60 participants in the Methadone Only clinic.

The Addiction Severity Index (ASI) (McLellan, Luborsky, Woody, & O'Brien, 1980) was part of the instrumentation administered to all study participants in this two-group pre–post design. The pretest interview protocol included: (1) an 18-item AIDS knowledge test; (2) frequency of exposure to high-risk events; (3) intentions to engage in safe sex and to avoid needle sharing; (4) high-risk behaviors in the past month; (5) intravenous drug use and needle sharing; (6) social relations as prompts to risk behavior; (7) relapse risk conditions; (8) a scale of Self-Efficacy in Avoiding Relapse; (9) preparedness for drug treatment; and (10) the ASI.

The posttest interview protocol was similar to the pretest but also included: (1) the General Acculturation Index (GAI), which was administered to Anglo-American as well as to Latino clients; (2) the drug user identity scales (Casual User, Drug Addict, and Recovering Addict); (3) an open-ended response item on effective needle cleaning techniques; and (4) questions on HIV sero status. At the posttest, the participants in the AIDS Prevention Program were also asked to respond to: (1) evaluations of program components; (2) comfort in working with the counselors;

(3) ratings of helpfulness of the counselors; (4) motivation for treatment; (5) effects of significant others in relapse avoidance; and (6) the Lifestyle Survey, a survey of health-related behaviors (Castro, 1991).

Demographic Characteristics—Total Sample

Only Anglo-Americans (non-Hispanic Whites) and Mexican Americans were included in this study sample, which totaled 101 participants. This total sample consisted of 51 clients from the AIDS Prevention Program and 50 clients from the Methadone Only condition. Table 11.1 shows the demographic characteristics of the sample for the present study. The frequency and percentage values in Table 11.1 are segmented by Treatment Group (AIDS Prevention or Methadone Only). This sample of 101 participants consisted of 66 Anglo-Americans and 35 Mexican Americans. Of these, 61 were male and 40 were female. Approximately half or 52 (51%) of the participants had full- or part-time employment, and 49 (48.5%) were unemployed. Regarding their living situation, 55 of these (54.4%) were living

TABLE 11.1   Demographic Characteristics of the Sample

| | Treatment Group | | | | |
| | AIDS Prevention | | Methadone Only | | Total Sample | |
	N	(Pct)	N	(Pct)	N	χ^2
Ethnic group:						0.78
Anglo-American	34	(51.5)	32	(48.5)	66	
Mexican American	17	(48.6)	18	(51.4)	35	
Sex:						0.63
Male	32	(52.5)	29	(47.5)	61	
Female	19	(47.5)	21	(52.5)	40	
Employment status:						0.17
Full	19	(59.4)	13	(40.6)	32	
Part	12	(60.0)	8	(40.0)	20	
Unemployed	20	(40.8)	29	(59.2)	49	
Living status:						0.59
Family	27	(49.1)	28	(50.9)	55	
Friends	11	(61.1)	7	(38.9)	18	
Alone	13	(46.4)	15	(53.6)	28	
Marital status:						0.76
Married	19	(54.3)	16	(32.0)	35	
Widowed	2	(66.7)	1	(33.3)	3	
Separated	7	(58.3)	5	(41.7)	12	
Divorced	11	(40.7)	16	(59.3)	27	
Never married	12	(50.0)	12	(50.0)	24	

*Note:*The total sample consisted of 101 heroin-addicted clients, 51 in the AIDS Prevention Program and 50 in the Methadone Only group. This sample consists of Anglo-American and Mexican-American clients.

within a family, 18 (17.8%) were living with friends, and 28 (27.7%) were living alone. Regarding marital status, 35 (34.6%) were married, 24 (23.8%) were never married, 27 (26.7%) were divorced, and the rest were separated or widowed. Chi-square analyses for these variables indicated that there were no differences in the distribution across treatment groups on ethnic group status, gender, employment status, living status, and marital status.

Demographic Characteristics, Mexican-American Sample

Table 11.2 shows the demographic characteristics of the Mexican-American sample for the present study. The frequency and percentage values in Table 11.2 are segmented by Treatment Group (AIDS Prevention Program or Methadone Only). The Mexican-American sample consisted of 17 clients from the AIDS Prevention Program and 18 clients from the methadone clinic, a total of 35 Mexican-American participants. Of these, 24 were male and 11 were female. Although the majority (57%) of the participants had full- or part-time employment, 15 of them (43%) were unemployed. Regarding marital status, 12 (34.3%) were married, 15 (43%) were separated or divorced, and the rest were never married. Chi-square analyses for these variables indicated that there were no differences in the distribution across treatment groups on gender, employment status, and marital status.

TABLE 11.2 Demographic Characteristics of the Mexican-American Sample

| | Treatment Group | | | | | |
| | AIDS Prevention | | Methadone Only | | Total Mexican-American Sample | |
	N	(Pct)	N	(Pct)	N	χ^2
Sex:						0.63
Male	11	(45.8)	13	(54.1)	24	
Female	6	(54.5)	5	(45.5)	11	
Employment status:						0.47
Full	7	(63.6)	4	(36.3)	11	
Part	4	(44.4)	5	(55.6)	9	
unemployed	6	(40.0)	9	(60.0)	15	
Marital status:						0.92
Married	7	(58.3)	5	(41.7)	12	
Widowed	1	(50.0)	1	(50.0)	2	
Separated	3	(42.9)	4	(57.1)	7	
Divorced	3	(37.5)	5	(62.5)	8	
Never married	3	(50.0)	3	(50.0)	6	

Note: The total sample consisted of 101 heroin-addicted clients, 51 in the AIDS Prevention Program and 50 in the Methadone Only group. This sample consists of Anglo-American and Mexican-American clients.

Characteristics of Clients at Treatment Entry

Table 11.3 shows other characteristics of these clients at treatment entry also as segmented by Treatment Group: the AIDS Prevention condition versus the Methadone Only condition. Data shown in Table 11.3 were obtained from the ASI. Regarding educational status, members of both groups had approximately 12 years of education. Regarding days of paid work, members of both groups reported fewer than 6 days of paid work in the last 30 days. Regarding the use of various illicit drugs, at the intake interview (the pretest) the AIDS Prevention group had a significantly higher number of days of heroin use (17.86) as compared with the Methadone Only group, which reported 7.98 days of heroin use in the last 30. Regarding methadone maintenance, the opposite pattern was observed across these two treatment conditions. Members of the AIDS Prevention group reported 15.61 days of methadone use in the past 30, relative to 25.8 days for the Methadone Only group. Thus, at entry into treatment, members of the AIDS Prevention group relative to the Methadone Only group reported more days of heroin use ($t = 4.29$, $p < .001$), but fewer days of methadone use ($t = -4.56$, $p < .001$).

The AIDS Prevention condition and the Methadone Only condition did not differ on days of cocaine use, where both used fewer than 3 days per month, or on the use of alcohol to intoxication, where both reported fewer than 4 days per month. However, regarding days of illegal activity for profit, at the intake/pretest

TABLE 11.3   Characteristics of Treatment Entry

| | Treatment Group | | | | |
| | AIDS Prevention | | Methadone Only | | |
	M	(SD)	M	(SD)	t
Age	37.24	(8.13)	40.62	(10.43)	−1.82*
Education	11.80	(1.96)	12.04	(2.32)	−0.55
Acculturation					
Anglo-Americans	4.67	(0.33)	4.67	(0.26)	0.03
Mexican Americans	3.18	(0.55)	3.21	(0.24)	−0.24
Days of paid work	3.84	(8.34)	5.94	(9.73)	−1.16
Days of heroin use	17.86	(12.24)	7.98	(10.85)	4.29***
Days of methadone use	15.61	(13.31)	25.88	(8.95)	−4.56***
Days of cocaine use	2.26	(6.19)	2.52	(6.33)	−0.21
Days of alcohol to intoxication	2.94	(7.81)	3.20	(8.37)	−0.16
Days of illegal activity for profit	7.18	(11.18)	1.88	(5.54)	3.03**
Days troubled by family problems	1.41	(1.56)	0.94	(1.53)	1.53
Days troubled by emotional problems	1.29	(1.64)	1.22	(1.64)	0.21

Note: This sample consists of 101 heroin-addicted clients with 51 clients in the AIDS Prevention Program and 50 clients in the Methadone Only group. This sample consists only of Anglo-American and Mexican-American clients. Variables and data are from the Addiction Severity Index (ASI) as administered to this sample of participants at treatment entry.

*$p < .10$. *$p < .05$. **$p < .01$. ***$p < .001$.

interview, members of the AIDS Prevention group reported 7.81 days of illegal activity in the last 30, relative to 1.88 days for the Methadone Only group ($t = 3.03$, $p < .01$). Finally, both conditions did not differ in the number of days troubled by family problems and days troubled by emotional problems. Here members of both groups reported fewer than 2 days of difficulties with family and emotions in the month before treatment entry.

Effect of Treatment Outcomes by Ethnic Group

A series of analyses of variance (ANOVAs) were conducted to examine the effects of Ethnic Group (Anglo-American or Mexican American) and Treatment Condition (AIDS Prevention or Methadone Only) on eight selected outcome measures. Table 11.4 shows the effects of Treatment and Ethnic Status on changes in these eight treatment outcomes. In Table 11.4, columns (1) and (2) present pretest-to-posttest change scores on these outcome measures for Anglo-Americans and Mexican Americans, respectively. The ANOVA factor effects are presented in columns (3), (4), and (5), where column (3) shows the effect for Ethnicity, column (4) the effect for Treatment, and column (5) the Ethnicity × Treatment interaction effect. Change scores on these eight outcome measures were generated from the difference between pre- and post scores on these measures, where specifically the pretest value was subtracted from the posttest. Accordingly, a *negative* change score indicated a *reduced* frequency or amount on the given outcome measure across the life of the intervention program, and a *positive* score indicated an *increase* on the given outcome measure.

Regarding days of heroin use in the last 30, an effect for treatment was observed ($F = 8.84$, $p < .01$) where a greater reduction in heroin use was observed both for Mexican Americans (−16.91), and for Anglo-Americans (− 9.04) in the AIDS Prevention Group relative to the decreases observed for the Methadone Only group. A trend was also observed here for the ethnicity factor ($F = 3.09$, $p < .10$). Moreover, for days of methadone use, a treatment effect was observed ($F = 4.04$, $p < .05$). Among members of the AIDS Prevention Program, the use of methadone increased both among Mexican Americans (+10.25) and among Anglo-Americans (+5.16) of the AIDS Prevention group relative to the Anglos (− 0.39) and among Mexican Americans (+2.23) in the Methadone Only group. This effect occurred as a complement to the observed decrease in the days of heroin use. Both effects operated in the direction that suggested that the AIDS Prevention Program was having an intended effect in increasing methadone use while decreasing heroin use. Similarly, regarding days of illegal acts for profit, there was a decrease in days for Mexican Americans (− 6.44) and Anglo-Americans (− 3.48) from the AIDS Prevention group relative to little change among members of the Methadone group ($F = 5.31$, $p < .001$).

Regarding psychological factors, on the scale of self-efficacy in avoiding relapse, an effect for ethnicity was observed where the Mexican Americans from the AIDS Prevention group (+0.71) and the Mexican Americans from the Methadone Only group (+0.39) exhibited an increase in self-efficacy, relative to little

TABLE 11.4   Effects of Treatment and Ethnic Status on Changes in Treatment Outcomes

	Ethnic Group		Effects		
	(1)	(2)	(3)	(4)	(5)
Change In:	AA	MA	E	T	ExT
Days of heroin use[a]:			3.09$^{\neq}$	8.84**	1.04
AIDS Prevention	−9.04	−16.91			
Methadone Only	−3.50	−5.59			
Days of methadone use[a]:			1.30	4.04*	0.13
AIDS Prevention	5.16	10.25			
Methadone Only	−0.39	2.23			
Committed illegal acts for profit[a]:			1.17	5.31*	0.19
AIDS Prevention	−3.48	−6.44			
Methadone Only	0.16	−1.09			
Self-efficacy in avoiding relapse:			9.27**	0.63	0.54
AIDS Prevention	−0.08	0.71			
Methadone Only	−0.10	0.39			
Had unprotected sex with different partners[b]:			3.48$^{\neq}$	3.24$^{\neq}$	1.20
AIDS Prevention	−0.20	−0.06			
Methadone Only	−0.07	−0.46			
Injected drugs[b]:			1.24	6.24*	0.88
AIDS Prevention	−2.04	−3.31			
Methadone Only	−1.07	−1.18			
Shared a needle while doing drugs[b]:			0.00	0.08	0.34
AIDS Prevention	−0.76	−0.50			
Methadone Only	−0.37	−0.64			
Used someone else's needle[b]:			0.59	7.09**	0.26
AIDS Prevention	−0.71	−1.06			
Methadone Only	−0.11	−0.19			

Note: Change scores range from negative values (e.g., −30) to positive values (e.g., +.30). AA refers to Anglo-American clients, and MA refers to Mexican-American clients.

[a.] Change in days in past 30.

[b.] Change in times in past month. Original scale values are: (1) = None, (2) = 1 to 5, (3) = 6 to 10, (4) = 11 to 15, (5) = 16 to 20, (6) = 21 to 25, (7) = 26 to 30.

$^{\neq}p<.10.$ *$p<.05.$ **$p<.01.$ ***$p<.001.$

change for the Anglo-Americans ($F = 9.27$, $p < .001$) from both groups. Regarding AIDS risk behavior, four risk conditions were examined: (1) frequency of unprotected sex with different partners, (2) frequency of drug use by injection, (3) frequency of needle sharing, and (4) frequency in the use of someone else's needle. A trend was observed only for unprotected sex with different partners, where changes in the direction of risk reduction were observed, but only as trends both for ethnicity ($F = 3.48$, $p < .10$) and for treatment ($F = 3.24$, $p < .10$).

Regarding the frequency in the last 30 days of drug use via injection, members of the AIDS Prevention group, Mexican Americans (−.3.31) and Anglo-Americans (−2.04), exhibited a greater *decrease* than the Methadone Only group ($F = 6.24$,

$p < .05$). By contrast, regarding needle sharing, there was little change across time, with no effect for ethnicity or treatment. Finally, regarding the use of someone else's needles, changes were small, although a significant treatment effect was observed in the direction of a *decrease* in the use of other people's needles ($F = 7.09$, $p < .01$) among Mexican Americans (−1.06) and Anglo-Americans (−0.71) from the AIDS Prevention group relative to their peers from the Methadone Only group.

The results observed for these selected outcome measures involving drug use, capacity for relapse avoidance, and reduction in behaviors that promote the risk of HIV infection, suggested some treatment effects for the AIDS Prevention Program. In summary, regarding the effects of ethnicity, a greater increase in self-efficacy for avoiding relapse was observed among Mexican Americans, as well as a trend toward fewer days of heroin use and less unprotected sex with different partners among the Mexican Americans.

Analyses of Predictors of Change in Heroin Use

To examine further the variables associated with changes in heroin use, three multiple regression analyses were conducted, one for the total sample, a second regression that examined only the Anglo-Americans as a group, and a third regression that examined only Mexican Americans. For the total sample, Table 11.5 shows the predictors of pretest-to-posttest changes in days of heroin use, where the significant predictors were days of methadone use ($\beta = -.49$), days of illegal activity for profit ($\beta = +.29$), days of alcohol use to intoxication ($\beta = +.19$), and confidant discouragement of heroin use ($\beta = -.16$).

Thus, for the total sample, an *increase* in heroin use during the 14-week program period (an undesired outcome) was associated with a *decrease* in days of methadone use, an *increase* in illegal activity for profit, an *increase* in alcohol use to

TABLE 11.5   Predictors of Increases in Heroin Use During Program Participation

Change In:	ΔR^2	F for ΔR^2	Final β	Total R^2	Equation F
Total sample:				0.46	20.81***
Days of methadone use	0.35	62.35***	−.49		
Days of illegal activity for profit	0.06	11.18***	.29		
Days of alcohol use to intoxication	0.03	5.46*	.19		
Confidant discourages use	0.23	4.26*	−.16		
Anglo-Americans:				0.53	23.45**
Days of methadone use	0.38	50.07***	−.60		
Days of cocaine use	0.03	10.61**	.28		
Days of alcohol use to intoxication	0.07	9.66**	.27		
Mexican Americans:				0.53	11.75***
Days of methadone use	0.28	18.45***	−.41		
Days of illegal activity for profit	0.13	8.88**	.50		
Acculturation level	0.12	7.91**	−.37		

$*p < .05.$ $**p < .01.$ $***p < .001.$

intoxication, and *less* confidant discouragement of heroin use (that is, greater encouragement to use heroin). When stated in the *therapeutic direction* (by reversing the sign of the regression variables for the total sample), a decrease in heroin use (a desired outcome) was associated with an *increase* in methadone use, a *decrease* in illegal activities, a *decrease* in heavy alcohol use, and *higher* levels of confidant discouragement of heroin use. For the Anglo-Americans, fewer days of methadone use ($\beta = -.60$) was also predictive of an increase in days of heroin use, as was days of cocaine use ($\beta = +.28$), and days of alcohol use to intoxication ($\beta = +.27$). Thus, for the Anglo-Americans, *reducing* heroin use was associated with *greater* methadone use, along with *fewer* days of cocaine and heavy alcohol use.

For Mexican Americans, again a *reduction* in days of methadone use was predictive of an *increase* in days of heroin use ($\beta = -.41$). In addition, a greater number of days of illegal activity for profit ($\beta = +.50$) was predictive of an increase in heroin use. For Mexican Americans, *lower* level of acculturation appeared as a significant predictor of increases in heroin use ($\beta = -.37$). Here the acculturation score served as a traitlike measure that was not expected to change across the sixteen-week period of the program. Acculturation scores in the "bicultural" and "low acculturation" ranges were associated with increases in heroin use.

From a therapeutic perspective, for the Mexican Americans, a *decrease* in days of heroin use was associated with an *increase* in days of methadone use, with a *decrease* in days of illegal activity, and with a *higher* level of acculturation. In summary, *fewer* days of illegal activities and a *decrease* in the use of other illicit drugs were observed as positive factors associated with a *decrease* in heroin use across the fourteen- to sixteen-week period of this treatment program. In addition, other effects were observed that were specific to Anglo-American and to Mexican-American heroin users.

Study Summary

In a large metropolitan city in the Southwest, an AIDS Prevention Program was developed for injection drug users who were addicted to heroin. The purpose of this program was to increase knowledge and to modify high-risk behaviors in order to reduce risk factors for HIV infection. An evaluation of this AIDS Prevention Program was conducted by comparing the activities of this program against a standard Methadone Only comparison group. This group was drawn from a local methadone maintenance dispensary. Participating clients were interviewed at three intervals. Only Anglo-Americans (non-Latino Whites) and Mexican Americans were included in this sample, which totaled 101 participants. This total sample consisted of 51 clients from the AIDS Prevention Program and 50 clients from the methadone clinic.

The results observed suggested minor treatment effects for the AIDS Prevention Program. Regarding the effects of ethnicity, Mexican Americans as compared with Anglo-Americans exhibited a greater increase in self-efficacy as well as a trend toward fewer days of heroin use and less unprotected sex with different partners.

Unexpectedly, acculturation scores in the bicultural and low acculturation ranges were associated with increases in heroin use across the sixteen-week life of the project. Moreover, for the AIDS Prevention group subjects, a *decline* in methadone use was associated with an *increase* in heroin use. By contrast, an increased involvement in illegal activities and the use of other illicit drugs appeared as negative factors that are associated with an increase in heroin use across the fourteen- to sixteen-week period of this treatment program.

Relapse Issues

For users of illicit drugs such as cocaine and heroin, relapse after undergoing drug treatment involves a return to drug use at pretreatment frequency and quantity levels. Regarding aspects of relapse, Marlatt and Gordon (1985) in relapse prevention theory (RPT) made an important distinction whereby a *lapse* is a brief episode of drug use (a slip) followed by an expeditious return to abstinence. By contrast, a *relapse* is a full-blown return to use for an extended period of time and typically at the original levels of use (quantity and frequency) or beyond. Besides amount and duration of use, the critical factor that governs whether a lapse progresses to a relapse is the attributional process by which the addicted person evaluates the *meaning* of an episode of drug use. Under this self-evaluation process, if an episode of use is followed by feelings of guilt and failure, the abstinence violation effect, then the individual is likely to continue drug use (Marlatt & Gordon, 1985).

In the treatment of cocaine- and heroin-addicted patients, the goal of relapse prevention is attained via skills training in recognizing, avoiding, and exerting control over events that produce relapse (Marlatt & Gordon, 1985). A complete program for relapse prevention in the clinical setting should address at least seven key areas: (1) addressing client ambivalence in treatment motivation; (2) reducing cocaine availability; (3) coping with high-risk situations; (4) overcoming cravings related to conditioned cues; (5) avoiding apparently irrelevant decisions; (6) modifying one's lifestyle toward more healthful behaviors; and (7) coping with the abstinence violation effect (Carroll, Rounsaville, & Keller, 1991).

In an extension of Marlatt and Gordon's RPT, Walton, Castro, and Barrington (1994) developed an eight-level scaling of lapse/relapse outcomes (abstinence, three levels of lapse, and four levels of relapse). In this scaling, the major measurable distinction between lapses and relapses is that a lapse is an isolated episode of use where such instances are separated by at least one week, whereas relapses are *clustered* episodes of use, binges that occur twice or more within a one-week period. These patterns of use aid in the classification of users as *Lapsers* and *Relapsers*. It has been observed that persons who ultimately remain as Lapsers, as compared with persons who go on to become Lapsers and Relapsers, make different cognitive attributions about their use, as evaluated by the attribution theory dimensions of *locus of causality*, *stability*, and *specificity*. For example, among cocaine users, a slip to cocaine use among Lapsers is seen as a unique event, one that is not likely to occur for other drugs (a specific attribution), whereas Relapsers see their use as likely to occur for other drugs as well (a global attribution) (Walton, Castro, & Barrington, 1994). Thus, as compared with clients who achieve total abstinence, those who experience a full-blown relapse also develop feelings of loss of control and self-blame. In a spiraling process, these negative views about self are perpetuated across time and, in turn, contribute to a greater likelihood of continuing to use (to relapse further). Clients who relapse, Relapsers, tend to see themselves as blameworthy for their own relapse, which they view as a failure at abstinence, whereas Lapsers see themselves as empowered to maintain control and to avoid relapse, despite suffering a brief slip—a lapse.

In preventing relapse among persons addicted to cocaine, education and training have focused on the identification of "triggers," events or situations (cues) that prompt or initiate a return to drug use. These cues, events, or triggers can include cravings that can occur when the recovering addict observes drug paraphernalia, or receives encouragement from others to use drugs as before. Developing skills for recognizing and avoiding these cues operates as a form of personal empowerment (self-control) that aids in avoiding relapse.

Relapse avoidance, however, is not always an individual or a rational process. Carroll, Rounsaville, and Keller (1991) have indicated that many users of cocaine (and users of heroin) also have coexisting Axis I and Axis II psychiatric disorders (such as depression or antisocial personality disorder) that complicate the process of coping with stressors that prompt a return to drug use. Drug-addicted persons who experience psychiatric complications cannot cope exclusively on their own but need even more stable and supportive sources of encouragement and support from family and friends.

To date, little work has been conducted on how the principles of RPT and the complications of psychiatric disorder may apply to various Latinos. Besides the need for the individual addict to make a formal commitment to sobriety and drug avoidance, a requirement for successful relapse prevention, issues involving the enhancement of self-concept and ethnic pride as well as family issues may require additional treatment focus for effective relapse prevention among recovering Latino drug addicts (Castro & Barrington, 1993). Instilling pride in family and ethnic heritage, where such pride may have been compromised by drug involvement, may foster a positive self-concept. In addition, establishing a new circle of friends (a sober reference group) and advising family on how to be supportive while also setting limits on maladaptive behavior are two critical system-oriented interventions that can provide a supportive context for drug avoidance (Castro et al., 1991). As observed in the study presented in this chapter, prompts by even one confidant that discourage heroin and other drug use may serve as a potent predictor of heroin avoidance, perhaps more so for Latinos, who place a strong cultural value on harmony (*simpatía*) in social and family relations (Marín & Marín, 1991). The presence of one or more significant others who discourage drug use would appear to be an important factor in successful relapse prevention among Latinos.

Treatment Implications

For work with various Latino populations, level of acculturation has been a useful, albeit limited, moderator variable, which should be refined further as it relates to drug abuse and treatment via advances in theory and measurement (Rogler, Cortes, & Malgady, 1991). The study presented in this chapter used the brief five-item General Acculturation Index (GAI) which was derived from the 20-item Acculturation Rating Scale for Mexican Americans (ARSMA) (Balcazar, Castro, & Krull, 1995; Cuellar, Harris, & Jasso, 1980). Both scales have the limitations involved in the use of scales with this format to assess acculturation issues. As discussed by Oetting and Beauvais (1991), cultural identification (the reciprocal of level of acculturation) is not clearly conveyed by a single continuum. That is, one can be acculturated to the mainstream culture while also being strongly identified with a minority culture.

As observed by Rogler, Cortés, and Malgady (1991), the use of a single-continuum model yields limited information for the purposes of research and assessment. That is, a single-continuum, *zero-sum* model assumes that as one's acculturation to Anglo-American culture increases, one's identification with one's own culture decreases. Clearly, this is not always the case. Thus, a person's rating on one scale may well be independent of the rating on the other scale, and a person could be highly acculturated to Anglo-American culture while remaining strongly identified with his or her own culture. On a single-continuum model, this profile (being bicultural) is reflected, but only partially so, by a mid-level rating—that is, an acculturation scale score of about 3 on the 1- to 5-point continuum. However, the confounding case occurs when a person exhibits low acculturation to the Anglo-American culture as well as a weak identification with his or her own culture. Unfortunately, this second profile (*marginal man* or acultural condition) would also result in a mid-level rating on the single continuum model. Although the single-continuum model may yield adequate assessment for those whose ratings fall at the poles (i.e., acculturation scores of 1.00 to 2.49, or of 3.70 to 5.00), important information may be confounded or ambiguous for those who rate at mid-levels.

There is a growing view that people who are truly bicultural are better equipped to operate within each of two cultures and typically have access to the resources and support necessary for treatment and recovery. By contrast, a person who is more acultural or culturally marginalized may not have the skills to gain access to resources and support in either culture (LaFromboise, Coleman, & Gerton, 1993). For this and other reasons, a bicultural person is likely to be better adjusted and may well have a more positive treatment outcome, whereas an acultural person is likely to be maladjusted and the prognosis for full drug rehabilitation may be less favorable. Thus, it is an important treatment consideration to know if one's client/patient is strongly identified as Mexican or Mexican American, is strongly identified as Anglo-American, is bicultural, or is acultural. Future research needs to address and to develop psychometrically sound methods of assessing level of acculturation and cultural identification for various Latino populations.

As discussed by Castro and colleagues (1994), acculturation to mainstream culture can have both positive and negative effects. Based on the coarse manner in which researchers now assess level of acculturation, it is difficult to predict under what conditions a high level of acculturation will facilitate or impede treatment outcomes. In the study presented in this chapter, however, ability to read English, one of the five items from the GAI, emerged as a predictor of positive drug treatment outcomes. Of importance here is the fact that the AIDS Prevention Program was available only to those participants who could speak English. Further, the Methadone Only comparison program was staffed primarily by English-speaking staff. It may well be that these monolingual, mainstream treatments were effective for the highest acculturated Mexican-American clients, while having a diminished relevance and effectiveness with the bicultural and less acculturated Latino clients. This interpretation suggests that in working with Latino heroin addicts, particularly those of bicultural or lower acculturation status, it is important for treatment programs to be available in the language(s) preferred by the client/patient and that they offer cultural and psychological activities that are culturally relevant and psychologically meaningful (LaFromboise, Trimble, & Mohatt, 1990).

Summary

This chapter examined general treatment factors and considerations for working with Latinos addicted to cocaine and/or heroin. These factors include level of acculturation, income level, level of education, barriers associated with general health care (such as having health insurance, language discrepancies, and access to services), and the drug user's system of family, friends, and fellow drug users. When a person who abuses illicit drugs realizes that treatment is necessary, a major unhealthy shift in lifestyle has occurred, marking a low point in his or her life (Washton, 1986). That is, the addicted individual may have lost or compromised work, social relations, and health, thereby indicating a clear need for treatment. Thus, addiction to an illicit drug, such as heroin or cocaine, induces a series of unhealthful life changes that constitute major disruptions to normal living. For Latinos addicted to illicit drugs, this lifestyle shift also occurs, although more research is needed to add further knowledge on the cultural, social, and psychological factors that may also contribute to the experience of drug addiction among Latinos.

A study was presented in this chapter that evaluated an AIDS Prevention Program in comparison with a Methadone Only treatment group. A greater increase in self-efficacy was observed among Mexican Americans, as well as a trend toward fewer days of heroin use and less unprotected sex with different partners. Acculturation scores in the bicultural and lower acculturation ranges were associated with increases in heroin use. In general, these analyses suggest that an increase in methadone use, which reflects compliance with the methadone program, is associated with a decrease in heroin use. Conversely, increases in the use of cocaine and/or alcohol and increases in illegal activity are associated with increases in heroin use.

For users of illicit drugs such as cocaine and heroin, *relapse* after undergoing drug treatment involves a return to drug use at levels high enough to signal a return to regular drug use. By contrast, a *lapse* is a brief episode of drug use followed by a return to abstinence and feelings of self-control and empowerment.

In the process of relapse prevention, developing skills for recognizing and avoiding cues that trigger a return to drug use operate as a form of personal empowerment. More research is needed to identify culturally relevant factors that may influence the process of relapse. In working with Mexican Americans, potential mediators of relapse may include a person's cultural identification with Mexican cultural values and traditions. It appears that acculturation to mainstream American culture can have both positive and negative effects. It is often difficult to predict under what conditions a high level of acculturation will facilitate or impede treatment outcomes. More process-oriented research is needed to clarify the ways in which the process of acculturation might contribute to the risk of illicit drug use among Latinos and how it might influence treatment outcomes. The availability of culturally relevant health promotion and drug treatment programs (i.e., programs that promote cultural identity and pride), as well as certain types of traditionalism, such as family loyalty and social responsibility, may help reduce the risks of illicit drug use among certain Latinos.

Within this context, how basic inpatient, outpatient, and aftercare programs should be modified to accommodate the unique needs of Latinos is an interesting and important treatment question in today's contemporary treatment arena. Currently, very few programs nationally include cultural factors as an integral part of their treatment and recovery program. For less acculturated (low acculturated and bicultural) Latinos, cultural issues such as Latino family dynamics, the importance of ethnic identity in recovery, and ways to avoid relapse might be affected by social obligations to *compañeros* (close friends). These are areas of importance that require further research and clinical work to clarify the unique needs and stressors faced by various Latinos who engage in the use of illicit drugs. Highly acculturated Latinos may not require the addition of culturally relevant intervention components, whereas bilingual/bicultural and especially low-acculturated Latinos may be in greater need of such culturally related intervention components in order to ensure enhanced recovery and a reduced risk of relapse.

Culturally sensitive relapse prevention efforts must also consider the supportiveness of the recovering addict's family and other aspects of preparedness of various Latino families to help their family member to avoid relapse. In working with Latino heroin addicts, it is important to offer an integrated program of treatment (LaFromboise, Trimble, & Mohatt, 1990), which for Latinos includes treatment in the language preferred by the client/patient, and also includes cultural and psychological activities that are relevant to the specific recovery needs of the specific subgroup of Latino clients who need drug treatment services.

References

Balcázar, H., Castro, F. G., & Krull, J. L. (1995). Cancer risk reduction in Mexican American women: The role of acculturation, education, and health risk factors. *Health Education Quarterly, 22,* 61–84.

Carroll, K. M., Rounsaville, B. J., & Keller, D. S. (1991). Relapse prevention strategies for the treatment of cocaine abuse. *American Journal of Drug and Alcohol Abuse, 17,* 249–265.

Castro, F. G. (1991). *Evaluation of Project PARA: An AIDS Education/Prevention Program.* Tempe, AZ: Hispanic Research Center.

Castro, F. G. (1994). Drug use and drug-related issues. In C. W. Molina & M. Aguirre-Molina (Eds.), *Latino health in the U.S.: A growing challenge* (pp. 425–446). Washington, DC: American Public Health Association.

Castro, F. G., & Barrington, E. H. (1993, July). *Client–treatment matching with a focus on ethnic identity.* Invited workshop presented at the 36th Annual Institute of Alcohol and Drug Studies, Texas Commission on Alcohol and Drug Abuse, Austin.

Castro, F. G., Barrington, E. H., Sharp, E. V., Dial, L. S., Wang, B., & Rawson, R. (1992). Behavioral and psychological profiles of cocaine users upon treatment entry: Ethnic comparisons. *Drugs and Society, 6*(3–4), 231–251.

Castro, F. G., Harmon, M., Coe, K., & Tafoya-Barraza, H. (1994). Drug prevention research with Hispanic populations: Theoretical and methodological issues and a generic structural model. In A. Cazares & L.A. Beatty (Eds.), *Scientific methods for prevention intervention research* (pp. 203–232). National Institute on Drug Abuse Research Monograph 139. DHHS Pub. No. (ADM) 94–3631. Washington, DC: U.S. Government Printing Office.

Castro, F. G., Sharp, E. V., Barrington, E. H., Walton, M., & Rawson, R. (1991). Drug abuse identity in Mexican Americans: Theoretical and empirical considerations. *Hispanic Journal of Behavior Sciences, 13,* 209–225.

Cuellar, I., Harris, L. C., & Jasso, R. (1980). An acculturation scale for Mexican American normal and clinical populations. *Hispanic Journal of Behavioral, Sciences, 2,* 199–217.

De La Cancela, V., & Guzman, L. P. (1991). Latino mental health service needs: Implications for training psychologists. In H. Myers et al. (Eds.), *Ethnic minority perspectives on clinical training and services in psychology.* Washington, DC: American Psychological Association.

Dole, V. P., & Nyswander, M. E. (1965). A medical treatment for diacetyl-morphine (heroin) addiction. *Journal of the American Medical Association, 193,* 80–84.

Enchautegri, M. E. (1995). *Policy implications of Latino poverty.* Washington, DC: Urban Institute.

Gearing, F. R. (1972). Methadone maintenance: Six years later. *Contemporary Drug Problems, 1,* 191–206.

Giachello, A. L. M. (1994). Issues of access and use. In C. W. Molina & M. Aguirre-Molina (Eds.), *Latino health in the U.S.: A growing challenge* (pp. 83–111). Washington, DC: American Public Health Association.

Ginzberg, E. (1991). Access to health care for Hispanics. *Journal of the American Medical Association, 265*(2), 238–241.

Hayes-Bautista, D. E., Shink, W. O., & Chapa, J. (1988). *The burden of support: Young Latinos in an aging society.* Stanford, CA: Stanford University Press.

Jessor, R., & Jessor, S. L. (1977). *Problem behavior and psychosocial development: A longitudinal study of youth.* New York: Academic Press.

Jorquez, J. S. (1984). Heroin use in the barrio: Solving the problem of relapse or keeping the Tecato Gusano asleep. *American Journal of Drug and Alcohol Abuse, 10*(1), 63–75.

LaFromboise, T., Coleman, H. L. K., & Gerton, J. (1993). Psychological impact of biculturalism: Evidence and theory. *Psychological Bulletin, 114*(3), 395–412.

LaFromboise, T. D., Trimble, J. E., & Mohatt, G. V. (1990). Counseling intervention and American Indian tradition: An integrative approach. *The Counseling Psychologist, 18,* 628–654.

Macías, R. F. (1977). U.S. Hispanics in 2000 AD: Projecting the number. *Agenda 1977, 7,* 16–20.

Maddox, J. F., & Desmond, D. P. (1992). Ten-year follow-up after admission to methadone maintenance. *American Journal of Drug and Alcohol Abuse, 18*(3), 289–303.

Marín, B. V. O., Marín, G., Padilla, A. M., & de la Rocha, C. (1983). Utilization of traditional and non-traditional sources of health care among Hispanics. *Hispanic Journal of Behavioral Sciences, 3*(1), 65–80.

Marín, G., & Marín, B. V. (1991). *Research with Hispanic populations.* Newbury Park, CA: Sage Publications.

Marlatt, G. A., & Gordon, J. (1985). *Relapse prevention: Maintenance strategies in the treatment of addictive behaviors.* New York: Guilford Press.

McLellan, A. T., Luborsky, L., O'Brien, C. P., & Woody, G. E. (1980). An improved evaluation instrument for substance abuse patients: The addiction severity index. *Journal of Nervous and Mental Disease, 168,* 26–33.

Molina, C. W., Zambrana, R. E., & Aguirre-Molina, M. (1994). The influence of culture, class, and environment on health care. In C.W. Molina & M. Aguirre-Molina (Eds.), *Latino health in the U.S.: A growing challenge* (pp. 23–43), Washington, DC: American Public Health Association.

Moore, J. (1990). Mexican American women addicts: The influence of family background. In R. Glick & J. Moore (Eds.), *Drugs in Hispanic communities* (pp. 127–153). New Brunswick, NJ: Rutgers University Press.

National Coalition of Hispanic Health and Human Services Organizations (COSSHMO). (1988). *Delivering preventive health care to Hispanics: A manual for providers.* Washington, DC: Author. As cited in *Journal of the American Medical Association Council Report.* (1991). Hispanic health in the United States. *Journal of the American Medical Association, 265*(2), 248–252.

National Institute on Drug Abuse. (1992). *National Household Survey on Drug Abuse: Population Estimates 1991.* DHHS Pub. No. (ADM) 92–1887. Washington, DC: U.S. Government Printing Office. As cited in *Drug abuse among racial/ethnic groups.* (1993). Rockville, MD: National Institute on Drug Abuse.

National Institute on Drug Abuse. (1993). *Drug abuse among racial/ethnic groups.* Rockville, MD: Author.

Newcomb, M. D., & Bentler, P. M. (1988). *Consequences of adolescent drug use: Impact on the lives of young adults.* Newbury Park, CA: Sage Publications.

Oetting, E. R., & Beauvais, F. (1991). Orthogonal cultural identification theory: The cultural identification of minority adolescents. *International Journal of the Addictions, 25*(5A, 6A), 655–685.

Orlandi, M. A., Weston, R., & Epstein, L. G. (1992). *Cultural competence for evaluators: A guide for alcohol and other drug abuse prevention practitioners working with ethnic/racial communities.* Rockville, MD: Office for Substance Abuse Prevention.

Peele, S., & Brodsky, A. (1991). *The truth about addiction and recovery: The life process program for outgrowing destructive habits.* New York: Simon & Schuster.

Pérez-Stable, E. J. (1987, February). Issues in Latino health care—Medical Staff Conference. *Western Journal of Medicine, 146,* 213–218.

Platt, J. J. (1988). *Heroin addiction: Theory, research, and treatment.* (Vol. 1). (2nd ed). Malabar, IL: Krieger.

Rawson, R. A., Obert, J. L., McCann, M. J., Castro, F. G., & Ling, W. (1991). Neurobehavioral treatment for cocaine dependency. In F. Tims & C. Leukfield (Eds.), *Advances in cocaine treatment* (NIDA Research Monograph). Rockville, MD: NIDA.

Rogler, L. H., Cortés, D. E., & Malgady, R. G. (1991). Acculturation and mental health status among Hispanics: Convergence and new directions for research. *American Psychologist, 46*(6), 585–597.

Schilling, R. F., Schenke, S. P., Nichols, S. E., Zayas, L. H., Miller, S. O., Orlandi, M. A., & Botvin, G. J. (1989). Developing strategies for AIDS prevention research with Black and Hispanic drug users. *Public Health Reports, 104,* 2–11.

Solís, J. M., Marks, G., García, M., & Shelton, D. (1990). Acculturation, access to care, and use of preventive services by Hispanics: Findings from HHANES 1982–84. *American Journal of Public Health 80* (Suppl.), 11–19.

Szapocznik, J., & Kurtines, W. M. (1989). *Break-throughs in family therapy with drug abusing and problem youth*. New York: Springer.

U.S. Bureau of the Census. (1993). *1990 census of population: Persons of Hispanic origin in the United States*. Washington, DC: U.S. Government Printing Office.

U.S. Department of Health and Human Services. (1994). *Health—United States—1993*. DHHS Publication No. (PHS) 94–1232. Hyattsville, MD: Author.

Walton, M. A., Castro, F. G., & Barrington, E. H. (1994). The role of attributions in abstinence, lapse, and relapse following substance abuse treatment. *Addictive Behaviors, 19*, 319–331.

Washton, A. M. (1986). Nonpharmacologic treatment of cocaine abuse. *Psychiatric Clinics of North America, 9*(3), 563–571.

Westermeyer, J. (1985). Psychiatric diagnosis across cultural boundaries. *American Journal of Psychiatry, 142*(7), 798–805.

Chapter 12

Socioeconomic and Cultural Factors in Rehabilitation of Latinos with Disabilities

MARÍA CECILIA ZEA
FAYE Z. BELGRAVE

JORGE G. GARCÍA
TIRSIS QUEZADA
The George Washington University

In this chapter we present socioeconomic and demographic information about Latinos with disabilities, a group that only recently has begun to be studied. Socioeconomic and employment barriers due to disability are also discussed. The remainder of this chapter focuses on factors that may affect adjustment to disability and rehabilitation outcomes among Latinos. The interaction among socioeconomic issues, cultural values, and disability is also discussed (see Figure 12.1).

Sociodemographic Factors

There are 3,343,000 Latinos with disabilities in the United States, who represent 15.3% of the Latino population living in this country. This compares to a disability rate of 19.7% for non-Latino Whites, 20% for African Americans, and 9.9% for Asian Americans (McNeil, 1993). But, perhaps most important, the number of Latinos with a disability has grown 31% in just seven years, five times higher than the growth rate of non-Latino groups (Bowe, 1992).

The last part of this chapter was published in the *Journal of Social Behavior and Personality, 9,* 185-200.

			Sociodemographic -Place of residence -Median age -Educational level -Median income -Employment status -Language preference
	Socio- economic status	Commonalities	
Place of origin (United States or a Latin American country)		Latino charac- teristics in the United States	*Cultural Values* -Allocentrism, personalism -Familialism -Interdependence -Defined gender roles -*Simpatía* -Respect -Power distance -Present-time orientation -Informality -Spirituality
	Cultural roots: -Religion -Language -Race -Ethnicity		
		Differences[a]	-Historical -Racial -Geographical -Linguistic -Acculturational -Socioeconomic

FIGURE 12.1   Variables That Contribute to Latino Characteristics in the United States

Source: Adapted from Zea, M. C., Quezada, T., & Belgrave, F. Z. (1994) Latino cultural values: Their role in adjustment to disablility. *Journal of Social Behavior and Personality*, 9, 18–20, with permission.
[a] Although these differences contribute to the diversity of the Latino population, mentioned earlier, they are not within the scope of this chapter.

Statistics across ethnicity for individuals aged 16 through 64 with a work disability show that approximately 8.2% of Latinos have a work disability, compared to 7% for non-Latino Whites and 13.7% for African Americans (Schick & Schick, 1991). These data seem to indicate that the disability rate for Latinos is more similar to the disability rate for non-Latino Whites than for other groups. If we examine the data on Latinos with severe disabilities, however, this similarity ends drastically. According to Bowe (1992), 68.3% of Latinos with a work disability are severely disabled, compared to 52% for non-Latino Whites.

Employment information shows that only 28% of Latino males with a work disability are in the labor force (compared to 74% without a disability). Of these, 14% are employed full time. For non-Latino White males with a work disability,

39% are in the labor force (compared to 79.5% without a disability), and 26% are employed full time. Regarding unemployment, 28% of Latino males with a work disability are unemployed, whereas this figure is 13% for White males with a work disability. A lower percentage of females with a disability are represented in the labor force, although differences remain across ethnic groups. Only 18% of Latino women with a work disability are in the labor force, whereas this number is 29% for non-Latino White females with a work disability. As for unemployment rates for females with a work disability, these percentages are 11% for non-Latino Whites and 18% for Latinas (NIDRR, 1992).

Occupation also changes after a disability. Latino males experience about a 50% drop in managerial/professional positions after a disability. Only 6.7% of Latino males with a disability hold these positions, compared to 13% of Latino males without a disability. On the other hand, Latino females with a disability experience a 32% drop in clerical positions after a disability (Bowe, 1992). By and large, Latino males with a disability hold labor-type occupations (32%), whereas females hold service (32%) and clerical (29%) positions.

The mean earnings of workers with a disability vary across ethnic groups. The mean income for Latino males is about $12,223, which represents about 77% of the mean income for non-Latino White males with disabilities ($15,869). Income drops substantially in the case of females with a work disability, for all ethnic groups, and there is less variation across ethnic groups. The mean earnings of Latinas is $7,559 and represents about 90% of the mean income for non-Latino White females with disabilities ($8,340) (NIDRR, 1992). According to Bowe (1992), the majority of Latinos with a disability live under the poverty level, regardless of gender. As an illustration, 27% of adult Latinos with a disability who are in the labor force live under the poverty level, and this is the segment with the highest earnings among Latinos with disabilities.

Latinos with a work disability are also more dependent on food stamps and Medicaid than non-Latino Whites with a disability. About 32% of Latinos receive food stamps compared to 14.4% for Whites, and about 33% of Latinos receive Medicaid, compared to about 18% for non-Latino Whites. Data on Social Security Insurance (SSI) are different, with about 30% of non-Latino Whites with a work disability receiving this benefit, compared to about 23% for Latinos with a work disability (Schick & Schick, 1991).

Insurance coverage rates of Latinos with disabilities are low. Only 41% of men and 46% of women with a disability who have jobs are covered by a pension or health plan (Bowe, 1992). However, non-Latino Whites with disabilities have similar insurance rates (41% for men and 51% for women). Insurance rates for Latinos with disabilities are lower if we include those individuals who are unemployed.

The educational level of Latinos with disabilities is low, though similar to the educational level of Latinos without a disability. About 24% of Latinos with a disability never complete eighth grade compared to 21% for those without a disability. Just 6.6% of Latinos with a disability graduate from college, compared to 13.5% of Latinos without a disability (Bowe, 1992). The statistics on education, employment, and occupational status suggest that Latinos with disabilities are not faring well on any indicator. More research is needed in order to address the specific concerns and challenges of Latinos with disabilities.

Data on Latinos with disabilities is often confounded by race. According to Summers and Jackson (1992), information about type of disability for Latinos is limited by classification problems, because in many health surveys Latinos are considered White. In general, Latinos have lower mortality rates from all causes combined than other population groups, with the exception of diabetes and cirrhosis. Primary causes of death are coronary heart disease and strokes, followed by cancer. Latinos also have excess cancer rates, especially for stomach and prostate cancer. Diabetes mellitus has a high incidence rate in the Latino population. The risk of AIDS is three times higher for Latino males than for White males, and 19% of AIDS cases are found in Latino women (Summers & Jackson, 1992). In terms of mental and emotional disability, there are few differences between Latinos and non-Latino Whites, although the incidence of depression is higher for non-Latino Whites than for Latinos.

Summarizing the data for Latinos with disabilities, Bowe (1992) presented a *typical* demographic profile of an adult Latino with a disability. This person is about 43 years old, is married, lives in an urban area, is a high school graduate, has a severe disability, is likely to be unemployed, holds a blue-collar job, and has a mean income of about $11,000.

Despite a high incidence of disability, Latinos have yet to obtain the full benefit of state/federal vocational rehabilitation services. According to Giles (1992), Latinos with disabilities are likely to remain in referral or applicant status for a longer period of time than members of other groups, and they are more frequently ineligible for services. At the same time, the amount of money spent toward their rehabilitation is low, and they receive significantly less academic training. Consequently, rehabilitation rates and outcomes for Latinos with disabilities can be expected to be poor.

Socioeconomic and Employment Barriers

In the introduction to this chapter we described the demographic characteristics of Latinos with disabilities, including key socioeconomic variables such as educational level, labor force participation, income, poverty level, insurance coverage, and occupational status. Statistics on these variables depicted a disadvantaged situation for Latinos with disabilities. Insufficient education, low earnings, poverty, unemployment or part-time employment, and positions in unskilled labor occupations jeopardize the potential for successful rehabilitation outcomes. The generally accepted goal of rehabilitation in the United States today is the full reinsertion of individuals with disabilities in the work force via their placement in competitive employment with salaries comparable to those of individuals without a disability. This goal has proved difficult to achieve for the population with disabilities as a whole, let alone for disadvantaged minority groups such as Latinos. Several barriers to employment interact with the socioeconomic factors discussed earlier in this chapter. Frequently mentioned barriers are work disincentives, lack of transferable skills, discrimination, standardized testing, and labor market trends, among others. These factors are discussed next.

Work Disincentives

Latinos receiving direct and indirect disability benefits realize that these would be lost if they regain employment. This is actually the case for all individuals with disabilities in the United States. Data presented earlier in this chapter show that a considerable percentage of Latinos with disabilities receive SSI, food stamps, and Medicaid. They also qualify for other indirect benefits such as rent subsidies and educational and social services. The fear of losing these benefits translates into an unwillingness to find a job and a tendency instead just to be satisfied with the disability benefits they receive. Work disincentives are particularly strong for this population group because disability benefits give them a financial stability that they traditionally have not enjoyed, and access to insurance and health care has traditionally been limited (Smart & Smart, 1991).

The problem may be compounded by the family if they react to protect the member with a disability by caring for him or her. This overcaring may in fact discourage productive work outside the home. Moreover, the burden of caring for a family member is alleviated if the member with a disability contributes to the household a stable disability payment and other benefits. In our experience, this may be a common compromise that benefits all family members involved, especially given that obtaining well-paid jobs is so difficult. It should be emphasized that the problem is not that Latinos prefer welfare but that there is a lack of structural incentives to work. The low number of Latino applications for rehabilitation services and the low percentage who are considered rehabilitated after receiving services may in part be the result of this phenomenon. Further research is needed to investigate this relationship.

Lack of Transferable Skills

As the statistics presented earlier indicate, the majority of Latinos in the work force hold positions involving labor or domestic work. These types of jobs may become impossible to perform for people who acquire a disability that precludes them from doing strenuous work. Suddenly the range of job opportunities becomes even more limited because Latinos have not learned advanced technical skills and do not have the appropriate educational qualifications to apply to and perform the jobs available in the labor market today. As indicated by Smart and Smart (1991), the fastest growing jobs are those of technicians and support occupations that provide technical assistance to professional workers. In these jobs, one has to be able to operate and program increasingly sophisticated equipment. The second fastest growing jobs involve professional occupations, especially computer scientists, engineers, health technicians, lawyers, and social workers. These occupations require bachelor and graduate degrees that most Latinos do not possess. To worsen matters, the types of occupations that frequently are held by Latinos are projected to decline in the future. These occupations include handlers, helpers, and laborers, which require the least education (Smart & Smart, 1991).

The fastest growing occupations today maximize the need for workers with good English skills as well as technological skills. Level of acculturation becomes an important factor in that Latinos who are more highly acculturated are more likely to succeed in these jobs. Recent immigrants, such as Salvadorans and other Central Americans, are the most disadvantaged because of their limited English skills. These are limitations for Latinos in general, but they become particularly relevant for Latinos with disabilities who need to transfer to new jobs.

Discrimination

Researchers have documented different forms of discrimination against Latinos as well as against other minority groups. Dziekan and Okocha (1993) conducted a large study in which they reviewed the acceptance rates of minorities for rehabilitation services. They reviewed 60,000 cases and found that the total pool of applicants included only 2.5% of Latinos and their acceptance rate was only 44%, well below the 61% for non-Latino Whites.

Statistics shown earlier in this chapter also illustrate structural discrimination. Latinos with disabilities are more frequently unemployed, earn less money, and are more frequently occupied in part-time jobs than non-Latino Whites. Studies on employer attitudes confirm a discriminatory view of Latinos as workers. Smart and Smart (1991) cited research studies concluding that many employers stereotype Latinos as "preferring welfare to hard work, tend to be lazy, are inclined to violence, are less intelligent, and are less patriotic" (p.176).

Other manifestations of discrimination may occur on the job. Even if Latinos with disabilities manage to find a job, they may encounter negative attitudes from employers and co-workers afterwards. One such case involves *tokenism*. This concept can be defined as the experience of a minority individual in a job environment dominated by another culture, whose members encapsulate the individual into a stereotyped role (see Chapter 9 by Comas-Díaz). The individual feels isolated and misunderstood, and co-workers resent "token" individuals because they perceive that their hiring and promotion were based not on merit but on ethnicity. In the case of Latinos with disabilities, they may be encapsulated into two token roles, that of a person with a disability and that of an ethnic minority, further compounding the problem (Smart & Smart, 1991).

Discrimination and prejudice also may worsen the problem of lack of work incentives. Because of past experiences with discrimination, stereotyping, and prejudice, Latinos may develop lower placement expectations and prefer jobs that are less demanding and challenging. The worst-case scenario would be one in which Latinos separate themselves from the work force altogether. This is especially likely to occur if they are able to negotiate a financial arrangement.

Standardized Testing

In describing the significance of language as a cultural factor mediating the practice of testing Latinos with a disability, Kunce and Vales (1984) stated that language affects the evaluation of intelligence, abilities, rehabilitation potential, emotional and motivational status, mental and personality assessment, and vocational interests and expectations. This is not only because clients who are Spanish speakers may not be able to understand verbal or written instructions, but because cultural bias is inherent in all tests. Translations involve both translating the language and translating the cultural elements of a test. This relates to the issue of standardization. Very few tests commonly utilized in the assessment of people with disabilities have been standardized for Latinos. This means that the results of these tests may not be valid and reliable when used as a primary tool for psychological diagnosis, vocational evaluation, or job placement.

In Chapter 13, Preciado and Henry describe different techniques that may be used to override language barriers faced by professionals administering verbal or written tests to Latinos, including those with disabilities. The authors discuss different translation techniques that allow the immersion of relevant cultural elements into the test, and proper training and utilization of interpreters.

Labor Market Trends

Earlier in the chapter we discussed the market trends delineated by Smart and Smart (1991). The fastest growing jobs are in technical and professional fields that require refined technological skills and advanced educational qualifications, which most Latinos do not possess. This poses a significant barrier to individuals with disabilities who aspire to change to a career that will accommodate their abilities. More and more, Latinos have to face the reality of having to undergo substantial training in order to meet the requirements of these jobs. Otherwise, they will inevitably become dependent on family and government support.

However, Suazo (1991) suggested that Latinos with disabilities can utilize some recent labor changes to their advantage. Individuals with physical disabilities, largely the major cause for which Latinos seek rehabilitation services, can benefit significantly from changes in the work structure that allow more time and scheduling flexibility. The physical demands of jobs are decreasing with the rapid incorporation of advanced communications technology such as e-mail, fax machines, word processors, advanced computer technology, and checkout scanners. This technology is becoming increasingly accessible for individuals with disabilities, even those with sensory limitations such as visual or hearing impairments. With proper job skills training, Latinos with disabilities can take advantage of these technological developments and actually enhance their career choices. Rehabilitation professionals will have to keep pace with these changes and be able to help their clients by facilitating access to the new technology and adapting it to their specific needs.

Diversity among Latinos

Several factors may affect adjustment to disability and rehabilitation outcomes among Latinos, especially the interaction between socioeconomic factors, cultural values, and disability. It is misleading to refer to a common "Latino" culture. Cultural diversity is the rule, and this diversity is deeply rooted in historical, racial, geographical, linguistic, acculturational, and socioeconomic differences. Although Latinos are commonly described as one distinctive racial group, and most research refers and applies to one particular Latino group (e.g., Mexican Americans), Latinos are indeed multiracial because of the varying degrees of mixing of indigenous Latinos with European colonizers or with African descendants. This multiracial diversity follows a different pattern in each country or region.

Intragroup socioeconomic disparity is also characteristic of this population group. For example, Latinos of European descent or with lighter skin tend to belong to a higher socioeconomic status, whereas higher levels of poverty are found among Afro-Latinos and indigenous groups. European-descent Latinos usually control power and resources, whereas Latinos of African and indigenous descent are mostly laborers. Even today, many of these disparities remain. Some researchers have suggested that socioeconomic factors may play a larger role in how well a person does than culture (Garza & Ames, 1974; Zea & Tyler, 1994).

Another factor that influences adjustment to disability and rehabilitation status is level of acculturation (Smart, 1993, 1995). This concept has been defined as the process by which behaviors, attitudes, and customs of the dominant culture are incorporated by the nondominant group (Berry, 1990). The interaction with Anglo culture strengthens either Latinos' self-identification or its opposite, assimilation into the dominant culture. A positive product of acculturation is *biculturalism*, which describes individuals who maintain a strong psychological Latino identity while acquiring attitudes and behaviors characteristic of the Anglo culture. This type of biculturalism has been associated with positive outcomes, such as better adjustment and rehabilitation outcomes (Rivera, 1983; Szapocznik, Kurtines, & Fernandez, 1980). But acculturation may also play a role in augmenting disability. Research has shown that certain stages or forms of acculturation lead to stress, which correlates with an increase of mental and emotional disorders such as depression, interpersonal difficulties, and alcoholism (Cuéllar & Arnold, 1988).

Cultural Values and Adjustment to Disability

In the remainder of this chapter we discuss how Latino cultural values influence adjustment to disability and rehabilitation outcomes. Culture has been defined as the integrated pattern of behavior acquired by humans, including knowledge, beliefs, values, and behaviors, which condition further actions (Kroeber & Kluckhohn, 1952). These culturally determined actions include health beliefs, health practices, and attitudes toward disabilities. Although this definition of culture seems static and could lead to cultural stereotyping, the authors of this chapter sustain the notion that any definition of culture applied to Latinos in the United States ought to include an understanding of genesis of culture as arising from an adaptation to a new group, out of social interaction, and out of a creative process (Berry, Poortinga, Segall, & Dasen, 1992). In this sense, Latinos may constitute a group in perpetual cultural transformation and creation. The processes of ethnic identity development and acculturation as applied to adjustment to disability are clear examples of a dynamic definition of culture. Some health beliefs and cognitions are based on the Western medical model, particularly among educated Latinos. Other health beliefs and cognitions are based on indigenous and African folk practices and explanations. An example of the former type of belief is the explanation that poliomyelitis is caused by several viruses, preventable through vaccination. An example of the latter type of belief is the explanation that poliomyelitis is caused by *mal de ojo* or evil eye, treatable by a *curandero* or healer.

A framework for understanding how cultural values influence disability-related attitudes and behaviors in the Latino population is presented in Figure 12.2.

Cultural values such as allocentrism, familialism, defined gender roles, a *simpatía* or congeniality orientation, deference to power, preference for interdependence over dependence, time orientation, informality, and a spiritual orientation have been described as cultural characteristics of Latinos (Kunce & Vales, 1984; Marín & Marín, 1991; Zea, Quezada, & Belgrave, 1994). These cultural values can have an impact on how Latinos adjust to disability and on their participation in the rehabilitation process. The authors have observed examples of how these cultural values influence adjustment to disability and rehabilitation outcomes in their work with Latinos with disabilities. This work has consisted primarily of interventions with groups of Latinos with disabilities in community settings. These individuals for the most part are relatively poor; many do not speak English; and they come from Central America, the Dominican Republic, and South America. Generally, intervention programs involving Latinos with disabilities have been designed to improve employment and other functional outcomes by teaching clients how to obtain access to social support and gain psychosocial competence.

Additional examples of the influence of cultural values on adjustment to disability and rehabilitation are derived from the authors' experiences with other diverse groups of Latinos who are not disabled. These core values and beliefs are discussed next.

Familialism and Allocentrism

Latino culture is mostly relational and oriented toward the family. The needs of the family and the group may be more important than those of the individual. The family unit is tightly knit. Values that support allocentrism and familialism account for the attachment to the nuclear and extended family and the emphasis that is placed on the needs and points of view of all members of the group (Comas-Díaz, 1989; Marín, 1990; Triandis, Marín, Lisansky, & Betancourt, 1984).

Cultural Values	Impact on Rehabilitation Process
Allocentrism	Attitudes and behaviors toward family member with disability are supportive.
Familialism	Overprotective nuclear and extended family inhibit independence.
Interdependence	Inclusion of friends increases support network.
Family and community centered	Interdependence and interconnectedness promote acceptance of help, but may also promote dependence.
Defined gender roles	Disability may not be acknowledged as such, unless it impedes productivity or reproduction.
	Aguante, endurance of the disability, is promoted.
Simpatía	Attitudes and behaviors toward those in need are supportive.
	Apparent compliance with health care providers avoids conflict.
Power distance	Relationship with health-care provider is hierarchical. Solutions
Personalismo/respect	to problems may be perceived as outside the client's domain.
Present-time orientation	There is concern for immediate, practical problems. Too strong present-time orientation may interfere with long-term planning of treatment.
Informality	There is little concern for formal structures such as timeliness and orderliness.
Spirituality	Faith in God's will can lead to positive acceptance.
	Disability is explained as a "trial" that the individual has to endure, or as punishment for wrongdoing.

FIGURE 12.2   Latino Cultural Values and Their Impact on the Rehabilitation Process

Allocentrism and familialism are translated to supportive attitudes and behaviors toward the person who may have a disability or who is in need within the group. For a person with a disability, the Latino family and the community can provide much support. For example, Mexican-American families have been described as supportive and protective of individuals with disabilities (Smart & Smart, 1991). In fact, support may be expected from the family more than from the rehabilitation professional. Generally, the support from family and others within the group has a positive impact on functioning. Research indicates that social support from the family has a favorable impact on outcomes such as employment for ethnic minorities and others with disabilities (Walker, Belgrave, Jarama, Ukawuilulu, & Rackley, 1995). "Overprotectiveness" on the part of the family may hinder movement towards independence among Latinos with disabilities, but this can be avoided by including the family in the rehabilitation process. This might mean, for example, having a member of the family involved in rehabilitation sessions with the individual.

Support from families is valued among Latinos, but many immigrants, particularly those escaping political violence, have come to the United States without families. Individuals with disabilities may not have the support of family members that benefits Latinos who have immediate and extended family in the United

States. For the immigrant, the community or friends may replace the family. In our work with Latinos with disabilities, we found that when they were asked who provides support, friends were more often mentioned than family, unlike the case of those Latino groups whose families were more readily available. In this case, many Central Americans migrated without their families and consequently do not have this source of support. Yet, because of relational and communal values in the community, they were able to identify others in the community who provide support. This implies that a community-oriented intervention where friends and neighbors become involved in providing support may be effective.

Interdependence

Closely related to values of familialism and allocentrism are values of interdependence among Latinos. These values differ from those of Anglo-Americans, who may value individualism and independence. Kerr and Meyerson (1987) pointed out that independence and self-sufficiency are as American as apple pie. Latino culture, being more relational, places more emphasis on interdependence. Interdependence reflects the fact that the well-being of the group is more important than that of the individual, and that individuals cannot progress without the help of others and reciprocation for the support received. The individualist axiom "I did it on my own" has less merit for Latinos than "I did it thanks to others." Interdependence may be interpreted by the dominant culture as dependence, and Latinos may be criticized for not having the "rugged individualism" characteristic of Americans.

Interdependence, however, may be a more appropriate way of adapting to disability, particularly when professional rehabilitation services are not readily available. Clients may be more readily able to participate in rehabilitation programs than if the cultural pressure was to "do it" on their own. From this perspective, the cultural value of interdependence may facilitate adaptation among Latinos with disabilities. All members of a functioning family or relationship are interdependent with one another. One implication of an interdependent orientation is that the disability may be *owned* by several persons. Hence the problems and solutions associated with having a disabling condition are shared by many. One practical implication of a value of interdependence is that the coordination of rehabilitation services for Latinos with disabilities may be facilitated by including those with whom the individual functions interdependently.

Clearly Defined Gender Roles

Gender roles are well defined among the Latino population. Men are expected to be material providers, fulfilling a productive role. Women are expected to fulfill a reproductive and emotional-bonding role but, in fact, may also serve a productive function. Clearly defined gender roles constitute one value that seems to be mediated by socioeconomic status, with more clearly defined gender roles among those of lower rather than higher socioeconomic status. Traditional gender-role differentiation may also change because of the effect of acculturation. Census data clearly indicates that Latino women participate equally in the work force, and this phenomenon could eventually trigger a redefinition of gender roles. Kunce and Vales (1984) already warned that this traditional view may be changing and could be misleading.

Despite research indicating a modification of traditional gender-role differentiation, it continues to play a role because it is still present. Rivera (1983) described clearly defined gender roles as one of the reasons males may have difficulty accepting disability. Thus, many Latinos with disabilities may deny or minimize their disability as long as they can function within these roles. On the one hand, this denial may serve an adaptive function in that the person's energies are not focused on the disability. On the other hand, minimizing the disability may interfere with the person's ability to acknowledge the beneficial aspects of participation in rehabilitation programs. For example, many of the Latinos who participated in our community interventions had the perception that they were disabled not by having an impairment but by their lack of English, which in this country interferes with their productivity and their ability to perform certain jobs. It is possible that the lower percentage of disabilities among Latinos compared to other ethnic groups is due to underreporting because their definition of disability might be different, as evidenced in our community interventions.

Machismo, defined as maleness or virility (Comas-Díaz, 1989), also may contribute to denial of disability. Beliefs among men that they should be physically dominant may be counter to the reality that the physical and mental sequelae of a disabling condition can be limiting. Men may feel that participation in a rehabilitation program is a sign of weakness. In this context, denial of disability may be counterproductive if men do not recognize that rehabilitation may be beneficial and lead to their ability to function even better within the prescribed role. A frequent consequence of denial is to attempt to return to work too soon in an attempt to hide or minimize the disability, which may result in failure and a possible aggravation of the disability (Kunce & Vales, 1984).

Some research indicates that a primary expression of *machismo* after a disability is the impact on Latino males' self image, the feeling of being threatened by a loss of authority, and the fear of no longer playing the role of *patrones*. When compared with Anglo males with a disability, however, Latino males do not feel as threatened by becoming financially dependent after a disability (Smart & Smart, 1991).

Women are supposed to endure, *aguantar*. Tolerating adversity is considered an important positive quality for Latinas (Comas-Díaz, 1989). Thus, although the outcome for both men and women may be denial of disability, the process by which this occurs differs for women and men. Women may in fact be considered to have adapted successfully if they can *endure* the hardships of a disabling condition. Here the praise of others in their network serves to reinforce beliefs that endurance is a positive quality. On the one hand, this value can be beneficial because, as noted earlier, their energies may be used in a more adaptive way. On the other hand, this passive resignation may prevent women from benefiting from rehabilitation programs that could contribute to more adaptive functioning.

Simpatía

A *simpatía* orientation among Latinos also may influence adjustment to disability and rehabilitation. *Simpatía* has been defined as "a general tendency toward avoiding interpersonal conflict, emphasizing positive behaviors in agreeable situations, and deemphasizing negative behaviors in conflictive circumstances" (Triandis et al., 1984).

This *simpatía* orientation can be reflected in different types of health-related behaviors that relate to how Latinos adjust to their disabilities. These include (1) supportive attitudes and behaviors toward those in need and (2) apparent compliance to health care providers and other persons of perceived authority. The first implication of *simpatía* is that there is a climate of support toward people with disabilities. The second implication is that clients may interpret disagreement as a sign of conflict, which is to be avoided. For example, a rehabilitation client may give the impression of being in complete agreement with the recommendations of the rehabilitation specialist and not show any apparent signs of disagreement, but this is no guarantee that the recommendations of the rehabilitation specialist will be followed. The value placed on *simpatía* may result in Latinos seldom disagreeing or questioning the advice of health care or rehabilitation experts and thus not benefiting from full participation in the rehabilitation process.

Another implication of a *simpatía* orientation is that interpersonal conflict with family members and significant others is to be avoided at all costs. In situations where a significant family member disagrees with the recommendations of rehabilitation specialists, the rehabilitation client is likely to comply with the wishes of family members to avoid interpersonal conflict. Ensuring that the family or significant others understand and agree with the recommendations of the rehabilitation specialist may require additional time and effort, but it will guarantee that they will play the role of advocates instead of opponents of the treatment.

Respect for and Deference to Power and Authority Figures

Respeto (respect) is another Latino cultural value, which is somewhat related to the value of *simpatía*. Values that center around unquestioning deference to authority figures may affect the relationship persons with disabilities have with rehabilitation specialists and other professionals. This hierarchical relationship, in which care providers are perceived as the ones who have the knowledge, is characterized by respect and attribution of the power to heal, frequently disempowering the client. Hence, in a situation in which the client disagrees with the recommendation of the provider, the Latino client is less likely to question the provider. On the other hand, respect for authority figures may facilitate recommendation to rehabilitation regimens, although, as noted previously, this may not be genuine internalization of the advice of professionals.

Time Orientation

Emphasis on a past, present, or future time orientation is culturally determined. Latinos, like those from many other collectivist cultures, are focused on past orientation (tradition) and on present-time orientation. Long-term planning, characteristic of future-time orientation, is a characteristic of more individualistic cultures (Triandis, 1994). How time is perceived and used may have an impact on the rehabilitation outcomes of Latinos. Long-term planning may not be a major consideration for Latinos participating in the rehabilitation process.

A present-time orientation also is determined to a certain extent by socioeconomic status (i.e., a present-time orientation is associated with lower socioeconomic status). Immediate, daily needs—such as providing for the family—require attention that may impede long-term planning because long-term plans may seem less vital for subsistence. Present-time orientation affects adherence to treatment and, consequently, the relationship with the rehabilitation specialists or other health care providers. Weekly appointments with a physical therapist may be of low priority (even if such treatment is affordable and accessible) to a person with concerns over subsistence. Maintaining long-term treatments becomes a difficult task. One recommendation is for rehabilitation specialists to connect long-term treatment to more immediate needs.

Informality

Latinos generally place less emphasis on formality than Anglos. This is manifested in the way they establish interpersonal relationships and on the emphasis they place on orderliness. A positive consequence of informality as a cultural value is that it allows the rehabilitation professional to establish a working relationship with the client more quickly. Some practitioners may interpret informality as relaxed boundaries. However, an informal relationship may help the professional connect with and subsequently motivate the client in a way that would be more difficult in a very formal atmosphere. The implication here is that the rehabilitation professional should take the lead and balance formal and informal aspects of the interaction.

A negative consequence of informality is being late for appointments, along with insufficient regard for schedules, routines, rules, and regulations (Kunce & Vales, 1984). This may have a detrimental effect on the professional–client relationship and on compliance with rehabilitation plans. Further, it is not uncommon to expect professionals to go beyond the professional relationship by providing personal favors in the name of *amiguismo* or *compadrismo*. This value may extend to the expectation that professionals will waive rules and regulations to accommodate the personal needs of the client. One limitation of this view is that clients may feel frustrated and reject professionals who fail to fulfill this expected role. Professionals also may misinterpret the value of *amiguismo* and feel exploited by the clients' personal requests, which may further deteriorate the crucial relationship with the client.

Spirituality

Spirituality, a belief in a power higher than oneself, is often rooted in religiosity. Latinos are basically spiritual people. This cultural value may explain disability as a trial or tribulation that the individual must endure in order to demonstrate that he or she is deserving or worthy of spiritual reward. This approach may promote *aguante*, which may contribute to more favorable adjustment to disability. Spirituality also may contribute positively by encouraging faith in that the person will get better if it is God's will. The negative side to spirituality is that it may contribute to the perception that disability is punishment sent by God because of the individual's or the family's wrongdoing. Consequently a passive, resigned attitude may prevail throughout the treatment.

Beliefs about Causation of Disability

Some culturally specific general values have an impact on adjustment to disability and the rehabilitation process. Beliefs about the cause of disability may range from having (1) a supernatural etiology, for example as punishment for some unnamed wrong (Cruz, 1979), to (2) medical causes (Hershenson, 1992) or (3) natural causes such as an accident, outside the control of the individual, independent of his or her actions.

Beliefs regarding the changeable nature of the disability also may influence attitudes toward disability. If the disability is perceived as something that one cannot change but simply must live with, more emphasis may be placed on adjusting to living with the disability than on participating in any form of rehabilitation. After all, endurance or *aguante* is a cultural value, sometimes rooted in the belief that nature and society are not changeable. This is an important difference from Anglo culture, in which people "conquer" and change nature. In Latino culture, you "live with nature." Acceptance of the disability can have both positive and negative effects. It may reduce any stress associated with trying to change and thus be quite adaptive. On the other hand, such acceptance may inhibit the person from engaging in meaningful rehabilitation.

Knowledge of Latino and other cultures needs to be incorporated in the training of rehabilitation experts. It is important that these experts understand the role of culture in the rehabilitation process. This understanding should facilitate the development of viable, appropriate interventions for Latinos with disabilities. If a program does not consist of culturally congruent interventions, attendance rates may be low and individuals may not benefit from treatment. Instead of implementing interventions based on individualistic models, the richness of Latino support networks may enhance rehabilitation outcomes.

Summary

We assume that Latinos' adjustment to disability and participation in rehabilitation can be facilitated by understanding core Latino values and socioeconomic and demographic factors. Although there is a great deal of diversity among Latinos, a substantial number adhere to these core values. In this chapter, we have attempted to illustrate how these culturally specific values influence adjustment to disability and the rehabilitation process. Moreover, we have tried to point out how these values can either facilitate or impede the rehabilitation process. Rehabilitation specialists and other professionals working with Latinos with disabilities need to understand these values in order to facilitate competent functioning.

Familialism and allocentrism among Latinos emphasize the importance of family and relationships. Thus, the beliefs and attitudes of the family and community regarding disability and rehabilitation will influence how individuals perceive their disability and subsequent adjustment. One implication is that families and significant others from the community should be involved in the clients' rehabilitation in order to maximize the benefits that can be gained.

Closely related to allocentrism and familialism are Latino values oriented toward interdependence. These values can be quite adaptive given that the problems and the solutions are *owned* and shared by all members within a functioning network. However, these values can be counterproductive if the family and significant others do not share the client's need for rehabilitation.

Clearly defined gender roles also may have an impact on adjustment to disability and rehabilitation. To the extent that individuals with a disability can function within their prescribed roles, the disability may be minimized, which may be adaptive. However, these clearly defined gender roles may be maladaptive if they interfere with the individuals' recognition that they can benefit from rehabilitation. One suggestion is that the rehabilitation plan be congruent with the prescribed gender roles.

In understanding a *simpatía* orientation, it is important to acknowledge that Latino clients will minimize confrontation and disagreement. With this in mind, rehabilitation professionals may need to work to create an atmosphere in which disagreement is minimized and harmony is emphasized. Cooperative decisions made between Latino clients, their families, and rehabilitation professionals should be helpful. Respect and deference for power is closely tied to the *simpatía* orientation. Because questioning by clients may be limited, rehabilitation specialists need to make sure their recommendations are understood by presenting information using clear, simple words in the language of the participants.

Informality is another value that Latinos have learned through their socialization process. This value translates into a reluctance to follow rules and regulations that can impede or delay the accomplishment of the rehabilitation goals. Likewise, *amiguismo* and *compadrismo*—viewing the rehabilitation professional as a friend instead as of a professional helper—can both impede and benefit rehabilitation, depending on how this informal relationship is oriented and understood by both parties.

Finally, Latinos may have culturally specific beliefs regarding disability, which may include a supernatural or a spiritual explanation for the disability. For example, the person may believe his or her disability to be God's will. On the one hand, beliefs in spirituality may be adaptive in that they promote acceptance of the disability and reduce stress associated with trying to change it. On the other hand, they could lead to passive resignation about the disability and limited participation in a rehabilitation program.

Adjustment to disability and rehabilitation also may be mediated by a number of other socioeconomic factors in addition to cultural values. These may include acculturation, age, education, income, employment, type of occupation, and labor force participation. These interconnected factors may foster the development of specific barriers to employment after a disability. Among these, we discussed the issues of work disincentives, transferable skills, discrimination, testing validity, and labor market changes.

In summary, an understanding of culture and the role it plays in adjustment to disability and rehabilitation is essential to providing appropriate programs and services for Latinos with disabilities. Programs based on models developed for other cultural and ethnic groups are likely to be less effective. There has been limited research on Latinos with disabilities and even less on how culture influences adaptation to disability and rehabilitation. There is a need for future studies in a number of areas. For example, what specific cultural factors promote positive adjustment to disability and rehabilitation? How does adjustment to disability differ for Latinos and other ethnic groups? How can culturally congruent interventions promote adjustment to disability and positive rehabilitation outcomes among Latinos? We hope our comments will stimulate culturally congruent research and interventions with Latinos with disabilities.

References

Berry, J. W. (1990). Acculturation and adaptation: A general framework. In W. H. Holtzman & T. H. Bornemann (Eds.), *Mental health of immigrants and refugees.* (pp. 90–102). Austin: University of Texas.

Berry, J. W., Poortinga, Y. H., Segall, M. H., & Dasen, P. R. (1992). *Cross-cultural psychology: Research and applications.* New York: Cambridge University Press.

Bowe, F. (1992). *Disabled adults of Hispanic origin: A portrait.* Washington, DC: President's Committee on Employment of People with Disabilities.

Comas-Díaz, L. (1989). Culturally relevant issues and treatment implications for Hispanics. In D. R. Koslow & E. P. Salett (Eds.), *Crossing cultures in mental health* (pp. 31–48). Washington DC: SIETAR International.

Cruz, D. (1979). Outreach problems in Puerto Rico. In G. Dixon & C. Bridges (Eds.), *On being Hispanic and disabled: The special challenges of an underserved population.* Conference Report (pp. 33–34). Washington, DC: Partners of the Americas. (ERIC Document Reproduction Service No. ED 210893).

Cuéllar, I., & Arnold, B. R. (1988). Cultural considerations and rehabilitation of disabled Mexican Americans. *Journal of Rehabilitation, 54,* 35–40.

Dziekan, K. I., & Okocha, A. G. (1993). Accessibility of rehabilitation services: Comparison by racial-ethnic status. *Rehabilitation Counseling Bulletin, 36,* 183–189.

Garza, R. T., & Ames, R. E., Jr. (1974). A comparison of Anglo- and Mexican-American college students on locus of control. *Journal of Consulting and Clinical Psychology, 42*(6), 919.

Giles, F. (1992). The vocational rehabilitation of minorities. In T. Wright & P. Leung (Eds), *The unique needs of minorities with disabilities: Setting an agenda for the future* (pp. 83-97). Jackson MS: National Council on Disability and Jackson State University.

Hershenson, D. B. (1992). Conceptions of disability: Implications for rehabilitation. *Rehabilitation Counseling Bulletin, 35,* 154–160.

Kerr, N., & Meyerson, L. (1987). Independence as a goal and a value for people with physical disabilities: Some caveats. *Rehabilitation Psychology, 32,* 173–180.

Kroeber, A. L., & Kluckhohn, C. (1952). *Culture: A critical review of concepts and definitions* (Vol. 4, p. 1). Cambridge, MA: Peabody Museum.

Kunce, J. T., & Vales, L. F. (1984). The Mexican American: Implications for cross-cultural rehabilitation counseling. *Rehabilitation Counseling Bulletin, 28,* 97–108.

Marín, B. V. (1990). AIDS prevention for non–Puerto Rican Hispanics. In C. G. Leukefeld, R. J. Battjes, & Z. Amsel (Eds.), *AIDS and intravenous drug use: Future directions for community-based prevention research* (pp. 35–52). Rockville: NIDA Research Monograph.

Marín, G., & Marín, B. V. (1991). *Research with Hispanic populations.* Newbury Park, CA: Sage Publications.

McNeil, J. M. (1993). *Americans with disabilities: 1991–92.* U.S. Bureau of the Census Current Population Reports, P70-33. Washington, DC: U.S. Government Printing Office.

National Institute of Disability and Rehabilitation Research. (1992). *Digest of data on persons with disabilities.* Washington, DC: U.S. Department of Education.

Rivera, O. A. (1983). Vocational rehabilitation process and Hispanic culture. *The special rehabilitation and research needs of disabled Hispanic persons.* Washington, DC: National Institute of Handicapped Research and the President's Committee on Employment of Persons with Disabilities.

Schick, F. L., & Schick, R. (1991). *Statistical handbook on U.S. Hispanics.* Phoenix, AZ: Oryx Press.

Smart, J. F. (1993). Level of acculturation of Mexican Americans with disabilities and acceptance of disability. *Rehabilitation Counseling Bulletin, 36,* 199–211.

Smart, J. F. (1995). Acculturative stress of Hispanics: Loss and challenge. *Journal of Counseling and Development, 73*(4), 390–396.

Smart, J. F., & Smart, D. W. (1991). Acceptance of disability and the Mexican American culture. *Rehabilitation Counseling Bulletin, 34,* 357–367.

Suazo, A. (1991). Hispanics with disabilities in the work force: A window of opportunity. In S. Walker, F. Belgrave, R. W. Nicholls, & K. A. Turner (Eds.), *Future frontiers in the employment of minority persons with disabilities* (pp. 50–55). Washington, DC: President's Committee on Employment of Persons with Disabilities and Howard University Research and Training Center.

Summers, T., & Jackson, G. (1992). Mental health and minorities: Emerging issues. In T. Wright & P. Leung (Eds), *The unique needs of minorities with disabilities: Setting an agenda for the future* (pp. 57-67). Jackson, MS: National Council on Disability and Jackson State University.

Szapocznik, J., Kurtines, W. M., & Fernández, T. (1980). Bicultural involvement and adjustment in Hispanic-American youths. *International Journal of Intercultural Relations, 4,* 353–365.

Triandis, H. C. (1994). *Culture and social behavior.* New York: McGraw-Hill.

Triandis, H. C., Marín, G., Lisansky, J., & Betancourt, H. (1984). *Simpatía* as a cultural script of Hispanics. *Journal of Personality and Social Psychology, 47,* 1365–1375.

Walker, S., Belgrave, F. Z., Jarama, S. L., Ukawuilulu, J., & Rackley, R. (1995). *The effectiveness of a support group intervention on employment efficacy among ethnic minorities with disabilities.* Manuscript submitted for publication.

Zea, M. C., Quezada, T., & Belgrave, F. Z. (1994). Latino cultural values: Their role in adjustment to disability. *Journal of Social Behavior and Personality, 9,* 185–200.

Zea, M. C., & Tyler, F. B. (1994). Illusions of control: A factor analytic study of locus of control in Colombian students. *Genetic, Social, and General Psychology Monographs, 120,* 199–221.

Chapter 13

Linguistic Barriers in Health Education and Services

JUAN PRECIADO
Hostos Community College

MANUEL HENRY
University de la Laguna, Islas Canarías

Language is the most salient factor identifying Latinos in this country (Ramírez & McAlister, 1988). The 1990 census estimated that there are 17 million Spanish-speaking Latinos in the United States. Of these, 8.3 million or 37% of the total Latino population either do not speak English well or do not speak it at all (U.S. Bureau of the Census, 1993).

Latinos can be classified into four groups according to their language dominance: (1) monolingual English speakers (proficient only in English); (2) English-dominant bilinguals (more proficient in English than in Spanish); (3) Spanish dominant bilinguals (more proficient in Spanish than in English); (4) and monolingual Spanish speakers (proficient only in Spanish). Latinos also vary in their ability to read and write in either language. According to degree of literacy, they can be classified into four groups: (1) Literates in English and Spanish; (2) literates in English only; (3) literates in Spanish only; and (4) illiterates in both English and Spanish. There are no statistics on the proportion of Latinos falling into each of these categories.

Spanish monolingualism and limited English-speaking skills are factors that limit Latinos' access to health care services and information. Researchers and practitioners advocate that these services be provided in Spanish (Altarriba & Santiago-Rivera, 1994; Stein & Fox, 1990). Such a recommendation to improve services may be too broad given the fact that each Latino subgroup speaks a different vari-

The authors would like to thank Ron Sitter and the editors for their valuable suggestions on the manuscript.

ety of the Spanish language. Simply tailoring the Spanish variety to the specific Latino subgroup is not enough. In order to ensure a particular Latino subgroup's comprehension of health information, one needs to determine the literacy level of the audience and adjust the material accordingly. However, the impact of literacy levels on health information has not been fully addressed in the literature (Richwald, Schneider-Muñoz, & Valdez, 1989).

The inability of most psychotherapists to communicate effectively with patients who have limited English-language skills seriously compromises the quality of services provided to this population (Bamford, 1991; Padilla et al., 1991). The mental health needs of Spanish-dominant Latinos are not being met because of the scarcity of linguistically competent professionals and a lack of valid tools to assess and treat them using their language. Even in cases where patients may be proficient in both languages, it is still unclear which language should be used (Rozensky & Gómez, 1983).

This chapter focuses on those Latinos with limited English skills, spoken and/or written, those who are most likely to encounter linguistic barriers in English-dominant health care settings and services in the United States. For the purpose of this discussion, Latinos with limited English skills are those who are either monolingual Spanish speakers (literates or illiterates), or Spanish-dominant bilinguals who may speak English well but face linguistic barriers when required to read and write in English. Illiterate monolinguals, those Spanish speakers who cannot read or write in either language, may present the most serious challenge to health care professionals.

Impact of Language Barriers

The following section explores the problem of mismatched communications between English-monolingual health professionals and Spanish-monolingual Latinos.

Public Health Education

Mainstream public health education campaigns conducted in English do not reach Spanish-monolingual Latinos. A troublesome implication of this problem is that Latinos who are not proficient in English may not have access to prevention information that otherwise could help them make informed decisions about their health. In a study of Spanish-monolingual Mexican women, Rapkin and Erickson (1990) found that these women were less knowledgeable about AIDS and HIV infection than their English-monolingual counterparts. In addition, Spanish monolinguals scored lower on items measuring their knowledge of such basic information as prevalence of HIV, probability of women and children acquiring HIV, and low-risk behaviors. Stein and Fox (1990) found that Spanish monolinguals have less access to preventive health information. They reported that Latinos who have mastered only the Spanish language were less well informed about preventive health practices than were Latinos whose dominant language was English. Specifically, Spanish-dominant women were less likely to have had a mammogram and to have discussed early cancer detection and breast self-examination with their physicians than were English-dominant Latino females.

The dissemination of public health information in Spanish may prove empowering for Spanish-monolingual Latinos. Ramírez and McAlister (1988) showed that a mass media public health education campaign conducted in Spanish was found effective in promoting changes in health-related behaviors. In this study, a health education program using television, radio, and print media in Spanish was implemented to increase knowledge about cancer, alcohol, and nutrition and to discourage smoking. A preliminary evaluation of this program showed that a multilevel approach including mass media, community organization, individualized attention, and social support systems increased the participants' level of knowledge about the targeted subject matters (Ramírez & McAlister, 1988).

Health care providers should not assume that health education campaigns via pamphlets and billboards written in Spanish will reach all Latinos, because a significant proportion of this population is either English monolingual or English-dominant bilingual, and may be Spanish illiterate. Therefore, individual or community interventions ought to consider both language dominance and literacy levels of Latinos in both languages before rendering services to them.

Health Services Utilization

Lack of health insurance coverage, underemployment, low educational attainment, and poverty contribute to a low utilization of health services by Latinos. The Hispanic Health and Nutrition Examination Survey (HHANES) studied insurance coverage in a sample of three Latino subgroups in selected regions of the country and found that one-third of Latinos do not have insurance coverage (Treviño, Moyer, Valdez, & Stroup-Benham, 1991). Although insurance coverage varied across Latino groups, it was apparent that limited speakers of English had the lowest insurance coverage. Indeed, Treviño (1991) found that Spanish-monolingual Mexicans in California were twice as likely to be uninsured as English-dominant Mexicans. Low educational levels also may limit the ability of Spanish-dominant Latinos to use the health care system (Council on Scientific Affairs, 1991). Census data indicate that Latinos as a group have significantly fewer years of education than the population of the United States as a whole (U.S. Bureau of the Census, 1993). According to these data, 31% of Latinos had less than nine years of education compared to only 8% for non-Latinos. Furthermore, a study of a random sample of Mexican Americans in a southwestern region found that Spanish monolinguals had significantly less education than their English-dominant peers (Ortiz & Arce, 1984).

Income level is another variable that compounds the problem of insurance coverage for Latinos. Census data indicate that Latino families are more likely to fall under the poverty level (26.5%) than non-Latino families (10.2%) (U.S. Bureau of the Census, 1993). Sorenson (1988), in a study conducted in the Southwest, suggested that Mexican Americans whose only language is Spanish are very likely to have a low income, which makes access to health care even more difficult.

Even though there is evidence that non-English-speaking Latinos actively seek treatment services in the event of a sudden illness or accident (Estrada, Treviño, & Ray, 1990), this is not necessarily true in the case of preventive services. Solis, Marks, García, and Shelton (1990) examined HHANES data from three Latino subgroups and found that Spanish-dominant Latinos use fewer preventive screening services than do English-dominant Latinos. This is consistent with a study by Hu, Keller, and Flemming (1989), who stated that individuals who are not proficient in English are less aware of prevention services and subsequently less able to take advantage of such services, including primary care for their children. Kirkman-Liff and Mondragón (1991) gathered data on health status, accessibility, consumer satisfaction, and barriers to health care on a representative sample of adults and children in Arizona. They found that Latino children with Spanish-monolingual parents had less access to health care and were more likely to come from families with financial problems than were Latino children whose parents spoke English.

Research

As indicated in Chapter 1, Latinos are a heterogeneous group with marked differences across several dimensions, including but not limited to historical origin, migration status, reception at point of entry into this country, and English-language proficiency. Although language proficiency is one of the most salient factors identifying Latinos, this variable has been one of the most neglected by researchers conducting health-related studies with Latinos. Kirkman-Liff and Mondragón (1991) reviewed 69 articles published from 1981 to 1991 and found that none included language of interview as a variable of their study.

Despite the linguistic diversity of the Latino population, nationwide research surveys often miss these differences because the information is collected in English. A significant portion of the Latino population, particularly those who are Spanish monolinguals, are severely underrepresented in that research. This situation could be reversed by offering to the respondents the option to answer these surveys in either English or Spanish. For example, the National Center for Health Statistics (NCHS) surveyed the health and nutritional status of three major Latino groups in the nation (National Center for Health Statistics, 1985). To collect the data, this study employed a team of bicultural professionals, which allowed participants the option of responding in either language.

Survey translation often presents a challenge to researchers because, as part of the norming process, both versions have to match in terms of meaning and content. Literal translations may result in an awkward and sometimes incomprehensible translation (Kegley & Savier, 1983). One could minimize this problem by using translation techniques derived from cross-cultural research that increase the likelihood that instruments presented in two or more languages are equivalent in meaning and content (Brislin, 1970; Marín, & Marín, 1991).

Additionally, professionals using health surveys need to exercise caution when translating instruments to be utilized with different Latino groups because cultural and linguistic variations within these groups may compromise their validity and reliability (Hendricson et al., 1989). Despite these difficulties, there are a few reliable and valid survey instruments in Spanish for collecting health care data on monolingual Latinos. The HHANES, a well-designed instrument for assessing health and nutritional status, was translated into a single Spanish-language version. Despite intragroup linguistic differences, the instrument was found valid by respondents from all three major Latino groups included in the study: Cuban-American, Puerto-Rican, and Mexican-American (Treviño, 1985). A second instrument, used to assess attitudes and knowledge about prenatal care, was translated into a Spanish variety spoken by a group of Mexican Americans living in San Diego, California. This instrument was found to be reliable and valid with members of this homogenous Latino group (Fullerton, Wallace, & Concha-García, 1993).

Accurate data collection not only requires reliable and valid instruments in Spanish but also must be conducted by bilingual/bicultural personnel. Surveys in which interviews are conducted require bilingual/bicultural researchers and field workers. The HHANES study employed bilingual interviewers and health personnel to make participants feel comfortable, to encourage participation, and to ensure the quality of the data collected. Berkanovic (1980) also used bilingual interviewers to examine the effects of an inadequate translation of a Spanish instrument on responses of a sample of Latinos. The bilingual interviewers were able to detect items that were inadequately translated by comparing the reactions of Latinos responding in English versus those responding in Spanish.

There are few Latino health professionals and even fewer Latino researchers, a reality that has an adverse effect on information available to the limited English speaker (Delgado & Estrada, 1993). The dearth of Latino health professionals in the higher policy levels of organizations makes access to funding for adequate research involving Latinos difficult (Marín, Amaro, Eisenberg, & Opava-Stitzer, 1993).

Health Service Personnel

Although Spanish-monolingual Latinos are better served by health professionals who know their culture and language, there are few Latinos in the health professions (Surgeon General's National Hispanic Health Initiative: Todos, 1993; U.S. Public Health Service, 1990). National data of applicants to medical schools show that Mexican Americans and mainland Puerto Ricans constitue only 2.4% of all applicants to U.S. medical schools, compared to 73% for non-Latino whites and 7.5% for African Americans (U.S. Department of Health and Human Services, 1991). There is a shortage of physicians regardless of ethnicity in areas with a high concentration of Latinos (U.S. General Accounting Office, 1992). Only 30 out of 800 physicians (3.75%) have practices in the poorest area of El Paso, Texas. Although data on Latinos in other health professions have not been fully analyzed, preliminary examinations suggest that Latinos are underrepresented in the allied health professions more so than in medical schools (U.S. Department of Health and Human Services, 1991).

There are not enough Latino health professionals to provide culturally and linguistically valid health services to the Latino population (American Public Health Association, 1986). The linguistic gap between English-monolingual health care providers and Spanish-monolingual Latinos will continue to grow unless there are systematic efforts to recruit Latinos into the health professions, including early interventions at the elementary and high school levels to motivate students to follow health career paths (Surgeon General's National Hispanic Health Initiative: Todos, 1993).

Patient-to-Health Professional Communications

Perhaps the most obvious impact of language on health occurs when Spanish-monolingual Latinos encounter health professionals who are not proficient in Spanish. The first problem arises in the intake session. The health history, which contains important information for diagnosis, planning, and treatment, may be invalid, as the patient or client may not be able to articulate clear and accurate descriptions of prior and current health conditions and problems. The health professional's diagnosis may be erroneous if it is based on an unreliable health history in which symptoms and other patient concerns may have been either omitted or misinterpreted. Even if the health professional makes a seemingly valid diagnosis, treatment plans could be hindered because monolingual Spanish patients may not understand, accept, and/or follow the English-monolingual health professional's recommendations (Poma, 1983).

Research has shown that a linguistic mismatch has a negative impact on the quality of health care of Latinos with limited English-speaking skills. Manson (1988) reported that when the language of the physician and that of the monolingual Spanish patient was the same, patient compliance with treatment increased. Monolingual Spanish patients seen by English-speaking physicians were twice as likely to make emergency visits than Spanish-monolingual patients seen by Spanish-speaking physicians. Seijo, Gómez, and Freidenberg (1991) found that monolingual Spanish patients treated by Spanish-speaking physicians had better information recall and asked more questions about their health care than did monolingual Spanish patients treated by English-speaking physicians.

Impact on Mental Health Services

Researchers have demonstrated that Latinos and other minorities for whom English is a foreign language underutilized mental health services as compared to other groups such as African Americans and Whites (Padgett, Patrick, Burns, & Schlesinger, 1994). It seems that the inability to speak English contributes strongly to this problem, along with the scarcity of bilingual professionals in the mental health work force (Malgady, Rogler, & Constantino, 1987).

Mental health service providers may not have the tools to assess accurately the mental status of Spanish-monolingual patients. Willig (1988) questions the validity of utilizing standard tests to assess mental health problems with Latinos, and other authors have stated that these tests "have been conceived, standardized, and validated from a non-minority, middle class, English-speaking perspective" (Malgady, Rogler, & Constantino, 1987, p. 229). Although professional organizations and federal, state, and local laws stress sensitivity to linguistic and cultural differences, Padilla et al. (1991) suggested that practitioners still need more cultural awareness training.

Psychological and psychiatric interviews conducted in English may bias the clinical diagnosis of the Spanish-speaking patient (Flaskerud & Hu, 1992; Padilla et al., 1991). The accuracy of the diagnosis will depend to a great extent on the language used during the clinical interview. In general, researchers agree that the perception of psychopathology is more accurate when patients are interviewed in their native language. This is because individuals apparently are able to express more emotion in their native language, thus allowing the clinician to render more accurate diagnoses (Price & Cuéllar, 1981; Cuéllar & Arnold, 1988). Guttfreund (1990) found that Spanish-speaking individuals scored significantly higher on depression and anxiety scores when the assessment was conducted in Spanish. On the other hand, Spanish-speaking individuals who are interviewed in their second language may display a poorer vocabulary, slower speech patterns, and longer pauses than individuals interviewed in their native language. This may lead to distortions by the clinician, who can misinterpret such verbalizations as signs of an underlying psychopathology (Bamford, 1991). Marcos, Alpert, Urcuyo, and Kesselman (1973) found that Spanish-dominant individuals interviewed in English were rated higher on measures of anxiety, depressive mood, and conceptual disorganization. Unfortunately, research findings on the interaction between language and clinical diagnosis have not yet been developed into comprehensive linguistic skill tests that could help assess the effect of language dominance on psychopathological measures (Altarriba & Santiago-Rivera, 1994).

Most psychotherapies can be identified as *talking therapies* because they rely on the patients' ability to verbalize feelings. When there is a linguistic mismatch, however, an English-monolingual therapist may misinterpret a Spanish-monolingual patient and vice versa. In such cases, patients may appear more stressed and less willing to disclose their feelings fully because of difficulties in expressing them in English. Nonetheless, therapists need to discriminate between the stress caused by a patient's inability to verbalize feelings in English and that which is caused by psychological distress. Furthermore, monolingual Spanish patients and those with limited English skills may appear more depressed and less motivated when seen by an English-monolingual therapist because of their inability to verbalize their feelings freely. Unless the therapist is attuned to the patient's paralinguistic behaviors expressing emotional pain, the therapist may not adequately assess the pain and deep emotions associated with the presenting problem. On the other hand, important paralinguistic clues from the therapist may be misinterpreted by patients because of their limited ability to understand the English language (Bamford, 1991). For example, the therapist's emotional tone may be missed by the limited speaker of English, who may concentrate on understanding the content of what is said rather than attending to the manner in which the message is conveyed.

Bilingual Patients

Bamford (1991) suggested that in order to provide effective services to Latinos, health professionals need to be able to understand their patients' linguistic background. The critical role that language plays in child development may be even more evident for bilinguals. Some authors have argued that the first language learned by bilinguals is associated with a particular set of deep emotions and feelings attached to early experiences in life (Marcos & Urcuyo, 1979). Thus, patients would express more affect when using their original language, and they would usually prefer using the language they learned first, unless they have not spoken it in a long time and have become more proficient in English (Rozensky & Gómez, 1983).

Monolingual and Bilingual Patients

There is substantial evidence that Spanish-monolingual patients who do not communicate effectively with monolingual English-speaking mental health professionals tend to drop out early from treatment (Laval, Gómez, & Ruíz, 1990; Sue, Fujino, Hu, & Takeuchi, 1991). An outcome study found that Latino patients served by Latino therapists in a community mental health center had lower dropout rates and remained in treatment longer than Latino patients seen by non-Latino therapists in other settings (O'Sullivan & Lasso, 1992). The authors argue that language was predominantly responsible for the dropout rates because most of the patients seeking services from that particular community mental health center were either Spanish monolingual or had limited English skills. However, missing data on linguistic match between therapist and client did not allow for an analysis of the effects of language on treatment outcomes. Nonetheless, this conclusion does not diminish the importance of assessing the patients' linguistic skills to determine the language in which they express themselves more effectively so that services can then be provided in this language. A significant implication of the impact of Spanish monolingualism and bilingualism is the need to recruit and train bilingual/bicultural staff. Recognizing this necessity, influential professional organizations such as the American Public Health Association have advocated the development of linguistically sensitive services for Spanish-monolingual and bilingual patients that include bicultural staff (Padilla et al., 1991; American Public Health Association, 1991).

Recommendations for Closing the Linguistic Gap

The following are recommendations to improve communications between English-monolingual health professionals and the limited-English-speaking Latino population.

Translation of Written Communications

Written communications in English targeted at the Spanish population are sometimes unidiomatic or inadequately translated (Fullerton, Wallace, & Concha-García, 1993; Hendricson et al., 1989). Unidiomatic translation, defined as style of language that is not used in a particular speech community, may be understood but taken less seriously (Berkanovic, 1980). Researchers and practitioners need to realize that inappropriately translated written communications may not be equivalent in content nor meaning. To avoid this, researchers recommend a multi-method approach using cross-cultural translation techniques to ensure that educational materials and survey instruments are appropriately translated and meaningful in Spanish (Brislin, 1970; Gilson et al., 1980). A description of each cross-cultural translation technique follows.

Blind Back-Translation

This method typically involves the use of two or more competent translators. One translates from English into Spanish; the other, without knowledge of the original English document, translates the Spanish document back into English. The original English document remains intact during the translation process. If both the original and final documents are similar in meaning and content, then the translation is equivalent (Brislin, Lonner, & Thorndike, 1973). If the Spanish product is not equivalent, then the translation is revised until both are similar in meaning and content. This technique involves a panel of bilingual experts who examine both the original in English and the final product in Spanish to determine their equivalence. Back-translation guards against the possibility that a translated document would make sense and be meaningful, yet be different from the original source. For example, if researchers want to compare the effects of treatment "X" on anxiety scores using two groups of patients (Spanish-only versus English-only), the anxiety instrument would have to be adequately translated and equivalent in both languages. This way the scores could be attributed to treatment "X" and not to differences in the way the instrument was translated.

Decentering

In this technique, one or several competent translators are employed to provide the best translation of the target language. There is no prescribed way of conducting this translation process. During the translation process both the Spanish and

English versions of the document are modified equally without trying to maintain fidelity to either language (Brislin et al., 1973). Terms for which a direct translation cannot be made into Spanish are modified in both the English and the Spanish versions to improve the quality of the translation. For example, if the original English version employs a colloquial term that does not translate well into Spanish (e.g.,"fooling around"), translators would replace the colloquial term with an expression in English (e.g., "not paying attention") that can be easily translated into Spanish.

Bilingual Committee

This technique evaluates the quality of a translated document in two ways. One way is to convene a panel of bilingual-bicultural individuals from a variety of backgrounds including community laypersons, researchers, and health care providers. Afterwards translators would make changes based on the panel's recommendations (Kerr & Ritchey, 1990). In a variation of this technique, a group of bilinguals would be recruited and tested for bilingualism. Each would receive English and Spanish versions of the instrument in a directionally counterbalanced fashion, with a lapse of time between the first and second administrations. Overall and category scores would be calculated for each of the participants in both the Spanish and the English versions. If the overall correlation between the English and Spanish versions is consistently high in each of the categories, the instruments would be considered equivalent and well translated. If not, a particular section with low correlation would be revised until it yields a predetermined acceptable high score (Brislin et al., 1973).

Pilot Testing

Although there is no empirical support for choosing one particular technique over another, there is consensus among researchers that a multimethod approach using blind back-translation and a bilingual committee might be the best way to approach the translation processes (Fullerton et al., 1993; Hendricson et al.,1989; Walker, Kerr, Pender & Sechrist, 1990). Once a translation has been completed using a multimethod approach, the final version should be pilot-tested to ensure that the end product is appropriate for the intended audience. Ideally, pilot testing should be done with people who match the profile and characteristics of the target population. Following are techniques used to pilot-test translations of written materials:

1. The *interviewing debriefing* technique is used to elicit respondents' opinions about the questions and intentions of the authors. If necessary, the translation is revised on the basis of the results of the interviews (Brislin et al., 1973).
2. The *item-editing* technique asks respondents to rewrite items they find unclear. Again, the written document may be revised on the basis of feedback from respondents (Fullerton et al., 1993).

3. Another pilot-testing technique involves direct observation of an interviewee's reactions to items being tested (Maurer & Hitchcock, 1985). If participants make any comments in reference to a particular item, translators can query them and revise the item accordingly.

Interpreters in Health Care Settings

The scarcity of bilingual health professionals often forces patients to use friends, relatives, and even children as interpreters, regardless of their ability to convey accurate and reliable information to the health professional. This practice also poses a problem of confidentiality because patients may hesitate to disclose their problems to someone other than the health professional. For example, a mother may be embarrassed to reveal her ailment to her child who is translating for her.

The use of interpreters without adequate translation skills often leads to distortions, misunderstandings, and undesired condensations of patients' verbalizations (Marcos, 1979). Furthermore, some studies show that even highly skilled interpreters sometimes are unable to convey such patient paralinguistic clues as intonation and emotionalism of expression (Bamford, 1991).

According to Haffner (1992), competent interpreters enhance the effectiveness of our health care because they have an intimate knowledge of both language and culture and the ability to communicate with individuals from different social and educational levels. They have mastered formal and informal styles of communication in Spanish, are familiar with the patient's culture, and have knowledge of medical terminology and procedures. Erzinger (1991) reported that this kind of knowledge significantly contributes to the interpreter's effectiveness in conveying information to the patient.

Pérez-Stable (1987) stated that an effective interpreter would be positioned equidistant from the patient and the health professional so that body language cues revealing the patient's perception of his or her condition could be easily noticed. The author suggests that the health professional face the patient and not the translator so that the patient does not feel that the translator is leading the session.

Despite the need for competent interpreters, there is no research on ways to standardize their training. Nonetheless, Acosta and Cristo (1981) developed a year-long training program for interpreters in mental health settings. For one year, trainees received a weekly course in psychotherapy terminology, role playing to develop interpreting skills, and feedback from peers and supervisors through video and audio tapes. An evaluation of the program found that patients helped by trained translators felt understood, but that therapists working with translators perceived themselves as ineffective. It was suggested that therapists must be trained in how to work effectively with interpreters. The authors did not provide information regarding the impact of interpreters' level of acculturation, education, intensity of training, skills, and treatment modality on dropout rates and treatment effectiveness. Perhaps future research might examine these issues further.

Formal training for bilingual translators would resolve some of the problems associated with using them in mental health settings. Highly skilled interpreters would be familiar with psychological terminology, could translate the language, and would provide the therapist with relevant cultural information about the patients. However, the degree of familiarity with psychotherapy terminology or the level of acculturation necessary to interpret patient verbalizations has not been established. Researchers recommend that competent interpreters have the following skills: (1) literacy in both Spanish and English; (2) knowledge of Latino cultural practices and beliefs; (3) interpersonal relations; (4) working knowledge of psychological, psychiatric, and medical terminology; and (5) knowledge of ethics and confidentiality issues (Acosta & Cristo, 1981; Bamford, 1991). At the same time, therapists need training to develop a good relationship with the interpreter. Bamford (1991) stated that trained therapists would not allow the interpreter to lead the session and would schedule post-session meetings with the interpreter to discuss nonverbal behaviors of patients that may be critical for the therapist to understand.

Spanish-Language Varieties

Standard Spanish

Despite differences in national origin, Spanish-speaking Latinos can understand one another because they speak the same language. Standard Spanish is the variety with no foreign interference, regionalisms, and colloquialisms associated with specific ethnic groups or regions of the country (Keller, 1983). The Spanish spoken by educated people of any Spanish-speaking country is considered standard Spanish and is also known as *broadcast Spanish*. The Spanish used in the media is generally free of regionalisms so that Spanish-speaking Latinos from different ethnic backgrounds can understand the broadcast (Weller, 1983).

Standard Spanish enables effective communication with the linguistically diverse Spanish-monolingual population. The popular Spanish language media have successfully conveyed messages in Standard Spanish. Indeed, movies, songs, and television programs that are produced in various Latin American countries (e.g., Mexico) have overcome linguistic differences to become instant hits all over Latin America and Spain, as well as in areas of the United States that are heavily populated by Spanish-speaking Latinos.

Standard Spanish may be the best way to communicate with a linguistically diverse Spanish-monolingual population, even though some words may have different meanings for different ethnic groups. For example, the word *guagua* means *baby* to a Chilean and *bus* to a Caribbean Latino. The developers of the Hispanic Health and Nutrition Examination Survey (HHANES) successfully measured health status in three linguistically diverse Spanish-speaking groups by eliminating the problem of words with multiple meanings by using descriptive phrases understood by all three groups (Treviño, 1985). For example, in order to avoid misunderstandings, the word *lunch*, which has different meanings across Latino ethnic groups, can be replaced with the descriptive phrase *the midday meal*.

Miscommunication may also arise when using different words for the same concept across Spanish varieties. To prevent this problem, the HHANES survey designers developed a technique in which alternative words used by each of the groups to refer to the same concept were incorporated within a given survey item (Treviño, 1985). For example, the survey item, "About how many cigars a day do you smoke?" was translated into Spanish as "*¿Cuántos (puros/tabacos/cigarros) fuma por día más o menos?*" This technique might be useful when communicating with a heterogeneous Latino audience using words that have different meanings for specific Spanish-speaking groups. Publishers of Spanish textbooks in the United States have used this approach to teach vocabulary to Latino children from different ethnic groups (Keller, 1983). For example, children learned that although the English word *bus* has different meanings in Spanish, they all convey the same concept: *camion* (Mexico); *guagua* (Caribbean); *autobus* (Standard Spanish); *autocar* (Spain); and *micro* (Chile). Regardless of the Spanish variety chosen, one should carefully pilot-test and revise any written message.

Spanish Varieties

Spanish is an evolving language with distinct varieties associated with specific ethnic backgrounds. Although all varieties share basic similarities, each one has unique linguistic patterns. For example, the Spanish spoken by Chicanos in East Los Angeles is different from the Spanish spoken by Caribbean Spanish speakers in New York City. For instance, Puerto Ricans may sometimes delete the *s* ending of some words and replace the letter *r* with the letter *l*.

Health professionals could enhance the effectiveness of their educational messages by conveying them in the appropriate Spanish variety. In other words, health education campaigns accommodating Spanish varieties may have a greater impact on the intended audience. Schultz and Rogers (1979) developed a videotape to provide cancer education to Spanish-speaking Latinos in New Mexico. Instead of using available videos in Spanish that were developed for other regions, the videotape package used the New Mexican Spanish variety spoken in the region in question. According to the authors, the videotapes presented information in a realistic manner and increased the audience's knowledge of cancer prevention.

Researchers recommend that the appropriate Spanish variety be used to translate interview protocols or questionnaires (Fullerton et al., 1993; Kirkman-Liff & Mondragón, 1991). For example, using cross-cultural research techniques and a team of translators familiar with the Mexican Spanish variety, a health status questionnaire was adequately translated into the Spanish variety commonly spoken in South Texas (Hendricson et al., 1989). The authors reported that the instrument was reliable and had strong face and construct validity for this particular population.

Literacy Levels

Those service providers who know their target audience is primarily Spanish monolinguals must also determine the degree of literacy in that population; otherwise, health education interventions may be inadequate. For instance, a clinic may spend thousands of dollars on designing well-written pamphlets in Spanish only to find their efforts in vain because their target audience can neither read nor write the language. Similarly, health evaluators in a hospital may be puzzled by the unresponsiveness of a migrant farm worker Latino population to a previously validated consumer satisfaction survey in Spanish. Evaluators may attempt to explain the lack of response with assumptions about the behavior and attitudes of Latinos toward evaluation. However, they may overlook the fact that this group has limited reading and writing skills, which prevent them from completing a survey. To complicate matters further, migrant workers may be embarrassed to disclose their illiteracy to evaluators.

Richwald, Schneider-Muñoz, and Valdéz (1989) conducted a study to assess the readability levels of Spanish instructions provided with condom packages. Readability tests conducted using seven different Spanish texts showed that instructions were written at readability levels that were well above the reading skills of most Spanish-speaking Latinos. Improper condom use resulting from misunderstanding written instructions could eventually increase the risk of contracting sexually transmitted diseases and HIV. This is especially critical because so many educational campaigns rely on written communication. Health professionals need to adjust the readability level of the written materials to match the reading level of the intended audience.

Although they are rarely mentioned in the literature, several authors have developed formulas to assess readability levels of written materials in Spanish. The interested reader is referred to the original sources for a description of three formulas: the Spaulding (Spaulding, 1956); Flesch (Flesch, 1948; Henkin, Singleton, & Nguyen, 1984); and Fry (Fry, 1968; Gilliam, Peña, & Mountain, 1980). These formulas are useful indexes to measure different degrees of reading difficulty in Spanish (Rodríguez Diéguez, 1989).

To adjust the readability level of written materials, health professionals need to identify the reading skills of the target audience. Reliable and valid diagnostic reading tests in Spanish have not yet been developed for adults. However, health professionals could estimate the reading level of the target audience by pilot-testing educational materials written at different reading levels (Robin, 1989).

Medium of Communication

There are linguistic issues that need to be addressed when selecting a medium of communication for Spanish-monolingual Latinos. An appropriate medium of communication requiring low literacy skills such as pictorial symbols, television, radio, and video would enhance comprehension of health messages. Researchers found that a smoking cessation program using a variety of media (radio, television, billboards, fliers, pamphlets, etc.) effectively reached Spanish-monolingual Latinos. Media messages relied heavily on photographs and illustrations and minimized written texts. The authors reported that the mass-media health education campaign increased the target population's knowledge about the hazards of cigarette smoking from previous baseline levels (Marín, Marín, Pérez-Stable, Sabogal, & Otero-Sabogal, 1990).

It appears that the selection of a medium of communication depends on the literacy skills of the intended audience. Means of communication that rely less on reading skills such as pictorial and graphic symbols are preferred for illiterate Latinos. Television, video, and radio have a larger impact when the characters and audience are from similar backgrounds (Key & Peres, 1979). The credibility of a message is diminished when non-Latino characters are dubbed in Spanish. In this sense, health education messages are more effective when media characters match the literacy level, voice, and ethnicity of the audience.

Discussion

The health care system does not address the linguistic needs of a significant portion of the Latino population, namely limited English speakers. This linguistic mismatch is reflected in low utilization of preventive health services and ineffective public health education campaigns. In the mental health arena, bias in the assessment and treatment of Spanish-monolingual Latinos and Spanish-dominant bilingual patients is common. There are few competent bilingual health professionals and researchers to provide services or to conduct research involving Latinos.

Language and individual language dominance has important implications for the delivery of health education and health services to Latinos with limited English skills. The following are some strategies to overcome the linguistic gap between English-monolingual health professionals and Spanish-monolingual Latinos: Although cross-cultural translation techniques would minimize problems associated with the translation of written materials, they are costly and time consuming in applied settings. Furthermore, service providers may not have the resources and background to employ such methodology. There is a need to develop cost-effective ways to translate written materials at a minimum cost.

Translation of oral communications demands not only competent interpreters but also the willingness of service providers to work with a translator as a third party. Studies document the detrimental effects of poorly trained interpreters, yet offer few recommendations to train competent interpreters. Future studies should be aimed at refining training protocols to prepare professionals in this area. Supervision, psychological and psychiatric terminology, interpersonal skills, and ethical issues are areas in which more research is needed.

Use of the appropriate Spanish language variety enhances the impact of health messages. A heterogeneous Latino population would benefit from messages in Standard Spanish, whereas a homogeneous population would benefit from messages in the language variety associated with that specific ethnic group. It is not known whether speakers of different varieties need a minimum literacy level in order to understand messages written in the standard variety. Therefore, further research is needed to measure reading abilities in adults and to assess readability levels of written texts. Other disciplines such as sociolinguistics and foreign language teaching may offer some insight into innovative methodologies to assess Spanish-language ability.

Efforts are underway to develop comprehensive assessment tools to render reliable and valid psychological and psychiatric diagnoses in Spanish (Padilla et al., 1991). However, diagnostic tools in Spanish are valid only for patients who have been tested and found literate in this language. Unfortunately, therapists have relied on their impressions rather than on tests to assess their patients' language abilities. Comprehensive linguistic tests need to be developed to ascertain the patient's specific levels of Spanish-language proficiency in clinical situations.

Selecting the most appropriate language for assessment and treatment presents a dilemma to the therapist treating patients with proficiency and literacy in both languages. Elsewhere in this chapter it was suggested that proficiency and patient preference be taken into account when selecting the medium of communication in mental health. However, the role of language preference in mental health settings has not been systematically examined, nor has the effectiveness of using bilingualism as a therapeutic tool.

Except for the HHANES study, Spanish-dominant Latinos have been underrepresented in nationwide surveys. To compensate for this, future studies should oversample this population to collect accurate data on their health needs. Respondents may be given the option of answering in English or Spanish, thus allowing for comparisons between Latinos interviewed in English and those interviewed in Spanish. The benefits of reliable and valid survey data would be greater than the costs of translating instruments and recruiting and training bilingual and bicultural professionals.

Eliminating linguistic barriers faced by Spanish-dominant Latinos might not be enough to empower them to improve their health. Spanish-dominant Latinos would continue to suffer from underemployment, poverty, low educational attainment, and lower insurance coverage, all which have an adverse impact on utilization of health care, health knowledge, and health status. Future studies should compare English- and Spanish-dominant Latinos while holding income, insurance coverage, and education constant. Such studies may reveal the variance contributed by language to key health indicators.

The linguistic diversity of Latinos with limited English skills cannot be overlooked when planning and delivering services, or conducting research. Simply knowing that the target audience is Spanish-monolingual would not enable the adequate planning and delivery of services. Service providers need to determine both the degree of language dominance and the literacy level in order to better serve the health education needs of the Latino population.

References

Acosta, F. X., & Cristo, M. H. (1981). Development of a bilingual interpreter program: An alternative model for Spanish speaking services. *Professional Psychology: Research and Practice, 12,* 474–482

Altarriba, J., & Santiago-Rivera, A. L. (1994). Current perspectives on using linguistic and cultural factors in counseling the Latino client. *Professional Psychology: Research and Practice, 25,* 388–397.

American Public Health Association. (1986). *Policy Statement 8514: Minority access to the health professions.* American Public Health Association, Public Policy Statements, 1948–Present. Washington, DC: Author.

American Public Health Association. (1991). *Policy Statement No 9009: A call to reject "English Only" legislation.* American Public Health Association Public Policy Statements, 1948–present, cumulative, Washington, DC: Author.

Bamford, K. (1991). Bilingual issues in mental health assessment and treatment. *Latino Journal of Behavioral Sciences, 13,* 377–390.

Berkanovic, E. (1980). The effect of inadequate language translation on Hispanic responses to health surveys. *American Journal of Public Health, 70,* 1273–1278.

Brislin, R. W. (1970). *Translation: Applications in research.* New York: Wiley.

Brislin, R. W., Lonner, W. J., & Thorndike, R. W. (1973). *Cross-cultural research methods.* New York: Wiley.

Council on Scientific Affairs. (1991). Latino Health in the United States. *Journal of the American Medical Association, 265,* 248–252.

Cuéllar, I., & Arnold, B. R. (1988). Cultural considerations and rehabilitation of disabled Mexican Americans. *Journal of Rehabilitation, 54,* 35–40.

Delgado, J. E., & Estrada, L. (1993). Improving data collection strategies. *Public Health Reports, 108,* 540–545.

Erzinger, S. (1991). Communications between Spanish speaking patients and their doctors. *Culture, Medicine and Psychiatry, 15,* 91–110.

Estrada, A., Treviño, F. M., & Ray, L. (1990). Health care utilization barriers among Mexican Americans: Evidence from HHANES 1982–1984. *American Journal of Public Health, 80*(Suppl.), 27–31.

Flaskerud, J. H., & Hu, L. (1992). Racial/ethnic identity and amount and type of psychiatric treatment. *American Journal of Psychiatry, 149,* 379–384.

Flesch, R. (1948). A new readability yardstick. *Journal of Applied Psychology, 32,* 221–233.

Fry, E. B. (1968). A readability formula that saves time. *Journal of Reading, 11,* 513–516.

Fullerton, J. T., Wallace, H. M., & Concha-García, S. (1993). Development and translation of an English–Spanish dual-language instrument addressing access to prenatal care for the border dwelling Hispanic women of San Diego County. *Journal of Nursing Midwifery, 38,* 45–49.

Gilson, B. S., Erickson, D., Chávez, C. T., Bobbitt, R. A., Bergner, M., & Carter, W. B. (1980). A Chicano version of the Sickness Impact Profile (SIP). *Culture, Medicine and Psychiatry, 4,* 137–150.

Gilliam, B., Peña, C. S., & Mountain, L. (1980). The Fry Graph applied to Spanish readability. *The Reading Teacher, 33,* 426–430.

Guttfreund, D. (1990). Effects of language use on the emotional experience of Spanish English and English Spanish bilinguals. *Journal of Consulting and Clinical Psychology, 58,* 604–607.

Haffner, L. (1992). Translation is not enough—interpreting in a medical setting. *Western Journal of Medicine, 157,* 255–259.

Hendricson, W. D., Russell, J., Prihoda, T. J., Jacobson, J. M., Rogan, A., & Bishop, G. D. (1989). An approach to developing a valid language translation of a health status questionnaire. *Medical Care, 27,* 959–966.

Henkin, A. B., Singleton, C. A., & Nguyen, L. T. (1984). Seeking goodness of fit: Measuring the readability of bilingual materials. *Bilingual Review, 11,* 9–24.

Hu, D. J., Keller, R., & Flemming, D. (1989). Communicating AIDS information to Latinos: The importance of media and language preference. *American Journal of Preventive Medicine,* 5, 196–200.

Kegley, C. F., & Savier, A. N. (1983). Working with others who are not like me. *Journal of School Health,* 53, 81–85.

Keller, G. D. (1983). What can language planners learn from the Latino experience with corpus planning in the United States? In J. Cobarrubias & J. A. Fishman (Eds.), *Progress in language planning.* Berlin, Germany: Mouton.

Kerr, M. J., & Ritchey, D. A. (1990). Health promoting lifestyles of English-speaking and Spanish-speaking Mexican American migrant farm workers. *Public Health Nursing,* 7, 80–87.

Key, D. B., & Pérez, F. R. (1979). Cómo te sientes? Preventing childhood problems. In T. J. Moore, A. G. Ramirez, & P. L. Slayton (Eds.). *Communicating with Mexican Americans: Por su buena salud* (pp. 27–32). U.S. Department of Health and Human Services, Public Health Service, NIH Publication No 81–1961. Washington, DC: U.S. Government Printing Office.

Kirkman-Liff, B., & Mondragón, D. (1991). Language of interview: Relevance for research of Southwest Hispanics. *American Journal of Public Health,* 81, 1399–1404.

Laval, R. A., Gómez, E. A., & Ruiz, P. (1990). A language minority: Hispanic Americans and mental health care. *American Journal of Social Psychiatry,* 3, 42–49.

Malgady, R. G., Rogler, L. H., & Constantino, G. (1987). Ethnocultural and linguistic bias in mental health evaluation of Hispanics. *American Psychologist,* 42, 228–234.

Manson, A. (1988). Language concordance as a determinant of patient compliance and emergency room visits in patients with asthma. *Medical Care,* 26, 1119–1128.

Marcos, L. R. (1979). Effects of interpreters on the evaluation of psychopathology in non-English-speaking patients. *American Journal of Psychiatry,* 136, 171–174.

Marcos, L. R., Alpert, M., Urcuyo, L., & Kesselman, M. (1973). The effect of interview language in the effect of psychopathology in Spanish American schizophrenic patients. *American Journal of Psychiatry,* 130, 549–553.

Marcos, L. R., & Urcuyo, L. (1979). Dynamic psychotherapy with the bilingual patient. *American Journal of Psychotherapy,* 33, 331–338.

Marín, G., Amaro, H., Eisenberg, C., & Opava-Stitzer, S. (1993). Development of a relevant and comprehensive research agenda to improve Hispanic health. *Public Health Reports,* 108, 546–550.

Marín, G., & Marín, B. (1991). *Research with Hispanic populations.* Applied Social Research Methods Series. Newbury Park, CA: Sage Publications.

Marín, G., Marín, B. V., Pérez-Stable, E. J., Sabogal, F., & Otero-Sabogal, R. (1990). Change in information as a function of a culturally appropriate smoking cessation community intervention for Hispanics. *American Journal of Community Psychology,* 18, 847–864.

Maurer, K. R., & Hitchcock, D. C. (1985). Pilot testing. In National Center for Health Statistics, *Plan and operation of the Hispanic Health and Nutrition Examination Survey, 1982–1984* (pp. 36–37). DHHS Publication No. (PHS) 85-1321. Vital and Health Statistics, Series 1, No. 19. Washington, DC: U.S. Government Printing Office.

National Center for Health Statistics. (1985). *Plan and operation of the Hispanic Health and Nutrition Examination Survey, 1982-1984.* DHHS Publication No. (PHS) 85-1321. Vital and Health Statistics, Series 1, No. 19. Washington, DC: U.S. Government Printing Office.

Ortíz, V., & Arce, C. H. (1984). Language orientation and mental health status among persons of Mexican descent. *Hispanic Journal of Behavioral Sciences,* 8, 127–143.

O'Sullivan, M. J., & Lasso, B. (1992). Community mental health services for Hispanics: A test of the cultural compatibility hypothesis. *Hispanic Journal of Behavioral Sciences,* 14, 455–468.

Padgett, D. K., Patrick, C., Burns, B. J., & Schlesinger, H. J. (1994). Ethnicity and the use of outpatient mental health services. *American Journal of Public Health,* 84, 222–226.

Padilla, A. M., Lindholm, K. J., Chen, A., Durán, R., Hakuta, K., Lambert, W., & Tucker, G. R. (1991). The English-only movement: Myths, realities and implications for psychology. *American Psychologist,* 46, 120–130.

Pérez-Stable, E. J. (1987). Issues in Latinos' health care–Medical staff conference. *Western Journal of Medicine, 146,* 213–218.

Poma, P. (1983). Hispanic cultural influences on medical practice. *Journal of the National Medical Association, 75,* 941–946.

Price, C. S., & Cuéllar, I. (1981). Effects of language and related variables in their expression of psychopathology in Mexican-American patients. *Hispanic Journal of Behavioral Sciences, 3,* 145–160.

Ramírez, A. G., & McAlister, A. L. (1988). Mass media campaign—A su salud. *Preventive Medicine, 17,* 608–621.

Rapkin, J. A., & Erickson, P. I. (1990). Differences in knowledge of and risk factors for AIDS between Hispanic and non-Hispanic women attending an urban family planning clinic. *AIDS, 4,* 889–899.

Richwald, G. A., Schneider-Muñoz, M., & Valdéz, R. B. (1989). Are condom instructions in Spanish readable? Implications for AIDS prevention activities for Latinos. *Hispanic Journal of Behavioral Sciences, 11,* 70–82.

Robin, A. T. (1989). Medida de dificultad de los materiales de lectura en los idiomas distintos al inglés. *Leer en la escuela: Nuevas tendencias en la enseñanza de la lectura* (pp. 261–273). Madrid: Fundación G. Sánchez Ruipierez.

Rodríguez Diéguez, J. L. (1989). Prediccción de la lecturabilidad de textos en castellano: una propuesta y sugerencia. *Leer en la escuela: Nuevas tendencias en la enseñanza de la lectura* (pp. 284–310). Madrid: Fundación G. Sánchez Ruipierez.

Rogler, L. H., Malgady, R. G., Constantino, G., & Blumenthal, R. (1987). What do culturally sensitive mental health services mean? *Journal of the American Psychological Association, 42,* 565–570.

Rozensky, R. H., & Gómez, M. Y. (1983). Language switching in psychotherapy with bilinguals: Two problems, two models, and case examples. *Psychotherapy: Theory, Research and Practice, 20,* 152–160.

Seijo, R., Gómez, H., & Freidenberg, J. (1991). Language as a communication barrier in medical care for Hispanic patients. *Hispanic Journal of Behavioral Sciences, 13,* 363–376.

Schultz, F., & Rogers, J. L. (1979). Esperanza: A videotape package to reach Latinos with cancer health education. In T. J. Moore, A. G. Ramírez, & P. L. Slayton (Eds.), *Communicating with Mexican Americans: Por su buena salud* (pp. 48–53). U.S. Department of Human Services, Public Health Service, NIH Publication No 81-1961. Washington, DC: U.S. Government Printing Office.

Spaulding, S. (1956). A Spanish readability formula. *Modern Language Journal, 40,* 433–441.

Solís, J. M., Marks, G., García, M., & Shelton, D. (1990). Acculturation, access to care, and use of preventive services by Hispanics. Findings from HHANES 1982-1984. *American Journal of Public Health, 80*(Suppl.), 11–19.

Sorenson, A. M. (1988). The fertility and language characteristics of Mexican-American and non-Hispanic husbands and wives. *The Sociological Quarterly, 29,* 111–130.

Stein, J. A., & Fox, S. A. (1990). Language preference as an indicator of mammography use among Hispanic women. *Journal of the National Cancer Institute, 82,* 1715–1716.

Sue, S., Fujino, D. C., Hu, L., & Takeuchi, D. T. (1991). Community mental health services for ethnic minority groups: A test of the cultural responsiveness hypothesis. *Journal of Consulting and Clinical Psychology, 59,* 533–540.

Surgeon General's National Hispanic Health Initiative: Todos. (1993, June). *Recommendations to the surgeon general to improve Hispanic health.* Washington, DC: U.S. Department of Health and Human Services.

Treviño, F. (1985). Cross-cultural aspects. In National Center for Health Statistics, *Plan and operation of the Hispanic Health and Nutrition Examination Survey, 1982–1984* (pp. 4–6). DHHS Publication No. (PHS) 85-1321. Vital and Health Statistics, Series 1, No. 19. Washington, DC: U.S. Government Printing Office.

Treviño, F. M. (1991). Letter. Reply to Dr. Minuth. The health insurance coverage of Hispanics. *Journal of the American Medical Association, 265.*

Treviño, F. M., Moyer, M. E., Valdéz, R. B., Stroup-Benham, C. A. (1991). Health insurance coverage and utilization of health services by Mexican-Americans, mainland Puerto Ricans, and

Cuban-Americans. *Journal of the American Medical Association, 265,* 233–237.

U.S. Bureau of the Census. (1993). *Hispanic Americans today.* Current Population Reports P23–183. Washington, DC: U.S. Government Printing Office.

U.S. Department of Health and Human Services. (1991). *Report to the secretary on a proposal for filling the empty educational pipeline for Hispanic health professionals.* Rockville, MD: Education Subcommittee of the Health and Human services Hispanic Health in America (HHS/HHA) Committee.

U.S. General Accounting Office. (1992). *Hispanic access to health care: Significant gaps exist.* GAO/92-6. Washington, DC: U.S. Government Printing Office.

U.S. Public Health Service. (1990). *Report of the surgeon general on the 1990 PHS Hispanic recruitment.* Rockville, MD: PHS Hispanic Officers' Steering Committee.

Walker, S. N., Kerr, M. L., Pender, N. J., & Sechrist, K. R. (1990). A language version of the health promoting lifestyle profile. *Nursing Research, 39,* 268–273.

Weller, G. (1983). The role of language as a cohesive force in the Hispanic speech community of Washington, D.C. In L. Elías-Olivares (Ed.), *Spanish in the U.S. setting: Beyond the Southwest.* National Clearinghouse for Bilingual Education. Rosslyn, VA: Inter American Research Associates.

Willig, A. C. (1988). A case of blaming the victim: The Dunn monograph on bilingual Latino children on the U.S. mainland. Special issue: Achievement testing: Science vs. ideology. *Hispanic Journal of Behavioral Sciences, 10,* 219–236.

Limitations of an Acultural Health Psychology for Latinos: Reconstructing the African Influence on Latino Culture and Health-Related Behaviors

MARÍA CECILIA ZEA

TIRSIS QUEZADA
FAYE Z. BELGRAVE
The George Washington University

Health psychology is an interdisciplinary field within psychology devoted to understanding psychological influences on how people stay healthy, why they become ill, and how they respond when they do get ill. Health psychology contributes to a better understanding and management of the behaviors that contribute to disease as well as to health promotion (Matarazzo & Carmody, 1986). Health psychology, following the tradition of other fields of psychology, has given scant attention to the influence of cultural values on behaviors. Consequently, this discipline has been limited in its application for understanding health behaviors among Latinos. We discuss some of those limitations in this chapter. A health psychology that does not examine cultural values will not contribute to an understanding of how people of different cultural groups develop theories of health and illness. Consequently, prevention and intervention efforts to increase health and prevent illness are not likely to succeed. The purpose of this chapter is to examine how

Latino values influence health attitudes and behaviors. Latino values based on African influence will be a particular emphasis.

In this chapter we provide a brief overview of Latino cultural values as well as the role that these values play in health-related behaviors, with particular emphasis on Afro-Latino culture. The influence of African culture on the beliefs and behaviors of some Latino groups has been overlooked by psychologists and has been more often examined by anthropologists and sociologists. Afro-Latino cultural values influence health-related behaviors by (1) contributing to the construction of theories of the etiology of health and illness, (2) influencing culturally specific manifestations of health or illness, (3) influencing treatment approaches, and (4) influencing attitudes and behaviors that lead to positive or negative health outcomes.

Culture is the integrated pattern of behaviors acquired by humans, including knowledge, beliefs, values, and behaviors, which condition further actions (Kroeber & Kluckhohn, 1952). These culturally determined actions include health beliefs, health practices, and attitudes toward the condition of health and illness. Cultural values that affect health-related behaviors of Latinos in the United States are determined by a host of significant socioeconomic, racial, ethnic, cultural, and historical factors (Sussman, 1992; Zea, Quezada, & Belgrave, 1994). Some of these factors are emphasized in this chapter, particularly the influence of Afro-Latino culture on health conceptualizations and behaviors.

Limitations of Health Psychology for Latinos

The health–disease process can be explained by the interrelation among biological, psychological, social, and cultural factors. However, health psychology researchers have not examined the cultural biases of health psychology theory or the interaction between culture and health behavior. Some studies have emphasized the role of cultural factors on prevention of chronic illnesses such as cancer (Bundek, Marks, & Richardson, 1993; González, Atwood, García, & Meyskens, 1989; Zapka et al., 1993) or risk factors associated with behaviors such as cigarette use (Lee & Markides, 1991). Unfortunately, for the most part, these studies have focused on disease and not on health as a positive value, social construction, or representation. In addition, very few studies have included a formal definition of culture (Kosko & Flaskerud, 1987; Thompson, Thompson, & House, 1990). By ignoring the effect of culture on illness-related behaviors, research on health psychology fails to provide an understanding of the way individuals articulate and understand their illness.

Inadequate solutions to health problems are likely to occur when cultural values are not taken into account. For instance, researchers may assume that an appropriate intervention to prevent breast and cervical cancer should emphasize the importance of breast self-examination, yearly Pap smears, and regular doctor's appointments. Even if barriers like literacy levels, excessive use of written information, and limited access to health services were removed, this preventive effort still exclusively targets the individual. Such effort may be sufficient for White women to start preventive behaviors, but may not be for Latinas. A microlevel, individualistic conceptualization of health that does not account for underlying cultural values such as collectivism, familism, and allocentrism, and for culture-specific etiological explanations of the health–illness continuum, may be less efficient and have less applicability (see Comas-Díaz, Chapter 9, this volume; Zea, Garcia, Belgrave, & Quezada, Chapter 12, this volume).

Because of the influence of the Western medical model, health psychology research has been based largely on the predominant health and illness views of the North American White upper-middle-class (Williams, 1992). Illness is viewed as "an episodic interpersonal deviation caused by microlevel, natural, etiological agents such as genes, viruses, bacteria and stress. Thus, many white American laypersons and professionals may assume that illness can be described and treated without reference to family, community, or the gods" (Landrine & Klonnoff, 1992, p. 267). Many prevention and intervention programs originating from these beliefs have been found useful for specific target groups, (i.e., nonminority middle-class participants). However, the same interventions may fail to affect health problems and diseases involving other cultures with different world views.

Interaction of Culture and Socioeconomic Status

It is fundamental to understand the interconnection between culture and socioeconomic status because researchers have often confounded these two variables. Some cases of health and illness behaviors may be explained by culture while others may be related to socioeconomic factors. Latinos in the United States (as a general group) have the lowest educational attainment of all ethnic minority groups, and very low income (O'Brien, 1993). Therefore, low socioeconomic status (SES) often is viewed as analogous with being Latino. Lower socioeconomic status also correlates with lack of participation in major institutions in this country. This is particularly the case with a considerable number of Latino immigrants who are not well integrated in major institutions that provide economic benefits (Comas-Díaz, Chapter 9, this volume; Stephen, Foote, Hendershot, & Schoenborn, 1994). Given a low SES among a sizable number of Latinos, many interventions targeted at Latinos are designed to address low educational or SES levels, on the assumption that this is the case for all Latinos. Thus, it is necessary to understand how culture and SES influence health attitudes and behaviors both independently and in interaction. In fact, there are many cross-cultural similarities in values, beliefs, and behaviors of Latinos and non-Latinos across groups of similar SES. For instance, upper-class Latinos may resemble more closely upper-class Anglos than Latinos of lower socioeconomic status in behaviors, aesthetic values, and attitudes (Garza & Ames, 1974).

Williams (1992) pointed out how public information campaigns designed for African Americans and Latino groups have failed because these audiences have been perceived by the planners as *homogeneous* in terms of their socioeconomic status, preferences, styles, and behaviors. One example of how SES may be confounded with ethnicity is found in the assumption by many in the mental health field that insight-oriented therapies are inadequate for Latinos, and that they need a more structured and directive type of therapeutic intervention (Acosta, Yamamoto, & Evans, 1982). This approach assumes that all Latinos may function better with directive therapy because they are similar to other low-income clients. Morris and Silove (1992) reported opposite findings: that South American refugees were more receptive to insight-oriented therapy than to directive therapy. These results may be explained by differences in socioeconomic status between Mexican-American clients as described by Acosta et al. (1982) and South American refugees.

Some authors have noted methodological problems in attempting to understand the confounding relationship between culture, socioeconomic status, and physical and mental health (Angel & Guarnaccia, 1989; Guarnaccia, De La Cancela, & Carrillo, 1989). These authors suggest the need to control for socioeconomic status in research involving ethnic minorities, by including SES as a variable or by using participants from the same SES group only. Betancourt and López (1993) also argue that most minorities share a similar low SES, and controlling for this variable could remove some of the variance associated with ethnicity. Therefore, researchers should carefully assess the specific contribution of culture, race, and socioeconomic status to their findings.

Latinos have also been considered culturally homogeneous, and the unique values and beliefs contributed by subgroups have not been investigated. An example of this void is that very few psychologists—including Latino psychologists—have studied the role of African culture on Latino health beliefs, which is addressed next in this chapter. This relationship has been extensively studied by anthropologists (cf. Brandon, 1993; Koss-Chioino, 1995; Murphy, 1993), and health psychology researchers have much to learn from their research.

The African Influence among Latinos

Although Latino groups share many cultural commonalities, there are also enormous differences among them. The African diaspora to the Americas due to slavery is one of the main contributors to such diversity. Latinos share a common cultural heritage, whose roots are traceable to the colonization of the Americas by Spain, to the amalgamation of Spanish and indigenous cultures, and subsequently to African culture. This process was not uniform throughout the Americas. For instance, in some countries (e.g., Cuba, Puerto Rico, the Dominican Republic, coastal areas surrounding the Caribbean Sea, and Brazil), Africans and their descendants still remain more numerous than in areas where the Spaniards did not deem it necessary to bring slave labor or failed in this attempt (e.g., parts of Andean regions).

Shortly after Spain colonized the Americas, the traffic in African slaves began as a way of *protecting* indigenous people from the hardships imposed by their oppressors (Zapata Olivella, 1989). Centuries of enslavement of Africans followed until Latin American countries gradually abolished slavery. Africans were brought from Senegal, Gambia, Ivory Coast, Benin, and Nigeria, among other countries (Friedemann, 1993). The degree to which African descendants were able to preserve their traditions varied from country to country. For instance, Colombia, Venezuela, Panama, and Perú experienced the Catholic Inquisition, which for the most part eliminated African religions and replaced them with Catholicism— except in *palenques*, communities created by runaway slaves throughout the continent (Friedemann, 1993). In Cuba, Puerto Rico, and Brazil, however, Africans were ingenious in preserving their practices despite all efforts by their oppressors to surpress these customs. This is why Nigerian Yoruba traditions—including language and religion—are very much alive in parts of Latin America and have flourished in the United States since the early 1940s (Brandon, 1993, González-Wippler, 1994).

Puerto Ricans and Cubans constitute the second and third largest Latino groups in the United States (see Chapter 1 by García and Marotta). Like many other immigrant groups, they have kept and transmitted many of their African-based spiritual beliefs and practices. In both groups, strong African influence is evident in the practice of Santería, the religion of the Yoruba people, which is very much alive in urban enclaves such as the Bronx, Harlem, and Miami (Murphy, 1993, 1994; Zapata Olivella, 1989). In Brazil, the same Yoruba influence gave origin to Umbanda, Candomble, and Macumba; in Curaçao, to Montamentu; and in Surinam to Winti (Zapata Olivella, 1989).

Despite Catholic hegemony in Latin America, Santería survived. In Cuba and Puerto Rico, Catholicism was *el camino de los blancos* (the way of Whites) and Santería *el camino de los negros* (the way of Blacks) (Murphy, 1993). These two religions coexisted, and Afro-Latinos were bicultural and could function competently in both worlds, the Catholic-dominated world of the master, as well as their own. Some authors suggest that *santeros* syncretized their African Orishas with Catholic saints. Thus, Changó was Santa Barbara, Obatalá was Santa Mercedes, Elegguá was Saint Anthony, Oshún was la Virgen de La Caridad del Cobre, Yemayá was Santa Regla, and Babalú Aye was San Lázaro. Other authors argue that these religious systems are not an amalgamation of African and European influences, but a new religion (Jorge, 1991).

Santería has been a well-kept secret for four hundred years, and only initiates have access to its complete body of knowledge (González-Wippler, 1994). Most of this knowledge has been transmitted through oral tradition; written publications about Santería have appeared only recently. In Cuba and Puerto Rico, some people dismissed Santería as *cosa de negros* ("a Black thing"), although many *santeros* are not Black. Still, despite a strong African presence in Latino culture, Santería does not extend to all groups; therefore, researchers need to be cautious and not generalize it to all Latino groups.

Respect for their ancestors and a belief in the interconnection between the living and the dead stand as some of the main teachings of the Yoruba tradition. The living are affected by their relationship with the dead and with the Orishas or *santos*, the Yoruba deities (Friedemann, 1993; Zapata Olivella, 1989). The honoring and recognition of the interconnections to one's ancestors is an African-American belief stemming from Africa (Nobles, 1986, 1991).

Nature and natural forces play an important role in Santería. Natural and supernatural forces are considered causes of physical suffering, emotional distress, or personal problems (Koss-Chioino, 1995; Zapata Olivella, 1989). Each Orisha or saint controls or represents a force of nature (González-Wippler, 1994). Yemayá represents the ocean and is also a symbol of motherhood; Changó controls fire, thunder, and lightning and also symbolizes force; Oshún symbolizes river waters and also represents eros and fertility; Elegguá is the Orisha of crossroads and symbolizes destiny; Obatalá created humankind at the physical level and symbolizes clarity and purity; Oyá controls the winds and symbolizes the awareness of death's existence (González-Wippler, 1994; Murphy, 1993). Life and death, health and illness, are a fluid process within Yoruba culture.

Afro-Latino cultural values seem to moderate interpretations about health and the development of health-related theories and behaviors, including prevention, help-seeking behavior, and compliance with treatment.

Impact of Latino Cultural Values on Health-Related Behaviors

Some Latino health beliefs and cognitions are based on the Western medical model, but many are based on indigenous and African folk practices and explanations. For example, Western beliefs would state that cancer is caused by genetic and environmental causes, whereas indigenous and African beliefs would attribute cancer to a physical trauma (*un golpe*) or to supernatural forces punishing the individuals or their families for some wrongdoing. These beliefs may determine the measures adopted by individuals to deal with health and illness. An important consideration for health care providers when there is incongruence between the health provider's and the client's view of the etiology of an illness is that the client may be less likely to comply with medical recommendations (Janis, 1984).

Consider the following example. *Daño* ("curse") is the belief that someone has brought a curse upon an individual by engaging the services of a witch. This curse can be ended by using the services of a *curandero* or indigenous healer. Without knowledge of Latino beliefs about *daño*, professionals cannot properly understand and treat this health syndrome. A health provider who lacks this knowledge may dismiss the services of an indigenous healer and try instead to engage the patient in treatment, only to find that the treatment is unsuccessful. Some health providers in the United States who are knowledgeable about the role of *daño* beliefs in health are beginning to involve healers in their treatment (Koss-Chioino, 1995).

Whereas some Latino groups (e.g., Caribbean and Brazilian) espouse theories originating from Africa such as Santería and Candomblé, other groups have remained faithful to more traditional indigenous theories such as the Cult of María Lionza, which originated among the Caquetío and Jirajara Indians of Venezuela (Pollak-Eltz, 1991), and Curanderismo, a synthesis of Mexican Indian and folk

Catholic traditions (Koss-Chioino, 1995). Other explanations of health and disease include supernatural forces (such as God, or the Orishas), curses from other humans (e.g., *mal de ojo* or the evil eye), folk explanations (e.g., *un golpe*), or Western medical explanations. Theories of disease etiology influence therapeutic treatment approaches. Traditional treatment may be combined with Western medicine—for example, by taking medication prescribed by a physician along with homeopathic medicine, herbs, and "a little prayer."

In African traditions, illness etiology can be related to natural and supernatural forces. Few distinctions may be made between physical and emotional disorders (Koss-Chioino, 1995). In Santería, diagnosis is made by the *santero* through divination, by throwing 16 shells onto a straw mat. The shells can form 256 possible patterns (Mason, 1993). Each pattern represents a particular legend, which is then used by the *santero* to interpret the client's problems (González-Wippler, 1994; Koss-Chioino, 1995).

Sandra, a Latina woman of Caribbean descent, was encouraged by some friends to consult an *italero* (shell reader) about some job-related concerns. Much to her surprise, the *italero* mentioned patterns in her reading associated with back pain, a problem Sandra had been struggling with since a car accident several years before. According to the reading, she needed to help herself before the Orishas would do anything for her. Although she had never been a believer in Santería, in her own words "this made me diet and exercise regularly in order to help my back pain." She received an *eleque* (necklace) for her health protection and job instability. In Sandra's case, although she was not brought up within the Santería tradition, this intervention motivated her to change health-related behaviors. A well-educated woman, she already knew that diet and exercise would help, but she had never complied with physicians' recommendations.

Lucy Cohen (1979), an anthropologist and social worker, conducted an extensive study on culture, disease, and stress among Latino immigrants living in the Washington, D.C., area. Not all these immigrants were Afro-Latinos, but the examples she provides illustrate issues of compliance with treatment that may apply to Latino immigrants of similar socioeconomic status, regardless of their ethnic background. In examining the role of beliefs about deference to power in treatment compliance, Cohen stated that deference to power could mean that prescribed treatment by a physician must be followed, but it could also mean that listening to *personas de confianza* (trusted persons) is more important than listening to the physician. Usually such trusted persons are family members, kin, friends, and *curanderos*. Cohen (1979) described an instance of a woman who acted "like a mother" (p. 143) toward a patient, suggesting plants with medicinal properties for an ailment. The patient valued these suggestions and followed them. From the patient's point of view, a person of trust, a *santera*, or a *santero*, may be in a higher position of authority than a physician; after all, these persons are in contact with the Orishas and take a more holistic approach to health issues, inclusive of both the natural and the supernatural. If the patient believes in the power of the *santero* over the physician, he or she will follow his or her recommendations over those of physicians, as exemplified by Sandra's case.

Other persons who may play a role as authority are herbalists, and *botánica* owners. *Botánicas* are stores that sell religious, health-related, and luck-related items. There are hundreds of *botánicas* in larger cities populated by Caribbean Latinos, including the Bronx, Brooklyn, New York City, Miami, and Washington, D.C. Many of these *botánicas* advertise in Latino newspapers or yellow pages, but for the most part they are frequented only by persons who know about Santería.

The cultural value of spirituality has a strong impact on health-related behavior. A spiritualist framework does not perceive health and illness as mere physiological phenomena, but as conditions connected with the supernatural. Hence, the type of cure the individual may seek might be to honor a higher power such as the Orishas. Individuals also would follow the suggestions made by the *santero* in addition to or instead of traditional medical care. For instance, González-Wippler (1994) describes that many people who come to the *santera* or *santero* are "elderly and frail, or ailing with some chronic or unusual disease that has been declared incurable by medical doctors…. The treatment and cure of several kinds of cancer has been known in Santería for many years" (p. 221). She also relates how *santeros* have used *higuereta* for centuries, and that only recently traditional medicine is researching this tropical plant also known as *Ricinus communis*. Aside from using herbs, a *santero* can "heal by blessing" (González-Wippler, 1994). Brandon (1991) also describes the use of plants in healing in Santería.

Latino clients believe that herbal treatments provided by *santeros* are very efficient, and therefore they are more receptive to nontraditional medical treatments such as herbs (Brandon, 1991; González-Wippler, 1994). Western-trained health practitioners may find it hard to agree with the use of herbs for treatment. Patients may avoid open and direct communication about their health beliefs to avoid being perceived as "crazy" by Western health care professionals. Health providers should refrain from communication that may appear judgmental or that includes misunderstandings of the client's perspective. Anthropologists (e.g., Koss-Chioino, 1995) cited experimental projects such as the Therapist-Spiritist Training Project in Puerto Rico and the employment of Spiritists at Lincoln Hospital in New York, in which cultural healers are invited to clinical settings. These are illustrations of cooperative work between health providers and healers that merit further exploration by health professionals and psychologists.

Africans have also contributed a collectivistic orientation to the Latino culture. Several authors have documented that among Latinos and Afro-Latinos a collectivist orientation is more prevalent than an individualistic orientation (Comas-Díaz, 1989; Marín, 1990; Triandis, Marín, Lisansky, & Betancourt, 1984). Values such as allocentrism, familialism, and preference of interdependence over independence are rooted on this collectivist approach. Latinos place a strong value on relationships. Some studies have described values such as *simpatía* or congeniality orientation and deference to power as important cultural characteristics of Latinos (Marín & Marín, 1991; Zea, Quezada, & Belgrave, 1994; Zea, García, Belgrave, & Quezada, Chapter 12, this volume).

Given the high value most Latinos place on relational orientation, developing a relationship with their health care provider becomes a critical treatment element. Only then will *confianza* (trust) take place, which is basic to complying with treatment recommendations. Under conditions of trust, Latinos feel that the health care provider is looking out for their best interests. In a time of shrinking resources, where managed care physicians are mandated to restrict the time they spend with patients, Latinos will not be well served if not enough time is spent in developing trust.

Because Latinas hold strong collectivist values (Comas-Díaz, 1989; Comas-Díaz, Chapter 9, this volume; Marín, 1990; Triandis et al., 1984), they are more likely to listen to messages that emphasize the importance of their health for the well-being of their family than to those emphasizing their own individual benefit. One manifestation of collectivist values is illustrated by group ritual sessions for healing purposes (Koss-Chioino, 1995). Among Afro-Latinos, these ritual sessions may include the family or groups of *ahijados* (godchildren) of the *santero* (Gonzalez-Wippler, 1994; Murphy, 1993). *Ahijados* are the individuals initiated into the religion by the *santero*, and they maintain close ties for the rest of their lives. For instance, in a *tambor* (drum ceremony) that took place within an Afro-Latino community in Brooklyn, when one of the participants was possessed by Obatalá, several family members brought their ailing mother to be blessed with health by the Orisha. Healing in the context of a *tambor* is far from being a private, individualistic process. Both family and community members took part in this event. This example also illustrates the interconnection between health and the spiritual world for this mostly Afro-Latino community.

Fernández (1994) suggests taking advantage of collectivist values for improving women's health by involving the family and having the partner play a significant role in encouraging the woman to take preventive measures. This may extend to working with the male partner in order to discourage sexual promiscuity, which can be an important source of prevention of sexually transmitted diseases that are associated with cervical cancer (Fernández, 1994).

As indicated in Chapter 13 by Preciado and Henry, Latinos prefer Spanish-speaking practitioners over non–Spanish speakers, particularly when their English is limited. Cohen (1979) illustrates instances of cross-cultural communication in which the practitioner overestimates his or her Spanish skills and misses subtle cues that indicate miscommunication, which may result in failed treatment efforts. She cites an instance of an interaction between a physician and her patient in which both assumed that the physician was "the sole purveyor and controller of knowledge. The result was that on the one hand Josefa never indicated her lack of understanding of what she was told and, on the other hand, the health personnel assumed that she would abandon her belief system and follow the physician's concluding recommendations" (Cohen, 1979, p. 151). This example illustrates the need to remain aware of cultural issues and the importance of understanding the limitations of not sharing the same culture than the client even if health providers can speak Spanish.

Conclusions

It is of utmost relevance for researchers and health professionals to adopt more culturally sensitive approaches for understanding the health–disease process among Latinos in order to develop appropriate prevention and intervention strategies. Other cultural groups can learn and benefit from understanding health outcomes with Latinos. Central to this purpose is that researchers and health professionals need to understand Latino values and how these values affect health behaviors.

One starting point is to take into account the contributions of disciplines such as anthropology and sociology to gain a deeper understanding of African and indigenous health beliefs and practices that are very much alive among Latinos. In the psychological literature there is very little documentation of this influence on Latino health beliefs and behaviors. More research needs to be oriented on this direction, yet efforts to encourage research in this area are limited by funding and the scarcity of Latino researchers. Marín, Amaro, Eisenberg, and Opava-Stitzer (1993) documented that of all the projects funded by the Department of Health and Human Services (HHS), less than 2 percent target Latino health issues or support Latino researchers. Moreover, few proposal reviewers can "judge the cultural appropriateness, sensitivity, or competence of proposals" (Marín et al., 1993, p. 547). Therefore, Latinos must be involved at every level as researchers, health care providers, and developers of programs for Latinos.

To understand Latino health beliefs and behaviors, health psychology researchers must consider the diversity of the Latino population. African influence contributes to this diversity, as do socioeconomic factors. Training of graduate students in psychology should also take into account the role that different cultural influences play in the way different Latino groups articulate their world views and behaviors. Efforts to understand better the degree to which African influence and other cultural and socioeconomic factors influence health beliefs and behaviors should be a priority in Latino health psychology's research agenda. Only then will interventions be effective and culturally appropriate.

References

Acosta, F. X., Yamamoto, J., & Evans, L. A. (1982). *Effective psychotherapy for low income and minority patients*. New York: Plenum Press.

Angel, R., & Guarnaccia, P. J. (1989). Mind, body, and culture: Somatization among Hispanics. *Social Science Medicine, 28,* 1229–1238.

Betancourt, H., & López, S. R. (1993). The study of culture, ethnicity, and race in American psychology. *American Psychologist, 48,* 629–637.

Brandon, G. E. (1991). The uses of plants in healing in an Afro-Cuban religion, Santería. *Journal of Black Studies, 22,* 55–76.

Brandon, G. E. (1993). *Santería from Africa to the New World: The dead sell memories*. Bloomington: Indiana University Press.

Bundek, N. I., Marks, G., & Richardson, J. L. (1993). Role of health locus of control beliefs in cancer screening of elderly Hispanic women. *Health Psychology, 12,* 193–199.

Cohen, L. M. (1979). *Culture, disease, and stress among Latino immigrants*. Washington, DC: Research Institute on Immigration and Ethnic Studies, Smithsonian Institution.

Comas-Díaz, L. (1989). Culturally relevant issues and treatment implications for Hispanics. In D. R. Koslow & E. P. Salett (Eds.). *Crossing cultures in mental health.* (pp. 31–48). Washington, DC: SIETAR International.

Comas-Díaz, L. (1997). Mental health needs of Latinos with professional status. In J. García & M. C. Zea (Eds.), *Psychological interventions and research with Latino populations.* Boston: Allyn and Bacon.

Fernández, M. E. (1994). *Evaluation of an interactive videodisc on breast and cervical cancer prevention and early detection for Hispanic women.* Unpublished Ph.D. dissertation, University of Maryland at College Park.

Friedemann, N. S. (1993). *La saga del Negro: Presencia Africana en Colombia.* Bogotá: Pontificia Universidad Javeriana.

García, J., & Marotta, S. (1997). Characterization of the Latino population. In J. García & M. C. Zea (Eds.), *Psychological interventions and research with Latino populations.* Boston: Allyn and Bacon.

Garza, R. T., & Ames, R. E., Jr. (1974). A comparison of Anglo- and Mexican-American college students on locus of control. *Journal of Consulting and Clinical Psychology, 42*(6), 919.

González, J. T., Atwood, J., García, J. A., & Meyskens, F. L. (1989). Hispanics and cancer preventive behavior: The development of a behavioral model and its policy implications. *Journal of Health and Social Policy, 1,* 55–73.

González-Wippler, M. (1994). *Santería: The religion.* St. Paul, MN: Llewellyn Publications.

Guarnaccia, P. J., De La Cancela, V., & Carrillo, E. (1989). The multiple meanings of *ataques de nervios* in the Latino community. *Medical Anthropology, 11,* 47–62.

Janis, I. L. (1984). Improving adherence to medical recommendations: Prescriptive hypothesis derived from recent research in social psychology. In A. Baum, S. Taylor, & J. Singer (Eds.), *Handbook of psychology and health* (pp. 113–148). Hillsdale, NJ: Laurence Erlbaum Associates.

Jorge, A. (1991). Cuban Santería: A New World African religion. In K. Davis & E. Farajaje-Jones (Eds.), *African creative expressions of the divine* (pp. 105–120). Washington, DC: Howard University School of Divinity.

Kosko, D. A., & Flaskerud, J. H. (1987). Mexican American, nurse practitioner, and lay control group beliefs about cause and treatment of chest pain. *Nursing Research, 36,* 226–231.

Koss-Chioino, J. D. (1995). Traditional and folk approaches among ethnic minorities. In J. F. Aponte, R. Y. Rivers, & J. Wohl (Eds.), *Psychological interventions and cultural diversity* (pp. 145–163). Boston, MA: Allyn and Bacon.

Kroeber, A. L., & Kluckhohn, C. (1952). *Culture: A critical review of concepts and definitions, 47* (1). Cambridge, MA: Peabody Museum.

Landrine, H., & Klonnoff, E. A. (1992). Culture and health-related schemas: A review and proposal for interdisciplinary integration. *Health Psychology, 11,* 267–276.

Lee, D. J., & Markides, K. S. (1991). Health behaviors, risk factors, and health indicators associated with cigarette use in Mexican Americans: Results from the Hispanic HANES. *American Journal of Public Health, 81,* 859–864.

Marín, B. V. (1990). AIDS prevention for non-Puerto Rican Hispanics. In C. G. Leukefeld, R. J. Battjes, & Z. Amsel (Eds.), *AIDS and intravenous drug use: Future directions for community-based prevention research* (pp. 35–52). Rockville, MD: NIDA Research Monograph.

Marín, G., Amaro, H., Eisenberg, C., & Opava-Stitzer, S. (1993). The development of a relevant and comprehensive research agenda to improve Hispanic health. *Public Health Reports, 108,* 546–550.

Marín, G., & Marín, B. V. (1991). *Research with Hispanic populations.* Newbury Park, CA: Sage Publications.

Mason, M. A. (1993). "The blood that runs through their veins": The creation of identity and a client's experience of Cuban-American Santería: A dialogùn divination. *The Drawing Review, 37,* 119–130.

Matarazzo, J. D., & Carmody, T. P. (1986). Health psychology. In M. Hersen, A. E. Kazdin, & A. S. Bellack (Eds.), *The clinical psychology handbook* (pp. 657–682). New York: Pergamon Press.

Morris, P., & Silove, D. (1992). Cultural influences in psychotherapy with refugee survivors of torture and trauma. *Hospital and Community Psychiatry, 43,* 820–824.

Murphy, J. M. (1993). *Santería: African spirits in America*. Boston: Beacon Press.

Murphy, J. M. (1994). *Working the spirit: Ceremonies of the African diaspora*. Boston: Beacon Press.

Nobles, W. W. (1986). *African psychology: Towards its reclamation, reascension, and revitalization*. Oakland, CA: Black Family Institute.

Nobles, W. (1991). African philosophy: Foundations for Black psychology. In R. L. Jones (Ed.), *Black psychology*. Berkeley, CA: Cobb & Henry.

O'Brien, E. M. (1993). Latinos in higher education. *Research Briefs, 4*(4) 1–15.

Pollak-Eltz, A. (1991). The cult of Maria Lionza in Venezuela. In K. Davis & E. Farajaje-Jones (Eds.), *African creative expressions of the divine*. Washington, DC: Howard University School of Divinity.

Preciado, J., & Henry, M. (1997). Linguistic barriers in health education and services. In J. García & M. C. Zea (Eds.), *Psychological interventions and research with Latino populations*. Boston: Allyn and Bacon.

Stephen, E. H., Foote, K., Hendershot, G. E., & Schoenborn, C. A. (1994). Health of the foreign-born population: United States 1989–90. *Advance Data from Vital and Health Statistics*, No 241. Hyattsville, MD: National Center for Health Statistics.

Sussman, L. K. (1992). Critical assessment of models. In D. M. Becker, D. R. Hill, J. S. Jackson, D. M. Levine, F. A. Stillman, & S. M. Weiss (Eds.), *Health behavior research in minority populations* (pp. 145–148). Washington, DC: U.S. Department of Health and Human Services. NIH Publication No. 92–2965.

Thompson, W. L., Thompson, T. L., & House, R. M. (1990). Taking care of culturally different and non-English-speaking patients. *International Journal of Psychiatry in Medicine, 20*, 235–245.

Triandis, H. C., Marín. G., Lisansky, J., & Betancourt, H. (1984). Simpatía as a cultural script of Hispanics. *Journal of Personality and Social Psychology, 47*, 1365–1375.

Williams, J. E. (1992). Using social marketing to understand racially, ethnically, and culturally diverse audiences for public health interventions. In D. M. Becker, D. R. Hill, J. S. Jackson, D. M. Levine, F. A. Stillman, & S. M. Weiss (Eds.), *Health behavior research in minority populations*. U.S. Department of Health and Human Services. NIH Publication No. 92-2965.

Zapata Olivella, M. (1989). *Las claves magicas de América: Raza, clase y cultura*. Bogotá: Plaza & Janes.

Zapka, J. G., Harris, D. R., Hosmer, D., Costanza, M. E., Mas, E., & Barth, R. (1993). Effects of a community health center intervention on breast cancer screening among Hispanic American women. *Health Services Research, 28*, 223–235.

Zea, M. C., García, J., Belgrave, F. Z., & Quezada, T. (1997). Socioeconomic and cultural factors in rehabilitation of Latinos with disabilities. In J. Garcia & M. C. Zea (Eds.), *Psychological interventions and research with Latino populations*. Boston: Allyn and Bacon.

Zea, M. C., Quezada, T., & Belgrave, F. Z. (1994). Cultural values and adjustment to disability among Latinos. *Journal of Social Behavior and Personality, 9*, 185–200.

Author Index

Subject Index